BYRON IN CONTEXT

George Gordon, the sixth Lord Byron (1788–1824), was one of the most celebrated poets of the Romantic period, as well as a peer, politician and global celebrity, famed not only for his verse, but for his controversial lifestyle and involvement in the Greek War of Independence. In thirty-seven concise, accessible chapters, by leading international scholars, this volume explores the social and intertextual relationships that informed Byron's writing; the geopolitical contexts in which he traveled, lived and worked; the cultural and philosophical movements that influenced changing outlooks on religion, science, modern society and sexuality; the dramatic landscape of war, conflict and upheaval that shaped Napoleonic and post-Napoleonic Europe and Regency Britain; and the diverse cultures of reception that mark the ongoing Byron phenomenon as a living ecology in the twenty-first century. This volume illuminates "Byron" not only in context but also *as* context.

CLARA TUITE is Professor of English at the University of Melbourne, a Co-Director of the Faculty of Arts Research Unit in Enlightenment, Romanticism and Contemporary Culture, and a Fellow of the Australian Academy of the Humanities. Her books include *Romantic Austen: Sexual Politics and the Literary Canon* (Cambridge University Press, 2002) and *Lord Byron and Scandalous Celebrity* (Cambridge University Press, 2015), which was awarded the Elma Dangerfield Prize of the International Association of Byron Societies.

BYRON IN CONTEXT

EDITED BY

CLARA TUITE
University of Melbourne

CAMBRIDGE
UNIVERSITY PRESS

CAMBRIDGE
UNIVERSITY PRESS

University Printing House, Cambridge CB2 8BS, United Kingdom

One Liberty Plaza, 20th Floor, New York, NY 10006, USA

477 Williamstown Road, Port Melbourne, VIC 3207, Australia

314–321, 3rd Floor, Plot 3, Splendor Forum, Jasola District Centre, New Delhi – 110025, India

79 Anson Road, #06-04/06, Singapore 079906

Cambridge University Press is part of the University of Cambridge.

It furthers the University's mission by disseminating knowledge in the pursuit of
education, learning, and research at the highest international levels of excellence.

www.cambridge.org
Information on this title: www.cambridge.org/9781107181465
DOI: 10.1017/9781316850435

First published 2020

Printed in the United Kingdom by TJ International Ltd, Padstow Cornwall

A catalogue record for this publication is available from the British Library.

ISBN 978-1-107-18146-5 Hardback

In memoriam Rolf P. Lessenich (1940–2019)

Contents

Illustrations

Contributors

BERNARD BEATTY is Senior Fellow in the School of English at the University of Liverpool, England, and Associate Fellow in the School of Divinity at the University of St. Andrews, Scotland. He is the author of two books and has edited four collections of essays on Byron. He has written on Romanticism, the Bible, many major authors and aspects of literary theory. He was editor of the *Byron Journal* from 1986 to 2004. Recent publications have been about Shelley and the theater; Byron, Pope and Newman; Browning and Newman; Romantic decadence; Byron and Cowper; Byron's temperament; and Byron and Italian Catholicism. Pending publications are on Byron's "dramatic monologues"; Byron and Spain; *Childe Harold's Pilgrimage*; and a collection of selected essays, "Mainly Byron."

JOHN BECKETT is Professor of English Regional History at the University of Nottingham, England. His book *Byron and Newstead: the Aristocrat and the Abbey* (Associated University Presses, 2001) was awarded the International Byron Society's Elma Dangerfield Award in 2003 for its contribution to the understanding of Byron and his life. He has subsequently worked further on Byron's estate and financial matters and more recently on his role as a member of the House of Lords before his abrupt departure abroad in 1816. John is a vice president of the Newstead Abbey Byron Society and a regular lecturer at the society's meetings.

MADELEINE CALLAGHAN is Senior Lecturer in Romantic Literature at the University of Sheffield, England. Her research specialty is the poetry of Wordsworth, Byron, Shelley and Yeats. Liverpool University Press published her first monograph, *Shelley's Living Artistry: The Poetry and Drama of Percy Bysshe Shelley*, in 2017. Her second monograph, *The Poet-Hero in the Work of Byron and Shelley* (2019), is published by Anthem Press. She has published various articles and chapters on Romantic and post-Romantic poetry. With Michael O'Neill, she co-authored *The Romantic Poetry Handbook* (Wiley-Blackwell, 2018).

ANNA CAMILLERI read for her doctorate under the supervision of Professor Seamus Perry at Balliol College, Oxford, England, where she remained as a lecturer in English until 2013. From 2013 to 2018 she held a Career Development Fellowship at Christ Church College. She completed the manuscript of her first book, *Byron, Gender, and the Heroic*, in 2018 and is currently revising it for publication with the Oxford English Monograph series. A second book on Byron is under contract with Harvard University Press. She currently holds a Visiting Research Fellowship at the Institute of English Studies in the School of Advanced Study, Senate House, London.

MARK CANUEL is Director of the Institute for the Humanities and Professor of English at the University of Illinois at Chicago, USA. He has written widely on Romanticism, aesthetics and critical theory. His most recent monograph is *Justice, Dissent, and the Sublime* (Johns Hopkins University Press, 2012).

WILLIAM CHRISTIE is Professor and Head of the Humanities Research Centre at the Australian National University and a Fellow of the Australian Academy of the Humanities. He was foundation president of the Romantic Studies Association of Australasia (2010–15) and is author of *Samuel Taylor Coleridge: A Literary Life* (Palgrave, 2006), which was awarded the New South Wales Premier's Biennial Prize for Literary Scholarship in 2008; *The Letters of Francis Jeffrey to Thomas and Jane Welsh Carlyle* (Routledge, 2008); *The Edinburgh Review in the Literary Culture of Romantic Britain* (Pickering & Chatto, 2009); *Dylan Thomas: A Literary Life* (Palgrave, 2014); and *The Two Romanticisms, and Other Essays* (Sydney University Press, 2016).

GERARD COHEN-VRIGNAUD is Associate Professor of English at the University of Tennessee, USA. He is the author of *Radical Orientalism: Rights, Reform, and Romanticism* (Cambridge University Press, 2015) as well as articles appearing in journals including *English Literary History, Modern Language Quarterly, differences* and *Nineteenth-Century Literature*. He is currently at work on a book about Romantic-era politics as aesthetic experience.

SPIRIDOULA DEMETRIOU is a doctoral student in the Art History program at the University of Melbourne, Australia. Her research topic is "The

Creation of Modern Greece: Mesologgi, Art and Philhellenism in the Nineteenth Century." The thesis investigates how artists projected Philhellene iconography involving the Christian patriot and vanquished hero onto revolutionary Missolonghi in order to promote Western intervention into the 1821 Greek War of Independence against Ottoman rule.

GARY DYER is Professor of English at Cleveland State University, Ohio, USA. His research focuses on British literature and culture during the years 1790 to 1830, the Romantic period. He has worked on satirical verse and fiction, transatlantic literary relations, law and literature, textual studies and the literature of sexuality. His first book, *British Satire and the Politics of Style, 1789–1832*, was published by Cambridge University Press in 1997, and reissued in paperback in 2006. He is currently working on a book titled *Lord Byron on Trial: Literature and the Law in the Romantic Period*.

LINDSEY ECKERT is Assistant Professor of English and the History of Text Technologies at Florida State University, USA. Her research and teaching focus on the intersections between British Romanticism and media history. Her research has appeared in *ELH*, *Nineteenth-Century Literature*, *European Romantic Review* and *Digital Humanities Quarterly*. She is currently at work on a book about the cultural value of familiarity in the Romantic period.

ERIC EISNER is Associate Professor of English at George Mason University in Fairfax, Virginia, USA. His book *Nineteenth-Century Poetry and Literary Celebrity* (Palgrave, 2009) explored reader–writer relationships in Romanticism and its wake, showing how poets including P. B. Shelley, John Keats, Letitia Landon and Elizabeth Barrett Browning negotiated the culture of literary celebrity shaped by (and shaping) Byronism. He edited the *Romantic Circles Praxis* volume "Romantic Fandom" (2011). He is currently working on a book on the surprising affiliations between John Keats and innovative recent American poetry.

THOMAS H. FORD is Lecturer in English at La Trobe University, Australia. His publications include *Wordsworth and the Poetics of Air: Atmospheric Romanticism in a Time of Climate Change* (Cambridge University Press, 2018), *A Cultural History of Climate Change* (Routledge, 2016), a translation of Boris Groys' *The Communist Postscript* (Verso, 2010) and articles on Romanticism and poetics in such journals as *ELH*, *New Literary History* and *Literature Compass*.

CAROLINE FRANKLIN is Professor of English Literature at Swansea University, Wales. She is the author of *Byron's Heroines* (Clarendon Press, 1992), *Byron, A Literary Life* (Palgrave, 2001), *The Female Romantics: Nineteenth-Century Women Novelists and Byronism* (Routledge, 2012) and edited *The Longman Anthology of Gothic Verse* (Routledge, 2010). She leads the Elizabeth Montagu Letters project, which aims to publish a scholarly digital edition of the correspondence of the bluestocking queen. www.elizabethmontagunetwork.co.uk/the-project.

ANDREW FRANTA is Associate Professor of English at the University of Utah, USA. He is the author of *Romanticism and the Rise of the Mass Public* (Cambridge University Press, 2007) and, most recently, of *Systems Failure: The Uses of Disorder in English Literature* (Johns Hopkins University Press, 2019).

LAURA J. GEORGE is Professor of English Literature at Eastern Michigan University, USA. She has published articles and book chapters on muslin and dandyism among other topics.

JASON GOLDSMITH is Associate Professor of English at Butler University, Indianapolis, USA, where he offers courses on Romanticism, art and nature and video game narrative. He has published articles on William Wordsworth, John Clare, James Hogg and Robert Louis Stevenson, as well as topics such as the picturesque tradition and the national contours of Romantic-era celebrity. He is currently completing an illustrated essay about the intersection of urban and natural spaces in Vienna, Austria.

JONATHAN GROSS is Professor of English at DePaul University in Chicago, USA, and author of *Byron's "Corbeau Blanc": The Life and Letters of Lady Melbourne* (Liverpool University Press, 1998) and *Byron: The Erotic Liberal* (Rowman & Littlefield, 2000). He has edited *The Sylph* (Northwestern University Press, 2007) and *Emma, or the Unfortunate Attachment* (State University of New York Press, 2004) both by Georgiana, Duchess of Devonshire and *Belmour* by Anne Damer (Northwestern University Press, 2011). Joint President of the International Association of Byron Societies, he has written *The Life of Anne Damer* (Rowman & Littlefield, 2012) and explored Thomas Jefferson's interest in British Romantic poetry in *Thomas Jefferson's Scrapbooks* (Steerforth, 2006).

MIRKA HOROVÁ is Senior Lecturer in English Literature at the Faculty of Arts, Charles University, Prague. She has published essays and articles on Byron and the Norwegian Romantic poet Wergeland, and has also edited several volumes and journals on Byron and other topics, including a special issue of the *Byron Journal* ("Byron and the Bible," 2015). In 2013–2019, she co-organized the annual spring Byron conference at Newstead Abbey. She is currently preparing a monograph on Byron's plays for publication, and is the incoming Editor of the *Byron Journal*. The work on her essay was supported by the European Regional Development Fund Project "Creativity and Adaptability as Conditions of the Success of Europe in an Interrelated World" (No. CZ.02.1.01/0.0/ 0.0/16_019/0000734).

CHRISTINE KENYON JONES is a Research Fellow in the Department of English at King's College, London, England. Her books include *Kindred Brutes: Animals in Romantic-Period Writing* (Ashgate, 2001) and (as editor) *Byron: The Image of the Poet* (University of Delaware Press, 2008) and (with Roderick Beaton) *Byron: The Poetry of Politics and the Politics of Poetry* (Routledge, 2016). She was joint organizer of the 39th International Byron Conference in London in 2013. Her work on Byron includes chapters and papers on his portraiture, religious heritage, parliamentary career, disability, relationship with John Murray, pronunciation, eating habits and criticism of Keats.

ADAM KOMISARUK is Associate Professor of English at West Virginia University, USA. He is the editor (with Allison Dushane) of Erasmus Darwin's two-volume *The Botanic Garden* (2017) and the author of *Sexual Privatism in British Romantic Writing: A Public of One* (2019), both published by Routledge.

ROLF P. LESSENICH was Professor of English (and Comparative) Literature, and later Professor Emeritus, in the Department of English, American and Celtic Studies of Bonn University, Germany. He received both his PhD and his "Habilitation" from the same university. Fluent in English, French, Spanish and Hebrew, he traveled extensively and presented visiting lectures at universities across Europe, America and Asia. His wide research interests in comparative literature were chiefly in literary history from the seventeenth to the nineteenth centuries. He published six monographs: *Dichtungsgeschmack und althebräische Bibelpoesie im 18. Jahrhundert* (Böhlau, 1967), *Elements of Pulpit Oratory in Eighteenth-Century England 1660–1800* (Böhlau, 1972), *Lord Byron and the Nature of Man* (Böhlau, 1978), *Aspects of English Preromanticism* (Böhlau, 1989), *Neoclassical Satire and the Romantic School 1780–1830* (Vandenhoeck &

Ruprecht, 2012) and *Romantic Disillusionism and the Sceptical Tradition* (V&R unipress GmbH, 2017).

GHISLAINE MCDAYTER is Professor of English at Bucknell University, Pennsylvania, USA. Her publications include essays on the Gothic, Byron, Shelley, Wollstonecraft and Caroline Lamb. She has edited a collection of essays on Romanticism and psychoanalysis entitled *Untrodden Regions of the Mind* (Bucknell Press, 2002). Her most recent book is *Byromania and the Birth of Celebrity Culture* (State University of New York Press, 2009) and she is presently completing her monograph *Licentious Tyrants: Feminism and Flirtation in Eighteenth- and Nineteenth-Century British Literature.*

OMAR F. MIRANDA is Assistant Professor in the Department of English at the University of San Francisco, USA, where he teaches and researches the literatures of the eighteenth and nineteenth centuries. His book manuscript in progress examines the revolutionary possibilities of exile and literary form in the Romantic period. He is editor of *On the 200th Anniversary of Lord Byron's* Manfred: *Commemorative Essays*, a bicentenary Romantic Circles Praxis volume. He has published essays in *European Romantic Review, Symbiosis* and *Romantic Circles*; a book chapter in *The Cambridge Guide to the Eighteenth-Century Novel* (forthcoming); and book reviews in *Eighteenth-Century Fiction, BARS Bulletin & Review* and *Review 19.*

TOM MOLE is Professor of English Literature and Book History at the University of Edinburgh, Scotland, where he is Director of the Centre for the History of the Book. He is the author of *Byron's Romantic Celebrity* (Palgrave, 2007), *What the Victorians Made of Romanticism* (Princeton, 2017), and (with Michelle Levy) *The Broadview Introduction to Book History* (Broadview, 2017).

JULIAN NORTH is Associate Professor of Romantic and Victorian literature at the University of Leicester, England, specializing in life writing. She is the author of *The Domestication of Genius: Biography and the Romantic Poet* (Oxford University Press, 2009), which includes a chapter on memoirs of Byron. She is currently working on visual and biographical portraits of Victorian authors.

MARY O'CONNELL is the author of *Byron and John Murray: A Poet and His Publisher* (Liverpool University Press, 2014) and co-editor of

Readings on Audience and Textual Materiality (Pickering & Chatto, 2011). In 2012 she was awarded a Leverhulme Fellowship to the University of St. Andrews, Scotland, and in 2015 won the National University of Ireland Postdoctoral Fellowship, which she held at University College, Cork. She is currently working on a biography of the publisher John Murray.

CARLA POMARÈ is Professor of English Literature at the University of Eastern Piedmont at Vercelli in Italy. Her main research interests are Anglo-American poetry from the Romantic to the Modernist period and Renaissance drama. In the field of Byron studies, she has edited and annotated the first complete Italian edition of Byron's *Hebrew Melodies* (Trauben, 2003) and has written on Byron's plays, his Italian correspondence and his uses of historiography in *Byron and the Discourses of History* (Ashgate, 2013).

NEIL RAMSEY is Senior Lecturer in English Literature at the University of New South Wales in Canberra, Australia. He works on literary and cultural responses to warfare during the eighteenth century and the Romantic era, focusing on the representations of personal experience and the development of a modern culture of war. His first book was *The Military Memoir and Romantic Literary Culture, 1780–1835* (Ashgate, 2011) and his most recent is a collection co-edited with Gillian Russell, *Tracing War in British Enlightenment and Romantic Culture* (Palgrave, 2015).

ALAN RAWES is Senior Lecturer in Romanticism at the University of Manchester, England. His publications include *Byron's Poetic Experimentation* (Ashgate, 2000/Routledge, 2016), *English Romanticism and the Celtic World* (co-edited, Cambridge University Press, 2003), *Romantic Biography* (co-edited, Ashgate, 2003/Routledge, 2016), *Romanticism and Form* (edited, Palgrave, 2007), *Reading, Writing and the Influence of Harold Bloom* (co-edited, Manchester University Press, 2010), a special issue of *Litteraria Pragensia* – *"Tears, Tortures and the Touch of Joy": Byron in Italy* (co-edited, 2013) and *Byron and Italy* (co-edited, Manchester University Press, 2017, winner of the 2018 Elma Dangerfield Prize). He is a past editor of the *Byron Journal* (2005–12) and a joint president of the International Association of Byron Societies. He is currently co-editing *The Oxford Handbook of Lord Byron* and writing a monograph on "Byron's Literary Conquest of Italy."

DIEGO SAGLIA is Professor of English Literature at the Università di Parma, Italy, and a member of the advisory committee of the "Museo Byron a Palazzo Guiccioli" project in Ravenna. His research interests center on the Romantic period and include representations of otherness, constructions of national identity and international literary relations. He is the author of *Byron and Spain: Itinerary in the Writing of Place* (Edwin Mellen, 1996) and *Lord Byron e le maschere della scrittura* (Carocci, 2009). He is also co-editor, with Alan Rawes, of *Byron and Italy* (Manchester University Press, 2017), which was awarded the 2018 Elma Dangerfield Award of the International Byron Society. His most recent publication is *European Literatures in Britain, 1815–1832: Romantic Translations* (Cambridge University Press, 2019).

MARIA SCHOINA is Assistant Professor of English Literature at Aristotle University of Thessaloniki in Greece. She is the author of *Romantic "Anglo-Italians": Configurations of Identity in Byron, the Shelleys, and the Pisan Circle* (Ashgate 2009; currently available through Routledge) and co-editor of *The Place of Lord Byron in World History: Studies in His Life, Writings, and Influence. Selected Papers from the 35th International Byron Conference* (Edwin Mellen, 2013). Her essays have appeared in journals such as the *Byron Journal, Romanticism, Litteraria Pragensia,* the *Wordsworth Circle* and *European Romantic Review,* as well as in essay collections.

RICHARD C. SHA is Professor of Literature and Philosophy at American University in Washington, DC, USA. A recipient of two National Endowment for the Humanities grants, along with fellowships at the Huntington Library, Yale Center for British Art and the American Philosophical Society, he is the author of three monographs, the latest of which is *Imagination and Science in Romanticism* (Johns Hopkins University Press, 2018). With Joel Faflak, he has edited *Romanticism and the Emotions* (Cambridge University Press, 2016). His new book project, *Modeling Emotion: Romanticism and Beyond,* features chapters on Voltaire, Leopardi, Goethe, Hume, Baillie and Wordsworth.

JANE STABLER is Professor of Romanticism and Head of the School of English at the University of St. Andrews, Scotland. Her books include *Byron, Poetics and History* (Cambridge University Press, 2002) and *The Artistry of Exile: Romantic and Victorian Writers in Italy* (Oxford University Press, 2013). In 2014–17 she held a Leverhulme Major

Research Fellowship to work on the *Don Juan* volume of the Longman Annotated English Poets edition of Byron. This seven-volume edition is scheduled for completion in 2037.

CLARA TUITE is Professor of English at the University of Melbourne, a Co-Director of the Research Unit in Enlightenment, Romanticism and Contemporary Culture, and a Fellow of the Australian Academy of the Humanities. Her books include *Romantic Austen: Sexual Politics and the Literary Canon* (Cambridge, 2002) and *Lord Byron and Scandalous Celebrity* (Cambridge, 2015), which was awarded the Elma Dangerfield Prize of the International Association of Byron Societies.

PETER VASSALLO is Professor of English and Comparative Literature at the University of Malta. He was educated at the University of Malta and the University of Oxford, where he obtained the degrees of MA and DPhil. He is currently chair of the Institute of Anglo-Italian Studies and general editor of the *Journal of Anglo-Italian Studies*, which he founded. He has published widely on the literature of the Romantic period, on writers in Italy and on the classical influence on English literature. He is a member of the advisory editorial board of *Romanticism*. His book *Byron: The Italian Literary Influence* (Palgrave, 1984) is considered an authoritative work on the subject. His recent monograph is on "British Writers and the Experience of Italy."

TIMOTHY WEBB is Senior Research Fellow and Professor Emeritus at the University of Bristol, England, where he was Winterstoke Professor and Head of the Department of English. He has written and lectured widely on Romantic topics (especially Shelley and Byron) and on Irish topics (especially Yeats and Joyce). His two-volume annotated edition of Leigh Hunt's *Autobiography* is now with Oxford University Press. Work in progress includes *The Book of Stones*, an investigation of English Romantic writers and Ireland, joint editing of the second volume of Shelley's prose, and the collection into six volumes of about a hundred essays and papers.

SUSAN J. WOLFSON is Professor of English at Princeton University, New Jersey, USA, and a specialist in Long Romanticism. She has been teaching, publishing and lecturing on Byron for about thirty years, publishing widely on issues, texts and authors in the Long Romantic era and giving the Byron Foundation Lecture in 2011. Chapters on Byron appear in *Formal Charges* (Stanford University Press, 1997), *Borderlines*

(Stanford University Press, 2006), *Romantic Interactions* (Johns Hopkins University Press, 2010) and *Romantic Shades and Shadows* (Johns Hopkins University Press, 2018). In addition to these chapters, and the periodical publications by which they were previewed, there is an article on Hemans and Byron in *European Romantic Review* (2001), a chapter on "The Vision of Judgment" in *The Cambridge Companion to Byron* (Cambridge University Press, 2004) and an essay on Byron in America in the *Byron Journal* (2017). With Peter Manning, she edited Penguin's *Selected Poems of Lord Byron* (2nd ed., 2004), wrote the introduction and editorial material for Penguin's *Don Juan* (2005) and developed the unit on Byron for *The Romantics and Their Contemporaries* in *The Longman Anthology of British Literature* (5th ed., Pearson, 2012).

Chronology

1788	January 22: Born George Gordon Byron in London to Captain John Byron (1756–91) and his second wife, Catherine Byron, *née* Gordon (1765–1811).
1789	Mrs. Byron takes son to spend his early years in Aberdeen, Scotland.
	July 14: Storming of the Bastille marks beginning of French Revolution.
1790	Captain Byron abandons family and moves to Valenciennes, France.
1791	Captain Byron dies in France.
1794–8	Attends Aberdeen Grammar School.
1796	Matthew Lewis' *The Monk* published.
1798	Inherits baronetcy and title of 6th Baron Byron of Rochdale through the death of his great-uncle, Lord William Byron, the fifth Baron Byron.
	May: Napoleon leads French invasion of Egypt.
	August: Accompanies mother to ancestral estate at Newstead Abbey.
	September: William Wordsworth and Samuel Taylor Coleridge publish *Lyrical Ballads*.
1799	Enrolled at Dr. Glennie's School in Dulwich.
1800	Falls in love with first cousin, Margaret Parker, during summer holiday in Nottingham and Newstead.
1801–5	Enters Harrow School.
1801	Thomas Moore's *Poetical Works of the Late Thomas Little, Esq.* published.
1803	February: Newstead leased by Lord Grey de Ruthyn.
	September–November: Falls in love with Mary Ann Chaworth.

	November: Lives at Newstead under the care of Lord Grey de Ruthyn.
1804	Breaks with Lord Grey, returns to Harrow.
	December: Napoleon crowned Emperor of France.
1805	June: Charlotte Dacre publishes *Hours of Solitude*.
1805–7	Goes into residence at Trinity College, Cambridge, where he meets John Edleston, John Cam Hobhouse and Charles Skinner Matthews.
	October 21: Admiral Lord Nelson defeats French and Spanish naval forces at the Battle of Trafalgar.
1806	November: First volume of poetry, *Fugitive Pieces*, privately printed by John Ridge of Newark; Byron immediately suppresses it.
1807	January: *Fugitive Pieces* reworked and privately published as *Poems on Various Occasions*.
	June: *Hours of Idleness* published by Ben Crosby in London.
	June: Joins the Cambridge Whig Club.
	October: Returns to Trinity.
	Germaine de Staël publishes *Corinne, ou l'Italie* and Thomas Moore publishes the first of his *Irish Melodies*, to appear in ten parts 1807–34.
1808	Leaves Cambridge and is awarded his MA.
	Engages Robert Charles Dallas as intermediary with his publishers.
1809	March: Takes his seat in the House of Lords.
	March: *English Bards and Scotch Reviewers* published by James Cawthorn.
	June: Commences grand tour to Portugal, Spain, Gibraltar, Malta, Greece, Albania and Turkey, accompanied by Hobhouse.
1810	July: Hobhouse returns to England from the Continent, while Byron remains in Greece.
1811	February: The Prince of Wales is installed as Prince Regent after his father, King George III, is afflicted permanently by mental illness.
	May: Learns of the death of his Harrow school friend John Wingfield.
	June: Returns to England.
	August 1: Death of Byron's mother, followed two days later by his Cambridge friend Charles Skinner Matthews.

October: Learns of the death of his close Cambridge companion John Edleston.

November: Meets Thomas Moore at dinner with Samuel Rogers.

November: Offers *Hints from Horace* to James Cawthorn before requesting its suppression. The work is eventually published posthumously.

1812   February: Delivers maiden speech in the House of Lords on the Frame Work Bill.

March 10: *Childe Harold's Pilgrimage* (Cantos I and II) published by John Murray.

March 25: First sees future wife, Annabella Milbanke.

April: Begins relationship with Lady Caroline Lamb.

May 11: Prime Minister Spencer Perceval assassinated in the lobby of the House of Commons.

June: Lord Castlereagh appointed Foreign Secretary.

July: Considers eloping with Lady Caroline Lamb.

October: Proposes to Annabella Milbanke, but is rejected.

1813   January 23: Coleridge's *Remorse* premieres at Drury Lane.

January: Jane Austen publishes *Pride and Prejudice*.

May: Visits Leigh Hunt in Surrey Jail, Southwark, where he has been imprisoned for libelling the Prince Regent in the *Examiner*.

June 1: Gives final speech to House of Lords, presenting Major John Cartwright's petition for liberal reform.

June 5: *The Giaour* published, the first of Byron's Eastern tales.

June 20: Meets Madame de Staël.

December: *The Bride of Abydos* published.

1814   February 1: *The Corsair* published, sells 10,000 copies in a day.

April: Napoleon abdicates and is exiled to Elba.

July: Walter Scott's *Waverley* published.

1815   January 2: Marries Annabella Milbanke.

March: Napoleon escapes from Elba and rallies forces in France.

April: *Hebrew Melodies* published.

May: Elected to Committee of Drury Lane Theatre.

June 18: Napoleon defeated at the Battle of Waterloo, marking the end of the Napoleonic Wars.

October: Napoleon abdicates a second time and is exiled to St. Helena.

December: Birth of Ada, Byron's child by Annabella Milbanke.

December: Jane Austen's *Emma* published.

1816 January 15: Annabella leaves Byron, and Byron agrees to a legal separation (formalized on April 21), leading to the public controversy of the Separation scandal.

February 13: *The Siege of Corinth* and *Parisina* published together.

April 23: Leaves Britain for the Continent.

May: Lady Caroline Lamb publishes *Glenarvon*.

May: Coleridge's *Christabel* published with *Kubla Khan* and *The Pains of Sleep*.

May 27: Meets Percy Shelley at Sécheron.

June: Rents Villa Diodati in Geneva. An evening with John Polidori, Percy Bysshe Shelley and Mary Shelley leads to the publication of Mary Shelley's *Frankenstein* (1818) and Polidori's *The Vampyre* (1819).

October: Arrives in Italy, at Milan.

November 10: Arrives in Venice.

November 18: *Childe Harold's Pilgrimage* (Canto III) published.

December: *The Prisoner of Chillon* published.

1817 January 12: Birth of Allegra, Byron's daughter by Claire Clairmont.

March–May: Thomas Moore's *Lalla Rookh* published.

June 16: *Manfred* published.

July: Jane Austen dies.

July: Coleridge's *Biographia Literaria* published.

November: Newstead Abbey sold to Major Thomas Wildman.

December: Shelley's *Laon and Cythna* published and immediately suppressed. Revised and published as *The Revolt of Islam* the following year.

December: Jane Austen's *Northanger Abbey* and *Persuasion* published posthumously.

1818 February 28: *Beppo* published.

April 28: *Childe Harold's Pilgrimage* (Canto IV) published.

July: Begins writing *Don Juan*.

September: Finishes writing first canto of *Don Juan*.

1819 January 22: First encounter with Countess Teresa Guiccioli (*née* Gamba), with whom he begins an affair.

June 28: *Mazeppa* published.

July 15: *Don Juan* (Cantos I–II) published anonymously. John Murray declines to be identified as publisher.

August 16: Peterloo massacre in Manchester.

October: Gives Moore his "Memoirs."

1820	January: Death of George III. The Prince Regent is crowned George IV the following year. February: Moves into the Palazzo Guiccioli, Ravenna, home of Count and Countess Guiccioli. March: Becomes the Cavaliere Servente of Teresa Guiccioli. March 15: Begins *Some Observations Upon an Article in* Blackwood's Edinburgh Magazine. July: Meets Teresa's brother, Count Pietro Gamba. July: Count and Countess Guiccioli separate; she leaves the Palazzo and moves into her father's country house in Filetto. July: Keats publishes *Lamia, Isabella, The Eve of St. Agnes, and Other Poems.* August: Becomes involved in the Carbonari revolutionary society through his friendship with the Gambas. August: Shelley's *Prometheus Unbound* published.
1821	January: Begins the "Ravenna Journal." February: Planned Carbonari uprising fails. March 31: Publishes *Letter to John Murray Esqre*, the first installment of the Pope–Bowles controversy. April 21: *Marino Faliero* and *The Prophecy of Dante* published together. May 5: Napoleon dies on St Helena. June: Lady Morgan's *Italy* published. July: Teresa's father, Count Gamba, arrested and banished, followed by her brother Pietro. July: Teresa leaves Ravenna to join her brother and father. August: Shelley arrives in Ravenna. August: *Don Juan* (Cantos III–V) published. October 15: Begins *Detached Thoughts*. October 29: Leaves Ravenna with Shelley to join Teresa and the Gambas in Pisa. December 19: *Sardanapalus, The Two Foscari* and *Cain* published together.
1822	January: Article by Robert Southey (then Poet-Laureate) attacking Byron appears in the *Courier*. February: Replies to Southey's attack. February: Challenges Southey to a duel in an undelivered note. April: Byron's five-year-old daughter by Claire Clairmont, Allegra, dies in a convent at Bagnacavallo (near Ravenna), where she had lived since March 1821. July 8: Shelley drowns in Bay of Spezia.

August: Attends Shelley's cremation at Viareggio.

August: Lord Castlereagh commits suicide.

October 15: John Hunt publishes Byron's *The Vision of Judgment* in the *Liberal*, no. 1.

October–November: Breaks with John Murray after Murray refuses to publish further cantos of *Don Juan*. Subsequent cantos and other works are published by John Hunt.

November 23: Murray publishes Byron's *Werner*.

1823   January 1: *Heaven and Earth* published in the *Liberal*, no. 2.

April 1: *The Age of Bronze* published.

April 26: *The Blues* published in the *Liberal*, no. 3.

Byron's friend John Cam Hobhouse is involved in the creation of the London Greek Committee.

May–July: Learns that he has been formally elected a member of the London Greek Committee.

June 26: *The Island* published.

July 15: *Don Juan* (Cantos VI–VIII) published.

July 16: Sails for Greece on the brig *Hercules*, along with Pietro Gamba and a small fighting force under his command.

July 30: Byron's translation of Luigi Pulci's *Morgante Maggione* published in the *Liberal*, no. 4.

August 3: Arrives in Greece.

August 29: *Don Juan* (Cantos IX–XI) published.

November: Lends £4,000 to the Greek government.

December 17: *Don Juan* (Cantos XII–XIV) published.

December 29: Sails for Missolonghi.

1824   January 22: Writes "On this day I complete my thirty sixth year" to mark his birthday.

February 15: Suffers fits, supposed to be epileptic convulsions.

February 20: *The Deformed Transformed* published.

March 26: *Don Juan* (Cantos XV–XVI) published.

April 19: Dies of fever in Missolonghi, aged thirty-six.

July: Hobhouse and others destroy the manuscript of Byron's "Memoirs."

The fragment of *Don Juan* Canto XVII is found among Byron's papers after his death, and is published in 1903.

Abbreviations and Note on the Text

Works by Byron

BLJ   *Byron's Letters and Journals*, ed. Leslie A. Marchand, 13 vols. (London: J. Murray, 1973–94)

CHP   *Childe Harold's Pilgrimage*

CMP   *Lord Byron: The Complete Miscellaneous Prose*, ed. Andrew Nicholson (Oxford: Clarendon Press, 1991)

CPW   *Lord Byron: The Complete Poetical Works*, ed. Jerome J. McGann, 7 vols. (Oxford: Clarendon Press, 1980–93)

DJ   *Don Juan*

DJVE   *Byron's Don Juan: Varorium Edition*, ed. Truman G. Steffan and Willis W. Pratt, 4 vols. (Austin: University of Texas Press, 1957)

Moore   *Letters and Journals of Lord Byron: With Notices of His Life*, ed. Thomas Moore, 2 vols. (London: John Murray, 1830). Available via hathitrust.org

WLB   *The Works of Lord Byron: With His Letters and Journals, and His Life*, ed. Thomas Moore, 17 vols. (London: John Murray, 1832–3). Available via archive.org

Other Works

BCH   *Byron: The Critical Heritage*, ed. Andrew Rutherford (London: Routledge & Kegan Paul, 1970)

Blackwood's   *Blackwood's Edinburgh Magazine*

Blessington   *Conversations of Lord Byron with the Countess of Blessington* (London: Henry Colburn, 1834). Available via archive.org

Dallas   Robert Charles Dallas, *Recollections of the Life of Lord Byron* (London: Charles Knight, 1824) Available via archive.org

ER	*Edinburgh Review*
Guiccioli	Teresa Guiccioli, *My Recollections of Lord Byron and those of Eye-Witnesses of His Life*, trans. Hubert E. H. Jerningham (London: Richard Bentley, 1869). Available via archive.org
HVSV	*His Very Self and Voice: Collected Conversations of Lord Byron*, ed. Ernest J. Lovell, Jr. (New York: Macmillan, 1954)
LJM	*The Letters of John Murray to Lord Byron*, ed. Andrew Nicholson (Liverpool University Press, 2007)
LMWS	*The Letters of Mary Wollstonecraft Shelley*, ed. Betty T. Bennett, 3 vols. (Baltimore: Johns Hopkins University Press, 1983)
LPBS	*The Letters of Percy Bysshe Shelley*, ed. Frederick Lafayette Jones, 2 vols. (New York: Oxford University Press, 1964)
Liberal	*The Liberal: Verse and Prose from the South*
MacCarthy	Fiona MacCarthy, *Byron: Life and Legend* (New York: Farrar, Straus & Giroux, 2002)
Marchand	Leslie A. Marchand, *Byron: A Biography*, 3 vols. (London: John Murray, 1957)
Medwin	Thomas Medwin, *Conversations of Lord Byron*, ed. Ernest J. Lovell Jr. (Princeton University Press, 1966)
OED	*Oxford English Dictionary*
QR	*Quarterly Review*
RR	*The Romantics Reviewed: Contemporary Reviews of British Romantic Writers, Part B: Byron and Regency Society Poets*, ed. Donald H. Reiman, 5 vols. (New York: Garland, 1972)
Southey	Robert Southey, *The Poetical Works of Robert Southey, Collected by Himself*, 10 vols. (London: Longman, Orme, Brown, Green & Longmans, 1838). Available via archive.org and Google Books

All quotations from Byron's poetry, unless stated otherwise, are taken from the *Complete Poetical Works* (*CPW*), ed. Jerome J. McGann. They are indicated by in-text references to *CPW* followed by page number and line number. Block quotations are indicated by canto, stanza and line number (followed by page number). All other editions are noted in the individual chapters. Block quotations from dramas are by act, scene and line number. Quotations from prose writings are by volume and page number for *BLJ* and *CPW* and by page number for *CMP*.

Figure I.1 Thomas Phillips, *Portrait of a Nobleman*, 1813. 88 x 70.5 cm, oil on canvas. Newstead Abbey Collection, Nottinghamshire, inv. no. NA 532 BLDIDNA000454-1.

Introduction

Clara Tuite

The literary canon notoriously ignores context. Canonization removes authors and texts from their particular domains of production and reception, ushering them into the transcendent realm of the classical pantheon – remote, unchanging and monumentalized. All those pesky contingencies of time and place fall away, and the canonized work is left, supposedly, to speak for itself.

But what does that mean? Can we so easily separate text from context? What if the text itself forms a context? Addressing these questions compels us to recognize that context is essential to understanding literary texts and the work they do. Paradoxically, even acts of canonization that willfully ignore context are themselves acts of contextualization – and are among the many frames of reference that "the work itself" solicits for its readers.

This book's cover image, Mathieu Barathier's *Lord Biron Dédié aux Romantiques* (1826), is an exuberant allegory of canonization. Like a traditional devotional tableau, it is divided into earthly and heavenly zones, and we read time spatially, following Byron's progress upward from death to commemoration to apotheosis. At the top, on a plume of billowing clouds illuminated by shafts of sunlight, is the eternally young Byron of the iconic "Cloak Portrait," Thomas Phillips' 1813 *Portrait of a Nobleman* (see Figure I.1). Below this transcendent image, the clouds darken to a serpentine line of smoke, which frames a tableau of Byron's body, recumbent on a sarcophagus, draped in a gossamer-thin shroud. Through a scrim of smoke or incense, we witness an intimate *levée*. The dedication is in progress. The muses of lyric poetry, in various states of semi-undress, wail and dash their lyres against their breasts, in agony and ecstasy. In this vaguely cosmic landscape, classical appurtenances officiate – a well-wrought urn and sleek sarcophagus, laurels and lyres. The horned lyres flaunt their biblical affinity, recalling the altar in the Book of Exodus whose brass horns frame the sacrificial smoke joining earth with heaven.

Beneath the muses' delicately sandaled feet, the waves of the Mediterranean dash the blackened shores of Missolonghi, where Byron died in April 1824, and where the invading Ottoman forces burnt the town two years later in the final stages of the Greek Revolution. Smoke, clouds and incense are all messed up together, echoing the poignant confusion of these tiny liturgical dancers; but amidst the frenzied unravelling, there is method, deliberation and ritual. A logic of working through predominates: in the resolution performed by canonization, the smoke rising from the ruins becomes devotional incense and then the clouds of ascension. Scandalous celebrity is burnished into transcendent canonicity. As its ambiguous title suggests, the image enacts the canonization it represents: Byron and the image alike are "dedicated to the Romantics."

Barathier's smoke machine generates a heady mixture of classical antiquity, baroque agitation, neoclassical mannerism and Romantic consecration. Byron has been wildly, exuberantly, lifted out of context. Or has he? For all its kitsch transcendentalizing, this engraving was timely, commemorating the fall of Missolonghi and Byron's death. By aligning the two, Barathier recruits Byron's magnificent stock of symbolic capital to the causes of Greece and Romantic poetry. And for all its studied neoclassical detail, this commemoration is also an act of mourning, drenched with emotion.

Barathier's image also seems to fulfill the prophecy in one of Byron's very last poems, "On this day I complete my thirty sixth year," written in Missolonghi to commemorate his birthday on January 22, 1824:

> The fire that on my bosom preys
> Is lone as some Volcanic Isle,
> No torch is kindled at its blaze
> A funeral pile!
> (3, ll. 9–12 [*CPW* VII: 79]).

Smouldering here is Byron's unrequited love for his fifteen-year-old pageboy Loukas Chalandritsanos. Mary Shelley, Byron's amanuensis, added at the end of her copy of the poem: "E Spento quel fuoco – e lo copre piciol marmo" ("that fire is dead – and the marble pediment covers him" [*CPW* VII: 152, n. 40]). The presence of this note reminds us that Shelley's husband, Percy Bysshe Shelley, had died just over eighteen months earlier (in July 1822), his remains cremated on the beach at Viareggio. The note also highlights Mary Shelley's role in the process of textual creation. Contexts are also summoned by what the old New Critics used to call the "words on the page" or "the work itself." Texts such as Byron's poem, Shelley's copy or

Barathier's drawing are themselves powerful agents, changing the context of what is read or seen, keeping open the question of when – if ever – a text is completed. Posthumous publication and commemoration rekindle the torch.

Far from being an ahistorical celebration of the universal spirit of poetry, Barathier's drawing commemorates and transfigures historical events. His scene recalls Byron's funeral in Missolonghi, with its effusive eulogy spoken by Spyridon Trikoupis (who later wrote the first Greek history of the Revolution) and the crown of laurels placed upon the coffin – transforming what was originally "a rude, ill-constructed chest of wood" into the pure white marble sarcophagus of classical antiquity (Pietro Gamba, quoted in Marchand III: 1235–6). In keeping with ancient Greek customs, the marble pediment provides a home for the departed spirit and also releases it into the transcendent space of immortal fame. As to the body, Dr. Millingen, the attending physician, thought it "vied with that of Apollo himself," while, according to Missolonghi legend, the local woman who laid out the corpse fancied it "white like the wing of a young chicken" (Marchand III: 1231, 1232).

The impulse to canonize Byron – in 1826 as now – was by no means universal. Indeed, it was only continental Europe that celebrated Byron posthumously as the poet laureate of liberty. In France, as Gilles Soubigou notes, Byron was immediately transformed into "one of Europe's 'great men' – a hero who helped make a nation, modern Greece."[1] In Britain, however, skepticism prevailed. Westminster Abbey turned away both Byron's body and his statue. Many contemporaries poured scorn on Byron's political aspirations. The radical William Hazlitt regarded his participation in the Greek War of Independence as "preposterous *liberalism*."[2] That reading remained influential well into the twentieth century, but recent criticism confirms that Byron's politics were far more complex than previously thought, and far more imbricated with his poetry. Many of the chapters in this volume reflect that understanding.

Byron's writings themselves are saturated with context. Even at their most intimate, they usher the reader into the wider world, from the social, political and literary circles of Regency London to the geopolitical spaces of Napoleonic and post-Napoleonic Europe, the Middle East, the Americas and the Pacific. These geopolitical contexts are overlaid by biographical narratives of travel and exile, sustained from the opening canto of Byron's first commercial success, *Childe Harold's Pilgrimage* (1812–18), to *The Island* (1823), the last verse narrative Byron completed, about the

Bounty mutiny, where the Polynesian setting channels Byron's travels in Greece and his childhood in Scotland. Such interpenetration of the biographical, aesthetic and geopolitical is one of the constitutive pleasures and challenges of Byron's *oeuvre*.

This book aims to guide students, readers and researchers through the intersecting fields of biography, literary culture and reception, and the intellectual and cultural movements informing the history and politics of the Romantic period. It offers many ways of understanding Byron's works and heightening the pleasure of reading them, while elucidating their power as contexts themselves and highlighting their claim to agency and historical enactment in the wider world. It assembles work by scholars from around the globe on a range of vital topics grouped in four key categories: biography and textual production; political, social and intellectual contexts; literary cultures; and Byron's ongoing reception and interpretation.

Part I: Life and Works begins with the exploration of Byron's life as a context for his writing, in three broadly biographical chapters: "The Early Years" by Jonathan Gross, "The Years of Fame" by Diego Saglia and "Exile" by Jane Stabler. These chapters emphasize the interrelations between the personal, the literary and the political that are a hallmark of the Byron phenomenon. They are attuned to the intimate, social and intertextual relationships informing Byron's life and work, and explain the significance of the sites where he traveled, lived and wrote. From the beginning, Byron's writing is imbricated with place. So, Jonathan Gross observes about Byron's early writing: "Poetry became a contract of celebrity, a form of advertising for the small town of Southwell" in Nottinghamshire where the young Byron lived with his mother. Later, Diego Saglia details how "Byron's life was closely associated with Regency London as a metropolitan hub of pleasure, politics, culture and consumption." Here Byron blended his "cosmopolitan aura … with his metropolitan and provincial identities" and "monitored the literary scene." In her chapter on exile, Jane Stabler notes that exile for Byron was a state of mind – and a desired identity – well before it became an experiential reality; the young poet "rehearsed going into exile in 1809" at the age of twenty-one. In Italy, he adopted the quintessentially Italian verse-form of *ottava rima*, through which he "recast" his "role as a brooding outsider" and mounted a sustained attack on English expectations.

The chapters in the second half of Part I discuss how Byron's manuscripts became published texts, often disseminated in multiple material forms. They also illuminate the social dimensions of textual production and circulation. Outlining the complexities of Byron's often baffling writing methods, Tom Mole notes that Byron "rarely finished a poem in manuscript and then submitted it" for publication, but often adopted the ideas of his collaborators such as Mary Shelley, whose intentions "in effect became his own." Hence Byron's "intentions for his works are not always straightforwardly 'his.'" In the next chapter, Mary O'Connell highlights how Byron and his publishers jointly produced Byronic celebrity as a commercial enterprise, in spite of Byron's sustained "ambivalence about writing, publishing and commercial success." Finally, Gary Dyer examines the fakes, forgeries and piracies that became a vital component of Byronic textual production. These "illegitimate" publications accelerated the circulation of Byron's work and helped him establish his extraordinary popularity.

Part II: Political, Social and Intellectual Transformations registers the social and political changes that marked Regency Britain and Napoleonic and post-Napoleonic Europe during the Romantic period. The chapters in this section follow interconnected lines of enquiry across political, geopolitical, cross-cultural, social and intellectual contexts; they engage the public-intimate spheres that are inflected by broader transformations.

Several of the chapters deal with geopolitical shifts. As John Beckett observes, Byron's active political career, which began in Britain's House of Lords in 1809–16, shifted focus during his years of exile to encompass "involvement with the liberal-nationalist causes of the Carbonari and Greece." Byron took his seat as a liberal Whig when "the Tories were in power" and the "country was at war with France, as it had been almost continuously since 1793." War too was undergoing major changes, as Neil Ramsey observes: it was becoming total and global, "the conflict extending across Europe and reaching into the Indian subcontinent, America, and the Middle East." Ramsey's chapter explores how this conflict is registered with extraordinary complexity in Byron's work.

The next two chapters deal with Greece and Italy, where Byron spent most of his exile. Spiridoula Demetriou examines Byron's involvement in the Greek War of Independence and his relationship with contemporary British Philhellenism. She explores not only how Greece forms a context for understanding Byron, but also how Byron's life, writing and death there offer a context for understanding modern Greece. Reviewing Byron's response to Italy, Timothy Webb details his engagement with Italian language and culture, social and sexual customs, and the rituals of daily life that had such a profound influence on Byron's life and work.

Currents of cross-cultural exchange are central to Byron's life and writings and to the broader geopolitical transformations mediated by his work. Gerard Cohen-Vrignaud's chapter on "Orientalism" explores Byron as "a writer whose writing and personal mystique are fundamentally defined by his mobilization of cultural difference." It ponders how far Byron's "cultural appropriation of Eastern peoples, habits and settings" contributed to "the emerging regime of British imperialism, which reached its ideological and territorial peak in the long nineteenth century."

The mobilization of cultural difference was connected to a growing recognition of the cultural relativity of religious belief. Here, Christine Kenyon Jones reviews Byron's "shifting and multiple religious identifications and sympathies ... not only in relation to his biography but also within the complex landscape of religious belief and the politics of religion in the Romantic period." Religion was entangled with the emergence of science as an alternative source of authority. Thomas H. Ford observes how the "speculative materialism of Byron's poetry from the late 1810s" drew on contemporary scientific ideas, "particularly those he could mobilize against traditional religious conceptions of divine benevolence and official morality." Byron's work often forged "startling links ... between scientific concepts and the wider cultural and linguistic practices that generated them."

The book next turns to chapters on social-intimate contexts: "Sexuality" (Richard C. Sha), "Libertinism" (Adam Komisaruk) and "Fashion, Self-Fashioning and the Body" (Laura J. George). Richard C. Sha outlines how Romantic-period scientific discourse sought to produce normative modes of sexuality based on supposedly "natural" paradigms such as the Linnaean system of plant sexuality, which was used to allegorize human sexuality. In the following chapter, Adam Komisaruk grapples with the elusive phenomenon of libertinism, which forms an important context for a range of Byronic concerns. The meaning of the term is unstable, Komisaruk emphasizes, but productively so, with a range of applications, depending on whether it was used contemporaneously or retrospectively; by its adherents or detractors; in England or elsewhere; and depending on "how its variously spiritual, philosophical, political and sexual contexts did and did not intersect." Laura J. George closes this section with an examination of the domains of fashion, self-fashioning and the body. These provide a context for understanding Byron's "oppositional explorations of masculinity" that register how "[r]elationships between masculine style, specularity and power shifted dramatically" in Regency Britain.

Part III: Literary Cultures engages the specifically literary contexts of Byron's vast and complex multi-generic *oeuvre*. Emphasizing how Byron's literary form is always intertextually and socially grounded, the chapters in this section focus on literary traditions, genres, influences and sociable circles and "schools," locating Byron's formal concerns in their social and historical contexts and extending the biographical narrative plotted in Part I. Byron's works are situated within contexts of ever-changing traditions and currents of literary innovation. What becomes clear is that experimentation and transformation are the hallmarks of Byron's approach to tradition and influence. So Bernard Beatty outlines the eighteenth-century reworking of classical traditions that Byron in turn reworks, primarily through Pope. Illuminating both the stylistic practices and the controversies that informed Byron's relationship with the neoclassical tradition, Beatty demonstrates how his rejection of Romanticism's devaluation of the Augustans had "as much to do with politics as literary taste."

Other chapters in this section concern particular genres: epic, romance, lyric, satire and drama, proceeding from the earliest literary practitioners through to Byron's Romantic contemporaries. On epic, Carla Pomarè observes that Byron's participation in the genre is "a long-debated issue." He did, however, manifest a particular interest in historiography, which is "relevant … to almost all the genres he experimented with." As a result, Byron's epic was marked by a "peculiar investment in the relationships between the world of fiction and the world of facts."

Demonstrating how the aesthetic and the geopolitical are interconnected in Byron's work, Omar F. Miranda observes of the romance: "In his hands, a genre that had once been confined to the courts of medieval Europe developed into a global form with a diversity of subject matter and settings across Europe and Asia." Byron's participation in many genres is equally transformative – looking backwards to older traditions and forwards to the innovations of the avant-garde. Anna Camilleri's chapter on "Byron's Lyric Practice" explains how Byron's mode of lyric has been neglected because it runs counter to expectations of the genre: where lyric was supposed to be private and unheard, "Byron's lyric voice is performative, insincere, insouciant and playful." Audience is the key. As Mark Canuel demonstrates in his discussion of satire, "Byron's satirical stance criticizes the production of normative aesthetic and political values while carving out an inclusive yet rigorously refined discourse that connects the satiric persona to his audience."

That satirical opposition to normative values influenced alliances and antagonisms as well as the groupings of various "schools." Mirka Horová's chapter on the Satanic School engages the controversy surrounding Robert Southey's coinage of the moniker – delivered with "the causticity of a manic street preacher" – and Byron's provocative backward look to earlier forms of sympathy with the devil such as Milton's Satan and Whig libertinism. Similarly, Madeleine Callaghan's chapter on the Lake poets explores Byron's rich inter-textual relations with Coleridge and Wordsworth, in particular, arguing that "even at their most apparently divergent, the conversation between the poets reveals the depth of the engagement across their works." In the next chapter, Susan J. Wolfson takes up Southey as a powerful case study of intertextual revision in the form of Byron's "muse," "to show a different 'Southey,' not the one in Byron's scathing sights but a surprising brother in song."

One of the most dynamic sites of intertextual influence is also one of the most contested. The question of how Byron was influenced, and by whom, is particularly fraught in relation to women writers, as Caroline Franklin demonstrates. Charting Byron's habitual anxieties and ambivalence about women writers, she illuminates how his attacks on them often functioned as a "smokescreen" to deflect the visible signs of their influence on his work. Rather than seeing this misogyny as "quaint belatedness," Franklin traces it to contemporary conflicts, showing how "[t]he bluestocking values of female intellectualism and philanthropy survived the antifeminist reaction following the French revolution."

Continuing Part III's discussion of schools, Maria Schoina notes in her essay on the Pisan circle and the Cockney school that some of the schools were coinages manufactured by "reactionary periodicals" channeling "Tory anxiety over the formation of 'free thinking' literary circles." Nevertheless, they often reflect shared poetic enterprises and political ideals based on active affiliations, sociable networks and friendships. So, for example, understanding Byron's involvement in the oft-derided "Pisan circle, and its affiliate, the Cockney School of poetry," sheds light on "certain phases of the poet's career [and] also Romantic literary and political culture in general."

In his essay on "Theater and Drama", Rolf P. Lessenich explores the relationship between publicity and closet drama that energizes Byron's drama and its perversely mediated relation to the London stage: "On the one hand, provocative heresy had to be made public in order to question received opinions and create scandalous celebrity; on the other, publication and public performance risked intervention" by the government. This is followed by chapters on autobiography (Alan Rawes) and literary theory (Clara Tuite), seemingly marginal genres in Byron's work. Both chapters trace how the structuring impulses of autobiography and theory animate Byron's oeuvre. Rawes' chapter locates Byron's "self-writing" in relation to two eighteenth-century models: Jean-Jacques Rousseau's confessional "unveiling" and the "fictional autobiographer" of Laurence Sterne's *Tristram Shandy* that reflects on the difficulties of any attempt to narrativize "a coherent self." Rawes identifies how these two modes of "revealing the intimacies of the self and/or reflecting on selfhood per se … were to become key tropes of Romantic autobiography." Part III closes with Andrew Franta's chapter on periodical culture, which examines how Byron's career developed in "close proximity to the developing culture of reviewing," and argues that "the literary world into which the new poet sought to introduce himself in the early nineteenth century was one that was in the process of being remade by the interconnection of poetry and the reviews."

Part IV: Reception and Afterlives considers the history of reception, reinvention and afterlife that Byron has inspired, from the original moment of production to our current moment – exploring the diverse cultures of reception that continue to mark the Byron phenomenon as a living ecology in the twenty-first century.

Picking up from Franta's chapter, William Christie surveys the critical reception of Byron's work during his lifetime in the major periodicals. Detailing how Byron's early collection *Hours of Idleness* (1807) suffered under the nominally Whig *Edinburgh*'s "labile, upper-class critical hijinks," Christie notes that the big reviews, such as the *Edinburgh*, the *Quarterly Review* and *Blackwood's Edinburgh Magazine*, "may have had barely concealed political priorities, but this did not always translate into predictable allegiances." Moving from mainstream reception, Jason Goldsmith takes us to the dynamic cultures of radical and labouring-class reception – a world that includes William Hone's parodies, John Clare's Byron poems and Chartist poems and manifestos of the 1830s and 1840s, all of which enthusiastically embraced Byron's politics and literature, in sharp contrast to mainstream Whig and Tory reception in England.

Peter Vassallo explores how Byron's European reception focused as much on Byron's political influence as his literary influence, particularly in Italy and Greece, where Byron was celebrated as "a champion of liberalism and nationalistic sentiment." Nevertheless, the European "reading and misreading" of Byron's poems and persona could be complex and contradictory, with Byron regarded in France, for example, as both a "pro-Bonapartist aristocrat" and a symbol of revolution.

Julian North discusses the vast archive of recollections, conversations and biographies of Byron that appeared after his death in 1824, arguing that "the many thousands of pages of biography devoted to Byron in the decades following his death formed the most substantial embodiment of his evolving cultural presence through the nineteenth century."

Eric Eisner addresses the later nineteenth-century reception and reworking of Byron in Britain and North America, where he finds a hardening separation between critical and popular reception. Ironically, he points out, "Within a strengthening critical hierarchy distinguishing commercial entertainment from 'serious' literature, however, Byron's very popularity told against him. Even by the early 1830s, critics spoke of the embarrassing excesses of 'Byromania' as a bygone fad." More recently, as Lindsey Eckert observes, Byron has displayed extraordinary endurance as both a subject of scholarly interest and a figure of popular culture in the twentieth and twenty-first centuries, across a range of cultural media. "Byron's popular reception history reveals itself most strikingly" when looking "beyond the literary and printed to the variety of quirky and kitsch, serious and sensational, digital and decorative adaptations indebted to his life and works."

In her account of contemporary scholarship, Ghislaine McDayter notes it is "one of the greatest ironies of literary studies that the poet most renowned for his 'self-conscious' biographical impulses and 'egotism' has nonetheless inspired a deep sense of mystery about the 'truth' of his character, his poetic process and his art." On the topic of truth, McDayter argues that "for many prior scholars, what makes Byron 'wanting' as a poet might have been the fact that he could not be situated within their own paradigms of Romanticism," but that "for a new generation of scholars … the poet's resistance to such universalizing theories is his greatest appeal."

Byron's writing, life and spectacular model of authorship transformed literary culture in the Regency period and inspired new reading practices. How does this writing and these changed modes of reading speak to us now in the twenty-first century? Every chapter in this volume shows how reading functions as an act of contextualization or recontextualization. Each contributor proposes an act of recontextualization. Ultimately, as each of these chapters illuminates a particular aspect of Byron's work, life and reception – providing frames of reference for reading the work and understanding Byron's vital place within Romantic literature – they also provide insights into how we might think of "Byron" not only in context but also *as* context.

In producing this book, my primary debt is to the contributors for their superb scholarship, professionalism and collegiality. It has been my privilege to work with and learn from such an inspired and inspiring group of Byron scholars. I thank them for their brilliance and creativity.

At Cambridge University Press, Linda Bree has been a guiding spirit and gifted enabler of Romanticist scholarship for many years. I am indebted to her for commissioning the volume, and for her sound advice and trusted support throughout the planning and early stages. Her successor, Bethany Thomas, has smoothly taken over the process and, with Natasha Burton, the assistance of Sarah Lambert and Carrie Parkinson, seen the volume into print with thoughtful and enthusiastic support. I also thank Emily Morgan, Jenny Slater and Kelly Derrick for their attentive professionalism. The anonymous readers for the Press offered constructive feedback and helpful suggestions.

The editing, editorial and research assistance, as well as research and writing of my own contributions, were partially funded by the Australian Government through the Australian Research Council. The School of Culture and Communication, University of Melbourne, and my Head of School, Jennifer Milam, provided generous financial support through a Publication Grant to assist with costs.

This book has been particularly well served by outstanding research and editorial assistance. Thomas Vranken assisted in the early stages, carefully shepherding and bedding the chapters down in the Press style with a fine eye for detail, and later managed the acquisition of illustrations. Caitlyn Lehmann was meticulous in preparing the typescript for the Press and skillfully compiled the Index. Jenny Lee provided expert assistance, reading every chapter with tireless acuity, insight, care and dedication, adding value to the editorial process at every turn. Their contributions have enhanced the book – and the process of its production – immeasurably.

NOTES

1 Gilles Soubigou, "French Portraits of Byron, 1824–1880," *Byron Journal* 36.1 (2008), 46.
2 William Hazlitt, *The Spirit of the Age: Or Contemporary Portraits* (London: Henry Colburn, 1825), 179.

PART I

Life and Works

CHAPTER I

Early Years

Jonathan Gross

George Gordon, the sixth Lord Byron (1788–1824), was the son of Captain John Byron (1756–91), known as "Mad Jack," and his second wife, Catherine, *née* Gordon (1765–1811). Lord Byron, the poet, inherited his title from his great-uncle, known as "Wicked Lord Byron," who killed one of his relatives in a duel in a poorly lit tavern, the Star and Garter in Pall Mall, on January 26, 1765. The victim was William Chaworth, father of Mary Chaworth, Byron's distant cousin and early beloved. Notorious for his poor treatment of his wife and for allowing crickets to crawl over his body unmolested, the uncle denuded Newstead of trees and escaped a sentence of capital punishment for his crimes.

Born in rented rooms in London (16 Holles Street), Byron traced his ancestry to the Buruns, contemporaries of William the Conqueror. In England, his ancestors fought bravely in the Civil Wars, with five members of his family participating. On his mother's side, Sir William Gordon, first of the House of Gight, fell at Flodden Field in 1513. Byron boasted of his Scottish descent from James I, but piqued himself more particularly on his paternal ancestry. He took pleasure in reviving the memory of his grandfather "Foul Weather Jack" (1723–86), an admiral who attracted sea storms, encountered a race of giant Patagonians in South America, and left a journal of a shipwreck that influenced Canto III of *Don Juan*.[1] As a young boy enrolled at Dulwich school, just south of London, Byron earned the epithet "the Old English Baron" for referring so often to his illustrious ancestry (Marchand 1: 59).

After her ill-fated marriage to Captain John Byron in 1785, Byron's mother Catherine Byron spent four unprofitable years attempting to live with her husband, enduring financial hardship, until she finally left in 1789 for Scotland, bringing her son up in Aberdeen and treating his deformed right foot with a special shoe recommended by the surgeon John Hunter (Marchand 1: 25). Though her name was connected to the lands of Gight, she would eventually occupy Newstead Abbey, which she first saw in 1798, when her son inherited the estate and they moved back to England. Catherine Byron stayed on the estate to oversee business and prepare the property for Byron's maturity, but rented lodgings for her son in Nottingham to enable him to continue his formal education. Here he lived alone with his nurse, May Gray. With Catherine Byron twelve miles away at Newstead, Gray "played tricks with his person," sexually molesting him, as John Hanson, the family lawyer, later confirmed (Marchand 1: 57). Byron had unburdened himself to Hanson, who promptly informed Byron's mother that the nurse was bad for her son but withheld specific details. Catherine Byron dismissed the servant, hearing only rumors of Gray's friends beating her son. (The truth came out as late as 1824, when Hanson told Byron's close friend, John Cam Hobhouse, after Byron's death.)[2] At this time, the east wing of Newstead Abbey had no roof, the monks' reception room and grand refectory were filled with hay, and "the entrance hall and monks' parlor were stables for cattle."[3] While Newstead underwent repairs, Mrs. Byron leased the property for five years to Lord Grey de Ruthyn and enrolled her son in Dr. Glennie's school in Dulwich. At fourteen, the young boy wrote his first poem to his cousin Margaret Parker: "Hush'd are the winds, and still the evening gloom, / Not e'en a zephyr wanders through the grove" (*CPW* 1: 125, ll. 1–2).

Byron's emotional intensity was also evident in school at Harrow, where he enrolled in 1801. He cut a more social figure than the misanthropic pose he was later to strike as Childe Harold. In addition to "P. Hunter, Curzon, Long and Tatersall," he befriended "Clare, Cs Gordon, De Bath, Claridge, and John Wingfield" (Moore 1: 36). His attachment to Lord Clare and William Harness was lifelong. "Harness, if any fellow bullies you, tell me; and I'll thrash him if I can," he wrote to his school friend (Moore 1: 39). Mrs. Byron's friendship (from 1803) with Lord Grey de Ruthyn, who allegedly took an inappropriate sexual interest in Byron, shaped the poet's views of love for years to come and found poignant expression in the "satiety" of Childe Harold.

There were also more conventional relationships. He spent the summer of 1802 in Malvern Hills near Cheltenham, and the next at Annesley Hall in Nottinghamshire, a few miles west of Newstead, with Mary Ann Chaworth, who inspired Byron's "The Dream." From 1803 to 1807, when he was not away at school or university, Byron stayed with his mother at Burgage Manor, the property she rented at Southwell, the small Nottinghamshire town near Newstead. In October 1804, a young, fat and rather bashful Lord Byron returned to Harrow, emotionally wounded and embarrassed by Mary Ann's rejection of him in favor of a more athletic suitor, the twenty-six-year-old John ("Jack") Musters. "What! Do you think I could care anything for that lame boy" Byron supposedly overheard Mary Ann say.[4] What gave Byron the strength to return to school was the renewal of his intimacy at Southwell in 1806 with twenty-two-year-old Elizabeth Bridget (later Pigot) and her nineteen-year-old brother, John Margaret Becher Pigot, who was studying medicine at Edinburgh. Both Mrs. Byron and her son patronized the theatrical community at Southwell and the Pigot family as early as 1804. Elizabeth gave Byron confidence as a writer and as a man, encouraging his literary interests, flattering him into verse.

Byron cultivated a circle at Southwell, and then in London, that enabled him to gauge how his poetry would be received, and where and when it could best be disseminated. "I am sorry – but 'Childish Recollections' must be suppressed during this edition. I have altered, at your suggestion, the *obnoxious allusions* in the sixth stanza of my last ode," he wrote to John Becher (Moore 1: 117). In 1806, Byron reined in his own muse on the advice of friends like Becher; while he courted controversy, he was always aware of how his lordly postures would be read by the world beyond his immediate circles, which would later become a scandalized but fawning public. Byron created a chronology of impressions, of vivid tableaus, in which he would emerge as both an actor and a painter. In a letter to his half-sister Augusta Leigh, for example, he declared his intention to "*fall violently* in love, it will serve as an amusement pour passer le temps, and it will at least have the charm of novelty to recommend it, then you know in the course of a few weeks I shall be quite au desespoir, shoot myself and Go out of the world with eclat" (*BLJ* 1: 48). By the time he met Mary Chaworth, the pleasant theatrics of love had given way to some grim realities.

As a young boy at Harrow, Byron could still play at love, writing letters casting himself as a charming raconteur, master of the under-look (even in prose), traducer of intimacies, lover of animals. As his early poetry took shape, Byron provoked the very women who flattered him. "I hate Southwell," he wrote to the good-natured Elizabeth Pigot, setting the stage for later mercurial responses to Harrow, Cambridge and England itself. By posing as an eighteenth-century sentimentalist and hard-edged satirist, Byron freed himself from the provincialism of Southwell. "Half a Scot by birth" (*CPW* v: 442, ll. 135–6), Byron cultivated his status as sexual and national outsider. Poetry became a contract of celebrity, a form of advertising for the small town of Southwell. He divided those who could promote his career from those who he thought seemed intent on destroying him.

When Byron started school at Dulwich, his cousin, Lord Carlisle, had been persuaded by Hanson to become Byron's nominal guardian. Carlisle's apparent condescension, neglect and dismissive tone particularly rankled. First, when Byron sent him a copy of *Hours of Idleness*, Carlisle replied with a perfunctory note. He increased the offense by not introducing Byron personally to the House of Lords when Byron came of age on January 22, 1809, his twenty-first birthday, forcing Robert Dallas to do so (Moore 1: 134–5). Byron took his revenge by dismissing the "paralytic puling" of Carlisle's verses in a new edition of *English Bards and Scotch Reviewers*. Upon taking his seat before going abroad, Byron refused to shake the hand of Lord Eldon, the Lord Chancellor and chair of the House, offering only his fingertips. Some might ascribe Byron's thin-skinned hauteur to the broken family from which he hailed, his late ascendancy to aristocracy and his outsider status as an impoverished Lord. Not until he published *Childe Harold's Pilgrimage* (1812) and began his liaisons with Lady Caroline Lamb and Lady Oxford, and his epistolary friendship with Lady Melbourne, did he become comfortably ensconced in Whig society, the same society that would cast him out four years later.

How did all this transpire? How did Byron make this transition? At Burgage Manor and under the auspices of Elizabeth Pigot in Southwell, Byron performed in various amateur theatricals, portraying himself as a charming and world-weary roué. When he took residence in Newstead Abbey in the fall of 1808, he directed an all-male cast in Edward Young's *The Revenge* (*BLJ* 1: 170). Byron's theatrical performances at Harrow and Newstead were secluded, striking an unconventional note in his development. Not for him William Kent's Temple of Virtue, which included gardens, grottoes and sculptures celebrating political luminaries. Byron, by contrast, followed the lead of the dissolute Charles James Fox. He went a step further toward the Gothic than Fox in encouraging his friends to drink wine out of skulls and engage in activities reminiscent of Francis Dashwood's "Hell-Fire Club," once frequented by Benjamin Franklin. Half-masonic ritual and half-religious scoffing, the male bonding that occurred in Nottingham anticipates the third act of *Manfred*, and Byron's intense involvement with the Cacciatori Americani, a branch of the Carbonari in Ravenna.[5] At Newstead, Byron rehearsed for his subsequent performances on the stage of life and letters.

In moving from Southwell to London in 1808, Byron watched his weight and burnished his self-regard, which eventually made him popular with dandies like Beau Brummell. His associates included the ballet master

D'Egville and Grimaldi the clown. He continued with the fencing lessons from Henry Angelo that he had taken at Harrow and Cambridge, and from 1806 took boxing lessons from the heavyweight champion Gentleman Jackson at the Pugilistic Club at 13 Bond Street. Jackson was significant enough to appear as the subject of a note in *Don Juan* 11: "I refer to my old friend and corporeal pastor and master, John Jackson, Esq. Professor of Pugilism, who I trust still retains the strength and symmetry of his model of a form, together with his good humour and athletic, as well as mental accomplishments" (Moore 1: 121).

As he prepared *English Bards* for the press, Byron fluctuated between a manly defiance of reviewers like Henry Brougham, who would dismiss his talent (though Byron thought his first hostile reviewer of *Hours of Idleness* [1807] was Francis Jeffrey), and a facetious relationship to his own aristocratic privileges: his associates included John Cam Hobhouse, Scrope Berdmore Davies, Charles Skinner Matthews and other highly intellectual, thoughtful Cambridge students who excelled in their respective fields. Hobhouse founded the Whig club at Cambridge, and Davies and Matthews hid their academic gifts beneath a patter of high-jinks behavior.

On July 2, 1809, having come of age in January, Byron set off on his grand tour, a traditional rite of passage for young eighteenth-century upper-class men. Davies guaranteed the loan that made the trip possible, and Byron traveled with Hobhouse, who would become his lifelong friend. The conventional tour to Italy and France was ruled out by the Napoleonic wars; Byron initially suggested visiting Germany, Austria and Russia, but eventually took a less conventional route around the eastern Mediterranean. He had an abiding interest in the Islamic world, and had written to Hanson in 1808 of his wish to study "India and Asiatic policy and manners" (*BLJ* 1: 175). In 1807, he had compiled a "*Cosmopolite* account" of his reading that took in a vast range of cultures and "works of the European & ... the Asiatic" (*CMP* 3), ranging across Spain, Portugal, Arabia, Turkey, Persia, Hindostan, the Birman Empire, China and Africa, as well as writing in Latin and ancient Greek. Traveling for two years, Byron visited Portugal, Spain, Gibraltar, Malta, Greece, Albania and Turkey. These travels inspired his first great literary success, *Childe Harold* 1–11, which appeared in 1812, and the Eastern tales (*The Giaour* and *The Bride of Abydos*, [1813], *The Corsair* and *Lara* [1814] and *Siege of Corinth* [1816]), and later *Sardanapalus* (1821) and the Greek and Turkish cantos of *Don Juan* (1819–1823).

Another attraction of the East seems to have been the opportunities for sexual relationships with other young men and boys available in Greece, Albania and Turkey. In September 1809, Byron and Hobhouse visited

Albania, one of the least accessible parts of Europe, and met its quasi-independent ruler, Ali Pasha, legendary as a ruthless tyrant, but who Byron found a charming host (and who he would use as a source for Lambro in the *Bride of Abydos*). The travelers arrived in Athens on December 25, 1809 and stayed with the Macri family until March 1810 and again briefly in July, before Hobhouse returned to England. For much of the time between mid-August 1810 and April 1811, Byron lived at the Capuchin Monastery in Athens, where in March he began writing *The Curse of Minerva*, which dealt with Elgin's removal of the Parthenon frieze. Here, he met the young boy Nicolò Giraud, who instructed Byron in Italian and with whom he developed a relationship. When Byron returned to England in July 1811, he remembered Giraud with a generous bequest.

Byron was not as indifferent to social causes as his aristocratic poses suggested. In the House of Lords, after returning from Europe, Byron would eventually defend the frame-breakers of Nottingham (February 27, 1812) and support Catholic emancipation (April 21, 1812). Perhaps these liberal tendencies grew out of his engagement with talented friends like Matthews, Edward Long and John Edleston, some of whom were not as well off as he was; and even Byron recognized that his aristocratic position was not matched by a ready flow of capital. He was "dipp'd," as he confessed to his Cambridge friend Francis Hodgson, before boasting that the sale of Newstead would set him to rights.

In 1807, Byron reviewed William Wordsworth's poetry in the jargon of the day. "The characteristics of Mr. W.'s muse are simple and flowing, though occasionally inharmonious verse," Byron wrote loftily (*CMP* 8). Two years later, however, *English Bards* attacked almost every living contemporary, including some he had praised in his letters: Wordsworth, Hodgson, Coleridge. Nor were poets the only target. He had a much-flaunted rivalry with the headmaster of Harrow, Revd. Dr. Butler, who he satirized as "Pomposus" (*CPW* i: 132), a barb he later rescinded. Not everyone was impressed by the self-regarding figure Byron cut at this time. Isaac D'Israeli, for example, contrasted the Byron of 1808 with the Byron of 1812. The first was an affected figure, stabbing the air with his cane, and wearing perfumed shirts with lacy ruffles; the latter was far more impressive because subdued, graceful and understated.[6]

Above making money in literary concerns, he was not afraid to obtain profits from his lands, raise his rents and drive a hard bargain: "Hanson, my agent, intimated my Lancashire property was worth three Newsteads," he gloated to Francis Hodgson. Despite such wealth, Byron was short of cash. He dined on the modest fare of eggs and ale for his twenty-first birthday (Moore 1: 130), and apologized to his mother for fitting up Newstead Abbey in a lordly style. She would be the true beneficiary of Newstead's redecorations, he explained, especially when he traveled abroad. This may not have been the whole truth. Byron's self-exculpations had become habitual at this point. His easy habit of overlooking the sacrifices of others while pursuing his own pleasure shaped his subsequent behavior with Caroline Lamb, Anne Isabella Milbanke, Claire Clairmont and even Teresa Guiccioli, when he departed or ended relationships at times that suited his convenience.

Such strikingly different postures raise other questions about what Moore called "the sincerity of his gloom" (Moore 1: 152). His Gothic posturing inspired comment and was meant to do so, as were the wolf and bear that his friend Matthews found when visiting Newstead (Moore 1: 142). In his letters, he announced even more stagey transformations, such as his loss of four stone in weight between leaving Southwell and arriving at college: some of his friends could no longer recognize him. At Cambridge, he brought a tame bear to Trinity College, and imitated the witty and insolent repartee of Brummell when he announced that it would sit for a fellowship. The cultivation of wild animals was sincere, however, as was his sadness when his beloved Newfoundland dog Boatswain died of rabies. Byron constructed a monument with a poetic epitaph, which Hobhouse mocked by writing the following prose lampoon of the genre, which has always been assumed to be Byron's: "Near this Spot /Are deposited the Remains of one / Who possessed Beauty without Vanity / Strength without Insolence / Courage without Ferocity, / And all the Virtues of Man without his Vices." Like Alexander Pope, William Beckford and Edward Young, Byron had a striking attachment to animals, even if his misanthropic sentimentality was sometimes mocked by his closest friend. Samuel Jackson Pratt wrote a sentimental poem ("The Partridges – An Elegy," 1771) about a mother bird worried about her chicks, and became one of Byron's early advocates, sending him a consolatory poem after Brougham's negative review of *English Bards*. William Wilberforce presaged the serious side of Byron's politics, with his sympathy for the underdog, for animals and for the politically disenfranchised such as Catholics and Jews. Again, Byron's behavior was a reflection, rather than a departure, from late eighteenth-century England and the cult of sensibility popularized by Henry Mackenzie's *Man of Feeling* (1771) and Laurence Sterne's *A Sentimental Journey Through France and Italy* (1768). Byron knew that praising dogs was a way of dispraising humans. Whether he was commemorating the tears he shed at parting with his Cornelian,

John Edleston, or the death of Boatswain, Byron exhibited a capacity for emotion that was bound to end in disappointment.

That disappointment was soon channeled into outrage at the complacency of Spain, Portugal and Italy succumbing to Napoleonic bullying. For Byron, and even for Wordsworth, England won the battle of Talavera and lost the peace during the 1808 Convention of Cintra, an important part of the divisive Peninsular War that affected the growth of the *liberales* party in Spain and liberalism generally for a generation (especially in the Holland House circle, which cultivated the Spanish émigré Joseph Blanco White, who advocated independence in South America). On the continent, the revolution of feeling expressed itself in an interest in political revolutions (Moore 1: 145). Byron combined his own first-hand observations of war-torn Europe with deep reading in such diverse works as John Moore's *Zeluco* (1789) and Louis-Charles Fougeret de Monbron's *Le Cosmopolite* (1750), which he used as the epigraph to *Childe Harold* (1812), the poem that made him famous overnight. Early drafts include the self-identifying phrase "Childe Burun," modified to Childe Harold as the poem developed. When he returned to England in July 1811, complete with the manuscript of his revelations in hand, it was clear to Robert Dallas and other relatives that Childe Byron had grown up at last.

Notes

1 *Oxford Dictionary of National Biography*, s. v. "Byron, John (1723–1786), naval officer," by Alan G. Jamieson, accessed December 7, 2017, https://doi. org/10.1093/ref:odnb/4282.

2 Violet W. Walker, *The House of Byron* (London: Quiller Press, 1988), 184.

3 William W. Pratt, *Byron at Southwell: The Making of a Poet, with New Poems and Letters from the Rare Books Collections of The University of Texas* (New York: Haskell House, 1973), 1.

4 Quoted in Benita Eisler, *Byron: Child of Passion, Fool of Fame* (New York: Alfred A. Knopf, 1999), 68.

5 Iris Origo, *The Last Attachment: The Story of Byron and Teresa Guiccioli* (Brooklyn, NY: Helen Marks Books/Books & Co., 2000), 215.

6 James Ogden, *Isaac D'Israeli* (Oxford: Oxford University Press, 1969), 117.

CHAPTER 2

The Years of Fame

Diego Saglia

On November 4, 1811, the Whig poet and banker Samuel Rogers invited Byron to dine at his house together with fellow poets Thomas Campbell and Thomas Moore. To his host's consternation, Byron declined all offers of food and drink, seemingly pleased with "potatoes bruised down on his plate and drenched with vinegar." A few days later, on meeting Byron's friend John Cam Hobhouse, Rogers enquired: "How long will Lord Byron persevere in his present diet?" The answer was: "Just as long as you continue to notice it" (*HVSV* 41). This anecdote, from a few months before Byron became the most talked-about poet in Britain, significantly catches him in the process of learning to "act famous." Not yet a literary star, he comes across as a moody *poseur*, knowingly playing with his audience and their intersecting gazes, at the center of which is his own body, that pivotal and hugely problematic part of the Byronic myth.

The twenty-three-year-old Byron had returned from his two-year tour of the Mediterranean, landing at Sheerness, Kent, on July 14, 1811. Between then and the publication of *Childe Harold's Pilgrimage* I–II on March 3, 1812, he moved restlessly from London to Canterbury, Cambridge, Rochdale and the family's ancestral home at Newstead in Nottinghamshire; was persecuted by his creditors; had a mismanaged affair with the Newstead maid, Susan Vaughan; and delivered his maiden speech in the House of Lords on February 27, 1812. On publishing *Childe Harold* I–II, he became an overnight success, awoke and "found [himself] famous": his years of fame had thus officially started (Moore 1: 347). Popularized by Peter Quennell's homonymous book of 1935, the phrase "the years of fame" describes the period between Byron's return from the grand tour of 1809–11 and his departure into exile in 1816. More recently, scholars have investigated these years in light of the onset of "Byromania" and Byron's transformation into an icon of celebrity culture, which generated a new mode of celebrity offering a "perverse insight into – and ability to manipulate – an economy of desire" and combining "glamor with notoriety."[1] These categories and phenomena converged and interacted within the web of contexts characterizing Byron's years of fame.

Between 1811 and 1816, Byron's life was closely associated with Regency London as a metropolitan hub of pleasure, politics, culture and consumption. However, placed between his Mediterranean tour and later "exile tour," this very English period was also characterized by Byron's distinctive restlessness and "*mobilité*" (Blessington 110). Coming under pressure from various fronts (especially financial problems and the loss of his mother and some close friends), after his return in 1811 he repeatedly declared his intention to leave the country. On August 30, 1811, he wrote to his half-sister Augusta Leigh: "I shall leave England & all it's clouds for the East again" (*BLJ* 2: 85). In fact, he stayed; yet this was only an apparently static phase in his life. In these years, his cosmopolitan aura blended with his metropolitan and provincial identities: the English Byron of this period (which he later reworked in "Detached Thoughts" and the English cantos of *Don Juan*) was still typically on the move. He traveled between London and the provinces, and faced a series of troubling events; he also abandoned himself to pleasure, making new experiences and acquaintances – all of this, wrapped up in the exhilarating, challenging condition of fame.

A series of deaths afflicted Byron soon after his return from the East. In early August, his mother died aged forty-six before he could travel to Newstead to visit her. Despite their tempestuous relationship, Byron was devastated. In the same month, he learnt that his Cambridge friend and role model Charles Skinner Matthews had drowned in the Cam and his schoolfriend John Wingfield had died in Spain. Then, in October, he discovered that his beloved Cambridge choirboy John Edleston had died in May. When revising *Childe Harold* I–II for publication, Byron added an elegy to Wingfield, a tribute to Matthews in a note, and some melancholy closing stanzas that gave the poem a much gloomier tone. Addressing himself, he wrote: "Soon shall thy voice be lost amid the throng / Of louder minstrels in these later days," dejectedly concluding that "none are left to please when none are left to love" (*CPW* II: 75, ll. 884–5, 890). Edleston inspired him to write a sequence of poems addressed to a pseudonymous Thyrza, six of which appeared in the first and second editions of *Childe Harold* I–II (and were read as addressing a woman). By early September 1811, believing himself hounded by death and a cause of unhappiness to others, he felt irredeemably alone and wrote to Robert Charles Dallas, his early editor and agent: "my friends are dead or estranged, and my existence a dreary void" (*BLJ* 2: 92). These preoccupations unsurprisingly resurfaced in poem after poem, from the Oriental tales to *Parisina* and eventually *Manfred*.

Byron's exposure to death informs one of his most curious writings from this period. In a letter of August 12, 1811, he forwarded to his Nottingham lawyer the draft of a will – a genuine expression of despair, though characteristically filled with extravagant and theatrical gestures *(BLJ* 2: 71–2). The will throws into relief another of Byron's preoccupations in these years – cash – as he contemplates the sale of the family's property in Rochdale and leaving money to Nicolò Giraud, a boy he had befriended in Athens; his solicitor John Hanson; his Cambridge friend Scrope Berdmore Davies and his valet William Fletcher. He also stipulates that he should be "buried in the vault of the garden at Newstead" *(BLJ* 2: 72) together with his dog Boatswain, an irreverent statement that once again draws attention to Byron's body, a crucial focus of interest for himself and soon for his adoring public too. Shot through with a heavy dose of theatricality, the will uncovers a nexus of money, body and death that bespeaks his concerns with materiality and mutability, as well as with the transcendental significance of everyday facts or "common things" (one possible interpretation of *communia* in the Horatian epigraph to *Don Juan*).

Money was a constant cause of anxiety for Byron, whose creditors beset him as soon as he set foot back in England. In July 1811 he examined his finances with his banker John Hanson *(BLJ* 2: 62); in September he wrote to Dallas: "my circumstances are become involved" *(BLJ* 2: 92); and in October he admitted to Hobhouse: "my situation is perplexing" *(BLJ* 2: 115). Circumstances were compounded by the sale of Newstead Abbey to Thomas Claughton the following year, a failed operation that dragged on until August 1814 (Byron made £25,000 from this unsuccessful negotiation; the property was eventually sold to Colonel Thomas Wildman in 1817 for £94,500, roughly £4.4 million in today's currency). Money also partly drove Byron's search for a wife. He toyed with the idea of marrying a rich woman, and some of the attraction of Anna Isabella (Annabella) Milbanke lay in her prospective inheritance as the niece of the wealthy, childless Thomas Noel, Viscount Wentworth – beside her intellectual accomplishments and social connections as Lady Melbourne's niece. When Byron's creditors heard of the couple's wedding on January 2, 1815 and their elegant London lodgings at 13 Piccadilly Terrace, they teamed together in April 1815 to bring legal action and demand payment of his arrears. In November, a bailiff entered the Byrons' house and installed himself there. Undoubtedly, the fact of being constantly "embarrassed" *(BLJ* 3: 32) bore on the poet's mood and mental stability, and was a factor in the rapid failure of his marriage and final separation from his wife. Money matters also involved his complex psychological relationship to the staggering sales of his works and his refusal of the proceeds and copyrights, which he extravagantly bestowed or tried to bestow on acquaintances such as Dallas, William Godwin and Samuel Taylor Coleridge.

More broadly, money points to Byron's conflicted relation to transactions and exchanges, and the obligations that money and generosity establish between individuals. The resulting picture is the highly contradictory one of a dashing cosmopolitan and literary lion dealing with prosaic questions, and an aristocrat desperately trying to sell his ancestral seat. This panorama also reflects the significance of money in Regency London with its culture of aristocratic consumption, which Byron eagerly embraced as befitting his status. He adopted expensive dandyish habits, frequented exclusive clubs and partook in the high and low pleasures offered by the metropolis, eventually ensconcing himself at the heart of exclusive Mayfair when he moved into the Albany residential complex, off Piccadilly, in 1814.

The backbone of this culture of consumption, London's upper classes, made Byron a star. A provincial aristocrat without social connections, he became, as the Duchess of Devonshire wrote, the "subject of conversation, curiosity, of enthusiasm almost," being "courted, visited, flattered, and praised" everywhere he went (*BCH* 35). Taking an active part in the networks of Regency London, he attended clubs, coteries, aristocratic houses and salons: Almack's, Watier's, the dandies and Melbourne House, among others. As his popularity spread, his circle of literary acquaintances and friends expanded correspondingly. In 1812, also owing to the success of *Childe Harold* I–II, his publisher John Murray moved his premises from the Strand to Albemarle Street in Mayfair, and there Byron met Walter Scott, who became his friend and correspondent, and William Gifford, Murray's literary adviser and a staunch Tory, whom Byron nevertheless liked and respected. The literary connections he forged in these years were distinctly bipartisan: Gifford and Scott among the Tories, whereas among the Whigs, Thomas Moore became possibly his most important new friend after Rogers effected their reconciliation over a quarrel dating back to Byron's satirizing of Moore in *English Bards*. A society poet, and often excoriated for it, Moore was linked to the Whig political and cultural hub of Holland House. Though rather desultorily, Byron himself gravitated around Lord Holland and his circle. He sought Holland's advice in preparing his maiden speech in the Lords, and through Holland and the Whig oligarchy he developed his interest in the stage.

Byron's characteristic alertness to the link between politics and theater was at its most intense in this period. On March 26, 1813, he wrote to Augusta of his disappointment in the House of Lords; rehearsing a well-established metaphor, he declared his intention not "to 'strut another hour' on that stage" (*BLJ* 3: 32). A year earlier, he had made his parliamentary debut with a speech against the Frame Work Bill, with which the Tory government aimed to impose the death penalty on anyone guilty of destroying textile machinery. Lord Holland found his speech "not exempt from affectation" and "not at all suited to our common notions of Parliamentary eloquence" (Marchand 1: 322). It was more a stage-worthy piece of oratory than serviceable political rhetoric. Byron himself acknowledged he had spoken "very violent sentences," his delivery "perhaps a little theatrical" (*BLJ* 2: 167). Overall, the world of politics proved to be less satisfactory than expected. In June 1812, he was introduced to the Prince Regent, but never aligned himself with his followers. He had already satirized the prince's discarding of his earlier Whig allies on becoming regent in "Lines to a Lady Weeping," published in the *Morning Chronicle* on March 7, 1812. Instead, he supported the Regent's estranged wife Caroline, Princess of Wales, who became a focus of interest for the parliamentary opposition.

In 1812, Holland's chaperoning of Byron took a theatrical turn. The Whig leader invited the ostensibly Whig poet to write the address for the reopening of the Whig-sponsored Drury Lane Theatre on October 20, after all the submissions to the competition organized for the occasion had proved unsuitable. Byron's propensity for acting went back to his youth ("I was reckoned a good actor," [*BLJ* 9: 37]) and his lifelong passion for eloquence, which originated at Harrow and underpinned his repeated celebrations of action over writing. (Aptly, in his 1813–14 journal he praised it by invoking one of the greatest classical rhetoricians: "'Action – action – action' said Demosthenes," [*BLJ* 3: 220].) Also, he considered England and London as one vast "illegitimate" stage, imagining his old school friends with professional careers as "walk[ing] about in monstrous disguises" and "other masquerade dresses" (*BLJ* 2: 19).

Regency London was the theatrical epicenter of Britain, and Byron reveled in its vibrant life. An inveterate theatergoer, he went to see sensations such as the hugely camp Robert "Romeo" Coates and acclaimed stars including Sarah Siddons, John Philip Kemble and Edmund Kean. (Famously, Byron was so affected by Kean's powerful acting in Philip Massinger's *A New Way to Pay Old Debts* that he had a convulsive fit [*BLJ* 6: 206].) He also mixed with thespians. In October 1812, he made the acquaintance of the King of Clowns, Joseph Grimaldi, and exchanged pantomimical antics with him. He met Kean on various occasions during 1814 and presented him with money, a watch, a snuffbox and a Turkish sword. In November 1815, after drinking heavily at his friend Douglas Kinnaird's house, he had an argument with Alexander Rae, actor and stage manager of Drury Lane (see Marchand 11: 551–2). Appointed to the five-man management subcommittee of Drury Lane in May 1815, Byron was soon inundated by scripts from authors, who also solicited him in person. In this capacity, he asked Scott and Coleridge to submit plays, attempted to have Joanna Baillie's *De Monfort* revived, and, on Scott's suggestion, succeeded in having Charles Robert Maturin's *Bertram* performed in May 1816 (by which time he was on the Continent). During the London season, Byron attended masked balls and, most famously, a masquerade at Watier's on July 1, 1814, which was recreated in Thomas John Dibdin's *Harlequin and Fancy* at Drury Lane in 1815, when Byron and other members of the subcommittee appeared on stage as extras.

Byron's theatrical experiences left him with ambivalent feelings for the stage. On February 20, 1814, he wrote in his journal: "I wish that I had a talent for the drama; I would write a tragedy *now*" (*BLJ* 3: 245), but in a letter to Murray in February 1817, he declared that Drury Lane had given him "the greatest contempt" for theater (*BLJ* 5: 170). If his anti-theatrical prejudices and plans for a "mental theatre" were colored by the theatrical connections of his London years, these connections also left a deep mark on his imagination and resurfaced in *Manfred*, which bears conspicuous traces of contemporary theatrical practices.[2]

Theater, expenditure and politics also characterized Byron's voracious, undisciplined sexual life. Theater featured not only in his liaisons with the actresses Mrs. Mardyn and Susan Boyce, but also in Lady Caroline Lamb's cross-dressing and other stage-like subterfuges during their stormy affair in 1812. His sexual entanglements increased exponentially in these years, when he frequented women from a variety of social backgrounds. And politics bore on his affairs with women from the Whig oligarchy, most notably Lady Oxford. Byron's sexual desire was also bound up with his desire to leave England: after reconnecting with his half-sister Augusta in July 1813, in August he was already making plans to escape to Europe with her. A distinctive feature of the years of fame, his free-wheeling sexual activity belonged in that tendency to excessive, ephemeral passion that Annabella Milbanke deplored in a letter of August 22, 1813: "No longer suffer yourself to be the slave of the moment, nor trust your noble impulses to the chances of Life. Have an object that will permanently occupy your feelings & exercise your reason. Do good" (Marchand 11: 405). After refusing Byron's first proposal in October 1812, Annabella accepted him on his second attempt in September 1814. Their disastrous marriage was followed by a protracted separation, which years later Byron theatrically defined as "Lady Byron's farce" (*BLJ* 8: 237). Finally, eroticism and spectacle mingled in his visits to the boxing saloon run by the pugilist John "Gentleman" Jackson in London's fashionable Bond Street and used by Byron's fencing master Henry Angelo, where the celebration of the male body could lead to homoerotic contacts (though, since homosexuality was a capital offence, Byron seems to have abstained from same-sex intercourse in his English years).[3]

Sex also arguably weighed on Byron's reflections on writing. In a letter to Annabella of November 29, 1813, he described literary composition as "the lava of the imagination whose eruption prevents an earth-quake" (*BLJ* 3: 179). This view of composition as dominated by an "ejaculatory imperative" was not Byron's only pronouncement on the subject in these frenetic years.[4] He defined poetry as inherently political in some remarks to Murray on *Childe Harold* I–II (*BLJ* 2: 90–1) and as an instrument to provoke controversy to his friend Francis Hodgson (*BLJ* 2: 106). He prided himself on his skill for peddling modish "oriental*ities*" (*BLJ* 3: 233) and the speed of his compositional skills (*BLJ* 4: 77). By contrast, *The Giaour*, which doubled in length between the first and seventh editions, testified to a more gradual, revisionist mode of poetic creation.

Byron's letters and diaries from these years are characteristically filled with opinions about contemporary literature. In the journal he kept in 1813–14 he drew a pyramid-like "Parnassus" of present-day poetry, with Scott at its apex, Rogers below, followed by Moore and Campbell, the three Lake poets, and then "the many" (*BLJ* 3: 220). This, however, soon proved to be a far from definitive scheme, since Byron constantly monitored the literary scene and assessed the new, experimental poetries of the period, as in his evaluations of Coleridge's *Christabel* (*BLJ* 4: 318–19), Wordsworth's recent productions (*BLJ* 4: 324) or Leigh Hunt's *Story of Rimini* (*BLJ* 5: 35). While positioning him within this mutable panorama, these reflections doubled as occasions for self-analysis. A cultural and economic activity linked with sociability and celebrity, writing also had a deeply intimate significance for Byron. In a journal entry for December 10, 1813, he defined *The Giaour* as "my Fragment" and tellingly noted: "It is no wonder that I wrote one – my mind is a fragment" (*BLJ* 3: 237). Writing is therefore a manifestation of the self that stems from a dialogue within the self. However, Byron also envisaged writing as an antidote to overwhelming self-obsession: "To withdraw *myself* from *myself* … has ever been my sole, my entire, my sincere motive in scribbling at all" (*BLJ* 3: 225).

During his years of fame, Byron lived and wrote at a furious pace. While experiencing the intoxicating pleasures of celebrity, he also reflected on its vagaries. On April 9, 1814, he wrote to Moore that he rejoiced in the fact that the "temporary celebrity I have wrung from the world has been in the very teeth of all opinions and prejudices" (*BLJ* 4: 92–3). Later, in "Detached Thoughts," he mused: "As far as Fame goes (that is to say *living* Fame) I have had my share – perhaps – indeed – *certainly* more than my deserts," to which he added: "I doubt sometimes whether after all a quiet & unagitated life would have suited me – yet I sometimes long for it" (*BLJ* 9: 24). Apparently originating from "sincere motive," these words also express Byron's self-staging and awareness of an expectant audience. Thus, even as he ponders fame, Byron plays the game of self-revelation to offer his readers the "impression of unmediated contact" characterizing the "hermeneutic of intimacy" of Romantic-era celebrity culture.[5] At the same time, his words capture the oppositional nature of his identity as a cultural icon, one that proved deeply contentious and much more than temporary.

Notes

1 Clara Tuite, *Lord Byron and Scandalous Celebrity* (Cambridge, UK: Cambridge University Press, 2015), xviii, xxiv.
2 See Philip W. Martin, *Byron: A Poet Before His Public* (Cambridge, UK: Cambridge University Press, 1982), 109–11.
3 Gary Dyer, "Thieves, Boxers, Sodomites, Poets: Being Flash to Byron's *Don Juan*," *PMLA* 116 (2001), 570.
4 Sonia Hofkosh, *Sexual Politics and the Romantic Author* (Cambridge, UK: Cambridge University Press, 1998), 36–7.
5 Tom Mole, *Byron's Romantic Celebrity: Industrial Culture and the Hermeneutic of Intimacy* (Basingstoke, UK and New York: Palgrave Macmillan, 2007), 22.

CHAPTER 3

Exile

Jane Stabler

Byron rehearsed going into exile in 1809, when he was twenty-one years old. Before setting sail for Lisbon, he wrote, "I leave England without regret, I shall return to it without pleasure. – I am like Adam the first convict sentenced to transportation, but I have no Eve, and have eaten no apple but what was sour as a crab and thus ends my first Chapter" (*BLJ* I: 211). Byron's sardonic perception of himself as a biblical exile foreshadowed the allusive character of his second longer-term exile at the age of twenty-eight, when his carefully staged exit required an audience (some of the same friends and servants), expensive props (a replica of Napoleon's carriage) and a literary precursor. On his last evening in England, Byron visited the burial place of the satirist Charles Churchill, and lay down on his grave. It was a performance of immense weariness with life and solidarity with an embittered outcast.

In 1816, Byron was the most famous (and infamous) writer of the day, but he continued restlessly to try out different roles. Visiting the site of Waterloo, he invoked non-Wellingtonian military heroism. John Polidori, who was then accompanying Byron, recorded that they went "cantering over the field … my companion singing a Turkish song."[1] Lyrical descriptions of Greece and Albania in *Childe Harold's Pilgrimage* II had created a new kind of romance; as Byron reentered battle-scarred Europe after the defeat of Napoleon, he turned again to the persona of the Childe and the alliterative pulse of his Spenserian stanzas. For the first part of summer 1816 in Switzerland, *Childe Harold* III provided a vehicle for Byron's projection of his subjectivity onto external forms. Releasing his inner Albanian was something that Byron performed at least once more in front of an audience, as Mary Shelley remembered from a joint rowing-boat excursion:

> The waves were high and inspiriting – we were all animated by our contest with the elements. "I will sing you an Albanian song," cried Lord Byron;

"now, be sentimental and give me all your attention." It was a strange, wild howl that he gave forth; but such as, he declared, was an exact imitation of the savage Albanian mode, – laughing, the while, at our disappointment, who had expected a wild Eastern melody. (*WLB* 3: 270–1)

Byron's time with the Shelley party in 1816 involved intense conversation, shared reading, writing and copying out. Byron used Mary and her half-sister, Claire Clairmont, as amanuenses. For Clairmont, who had initiated an affair with Byron in London and engineered the meeting in Switzerland, making fair copies of his poetry was a way of maintaining a relationship that Byron was disinclined to continue. Byron's temporary home, Villa Diodati, invoked their sublime literary predecessor, John Milton, who had visited the Diodati family on his Italian tour; voyages around Lake Geneva paid homage to scenes from Rousseau's *Julie, ou la Nouvelle Héloïse* (1761) and Edward Gibbon's writing of *The Decline and Fall of the Roman Empire* (1776–88); they perused Voltaire, aware that he too had lived in exile nearby, and Byron briefly rejoined the salon of Madame de Staël, who made what was probably the last serious attempt to reconcile him with Lady Byron. Percy Bysshe Shelley's translation of *Prometheus* initiated a long-running debate about what was right about Greece and wrong with the English stage; the young writers devoured what fragments they could of Goethe's *Faust* (1808), Gothic tales (which initiated the ghost-story pact), more Wordsworth than Byron wanted, and the long-awaited *Christabel* by Coleridge. The serendipitous mixture of books and the heady excitement of "Glacier … Storm … thunder – lightning – hail – all in perfection – and beautiful" contributed to the hybrid nature of that summer's creations (*BLJ* 5: 101). Everything that they wrote pushed formal experimentation to the limit. Mary Shelley's *Frankenstein* (1818) provided a commentary on the heedless brinksmanship of it all. To external viewers, Byron seemed on the edge of insanity or suicide, but he wrote himself back into existence through works like *The Prisoner of Chillon* (1816) and *Manfred* (1817).

The summer of 1816 established a pattern for the first half of Byron's exile: a new place, a short stay in a hotel, determined avoidance of other English travelers, rental of an enormous house; transient sexual relationships (in Switzerland, he ended the affair with Claire Clairmont, leaving her pregnant); pilgrimages to the homes and graves of famous figures; new writing energized by the locality, and repeated backward glances to England, informed by Byron's sense of mythic injustice. His woundedness comes through in the prose piece he wrote in 1820 against a *Blackwood's* article that referred to his exile as "selfish and polluted." Byron pointed out that, while those who are exiled by political faction or debt have some hope of redress and return,

> he who is outlawed by general opinion ... whether he be innocent or guilty must undergo all the bitterness of Exile without hope – without pride – without alleviation ...
>
> This case was mine ... In other countries – in Switzerland – in the shadow of the Alps – and by the blue depth of the Lakes I was pursued and breathed upon by the same blight ... I crossed the Mountains – but it was the same – so I went little farther, and settled myself by the waves of the Adriatic. (*CMP* 94–5)

Arriving in Venice in November 1816, Byron embarked on a series of promiscuous sexual liaisons, accompanied by concentrated study of Armenian at the monastery, because "my mind wanted something craggy to break upon" (*BLJ* 5: 130). He started to restock the library he had been forced to sell off when he left England, and he attended operas, plays and Venetian *conversazione*. Something of Venice's spirit as a republic "which survived the vicissitudes of thirteen hundred years, and might still have existed" accorded with Byron's own sense of survival against the odds (*CMP* 91). He visited Venetian tombs and monuments, leased a palazzo on the Grand Canal, and asked for his grave to be "the foreigners' burying-Ground at the Lido ... I am sure my Bones would not rest in an English grave" (*BLJ* 6: 149).

He also began his memoirs. Canto IV of *Childe Harold* tracked the passage of human history through the dream-like decay of Venice and the ruins of Rome (which he visited in April–May 1817). In *Mazeppa*, Byron rediscovered his interest in story telling, blending the old piratical adventures of the Turkish tales with an unexpectedly humorous narrative closure. The chance arrival of new publications from London brought John Hookham Frere's playful *Whistlecraft* to Byron's attention, and in September 1817, he tried out comic *ottava rima* in *Beppo*.

Ottava rima enabled a creative recasting of Byron's role as brooding outsider. His allegiance to England had often seemed questionable to early reviewers, who felt that *Childe Harold* i–ii had not endorsed British values as wholeheartedly as travel writing by an Englishman ought. *Beppo* inclined to the continental way of doing things, but was seen as a *jeu d'esprit*. Byron's next work in *ottava rima*, however, attacked English expectations in a more sustained way. Byron's sense of grievance against the self-righteous Lake School had been rekindled in 1818 by the report that Southey had stirred up rumors about a "League of Incest" at Villa Diodati. Focusing all his resentment about the Separation scandal on Southey, Byron cast him as "a dirty, lying rascal; and [I] will prove it in ink" (*BLJ* 6: 83). Byron's robust Johnsonian adherence to empirical evidence always helped him to stand against what he saw as the characteristic hypocrisy of English life: "cant" or the utterance of things one doesn't really believe in order to pretend a virtue one doesn't really possess. Cant had forced Byron out of London society in 1816, and he now recognized it as an English version of the political hostility that had demonized freethinking writers across the ages – figures such as Rousseau, Voltaire, Hume, Dante, Galileo, Tasso and Boccaccio.

Don Juan was open about Byron's new intellectual center of gravity in Italy. When he moved from Venice to Ravenna in pursuit of a new lover, the Contessa Teresa Guiccioli, the poem's digressions detailed his daily route past the tomb of Dante, the site of the Battle of Ravenna, and his horse rides in Boccaccio's pineta. The narrative of *Don Juan* was interspersed with commentary on current affairs in England (culled from newspapers and reviews) and the smoldering Italian political unrest that led to an assassination outside his door in 1820. Byron had learnt of the nascent *Risorgimento* movement when he passed through Milan in 1816; but four years later, when he was established in the upper story of Palazzo Guiccioli in Ravenna, living "in the heart of their houses" and becoming "a portion of their hopes, and fears, and passions," Byron was captivated by the Italian struggle to shake off Austrian occupation (*BLJ* 7: 170). In the company of Teresa's brother, Pietro Gamba, he joined the local brotherhood of freedom fighters, stored their weapons and sent lively accounts of his new cause to English correspondents.

The anticipated Italian uprising of 1820–1 came to nothing, but Byron's opposition to tyrannical political authority did not diminish and was fueled by his increasing annoyance with John Murray's reluctance to publish more of *Don Juan*. Byron's European, cosmopolitan outlook sharpened his admiration for classical craftsmanship rather than Keatsian or Wordsworthian insular imaginings. He honed a translation of Luigi Pulci's *Morgante Maggiore* in February 1820, thought about resurrecting his old *Hints from Horace*, and participated vigorously in a prose pamphlet battle about the merits of Alexander Pope (which involved having another go at Wordsworth and Southey). He ventriloquized the voice of Dante in exile and turned to the idea of writing classical drama in the summer of 1820.

Canto v of *Don Juan* was the work of autumn 1820, but questions about political activism were uppermost in the winter of 1821, explored in *Sardanapalus*, followed by *The Two Foscari* and then *Cain*. In the summer of 1821, the Gamba family faced expulsion from Romagna for supporting the insurgents. Byron determined to go into exile with them and contemplated a move back to Switzerland. A visit by Percy Shelley in August 1821, however, rekindled the possibility of shared literary activism and persuaded Byron to move to Pisa. Shelley wanted to start a new periodical with the journalist Leigh Hunt that would counter reactionary forces with liberal energy "from the South." Byron agreed to join them, but delayed his departure and wrote another whole poem against "Rogue Southey" – *The Vision of Judgment* – before leaving Ravenna at the end of October 1821 (*BLJ* 8: 240).

The winter of 1821–2 in Pisa brought back English forms of sociability that Byron had not enjoyed since 1816. There were dinner parties, boating projects and participation in a closet theater production of *Othello*. Regular meetings between the Shelleys and the Greek independence leaders involved Byron at the fringes of this new liberation movement. Edward Williams and Percy Shelley were both laboring over stage plays; having written *Heaven and Earth* with apparent ease, Byron drafted *Werner* within a month, then began another prose response to Southey. Shelley noticed that the "canker of aristocracy" in Byron was still present (*LPBS* 11: 345). Shelley had been an unwilling party to Byron's separation of his daughter, Allegra, from her mother, Claire Clairmont; in April 1822, Allegra died in the convent where Byron had placed her. Claire's misery placed a severe strain on relations between Shelley and Byron. At the same time, Byron was warned by friends in England not to link himself with either the disreputable Hunts or Shelley. Teresa had asked him to discontinue *Don Juan*, but in 1822 Byron picked up Canto VI, this time determined not to make any concessions to female delicacy.

Hunt reached Italy at the beginning of July 1822. The journey had been a massive upheaval for his family and it proved to be one for Byron as well. Apart from the few days he had spent with Ada in his London home and the odd weeks that Allegra had been allowed to roam around his Venetian palazzo with the rest of the menagerie, Byron (an only child) had lived most of his adult life in child-free houses. His rented Palazzo Lanfranchi on the Arno was seen as "large & magnificent" by the Shelleys and "spacious" by Byron himself, but it turned out to be not quite big enough for the Hunt children, whose boisterousness came as something of a shock to a man who had only petted infant daughters for very limited periods of time (*BLJ* 8: 246). Percy Shelley might have been able to avert the inevitable falling out, but a week after Hunt arrived as Byron's house guest, Shelley drowned and Byron suddenly found himself responsible for Shelley's family as well as Hunt's, and for seeing through Shelley's political vision.

Byron escaped from the hideous details of Shelley's funeral, first by getting very drunk and then by writing furiously. He worked on *Don Juan* Cantos VI, VII and VIII "To occupy [his] mind," and suddenly in August 1822 resolved that Canto IX would "throw away the scabbard" and attack the English ruling class directly (*BLJ* 9: 187, 191). Byron felt that Shelley (like himself) had been maligned even beyond the grave by the Tory press. The Preface to Cantos VI, VII and VIII struck back against Establishment propaganda. The siege cantos and anti-Wellington stanzas that followed contain some of Byron's most excoriating satire. John Murray was horrified by the confrontational nature of the new cantos and said he could not publish them. Byron instructed Murray to place all his unpublished works in the hands of John Hunt, Leigh Hunt's brother, the publisher of the radical *Examiner* newspaper. The changed publishing affiliation had a significant impact on Byron's reputation; *Don Juan* passed completely beyond the pale of respectability, and several periodicals declined to review further installments. Byron did not flinch from his new war in words. Cantos X–XVI were written with astonishing speed in Genoa alongside *The Age of Bronze* and *The Island*. Byron also weighed up whether to join the liberation movements of South America or Greece. Shelley's memory and the urging of other friends in London sent him to Greece.[2]

Leigh Hunt recalled Byron's invitation to look at the Homeric helmets purchased as accessories for the Greek expedition: "'Have you seen my three helmets?' he inquired one day, with an air between hesitation and hurry. Upon being answered in the negative, he said he would show them me, and began to enter a room for that purpose; but stopped short, and put it off to another time" (*HVSV* 330). Hunt's account captures the conflicted nature of Byron's Greek venture – half eager and half reluctant, embracing a new heroic role and wryly aware of the clichéd territory, always sensitive to audience reaction. Despite his specially fitted-out schooner and the helmets, Byron's mission to Greece was one of the least ostentatious parts he ever played. His party set sail, after several false starts, on July 16, 1823. They landed on Cephalonia in August, at which point Byron realized the messiness of the situation. He advised Hobhouse in September 1823:

> Great divisions and difficulties exist – and several foreigners have come away in disgust as usual – it is at present my intention to remain *here* or *there* as long as I see a prospect of advantage to the cause – but I must not conceal from you ... that the Greeks appear in more danger from their own divisions than from the attacks of the Enemy. (*BLJ* 11: 23–4)

Back in 1810, when he visited Troy, Byron had reclined on the tomb of Achilles; the older poet's heroic model was no warrior idol, but a female reformer: "Whoever goes into Greece at present should do it as Mrs. Fry went into Newgate – not in the expectation of meeting with any especial indication of existing probity – but in the hope that time and better treatment will reclaim the present burglarious and larcenous tendencies" (*BLJ* 11: 32).

From his arrival in Missolonghi in January 1824 to his final illness, Byron took on the role of patient administrator, attending to finances, supplies, the management of his infuriatingly ill-disciplined brigade of Souliot soldiers and the humane treatment of prisoners. He had little time to write poetry, but he kept up his campaign against the rhetorical distortions of party ideology:

> I shall continue to pursue my former plan of stating to the [Greek] Committee [in London] things as they *really* are – I am an enemy to Cant of all kinds – but it will be seen in time – who are or are not the firmest friends of the Greek Cause … the Lempriere dictionary quotation Gentlemen – or those who neither dissemble their faults nor their virtues. (*BLJ* 11: 147)

Worn out by the vexations of Greek politics, Byron died from fever rather than in battle on April 19, 1824. Pietro Gamba noticed that in his delirious state, Byron thought that he was leading a military charge and tried to instill courage in his men. He spoke sometimes in English and sometimes in Italian, saying "Poor Greece!" and "why did I not go home before I came here?"[3] In his hours of fading consciousness, Byron believed that he had given his life to a lost cause, but Gamba saw his death as a sort of homecoming: "He died in a strange land, and amongst strangers; but more loved, more sincerely wept, he could never have been, wherever he had breathed his last."[4]

Notes

1 William Michael Rossetti, *The Diary of Dr. John William Polidori 1816* (Cambridge, UK: Cambridge University Press, 2014), 65.
2 Roderick Beaton, *Byron's War: Romantic Rebellion* (Cambridge, UK: Cambridge University Press, 2013), 139.
3 Count Peter Gamba, *A Narrative of Lord Byron's Last Journey to Greece* (London: John Murray, 1825), 264–5.
4 Gamba, *Byron's Last Journey*, 267.

CHAPTER 4

Texts and Editions

Tom Mole

Byron's works pose formidable challenges for textual scholarship. His manuscripts are sometimes barely legible. He usually wrote on whatever scraps of paper came to hand, with many words scratched out and second thoughts squeezed in between the lines. He sometimes turned the page sideways and wrote new lines of verse crosswise over the existing ones. He rarely dated his manuscripts. He wrote fast and not always carefully. He often relied on other people to copy his manuscripts and edit them for publication. He harassed his publishers with letters containing additions, corrections and revisions. He treated proofreading as an extension of composition, often making significant changes. Modern editors have a dauntingly large amount of material to work with, including multiple manuscripts of poems, fair copies in other hands, corrected proofs, and letters between Byron and his publishers. His mature works all appeared in several editions in his lifetime and the texts of these editions vary significantly. Sometimes Byron made revisions or corrected errors in new editions, and sometimes other people introduced changes, with or without his consent. Many spurious or dubious poems have at different times been considered part of Byron's *oeuvre*. For all these reasons, his works descend to us with very high levels of bibliographical and textual complexity.

These features of Byron's works don't simply provide a particularly interesting case for textual scholars to sink their teeth into: they also illuminate some key ideas in textual scholarship. The central tradition of Anglo-American editorial theory established the principle that editors should attempt to present a text of the work that, as closely as possible, reflects the author's final intentions. To do this, editors usually identify an early text of the work (whether in manuscript or print) to use as their copy-text, and then amend the copy-text in order to remove "corrupt" readings that reflect errors in transmission or interventions by people besides the author. They may also amend it to include later revisions by the author. In recent years, this tradition of editing has come under attack on a number of fronts. Paying attention to the textual history of Byron's works in manuscript and print reveals some of the reasons. As we will see in the examples discussed below, his intentions were often bewilderingly unstable, his collaborations were often complex and disorganized, and the bibliographical formats of his early editions were often significant in ways that modern editions find difficult to represent.

Byron did not usually make detailed plans for his longer poems: instead, his intentions shifted in the course of writing them. This is true at the micro level that Thomas Tanselle (following Michael Hancher) calls "active intention": the intention formed in the process of composition to write one word instead of another, or to use this piece of punctuation rather than that one. Byron's manuscripts show frequent second and third thoughts. But it is also true at the macro level that Tanselle calls "programmatic intention": the intention to write a certain kind of work, using a particular set of generic conventions, aimed at a specific audience.[1] In the course of his extended compositional process for some poems, Byron's understanding of the kind of work he was writing evolved, sometimes shifting quite significantly.

The Giaour underwent noteworthy changes in the process of composition. They not only drastically extended the poem's length, but also significantly altered its nature. In the earliest manuscript, it is a poem of 453 lines, which Byron sent to John Murray in March 1813 asking for fifteen copies to be printed for private circulation (two survive). Working from the printed text, Byron expanded the poem to produce a new version of 684 lines, which appeared in the first published edition in June. Byron continued to write new lines: over the first seven editions, the poem increased incrementally to 1,334 lines, roughly three times its original length (*CPW* III: 406–13). In the process it became a different poem. In the earliest version the Giaour speaks very few lines, and his character remains largely inscrutable. None of the poem's several narrators is sympathetic to him. In the final version, by contrast, the Giaour closes the poem with a monologue of about 350 lines and the monk to whom he confesses is more sympathetic than any of the original narrators. These changes make the character of the Giaour more central to the poem that bears his name, and render him more complex and sympathetic, as well as more closely aligned with Byron himself. Byron's conception of the poem changed over the course of the first seven editions, and his revisions and additions reflect this change.

The same is true of *Don Juan*, a poem that reinvented itself several times while Byron was writing it. When Byron began the poem, he may well have thought that he was writing a self-contained tale in *ottava rima* about a sexual misadventure in Spanish society. He had just finished a poem of this kind, *Beppo*. His primary English model was *The Monks and the Giants* by John Hookham Frere (1817). This fifty-five-page poem purported to be the "Prospectus and Specimen of an Intended National Work," but Frere never meant this claim to be taken seriously. When he began *Don Juan*, Byron may have been imitating Frere's mock-epic "specimen" rather than seriously embarking on a poem of epic length. As Byron got into his stride, however, his conception went through several reinventions. The poem became more romantic, even sentimental, in the Haidee cantos, more aggressively political in the battle cantos, more novelistic in the English cantos. Byron not only changed his active intentions as he revised individual lines of poetry, but also changed his programmatic intention as he rethought his conception of the poem.

Most editors would now agree that authors' intentions don't move in a linear fashion, with later improvements replacing earlier false starts as the work progresses toward its finished state. Borrowing a term from the historian Herbert Butterfield, Stephen Parrish criticized this teleological approach as "the Whig interpretation of literature."[2] Authors' intentions are usually much more complex: they often treat their own decisions as preliminary and they sometimes change their minds repeatedly. Byron's intentions for his poetry didn't simply develop in a straightforward fashion, and decisions that seemed settled at one time sometimes became unsettled later. Byron's "Ode to Napoleon Bonaparte" provides an example of an unstable text. The first draft contained ten stanzas, the fair copy twelve and the first edition fifteen. Murray asked Byron to write some additional stanzas so that the poem would occupy more than one sheet of paper, since stamp tax was payable on publications of less than one sheet. Byron obliged by providing four more stanzas: the received fifth stanza and three additional stanzas to add to the end of the poem. But the new fifth stanza was enough to extend the poem onto two sheets, and Murray never published the additional stanzas, which did not appear with the poem until 1832 (*CPW* III: 456). In this case, versions of the poem that Byron thought of as finished at one time were subsequently altered.

Byron's texts were also shaped by other people. He repeatedly collaborated with others to bring his poems to their published form, or deferred to others' opinions regarding revisions and additions. He completely reworked the third act of *Manfred* at William Gifford's suggestion. On the manuscript of Julia's letter from *Don Juan*, Canto 1, Byron wrote three alternative versions of one line, and wrote in the margin "take that which of these three seem[s] to be the best prescription" (*DJVE* 2: 131). Byron's habit of involving other people in his writing practice sometimes makes it difficult to distinguish his intentions from those of others. Byron worked with a number of collaborators, mostly women, to bring his works into a finished form. He employed a series of female amanuenses to produce fair copies of his poetry. Elizabeth Pigot copied poems for *Fugitive Pieces*; Lady Byron copied lyrics for *Hebrew Melodies*; Claire Clairmont and Mary Shelley both made copies of the manuscripts of *Childe Harold's Pilgrimage* III and *The Prisoner of Chillon*; and Mary Shelley copied large sections of *Don Juan* and other poems.

It is tempting to see these relationships as examples of a male poet exploiting the unpaid and uncredited labor of women to support his writing career. But Byron's amanuenses provided much more than clerical labor, and they should be recognized as playing an important collaborative role in his writing practice. Byron took his amanuenses seriously as creative partners, even though they didn't share the public recognition, or the profits, that the poems they worked on produced. Mary Shelley copied more of Byron's writing than anyone else, and they developed a working relationship that was genuinely collaborative. As a result, she made the greatest impact on the texts of Byron's poetry of any of his amanuenses. When copying the manuscripts of *Don Juan* from Canto VI onwards, she introduced dozens of minor changes. In some cases, these may be the result of her simply misreading Byron's handwriting, for example when she wrote "rapture" where Byron had written "rupture" (*CPW* v: 325, l. 678). Shelley also refused to copy out lines she thought were improper, leaving gaps in the manuscript for Byron to fill. But the extent and nature of the alterations she introduced show that she thought of her work not as mechanical copying, but as part of the creative process of composition. In many cases, she was clearly offering suggestions for improvement, for example when she substituted "batteries were erected" for "batteries were constructed" (*CPW* v: 352, l. 401) or "obliged to snatch" for "compelled to snatch" (*CPW* v: 373, l. 223). In these examples, the words Shelley wrote could not have been mistakes, and they could be understood as more accurate choices than the words in Byron's draft. On a few occasions, moreover, she changed the order of words, preferring, for example, "War cuts up not only branch but root" to "War not only cuts up branch but root" (*CPW* v: 349, l. 328). Where both Byron's draft and Shelley's fair copy are extant, we can see that Byron accepted almost half of Shelley's suggested changes, retaining seventy-four changes in three cantos, and rejecting seventy-seven (*DJVE* I: 112–13, 176–8; see also *CPW* v: xxi–ii). In these seventy-four cases, Shelley's intentions were endorsed by Byron, and in effect became his own.

Byron's willingness to work with others to bring his poems to their published form means that manuscripts in his hand often represent his texts in a condition that he would have viewed as unfinished or unsatisfactory in various ways. Byron rarely finished a poem in manuscript and then submitted it to the process of dissemination in print. Rather, he tended to view his manuscripts' progress through stages of editing, typesetting, proof correction and printing in multiple editions as part of the process of composition, so that his intentions were rarely "finalized" until he saw the poem in the first published edition, and sometimes (e.g. *The Giaour*) not even then. Pioneering editor Fredson Bowers argued that editors should reconstruct as closely as possible "an inferential authorial fair copy, or other ultimately authoritative document," before the work entered the corrupting process of transmission through manuscript copying or print.[3] But, as Jerome McGann argues, the interventions of others before publication can also be understood as "a process of training the poem for its appearances in the world."[4] Byron's poems were often not "finished" until they appeared in print, and even then sometimes not until they had gone through several editions.

Manfred offers the clearest example among many of Byron willingly making alterations to his poetry at the suggestion of Murray or Gifford. On at least four significant occasions, however, Murray changed Byron's writing or omitted lines from his publications without his consent. Murray and Gifford cut out all the more radical political content from the notes of *Childe Harold* Canto III and altered the text in five other places (*CPW* II: 299). Byron didn't learn about these textual changes until the poem was published. In *The Prisoner of Chillon*, Murray unilaterally left out the anti-monarchical lines "Nor slew I of my subjects one; / What sovereign hath so little done" (389–90), and these were not printed until the twentieth century. In *Manfred*, he left out Manfred's dying words, "Old man! 'tis not so difficult to die" (*CPW* IV: 102, l. 151). Byron complained "You have destroyed the whole effect & moral of the poem by omitting the last line of Manfred's speaking – & why this was done I know not" (*BLJ* 5: 257). Murray restored the line in collected editions from 1818 onwards. In *Don Juan*, Canto I, Murray omitted a stanza that mentioned Samuel Romilly's suicide (*CPW* I: 15) and another about syphilis (*CPW* I: 131). These stanzas were replaced by lines of asterisks in the first edition, which concealed the missing words while drawing attention to the fact that the poem included stanzas too improper to print. In all these cases, the first edition does not represent Byron's intentions for his poetry in important respects. Byron's editors therefore have to turn back to the manuscript or forward to a later edition to recover a text that reflects Byron's intentions.

One other challenge facing editors of Byron's works is how to convey to modern readers the extent to which the physical formats in which his poems were published inflected their meanings. The early editions of Byron's poems were carefully considered products, designed to prompt or reinforce certain ways of approaching their contents. The first edition of *Childe Harold*, for example, was a large, expensive and beautifully produced volume in quarto format targeted at an elite metropolitan audience. It included a fold-out facsimile of a letter in Romaic, thirty-five pages of shorter poems, twenty-three pages of appendices and two pages of advertisements for other books published by Murray. The bibliographical format of *Childe Harold* therefore played an important role in shaping the poem's reception and significance in 1812, in ways that are not readily apparent when readers encounter it in a modern edition.

Don Juan offers a more complex case. When publishing the first two cantos, Murray once again adopted a large, quarto format, with wide margins, fine printing and a high price. From Canto VI onwards, however, John Hunt published the poem in an innovative fashion, producing it simultaneously in three formats: an octavo format to match later editions of the first five cantos issued by Murray, a "small paper" format, and a much cheaper, "common" format, which sold in very large numbers.[5] The shift reflects a shift in Byron's audience, as he lost many of the upper-class readers who had helped to secure his fame, and gained a new audience across a wider social spectrum. Reading *Don Juan* in a modern, one-volume edition tends to obscure the very different kinds of formats in which it originally circulated by giving all cantos of the poem a uniform appearance.

Understanding the experience of its first readers is important to reconstructing the historical impact of a poem in its first publication. But the first readers are only a small subset of a poem's readership over time. Many readers from Byron's lifetime until today first encountered his poems in collected or selected editions. The landmark collected edition was produced after Byron's death. This was the seventeen-volume edition of 1832–3, edited by John Wright, which included Thomas Moore's *Life* of Byron (first published in 1830) as well as some of Byron's prose writings. Wright had the benefit of access to many of Byron's manuscripts, as well as the cooperation of people who had known the poet, and his work set a new standard of editing for Byron's works.

This edition supplied annotations to make Byron's poetry "intelligible throughout to the general reader, of what we must already consider as a new generation" (*WLB* 8: ix). As well as editorial glosses, the edition reprinted in its footnotes many critical judgments from reviews of Byron's poetry and other sources. Wright noted that "the time was come when the Public had a right to look for such notes and illustrations to Lord Byron's text, as are usually appended to the pages of a deceased author of established and permanent popularity" (*WLB* 13: v). This canonizing impulse caused the edition to swell from the planned fourteen volumes to seventeen. For the first time, readers encountered Byron in this multi-volume, annotated edition with all the trappings of a canonical author. Modern editions surround the text with their own apparatus, mediating it to new generations of readers. As a result, however, they cannot usually represent effectively the ways in which past editors such as John Wright undertook that process of mediation.

The textual history of Byron's works therefore opens up unsuspected dimensions of complexity in his poetry. His intentions are revealed as unstable: rather than developing toward fulfillment, they are often provisional and subject to change. Moreover, Byron's intentions for his works are not always straightforwardly "his." Instead, a number of other agents were involved in the textual history of his works, from amanuenses such as Mary Shelley to editors such as William Gifford and publishers such as John Murray and John Hunt. The editions in which his works appeared played a significant role in shaping his reception through their bibliographical formats and paratexts, in ways that are difficult for new editions to convey. Nonetheless, we need modern editions that bring Byron's poetry to new generations of readers and enable scholarly understandings of it. New interpretations of Byron's poetry must be built on detailed understandings of his works' textual histories.

NOTES

1 G. Thomas Tanselle, "The Editorial Problem of Final Authorial Intention," in *Textual Criticism and Scholarly Editing* (Charlottesville: Bibliographical Society of the University of Virginia, 1990), 27–71 (esp. 34–5).
2 S. M. Parrish, "The Whig Interpretation of Literature," *Text: Transactions of the Society for Textual Scholarship* 4 (1988), 343–51.
3 Fredson Bowers, "Textual Criticism," in James Thorpe (ed.), *The Aims and Methods of Scholarship in Modern Languages and Literatures* (New York: Modern Language Association of America, 1963), 26.

4 Jerome J. McGann, *A Critique of Modern Textual Criticism* (Charlottesville: University Press of Virginia, 1992), 51.

5 William St Clair, *The Reading Nation in the Romantic Period* (Cambridge, UK: Cambridge University Press, 2004), 327.

CHAPTER 5

Byron and His Publishers

Mary O'Connell

Of the publishers with whom Byron had a significant association, James Cawthorn was the first, John Hunt the last, and John Murray the one with whom he had the longest involvement. Their status reflected the trajectory of Byron's career: he began with a small publisher in Cawthorn, was with the influential Murray for the years of his most intense celebrity and allowed the radical Hunt to take over publishing *Don Juan* when his relationship with Murray broke down. His relationships with these men demonstrate his ambivalence about writing, publishing and commercial success.

Byron's first printed work was a collection of juvenile verse entitled *Fugitive Pieces*, written in the lively and satiric style of Thomas Moore's persona of Thomas Little and privately printed by John Ridge of Newark in November 1806. Stung by accusations that the verse was profligate, and very likely annoyed by the poor production of the book, Byron recalled all copies and destroyed them. He reworked the volume as *Poems on Various Occasions*, eliminating errors in the printing and altering the names of people who were easily identifiable in the original, showing his sensitivity to both public opinion and the material production of his work. His first dealings with a publisher were with Ben Crosby, a London bookseller who managed the sales of his early volume *Hours of Idleness*. The title of the volume expresses the image Byron wished to create at this stage of his career. He repeatedly professed his disdain for writing and publishing. In his journal, he asked: "Who would write, who had any thing better to do?" and recorded his belief that "the mighty stir made about scribbling and scribes, by themselves and others" was "a sign of effeminacy, degeneracy, and weakness" (*BLJ* 3: 220). It is therefore unsurprising that he wished his first published volume to be presented as the fruits of his idle hours.

A glance at Byron's correspondence from the period reveals this disdain to be largely affected. His first surviving letter to a publisher is to Crosby, dated July 21, 1807, and it is typical of his manner of communicating with publishers. He sends Crosby a "critique" of Wordsworth's *Poems* for the *Monthly Literary Recreations*, saying that Crosby and his editors can alter it as they please but should "commit it to the flames" if it is not to be published (*BLJ* 1: 129). In further letters, Byron discussed reports of the volume's circulation and the best time of the year to sell books. He also closely monitored the reviews. His next verse work was the lengthy satire *English Bards and Scotch Reviewers*, which attacked the literary establishment and mocked a host of popular writers. Byron's admiration of Alexander Pope and William Gifford is clear throughout the poem, which he presents as an addition to their efforts to cleanse the marketplace of substandard literature. He ridiculed Wordsworth and Coleridge for their incomprehensible verse, denounced Walter Scott for taking money for his work, and even targets Byron's future publisher, John Murray.

His professed contempt for authors receiving payment for their works would come back to haunt Byron, who would go on to be liberally rewarded in copyright fees. While the poem was partially motivated by a particularly brutal review of *Hours of Idleness* in the *Edinburgh Review*, Byron's satire also represented his antipathy toward the notion of literature as commerce. This is key to understanding his relationship with publishers, for the publisher is the figure who most obviously embodies the business transaction involved in writing and publishing. Numerous examples throughout Byron's correspondence demonstrate his struggle with the links between writing and commerce. He confessed that he did "not think publishing at all creditable to either men or women" and was often "ashamed of it." Later in his career, he wrote that he "thought that Poetry was an *art*, or an *attribute*, and not a *profession*" (*BLJ* 2: 175; 6: 47).

At this stage, a distant relative appeared and established himself as what we would now recognize as a literary agent. Robert Dallas knew that Byron thought well of *English Bards* and wanted a better-known outlet, but also wished to distance himself (or appear to distance himself) from the business of dealing with publishers. For a while, it suited the poet to have Dallas as an intermediary. Dallas first offered *English Bards* to Longmans, one of the major publishing houses of the day, but they declined to publish a satire that insulted most of the literary establishment. Byron did not forget the refusal; in later years, he would not allow the first cantos of *Childe Harold's Pilgrimage* to be submitted to them. *English Bards* was accepted and published by James Cawthorn. Cawthorn decided to print a first edition of 1,000 copies, which sold out quickly when it was launched in March 1809. The poem was well received critically and continued to be popular, going through another four official editions.

Byron, however, fell out with Cawthorn. He was furious with what he described as the publisher's "retrograde movements" and threatened to move to another firm (*BLJ* 2: 44). He was annoyed that Cawthorn had not written to him regularly (something that would aggravate him about every publisher he dealt with), and wrote complaining that he had to hear of his work's progress "through other channels" (*BLJ* 1: 253). He also accused the publisher – wrongly, it turned out – of failing to forward parcels. Cawthorn wrote to remind Byron that he had managed the publication and sale of *English Bards* well and was entitled to some credit. Byron readily apologized for his false accusation, and publisher and poet were once more on good terms. Cawthorn was delighted to learn that Byron had composed "a kind of Sequel" to *English Bards*, a satire entitled *Hints from Horace*. Byron told Cawthorn the volume was his to publish and suggested he print it in a joint volume with *English Bards*. At this stage, as far as Cawthorn was concerned, Byron was his poet.

Then, after he returned to England in July 1811 from his two-year Mediterranean tour, Byron began to distrust Cawthorn. Having made amends with some of the figures he abused in *English Bards*, he was embarrassed by the work and wanted it suppressed. Cawthorn was understandably reluctant to relinquish a steady seller and maneuvered his way around the suppression by printing editions with spurious title pages (of some 20,000 copies). Even before this, however, Byron warned his friend John Cam Hobhouse that he would encounter "sneaking conduct" from the publisher, denouncing Cawthorn as "a vendor of lampoons" (*BLJ* 2: 61). Byron's letters discussed the most eligible publishers (he thought highly of William Miller); and he was determined, against Dallas' initial objections, to find a superior publisher for *Childe Harold*. After Miller refused Byron's offer, Dallas took it to a publisher at 32 Fleet Street. Byron's next poem would be published by John Murray.

Murray had inherited his father's publishing business and was in the process of turning it from a reasonably successful publisher of medical texts into one of the most powerful publishing firms of the nineteenth century. Murray carefully cultivated associations with the influential Scottish firm of Archibald Constable and had a share in the publication of Walter Scott's *Marmion* (1808). The foundation for his success was his establishment of a journal to rival the *Edinburgh Review*. The *Quarterly Review*, launched in 1809, was one of the most important ventures of Murray's career, positioning him as a leading figure in the trade. On receiving Byron's manuscript of *Childe Harold*, Murray gave it to William Gifford, his chief literary adviser, editor of the *Quarterly Review* and one of Byron's literary heroes. Galvanized by Gifford's enthusiasm, Murray decided on a lavish quarto production and insisted that Byron's name appear on the title page. He also asked for alterations to the text.

Murray's first letter to Byron is full of praise and flattery, while articulating his reasons for requesting changes to the poem: some sections failed to "harmonize with the general feeling" and would "interfere with [its] popularity"; he was particularly concerned that the "religious feelings" would impact the sales. Murray employed a tactic he would use countless times with Byron, suggesting that the poet would jeopardize his future fame if he refused to make these changes: "[I]t were cruel indeed not to perfect a work which contains so much that is excellent – your Fame my Lord demands it – you are raising a Monument that will outlive your present feelings, and it should therefore be so constructed as to excite no other associations than those of respect and admiration for your Lordships Character and Genius" (*LJM* 3). Murray did not deny that he was motivated by the desire to secure as wide a readership (and profit) as possible for the poem, but he phrased his requests in such a way as to emphasize his desire for Byron's reputation and lasting fame. He also reminded Byron that their reputations would be at least partly entwined, assuring the poet of his "sincere regard for your lasting reputation, with, however, some view to that portion of it, which must attend the Publisher of so beautiful a Poem" (*LJM* 3–4).

Byron was pleased with Murray's praise; however, he was furious when he discovered that the publisher had shown the poem to Gifford, an act he described as a "begging, kneeling, adulating" affair, a "bookselling, backshop, Paternoster Row, paltry proceeding" (*BLJ* 2: 101, 105). This was the first, but by no means the last, time he would lose his temper with Murray. Byron was still leading Cawthorn to believe that *Hints from Horace* would be published, but once he realized that it was probably not a good idea to publish two such different poems simultaneously, he began to stall Cawthorn, claiming he did not wish to fire "on the Public with a *double Barrell*" (*BLJ* 2: 81). In the end, *Hints from Horace* was not published in Byron's lifetime.

Murray published the first two cantos of *Childe Harold* in March 1812 – the occasion when Byron awoke to find himself famous. The first edition of 500 copies sold out in three days. It was a lavish quarto, finely printed on heavy paper, and cost thirty shillings, an exorbitant sum, even considering the high price of new books. Murray had created a luxury, must-have item, helping to propel Byron to the height of fashion. The Duchess of Devonshire famously said that *Childe Harold* was "on every table," which gives us an idea of Byron's initial readership. Murray's first target market were a small group of wealthy fashionable readers. Byron was worried that a quarto was "a cursed unsaleable size," but the enormous success of *Childe Harold* demonstrated that he was right when he said "one must obey ones bookseller" (*BLJ* 2: 113).

Buoyed by the success of the poem, as well as some valuable copyrights, Murray moved his premises to 50 Albemarle Street, which quickly became a popular venue for writers to gather. Byron found that he enjoyed spending time with the Albemarle Street circle: "I have lately been leading a most *poetical* life with Messrs. Rogers Moore & Campbell … R[ogers] & Moore are very pleasing, & not priggish as poetical personages are apt to be" (*BLJ* 2: 128). Murray managed to effect a reconciliation between Byron and Scott, and in the years that followed, Byron wrote a series of wildly popular Eastern tales that consolidated his position as the leading poet of the day. His relationship with Murray became friendly and they conversed and corresponded regularly.

Murray began to show a strong sense of proprietorship over Byron and his works around this time. When Byron gave the copyright of *The Corsair* to Dallas, Murray's reaction can only be described as hysterical. Murray was not on the best of terms with Dallas and feared he would take the poem to another publisher or try to extract a huge fee. Murray wrote to Byron: "I feel nearly as little able to write to you, as I was to speak … I never felt [more] so bitterly unhappy … If you really meant to give the stab, you gave, to my feelings, may God, harden my heart against man, for never, never, will I attach myself to another" (*LJM* 64–5). Murray was an emotional person, but by any standards this was an extraordinary letter for a publisher to write to an author; it dramatized Byron's importance to him, both as an author and as someone he considered a friend.

After Byron left England in a cloud of scandal in April 1816, Murray was one of his principal correspondents. Byron continued to be as prolific as ever, and the publisher was thrilled by the composition of a third canto of *Childe Harold*, as well as *The Prisoner of Chillon*. It was not long, however, before difficulties arose in their relationship – principally caused by the distance and by Murray's habitual lateness in writing to Byron. One of their most serious disagreements occurred when Murray, on Gifford's advice, removed the last line of *The Prisoner of Chillon* ("Nor slew I of my subjects, one / What Sovereign hath so little done?"). Byron accused Murray "as a *Tory*" of tampering with his manuscripts (*BLJ* 5: 159). The publisher claimed he was acting on the advice of the "knowing ones," the writers and critics who gathered at Albemarle Street and formed what Byron called Murray's "illustrious Synod" (*LJM* 180; *BLJ* 7: 96). While Byron was abroad, his correspondence with Murray took the pattern of Byron being irritated by silences, misprints, omissions and Murray mollifying him with apologies, praise or gossip. Some of Byron's most engaging letters are addressed to Murray, and the publisher reveled in his position as the principal point of contact for the poet.

Murray's government connections, Tory leanings and role as publisher of the *Quarterly Review* might lead us to wonder how his association with Byron lasted so long. It lasted because both men were ambitious, commercially aware, and had a genuine regard for each other. The final breakdown in their relationship only came after a decade, and it happened because Murray gave into his tendencies to be swayed by the opinions of his advisers. Byron began what would be his greatest work, *Don Juan*, on July 3, 1818. Fearing that the "damned Cant and Toryism of the day may make Murray pause" (*BLJ* 6: 76–7), Byron sent the manuscript to his friend John Cam Hobhouse. Hobhouse was appalled at certain sections of the poem and felt it would be impossible to publish. Byron's confidence was shaken by this reaction, and Murray's continuing delay in writing led him to engage his attorney, Douglas Kinnaird, to mediate between himself and the publisher.

Murray was enthusiastic about the poem but feared prosecution. He published it in an expensive quarto edition with asterisks in place of offending lines. It was published anonymously, which Byron consented to, but Murray also omitted the publisher's name. Byron was outraged at what he perceived was Murray's disowning of both himself and the poem. The publisher had endeavored to create an air of mystery surrounding the publication, but only succeeded in giving ammunition to reviewers. William St Clair summarizes it well as "a book in rich dress presenting itself to Byron's previous readership ... but in other ways it looked like a gutter satire."[1]

Byron's late poetry moved away from what he had published earlier in his career. He turned to satire once again and wrote works on religious and political subjects, such as *Cain* and *The Vision of Judgment*. These poems were a far cry from the bestselling Eastern tales and Byron felt it would be in Murray's interests if they were published by someone else. Murray's indecision over *The Vision of Judgment* hastened his decision. Byron had been acquainted with Leigh Hunt for many years; in 1821, Byron, Hunt and Shelley discussed establishing a periodical called the *Liberal*, to be published by Hunt's brother John, and print *The Vision* in the first issue. John Hunt delivered a note from Byron to Murray asking him to surrender the manuscript. Murray was stricken and wrote telling Byron of his dismay. It is evidence of the two men's close connection that, even as their business relationship disintegrated, Byron wrote to the publisher to vent his growing frustrations over the Hunts, particularly Leigh, who he felt was a poor businessman. Byron never met John Hunt, but he thought him an honorable man. Hunt was in the difficult position of competing with John Murray, and critics were quick to seize on the material differences in the publication of the early and later cantos of *Don Juan*. Hunt wrote to Byron, exasperated at what he felt was an impossible task – to equal Murray in terms of influence and effectiveness.

Very few writers could compete with Byron for popularity and sales, and he was a coveted author for many publishers. Of those who managed to publish his work, Murray remains by far the most important. Murray was heavily implicated in the burning of Byron's memoirs in the drawing room at Albemarle Street after the poet's death, and this impacted the assessment of his role in Byron's career for many years. The truth was that the burning of the memoirs was a collective decision by Byron's friends and family, made in haste in order to protect the reputation of the poet, and of those mentioned throughout the memoirs. The manuscript was legally owned by Murray, and in consenting to its destruction, he denied himself what would have been one of the most sensational publications of the age. He did so to protect the reputation of the poet with whom his name will always be inextricably linked.

NOTE

1 William St Clair, *The Reading Nation in the Romantic Period* (Cambridge, UK: Cambridge University Press, 2004), 323.

CHAPTER 6

Piracies, Fakes and Forgeries

Gary Dyer

People attempted to benefit from Lord Byron's popularity while investing as little of their money as possible, and so they appropriated his writings or his name. Some of the resulting works were piracies, involving the publication of a composition without the copyright-owner's permission, such as the one-shilling edition of Byron's *Beppo* that William Dugdale published in 1823. Others were fakes, published works that misrepresented themselves (whether dishonestly or negligently) as being written by Byron, such as *Reflections on Shipboard* "by Lord Byron," published in 1816 by R. S. Kirby and W. Allason. Others again were forgeries, material artifacts crafted or altered so that they appear to have been created by Byron, such as the supposed Byron letters fabricated by "Major George Gordon De Luna Byron" in the mid-nineteenth century. Both Jerome J. McGann's *Complete Poetical Works* and Leslie Marchand's *Byron's Letters and Journals* include lists of dubia and apocrypha intended to repair the confusion created by fakes and forgeries. Piracies, fakes and forgeries are not just things to be weeded out, however, but are cultural works whose histories can be significant and illuminating.

There is no single comprehensive, reliable bibliography of unauthorized editions of Byron's writings. A researcher must move back and forth among WorldCat; Thomas James Wise's *A Bibliography of the Writings in Verse and Prose of George Gordon Noel, Baron Byron* (1932–3); Francis Lewis Randolph's *Studies for a Byron Bibliography* (1979); *Lord Byron: A Collection of 429 Items*, introduced by Jerome J. McGann (C. C. Kohler, 1980); the appendices in William St Clair's *The Reading Nation in the Romantic Period*; and book sale catalogs. Many questions can be answered only by examining copies at rare book libraries.

During Byron's productive years, the copyright statutes in the United Kingdom gave authors (or their assignees) the exclusive right to print and publish their books for a period of at least twenty-eight years. An author could license a publisher to print and sell a book, but authors

benefited most when publishers bought the copyright outright, and this
was the arrangement Byron preferred (see *BLJ* 10: 53). Byron retained the
copyrights of his earliest books, including *Hours of Idleness* (1807) and
English Bards and Scotch Reviewers (1809), but during his time with John
Murray, from 1812 to 1822, Murray purchased the copyrights of almost all
the Byron works he published. Byron's next publisher, John Hunt, could
not afford to buy copyrights, and therefore *The Vision of Judgment, The Age
of Bronze*, Cantos vi–xvi of *Don Juan* and other late works remained the
poet's property and belonged to his estate after his death. The owner of the
copyright of a popular work relied upon his or her legal monopoly; the
publisher could demand a much higher price if he was the only source for
the work than if multiple editions competed freely.

Pirates characteristically offered editions that were far less expensive
than those of the authorized publishers. Byron tempted pirate publishers
because of the wide demand for his works and because of Murray's high
prices. Murray usually published new Byron poems in octavo format,
often for 5s 6d, although a few works, such as the first two cantos of *Childe
Harold's Pilgrimage* (1812) and the first two cantos of *Don Juan* (1819), were
offered at first only as expensive quartos. Murray's original *Don Juan*, a
quarto that cost 31s 6d, was met with J. Onwhyn's piracy, "an exact copy
from the quarto edition" according to the title page, which was available
for 4s. (Murray soon put out an octavo for 9s 6d.) Whereas Murray's
only edition of *Sardanapalus, The Two Foscari* and *Cain* cost 15s, William
Benbow's piracy of *Cain* sold for 1s 6d and Thomas Keys' *Cain* sold for
"two shillings or some such price." Benbow charged less than one-third
the price per play, and he did not compel a customer who wanted *Cain*
to pay for two additional dramas. While Murray's book "was handsomely
printed … on good paper," Keys' was "badly printed … upon inferior
paper"; readers in general often remarked on the physical differences
between authorized and unauthorized editions, books of the latter kind
having been manufactured at much lower cost – using cheaper paper, with
less care devoted to printing.[1] Onwhyn's *Don Juan* included the same text
as Murray's, but Onwhyn economized otherwise. For example, he printed
four stanzas on each page, where Murray printed two stanzas surrounded
by white space.

When a piracy appeared, the only effective legal response available to
the copyright-owner was to petition the Court of Chancery to issue an
injunction restraining the sale. In 1820 the Lord Chancellor, Lord Eldon,
forbade W. T. Sherwin from selling Byron's *Hours of Idleness* (which could
no longer be obtained from the original publisher, S. & J. Ridge); and in

1823 he suppressed Dugdale's one-shilling *Beppo*.[2] One odd kind of piracy was the sale of books by a publisher whose authorization had expired. The original publisher of *English Bards and Scotch Reviewers*, James Cawthorn, continued to sell the book after 1812 against Byron's wishes, mostly by misrepresenting new printings as copies left over from the legitimate third or fourth editions. In May 1816 Murray went to court on Byron's behalf, and Eldon forbade Cawthorn "from printing & publishing any new Edition of the s[ai]d Poem or of any part th[ere]of."[3]

Byron and his authorized publishers were unusually vulnerable to pirates after 1817 because it could be difficult to enforce rights over his more transgressive works. The Court of Chancery would not restrain unauthorized publications if the chancellor had a reasonable suspicion that the work in question was seditious, blasphemous or obscene. This principle, which Eldon articulated for the first time in 1802, became notorious in 1817 when the chancellor applied it to Robert Southey's play *Wat Tyler*, a politically radical work composed (but not published) in the 1790s. These developments emboldened the pirates. From 1817 onward, Byron and his publishers knew they might be unable to prevent or suppress piracies of any writings that the Lord Chancellor or Vice Chancellor suspected were legally offensive.

In 1819 Murray and his legal advisers bore Eldon's principle in mind after piracies of the first two cantos of *Don Juan* appeared. *Don Juan* was notorious for its open eroticism and its impious appropriation of the Ten Commandments (in Canto 1, st. 204–6). Some of the barristers who were consulted predicted that Eldon would restrain the pirates, but Murray eventually decided against taking legal measures after he learnt that his affidavit would need to reveal the author's identity. In February 1822, however, he sought an injunction to suppress Benbow's and Keys' piracies of *Cain* (which had Byron's name on the title page). Eldon had to decide whether the "intent" behind *Cain* was "to bring discredit upon Scripture history and doctrines." After reading the work, he felt "a reasonable doubt" and therefore refused the injunction. In 1823 the vice chancellor dissolved an injunction suppressing Dugdale's piracy of *Don Juan. Cantos VI. – VII. – and VIII.* on similar grounds. Eldon did restrain Dugdale's piracy of *Beppo*, but only after interrogating Murray's counsel about the poem.

The most promising alternative to going to court was to attempt to defeat piracies in market competition by offering an authorized edition at the same, low price, and while respectable publishers shunned this tactic, Byron saw an opportunity. After John Hunt took over publishing *Don*

Juan, each installment of the later cantos appeared in three editions simultaneously, one of the three being an octodecimo costing just a shilling.

Pirates did not restrict themselves to works whose copyright was unprotected. In the 1820s Dugdale offered cheap editions not only of *Cain* and *Don Juan* but also of the unexceptionable *Childe Harold* (all four cantos could be had for 3s 6d) and *Hebrew Melodies* (for 6d). He even sold books that other publishers had been forbidden to sell, such as *English Bards*, *Hours of Idleness* and *Beppo*. (Injunctions restrain only specific defendants, so Dugdale was not in contempt of court.)

Pirate publishers had a special opportunity if no authorized edition was available. Some Byron poetry no one, not even Murray or Hunt, was legally permitted to publish in the United Kingdom: any of the poems from Byron's first four books (*Fugitive Pieces, Poems on Various Occasions, Hours of Idleness* and *Poems Original and Translated*), *English Bards, The Curse of Minerva, The Irish Avatar*, the nine poems included in John Cam Hobhouse's *Imitations and Translations from the Ancient and Modern Classics, Together with Original Poems Never Before Published* and numerous short poems. Two volumes that once had been read and reviewed widely, *Hours of Idleness* and *English Bards*, were no longer available except in a pirate edition or in whatever second-hand copies of legitimate editions might turn up on a bookstall. A gentleman who resolved in 1824 to have all Byron's works on his bookshelf would need to buy piracies; only there could he find in book form "A Sketch from Private Life," or the "Fragment" that begins "When, to their airy hall, my fathers' voice." The wealthy Byron admirer might pay 31s 6d for Murray's original *Don Juan*, then buy William Hone's 1s *Poems on His Domestic Circumstances* in order to have "A Sketch from Private Life" and *The Curse of Minerva* (which Hone included from the eighth edition onward), along with other poems believed likely to be Byron's.

Piracies offered customers other advantages. Only a committed pirate might pair Byron's *The Vision of Judgment* with the poem to which it responded, Southey's *A Vision of Judgement* (1821), because two copyright owners would not cooperate with each other (while a publisher who infringed one copyright might as well infringe two). Therefore some readers would welcome Dugdale's *The Two Visions: or, Byron v. Southey* (1822). Until 1830, only a publisher willing to stoop to piracy could offer a complete *Don Juan*, because the copyright of the first five cantos belonged to Murray and the last eleven belonged to the author or his estate. In 1828 Murray secretly co-published Thomas Davison's two-volume *Don Juan*, although neither he nor Davison had any right to publish Cantos VI through XVI. Only a pirate could provide a bowdlerized *Don Juan*, and it was Cawthorn who issued *The Beauties of Don Juan: Containing Those Passages Only Which are Calculated to Extend the Real Fame of Lord Byron* (1828).

One way to exploit Byron's popularity was to print and sell his poetry without permission and without compensating the copyright owner; another way was to attach his name to works written by someone else. In 1819 Byron observed wryly that it was his "destiny" to "bec[o]me the author of all unappropriated prodigies"; he had "been supposed the author of 'the Vampire' of a 'Pilgrimage to Jerusalem' – 'to the dead Sea' of 'Death upon the pale horse' of Odes to 'La Valette' to 'Saint Helena' to the Land of the Gaul – and to a sucking Child" (*CMP* 83). Byron's word "supposed" was humorous understatement: publishers had *misrepresented* these prodigies as Byron's (even if a few of these men were unaware of their misrepresentation). The most notorious instance was *The Vampyre*, published in the *New Monthly Magazine* as "A Tale by Lord Byron" and attributed to him on the title page of some book copies of the work. Both Byron and the real author, John William Polidori, stepped forward to contradict this claim.

The most brazen attempt to mislead the public occurred in November 1816, when publisher James Johnston not only advertised that *Lord Byron's Pilgrimage to the Holy Land: A Poem: In Two Cantos: To Which is Added, The Tempest: A Fragment* was composed by the noble poet, but also asserted that Byron himself had given him both poems and sold him the copyrights. Johnston's poems actually were the work of journeyman writer John Agg. Murray went to the Court of Chancery in Byron's name, and Eldon forbade Johnston from publishing the poems "in [Byron's] name or as his works."[4] (Eldon's injunction also applied to the four poems in Johnston's earlier *Lord Byron's Farewell to England; with Three Other Poems ...*). Frauds like these made it difficult for the public to know which published poems were actually composed by Byron.

Poems on His Domestic Circumstances, which first appeared late in April 1816, combined piracy with fakery: William Hone and other publishers sold genuine Byron poems without authorization and sold other writers' poems under Byron's name. Hone's first edition contained seven short poems, and the premise was that all were recent poems unavailable in any book Murray sold. Two of these were Byron's "Fare Thee Well" and "A Sketch from Private Life," both provoked by the collapse of his marriage, where he had ordered fifty copies of each printed for private distribution (*BLJ* 5: 58; 13: 42). The five remaining poems had appeared anonymously or pseudonymously in the *Morning Chronicle* or the *Examiner* between July

1815 and April 1816, and publishers of these poems might have believed that all were Byron's or were likely to be Byron's; actually, three were authentic.

Fakes can be hard to differentiate from imitations, and imitations from parodies. Not all imitations of Byron poems were crafted to mislead; some works appropriated his subject matter or continued his verse narratives without attempting to deceive. For example, in *Childe Harold's Pilgrimage to the Dead Sea: Death on a Pale Horse: and Other Poems* (1818) (a volume Byron disowned), "there is no attempt made to palm the work off as Byron's, for there is a dedication to the author's father and the memory of his mother," as Samuel Chew observed.[5] Because *Don Juan* appeared piecemeal (one volume in 1819, another in 1821, four between July 1823 and March 1824), it gave ambitious poets opportunities to write their own continuations. After Byron's death, writers could extend the poem past Canto XVI. Some of these continuations might be perceived to be genuine, at least by someone who only skimmed them. *Don Juan. Cantos XVII–XVIII*, published in 1825 by Charles Wiley in New York, pretends to have been composed by Byron, and *Don Juan: Canto the Third*, published by Greenlaw in 1821, might easily seem to be Byron's, whereas in *Continuation of Don Juan. Cantos XVII and XVIII*, published by G. B. Whittaker in 1825, the author actually eulogizes the late poet. Two prominent 1819 satirical poems dealing with Byron, Lady Caroline Lamb's *A New Canto* and William Hone's *Don Juan, Canto the Third!*, take the form of continuations of *Don Juan*. A poet who adopted Byronic themes, a Byronic subject, the Byronic style or Byron's persona risked seeing his work presented as that of Byron himself, so that imitation became imposture. Agg composed "Farewell to England" as "a speculative anticipation of [a poem] which was expected from the pen of lord Byron,"[6] but his publisher Johnston put the poem to less honorable uses.

People fabricated not only Byron's writings but also material artifacts. The value of a Byron manuscript was both "intellectual" (residing in its abstract content) and material (the letters inked by the poet, the paper that had been in his hands). Some forgers were able to imitate Byron's distinctive handwriting. "Major Byron" (also known as "De Gibler") concocted and sold many supposed manuscripts of Byron letters, beginning in the 1840s, often making use of the content of genuine letters he had seen, and he extended his talents to forging poetic manuscripts. Major Byron combined various kinds of fraud: for example, the soliloquy that he wrote on blank paper in a copy of *Manfred* was both a forgery, insofar as he counterfeited Lord Byron's handwriting, and a fake, in that he misled readers into thinking that the soliloquy had been composed by Byron when it really was the work of Leopold Bernays (who was translating Goethe).

McGann avers that "the detection of forgeries is not usually difficult" in the case of poems that "represent themselves as autograph manuscripts" because few would "deceive anyone who is even minimally familiar with Byron's handwriting styles" (*CPW* VII: 113). Yet Byron's handwriting is not the sole relevant factor when attributing a poem: "Epitaph on a Beautiful Boy" exists only as a fair copy manuscript at Trinity College Cambridge, and McGann observes that while the handwriting may (or may not) be Byron's, "we cannot be sure that the work is not a copy of a poem Byron liked" (*CPW* VII: 113–14). The proliferation of forgeries is more evidence of the appeal of Byron's name and image.

NOTES

1 Information on Benbow's and Keys' editions is taken from bills of complaint in the Chancery papers at the National Archives: *Murray v. Benbow* (1822), TNA C 13/1743/26; *Murray v. Keys* (1822), C 13/1743/28. On the price of Murray's octavo of the three plays, see *Monthly Review*, 2nd series 97 (January 1822), 83.

2 *Byron v. Sherwin* (Chancery, 1820), *The Times* (July 24, 1820), 3; *Murray v. Dugdale* (Chancery, 1823), *The Times* (July 23, 1823), 3. Byron was the plaintiff in the first case because he owned the copyright, whereas Murray had bought the copyright of *Beppo*. To be precise, Sherwin's *Hours of Idleness* reproduced the last authorized edition of Byron's book, which had been renamed *Poems Original and Translated*.

3 *Byron v. Cawthorne* [*sic*], order, TNA C 33/627, f. 768.

4 *Byron v. Johnston*, order, TNA C 33/637 f. 63. See also 35 Eng. Rep. 851–2; *The Times* (November 29, 1816), 3.

5 Samuel C. Chew, *Byron in England: His Fame and After-Fame* (New York: Scribner, 1924), 174.

6 "J. A." [John Agg], *The Ocean Harp: A Poem* … (Philadelphia: M. Thomas, 1819), vii.

PART II

Political, Social and Intellectual Transformations

CHAPTER 7

Politics

John Beckett

Byron's political interests and views can conveniently be divided between his active political career in the House of Lords (1809–16) and his years of self-imposed exile in Italy and Greece, associated most notably with the liberal-nationalist causes of the Carbonari and Greece.

Byron succeeded to the Barony of Rochdale, as the sixth baron, on the death of his great uncle, the fifth baron, in 1798. All peerage titles (Duke, Marquess, Earl, Viscount, Baron) were hereditary through the male line and automatically entitled the holder to membership of the House of Lords. Byron took his seat on March 13, 1809. He retained the seat in absentia from 1816 but did not attend the house or participate actively in political activities between 1816 and 1824.

Byron prepared himself for a political career. He read widely in political history, and at Cambridge he joined the Whig Club, where he met, among others, John Cam Hobhouse. Although he subsequently claimed to be above parties, Byron was by nature and inclination a Whig (*BLJ* I: 158). In the Lords, Byron started badly. According to Robert Dallas, Byron had no "friend" to explain the customs of the upper house to him. He caused offence by ignoring the Lord Chancellor, Eldon, who stepped down from the woolsack to welcome Byron through a handshake (Dallas 51–4). Between March and May 1809, Byron attended the Lords on seven occasions. In July 1809 he set off with Hobhouse on a European tour.

When Byron entered the House of Lords in 1809, the Tories were in power, and the Prime Minister was the third Duke of Portland. The country was at war with France, as it had been almost continuously since 1793 (as the French Revolutionary War 1793–1802 was followed by the Napoleonic Wars 1803–15), and the political issues of the day included parliamentary reform, political emancipation for nonconformists and Roman Catholics and the position of the monarch. On February 5, 1811, Prince George, the Prince of Wales, was given executive authority to act in his father's place as Regent, after George III lapsed into permanent mental impairment. The

Whigs continued to believe that the Prince would bring his "friends" into power. Byron anticipated his party forming a government, potentially with himself in an active role. This would certainly help to explain his regular attendance at the Lords between January and July 1812, as reflected in the daily presence lists, as well as his active role on several committees.

On Wednesday January 15, 1812, Byron attended the Lords for the first time since 1809. The House was sparsely populated, with only ten peers present and routine business (*BLJ* 2: 155). Byron returned the following day, January 16, when he was one of only four peers present. The Lords next sat on Monday, January 20, 1812, and Byron was there again, this time with Lords Grey and Grenville, two of the leaders of the Foxite Whigs, among the ten peers who were present.[1] He was in the House on the following Monday, January 27, Tuesday, 28 and Friday, 31. The last occasion brought a larger-than-usual turnout, with 110 peers present, including 11 bishops and 3 royal dukes (Cumberland, Cambridge and York). Byron claimed to be ill the following day: he told Francis Hodgson that he had "a vile cold, caught in the House of Lords last night." He had still to make his maiden speech and told Hodgson on February 1, 1812 that "the Catholic Question comes on this month, and perhaps I may then commence. I must 'screw my courage to the sticking place,' and we'll *not* fail" (*BLJ* 2: 160). Roman Catholic emancipation was not achieved until 1829, but legislation since 1778 had gradually given Catholics increasing social equality. William Pitt the Younger promised to deliver emancipation as part of the Act of Union between Britain and Ireland in 1800, and resigned when King George III refused his support. The issue subsequently came before parliament on a number of occasions, and tended to divide the pro-reform Foxite Whigs, who were known for championing the liberty of the subject and of the press, in opposition to the anti-reform Tories. As it transpired, a combination of a cold and "an attack of the *Stone* in the *kidney*" kept Byron out of the House until February 13, 1812 (*BLJ* 2: 160, 161). On February 27, Byron finally gave his maiden speech – on the second reading of the Frame Work Bill.

The fact that Byron had been preparing to make his maiden speech in favor of Catholic emancipation is significant. Byron's particular political alliance was with Henry Richard Fox (later Vassall), 3rd Lord Holland, nephew and spiritual successor of Charles James Fox, and Holland helped to shape Byron's political career between 1812 and 1816. Byron clearly saw himself as a Foxite Whig with a career in government ahead of him. Sadly Byron died before the Whigs returned to power in 1827 – the Prince Regent having failed to bring his "friends" into government either in 1812 or subsequently – so he never had the opportunity to advance his claims. His subsequent assertion that he had been "born for opposition" needs to be viewed in this light (*CPW* v: 595, l. 176).

Byron's decision to make his maiden speech on the Frame Work Bill rather than on Catholic emancipation was a matter of political expediency. On February 17, Byron was present together with all the leading Foxite Whigs, including Holland, and Lords Grey and Grenville. He was present again on February 20, when he was appointed to a committee to consider a Turnpike Road Bill in Devon, on February 24, when he was appointed to a committee to consider an enclosure bill for Erith, Kent (as was Lord Holland), and on February 27. Around February 4, 1812, he decided to make his maiden speech on the Frame Work Bill rather than the Catholic question (*BLJ* 2: 163, 165–6). He changed his mind when it became known that the Tories under Spencer Perceval intended to introduce legislation that would outlaw frame breaking, the Luddite practice of destroying wide frames used to undercut skilled workers in the stocking-knitting (hosiery) trade (*CMP* 284). The government concluded that only by making frame breaking a capital offence could the perceived threat to law and order in Nottinghamshire during the winter of 1811–12 be effectively countered (Marchand 1: 314).

In many ways the Luddite troubles were a stroke of political good fortune for Byron. His Newstead Abbey estate was just north of Hucknall, Bulwell and Basford, all of them villages subjected to frame breaking through the winter of 1811–12. Not surprisingly, Byron claimed that finding a solution to the problem of machine breaking was "a question in which I confess myself deeply interested" (*CMP* 22). The Frame Work Bill was brought into the Commons on February 14, 1812 and debated at length on February 17 before receiving its second reading. The following day it went into committee, and on February 20 received its third reading in the Commons. After this it went to the Lords, where its all-important second reading, when the principle of the bill was either accepted or rejected, was debated on Thursday, February 27. Byron was in the chamber, together with fifty-five other peers, among them Holland, Grey and Grenville, and the Tory leaders, Lords Liverpool and Harrowby. Holland put Byron forward to make the lead speech on behalf of the Whig opposition.

Arrangements for speaking were handled by the leader of the House, and those who wished to give notice of their intention to speak left their names with the leader. A high priority was always given to maiden speakers. Lord Liverpool, the Colonial Secretary, was leader of the Lords and he spoke first to introduce the measure. Byron knew the procedure and he was aware that behind-the-scenes preparations had been made for him to speak.[2] He knew it would be a nerve-racking experience. He had written out his speech, edited it and then practiced it in front of Dallas in an effort to boost his confidence: Dallas recalled that he "wrote an oration being afraid to trust his feelings in the assembly he was to address with extemporaneous effusion" (Dallas 202).

Liverpool argued that the bill was a temporary measure (two years) to counter what was expected to be a temporary situation, and that "the terror of the law would in many cases operate, where the apprehension of lesser punishments would be found ineffectual." Liverpool sat down, and Byron had the floor. He began by stating his credentials: "During the short time I recently passed in Notts, not 12 hours elapsed without some fresh act of violence" (*CMP* 22). He then provided something of a justification for these "outrages": "The perseverance of these miserable men in their proceedings, tends to prove that nothing but absolute want could have driven a large & once honest & industrious body of the populace into the commission of excesses so hazardous to themselves, their families, & the community" (*CMP* 22). This was fine, but Byron added little by way of detail, despite his claim to speak authoritatively on the bill because of his personal knowledge of the area. There was, for example, no mention of key problems in the trade that were central to the Luddites' activities, notably the issue of employers engaging people who had not completed the seven-year apprenticeship – "colts" as they were known.

Byron sat down to silence from across the House. Maiden speeches were not supposed to be controversial, and as Byron subsequently claimed: "I spoke very violent sentences with a sort of modest impudence, abused every thing & every body, & put the Ld. Chancellor very much out of humour" (*BLJ* 2: 167). Years later, Lord Holland was to recall: "His speech was full of fancy, wit, and invective, but not exempt from affectation nor well reasoned, nor at all suited to our common notions of Parliamentary eloquence. His fastidious and artificial taste and his over-irritable temper would, I think, have prevented him from ever excelling in Parliament."[3]

Normal debating practice was for a speaker from the government benches to be called to answer his speech, but no one offered themselves, and to prevent further embarrassment Holland stood up to support Byron's line of argument. After this, both Lord Eldon and Lord Harrowby spoke. None of those who followed Byron entered into the same flights of fancy that he had employed, particularly when he asked: "[A]re there not capital punishments sufficient in your statutes? is there not blood enough upon your penal code? that more must be poured forth to ascend to heaven &

testify against you?" (*CMP* 26). As regular debaters in the Lords they stuck to the points at issue, notably whether the new law would be beneficial – because of the terror it would induce – or detrimental – because informers would not come forward. The lack of reaction to his speech may not have troubled Byron, but it told his fellow Whigs that it had not gone down well. The bill was read for a second time and passed.[4]

Byron was just pleased to have delivered the speech. Dallas met him outside the chamber, and found him "glowing with success, and much agitated … He was greatly elated, and repeated some of the compliments which had been paid him, and mentioned one or two of the Peers who had desired to be introduced to him. He concluded with saying that he had, by his speech, given me the best advertisement for *Childe Harold's Pilgrimage*" (Dallas 204). Byron had assigned the royalty rights to Dallas, even before the poem was published. Byron was entertained to dinner by Lord Holland. In the days that followed he took great interest in the impact of his speech (*BLJ* 2: 166). He must have enjoyed the way *The Times*, for example, portrayed him as speaking "from local knowledge."[5]

Byron was back in the Lords on Friday February 28, along with the Foxite Whig leaders, doubtless hoping to pick up further (positive) feedback on his performance, and again on Monday March 2, when the Frame Work Bill was considered by a committee of the whole House. He was not present for the third reading the following day.

Byron relished receiving congratulatory letters from fellow peers, including a note on February 28 from his friend, and regular House of Lords "pair" for voting or nonvoting purposes, the Marquess of Sligo, "to congratulate you on the safe delivery of your first political bantling which has set the whole town talking."[6] On March 5, Byron told Hodgson "Lds. Holland & Grenville, particularly the latter paid some high compts. in the course of their speeches as you may have seen in the papers." "I have," he added, "had many marvelous eulogies repeated to me since in person & by proxy from divers persons *ministerial*." He may have recognized that this was all rather pompous because he closed the subject with the rather odd comment, "And so much for vanity" (*BLJ* 2: 167).

Byron's speech was never likely to change anything. It might add to information and provide a platform for a young peer, but he knew as well as anyone else that the bill would pass. He vented his frustration in an "Ode to the Framers of the Frame Bill," published anonymously in the Whig *Morning Chronicle* on March 2.

Byron continued with his political career, but scaled down. After March 2, he did not attend the Lords again until March 19, and then subsequently

April 16, 20 and 21, June 19 and July 1, 3, 6, 7, 10 and 14. He finally did give his speech in favor of Catholic emancipation on April 21, in a long and far more measured discourse than he had managed on February 27.[7] But he was not in the House on July 24, when a bill for preventing frauds and abuses in the framework knitting industry was thrown out by his fellow peers. He was also not in the Parliament building on May 11, 1812, when John Bellingham shot dead Spencer Perceval, the Prime Minister, although he rented a window from which to watch the public hanging of Bellingham on May 18.

In the 1812 parliamentary session, the Lords met for the last time on July 30. Byron's apparent cooling of interest may have been related to the Frame Work Bill. According to Dallas, the events of February 27 represented "an extraordinary crisis in [Byron's] life. He had before him the character of a Poet, and an Orator to fix and to maintain" (Dallas 202). Soon after, on March 10, *Childe Harold's Pilgrimage* was published, and overnight he became a sensation. Byron was clearly cooling when it came to the question of his political career, as opposed to his commitment to the cause of liberty expressed through his ongoing Whig philosophy.

None of this implies that Byron had given up. In the 1812–13 parliamentary session, he was in the Lords on twelve occasions and spoke once for what turned out to be the third and final time. This was a speech accompanying his presentation of a petition on behalf of Major John Cartwright, a Nottinghamshire man and a firm supporter of parliamentary reform who established the Hampden Clubs, and was well known to Byron's Radical friends including Sir Francis Burdett, William Cobbett and Francis Place.[8]

In truth, the political career that Byron appeared to be planning for himself at Christmas 1811 did not materialize. Byron remained on good terms with Holland, to whom he dedicated his poem *The Bride of Abydos* in 1813. Holland noted that Byron's "over-irritable temper" would probably have meant he lacked the patience to become a career parliamentarian.[9] In any case, Byron lost interest in politics after the publication of *Childe Harold*. In Malcolm Kelsall's view "Byron achieved nothing for reform, and was the determined opponent of the very radical forces who selectively misread his poetry to support their cause."[10] Certainly from 1816, Byron, the Whig patrician of 1811–12, who may even have entertained ideas of being a future minister of the Crown, had disappeared both literally and metaphorically.

Byron remained a champion of the cause of liberty, and of other Whig notions relating to the importance of the Glorious Revolution (1688), the right to resistance, and parliamentary and Catholic reform. In *Don Juan* he wrote of the European *ancien regime*. His Philhellenism was derived from a patrician education (Harrow and Cambridge), which led him to see events in the Peloponnese as if they were a continuation of classical antiquity, and from the usual Whig support for national liberation movements whether in the American colonies, Italy or Greece. Byron remained true to his political ideals, and his final venture, as it turned out, and death in Missolonghi on April 19, 1824, contrived to give him heroic status in Greece. In the words of the Greek Prime Minister, speaking at Newstead Abbey in 1931, "Childe Harold died like a Crusader."[11]

Notes

1 *Journals of the House of Lords* (London: HMSO), xlviii, 533, 546–7.
2 I am grateful to Sir John Sainty and Clyve Jones for advice on procedure.
3 Henry Holland, *Further Memoirs of the Whig Party 1807–1821*, ed. Lord Staverdale (London: John Murray, 1905), 123.
4 http://hansard.millbanksystems.com/lords/1812/feb/27/frame-work-bill.
5 *The Times* (February 28, 1812).
6 The Marquess of Sligo to Byron, February 28, 1812, http://petercochran .files.wordpress.com/2009/02/03-london-1811-18129.pdf.
7 http://hansard.millbanksystems.com/lords/1812/apr/21/answer-to-the-third-question-3.
8 S. D. Chapman, "The Pioneers of Worsted Spinning by Power," *Business History* 7.2 (1965), 103–5.
9 Holland, *Further Memoirs of the Whig Party*, 123.
10 Malcom Kelsall, *Byron's Politics* (Brighton: Harvester, 1987), 2.
11 *Nottingham Journal* (July 17, 1931), 4.

CHAPTER 8

War

Neil Ramsey

Born a year before the French Revolution, Byron grew up in a world ravaged by the French Revolutionary and Napoleonic Wars (1792–1815). The conflict began with Europe's ancien régime anticipating a swift victory over the fledgling French republic, but what ensued was nearly twenty-two years of war (broken only by the brief peace of Amiens in 1802–3). Dominated by the military genius of Napoleon Bonaparte, who declared himself emperor of France in 1804, the wars profoundly perturbed the existing political order of Europe. Warfare became so desperate and all-consuming for the contending nations that they were forced into unprecedented efforts to mobilize their resources and populations for war. The wars approached the scale and intensity of the total wars of the twentieth century.

Earlier in the eighteenth century, the full brutality of war had been tempered by Enlightenment views about the archaism of violence in human affairs. Such enlightened views did not wholly disappear as war became increasingly total, but they became entangled with a pervasive belief that what was at stake in the wars was the very future of civilization itself. Within the cultural view of war that Byron inherited, war had begun to be regarded as a cataclysmic interruption of the course of history, thus acquiring a millennial, apocalyptic cast.

If the era's wars were becoming total, however, they were also becoming global, the conflict extending across Europe and reaching into the Indian subcontinent, America and the Middle East. The wars curtailed travel outside Britain and led to the demise of the traditional grand tour. Instead, picturesque tours of Britain's native countryside became increasingly popular. The effect of the wars in isolating Britain cannot be divorced from the rise of a Romantic poetics of British rustic life and nature espoused by the school that became known as the Lake poets. In stark opposition to the Lake poets, Byron launched himself into a world beset by the upheavals of war. Marked by incessant wandering, turnings and border crossings, his poetry reflects an openness to the contingency that war had unleashed on European politics and society. War may have at one level horrified Byron, but it is also associated in his poetry with a degree of vigour, energy and freedom.

Childe Harold's Pilgrimage is marked by Byron's complex engagement with his era's wars. Begun in 1809, Canto I recounts Byron's travels across Spain during the Peninsular War (1808–14), when Britain allied itself with Portugal and Spain in an effort to resist French invasion of the Iberian Peninsula. His journey was unavoidably shaped by the wars. The traditional sites of the grand tour, France and Italy, were sealed off from a British Lord like Byron, and he could only travel in Spain itself because the allied forces had succeeded in driving the French from the cities he visited, Seville and Cádiz. Flooded with press accounts of the conflict, the British public during these years were fascinated by the Peninsular War, because it seemed to presage the possibility that the tide of war was finally turning against Napoleon.

While Byron's immediate success as a poet was undoubtedly due to this widespread interest, his poetry was devoid of the patriotic sentiments found in much of the British writing of this time. Drawing in part on his own experience of the war, and his discovery while traveling that "the barbarities on both sides are shocking," he focused on the despotism of empire and the immutability of ambition (*BLJ* I: 217). Shorn of glory, the battle of Talavera appears in his poem as a scene of slaughter:

> France, Spain, Albion, Victory!
> The foe, the victim, and the fond ally
> That fights for all, but ever fights in vain,
> Are met – as if at home they could not die –
> To feed the crow on Talavera's plain,
> And fertilize the field that each pretends to gain.
> (*CHP* I, st. 41, ll. 444–9 [*CPW* II: 25])

The battle having been fought in vain, Byron proposes that, far from shaping history, the soldiers are themselves shaped by the natural cycles of life and death: they do not "gain" the field of battle but are left as mere corpses rotting in the field.

Like many of his contemporaries, Byron drew on mythic associations to write about war, but, rather than identify the combatants with the heroism of chivalry and romance, he reinforces his concerns with death by referencing the book of revelations and its apocalyptic imagery, where "Death rides upon the sulphury Siroc, / Red Battle stamps his foot, and nations feel the shock" (*CPW* II: 24, ll. 421–2). Byron's account resembles Goya's

Disasters of War (1810–20), which similarly pictured the Peninsular War through apocalyptic scenes of death and barbarity.

The poem is not, however, wholly condemnatory of war. Although the war was widely applauded as an act of resistance to Napoleon, Whigs and radicals viewed the war as evidence that a revolutionary fervor for freedom had spread across Spain. Adopting this radical perspective, Byron expresses his disdain for the Convention of Cintra (1808), a treaty signed between the French and the ageing British commanders, Sir Harry Burrard and Sir Hew Dalrymple, who, having defeated the French at the battle of Vimeiro (1808), nonetheless allowed their forces safe passage back to France. Condemning their incompetence, Byron calls upon Spain to awaken to the cause of freedom, even as he recognizes the failures that their fighting has yet brought them:

> Not all the blood at Talavera shed,
> Not all the marvels of Barossa's fight,
> Not Albuera lavish of the dead,
> Have won for Spain her well asserted right.
> When shall her Olive-Branch be free from blight?
> When shall she breathe her from the blushing toil?
> How many a doubtful day shall sink in night,
> Ere the Frank robber turn him from his spoil,
> And Freedom's stranger-tree grow native of the soil?
> (*CHP* I, st. 90, ll. 918–26 [*CPW* II: 43])

Byron may regard the battles of Talavera, Barossa and Albuerra as wasteful massacres of human life, but he nonetheless intimates that they were fought in the rightful effort to achieve Spanish independence.

As the canto shifts from battle to its other key scene, the bullfight at Cádiz, there is also a shift from a concern with death to a fascination with the power and pageantry of violence. Reflecting a common view in Europe that pictured the war in Spain as a bullfight, the poem describes the Sabbath day crowd of Cádiz delighting in the orgiastic violence of the fight as the bull is repeatedly lanced for an audience mainly composed of enthusiastic, ogling "dames" (*CPW* II: 35, l. 724). If war is here metaphorically linked to a sexualized spectacle, the poem establishes a wider analogy between peace and languor in the way that the eponymous hero relieves his ennui by traveling through scenes of war. The poem draws together sexuality, violence, energy and festival in ways that suggest Byron's poem is itself rather deeply in thrall to the spectacle of war.

Byron turned again to war in *Childe Harold* III, beginning the canto shortly after he visited the battlefield of Waterloo (1815), where Napoleon ended his final campaign against the allied forces. Representing the concluding act of the Napoleonic Wars, the battlefield was immediately transformed into a site for secular pilgrimages, visited in the months following the battle not only by hosts of tourists but also by Britain's leading poets: Scott and Southey in 1815, Byron himself in 1816, and Wordsworth in 1820. If other poets wrote of the battle as a heroic victory for the Duke of Wellington, Byron does not deign to even mention him. Rather than glorifying the battle as a decisive event in the grand politics of European history, he focuses on one individual who was killed, Major Frederick Howard, a family friend whose death was an inassimilable grief for Byron. As a battle, therefore, Waterloo was, like Talavera, a site of "carnage" that did nothing to advance the cause of freedom:

> While Waterloo with Cannae's carnage vies,
> Morat and Marathon twin names shall stand;
> They were true Glory's stainless victories,
> Won by the unambitious heart and hand
> Of a proud, brotherly, and civic band,
> All unbought champions in no princely cause
> Of vice-entail'd Corruption; they no land
> Doom'd to bewail the blasphemy of laws
> Making kings' rights divine, by some Draconic clause.
> (*CHP* iii, st. 64, ll. 608–16 [*CPW* ii: 100–1])

Byron contrasts that battle with what he regards as truly glorious and epoch-making victories fought for the sake of liberty and democracy, such as the Swiss victory over the Kingdom of Burgandy at Morat (1476) and the Athenian victory over the Persian empire at Marathon (490 BC). Crushing all hope of liberty, Waterloo simply restored monarchical power to Europe and erased the achievements of the French Revolution, leaving the world to tyranny, corruption and kings.

While he was appalled by the victory of those he detested, including Wellington and especially the British foreign secretary, Lord Castlereagh, Byron had a complex relationship with the defeated Napoleon. Byron's desire to find a hero for his own age was both impelled and thwarted by Napoleon, the French emperor who dominated his imagination like no other historical figure. Byron viewed Napoleon as a Miltonic Satanic hero, a fallen angel who initially championed the freedom of the revolution, but who had mutated into a parody of the very monarchical order he had helped to overthrow. By abdicating rather than dying in glory in battle, Napoleon had shirked his historical role as a beacon of hope for the world.

In Byron's postwar writing, however, he tempers his resentment to some extent, siding with his Whig associates, who by the end of the war had begun to admire Napoleon as a bulwark against the return of the ancien régime. In *The Age of Bronze* (1823), written as a satire on the Congress of Vienna in 1814–15 that formally ended the wars, Byron reclaims Napoleon as a figure of hope and defiance. Byron imagines Napoleon, imprisoned by the British at the remote Atlantic Island of St. Helena, as a Prometheus who challenged the gods but is now eternally chained to his rock. Byron at times identifies himself with Napoleon. He imagines his personal exile from England as though he is reenacting Napoleon's abdication, having an exact copy of Napoleon's carriage built for his departure.

As John Clubbe notes, Byron may partly have been prompted to write *Don Juan* by the expectation that Napoleon would soon publish his memoirs.[1] As a mock epic in which Byron chooses for his hero the comic lover Don Juan, familiar to British audiences from pantomime, the poem clearly turns away from war for the bulk of its material. Byron did, however, draft a preface (albeit one he eventually rejected) that would have established war as a key context for the poem. In the preface, he invites his readers to imagine that the poem is narrated "by a Spanish Gentleman in a village in the Sierra Morena in the road between Monasterio and Seville," who, notably, stands close to a "knot of French prisoners," a scene clearly set during the Peninsular War (*CPW* v: 82–3, ll. 54–5, 69).

So too the poem's turn to war in the seventh and eighth cantos, where he describes the siege of Ismail (1790), when Russian forces under general Alexander Suvorov massacred the Turkish garrison, marks a fundamental shift in Byron's overall conception of his poem. By including an account of the siege, Byron establishes a specific historical and political setting for the poem, allowing him to present an image of the barbarity and hypocrisy of the world as it existed on the cusp of the French Revolution – the world restored by Napoleon's defeat at Waterloo. It is notable in this context that Suvorov was the most successful allied commander to wage war against the French revolutionary forces in the 1790s. In turning to war, Byron positions himself as a poetic equivalent of Napoleon, calling himself the "grand Napoleon of the realms of rhyme," whose poetry could oppose the savagery represented by Suvorov (*CPW* v: 482, l. 55).

The siege is pivotal to the way that Byron imagines the full impact of war. Partly this is because the siege has a long tradition within epic poetry stemming from the *Iliad* and its account of the siege of Troy. But Byron also mocks this epic tradition, the siege providing him with a way to imagine forms of warfare that were no longer worthy of epic poetry because they had become total in their impact. During wars of the eighteenth century, military engineers such as the Marquis de Vauban had conducted sieges with a geometrical and mathematical precision designed to avoid the need to storm a besieged town or fortress by force. The Napoleonic Wars saw the end of this humane ideal, sieges from this time routinely ending with a bloody and terrifying massacre in which the assaulting soldiers would sack the town and kill its inhabitants. It is just such an assault that Byron depicts at Ismail, with Suvorov himself training his soldiers in the use of the bayonet while lecturing them on "the noble art of killing" (*CPW* v: 355, l. 460). As the town is assaulted, so war spills over any bounds of politics, masculinity, heroism or military professionalism, as soldiers, women and children are all caught in the terrifying butchery.

If he undermines epic traditions of martial poetry, Byron also delivers some of his most biting invectives against war by revealing how its violence is masked by military reports, propaganda, martial rhetoric and government gazettes. At the opening of the canto, Byron jokes that because it is too difficult to rhyme Russian names he must decline to commemorate their deaths in his verse, while he questions the idea of trying to construct a memory of fallen soldiers at all, asking: "Of all our modern battles, I will bet / You can't repeat nine names from each Gazette" (*CPW* v: 347, l. 272). He inserts his own language of war's physicality to oppose this rhetorical cant, asking "if a man's name in a *bulletin* / May make up for a *bullet in* his body?" (*CPW* v: 343, ll. 162–3). He instead presents scenes of war through what he terms "Hard words, which stick in the soft Muses' gullets" (*CPW* v: 361, l. 624) and belie all ideas of glory:

> Three hundred cannon threw up their emetic,
>   And thirty thousand musquets flung their pills
> Like hail, to make a bloody diuretic.
>   Mortality! thou hast thy monthly bills;
> Thy Plagues, thy Famines, thy Physicians, yet tick,
>   Like the death-watch, within our ears the ills
> Past, present, and to come; but all may yield
> To the true portrait of one battle-field.
>   (*DJ* VIII, st. 12, ll. 89–96 [*CPW* v: 368])

In his "true portrait," war appears as the site of the bodily abject, a battle resembling a bloody diuretic that exceeds all other causes of human mortality. Don Juan himself is compelled by Suvorov to join the assault, yet he also rescues a young girl from being killed by two Cossacks, his kindness offering a glimpse of how humanity might be retained amid war's destruction.

Byron's death in 1824 came while he was serving as a commander in the Greek War of Independence. Although his time in Greece was brief – he died a mere 100 days after his arrival in the country – the simple fact that he had supported the conflict acted as a powerful tonic to the fight for independence. The Greek War represented a new kind of revolutionary nationalism that would play a decisive role in shaping nineteenth-century Europe. Notably, however, this culmination of Byron's life as a man of political action and an inspiration for an armed national liberty sits at odds with the poetic persona he crafted, in which he revels in life's inconsistencies and laments the horrors of war. His account in *Don Juan* of the Russian storming of the Turks at Ismail sits somewhat uneasily alongside his own plans to lay siege to the Turkish-held fortress at Lepanto at the head of "two thousand men" (*BLJ* 11: 110). Byron was no pacifist, though, and his views on war were fundamentally shaped by his concerns with the advance of tyranny. He was both appalled by war as the work of murder, and yet equally held in thrall to its spectacle and the possibilities that war held open for realizing liberty in "freedom's battles" (*CPW* v: 366, l. 31).

Note

1 John Clubbe, "Napoleon's Last Campaign and the Origins of *Don Juan*," *Byron Journal* 25 (January 1997), 12–22 (12).

CHAPTER 9

Greece's Byron

Spiridoula Demetriou

Lord Byron was not the first foreigner to arrive in revolutionary Missolonghi, or to die there. What set Byron apart from other volunteers was his celebrity status, based on literary success and a notorious lifestyle. His sojourn in the town to represent the London Greek Committee, and his death there on April 19, 1824, became the foremost symbols of nineteenth-century Philhellenism.

Philhellenism, the political and cultural movement supporting the liberation of Greece from Ottoman rule, had gained traction in Greece and elsewhere in Europe after the Enlightenment and French Revolution. Philhellene public opinion campaigns circumvented provisions in the 1815 Congress of Vienna that sought to impose neutrality on Western governments as a means of quelling support for revolutionary activity across Europe after the turmoil of the Napoleonic Wars. The spark that encouraged Greek rebellion against Ottoman rule was a military campaign in late February 1821 by Alexander Ipsilantis, a Russian officer of Greek heritage, who assembled an army of several nationalities through the Danubian principalities and unsuccessfully bid defiance to the Ottomans. Political Philhellenism contributed to the success of the Greek War of Independence of 1821–7, as France, Russia and Britain eventually intervened in favor of Greece.

There has been extensive debate about Byron's benefit to Philhellenism and the Greek struggle for independence. Some commentators believe that Byron achieved nothing other than his own demise, while others view him as the savior of the Greek nation. A close examination of primary sources demonstrating Byron's material contribution to the war effort in Missolonghi contradicts the contention that his presence had no value and that he died before achieving much at all. A particularly illuminating source – and context – for the exploration of this debate is the 1861 painting *The Reception of Lord Byron at Missolonghi* by Theodore Vryzakis (see Figure 9.1), a painter renowned for his scenes of the Greek War of

Figure 9.1 Theodoros Vryzakis, *The Reception of Lord Byron at Missolonghi*, 1861. 155 × 213 cm, oil on canvas. The National Art Gallery and Alexander Soutzos Museum, Athens, inv. no. Π. 1298.

Independence. This chapter considers the political context of Byron's arrival in revolutionary Greece, and then examines Vryzakis' conception of the poet as the "Greek messiah," revealing the legacy of the Byronic legend of Greek nationalism.

Byron first traveled to Greece with John Cam Hobhouse in 1809 as part of their grand tour of Europe, and it was Hobhouse who suggested that Byron act as an agent for the London Greek Committee. Byron had been in exile in Italy for seven years when the London Greek Committee was formed on March 3, 1823 to support the Greek War of Independence. The insurgents had also been lobbying Philhellenes outside Greece for financial aid for the poorly resourced rebellion. Sir John Bowring, the committee's secretary, wrote to Byron with the proposal on March 14, 1823, and he responded with alacrity: "With great pleasure I accept this honour conferred upon me and shall be happy to contribute by every means in my power to forward the views of the Committee who have considered me worthy to become a member of their body."[1] Hobhouse suggested that Edward Blaquiere, a founding committee member, call upon Byron, when he was in Genoa en route to Greece for a fact-finding expedition. Byron gave an account of Blaquiere's visit in a letter to Hobhouse dated April 7, 1823, where he also expressed uncertainty about whether he could make any contribution, military or otherwise (*BLJ* 10: 142–4). This same letter provides a hint that the social stigma created in England by his acrimonious separation from Annabella and his intimate relationship with his half-sister Augusta Leigh did not leave his self-regard entirely unblemished. He confided to Hobhouse that he had told Blaquiere that the use of his name in London "would probably do more harm than good" (*BLJ* 10: 143). Ultimately this concern was hollow, because he had already stated his intention of proceeding to Greece in July. Curiously, Blaquiere did not call on Byron on his way back from Greece, nor did he tell the committee in his initial report on his return to England that he had met Byron. This indicates that Blaquiere may have only expected Byron to play a peripheral role.

The rapidity with which Byron was prepared to set off for Greece must have alarmed Hobhouse, because in a letter dated July 8, 1823 he tactfully rejected the idea of any military involvement for his friend and suggested he take an executive position at the seat of the provisional Greek government. There was no question of Byron taking an administrative role, because Greece at the time lacked a stable central government, army or treasury. The executive and legislative bodies were in a constant state of flux and kept moving between locations. Byron commented in his journal on November 23, 1813, "To be the first man – not the Dictator – not the Sylla, but the Washington or the Aristides – the leader in talent and truth – is next to the Divinity!" (*BLJ* 3: 218). It appears he held deep-seated desires to become a statesman and soldier.

Surprisingly, he made no mention of military or political ambitions when he wrote to Augusta Leigh on October 12, 1823 from British-governed Cephalonia, where he had arrived at the beginning of August. Byron explained that he was going to Greece both as an individual and as a representative of the committee to aid the Greek nation's "struggle for independence" (*BLJ* 11: 44). Doris Langley Moore coined the term "the siege of Byron" to describe the barrage of requests for material support coming from Greek military, civil and religious emissaries while he was on Cephalonia.[2] By the time he arrived in Missolonghi to an enthusiastic reception on January 5, 1824, Byron understood the complexity of a war that was largely being led by parochial factional leaders. The power struggles between governmental authorities and military leaders would eventually result in civil war. Through Percy Bysshe Shelley, Byron indirectly knew Alexandros Mavrokordatos, who had been staying with Shelley at the outbreak of the War of Independence and had hurried from there to Greece. At the first National Assembly that gathered in December 1821, Mavrokordatos had been appointed president; Missolonghi became the western seat of the provisional government and thus a strategic military and political location in revolutionary Greece.

On October 15, 1823, the legislative body of the provisional government wrote to Mavrokordatos asking him to proceed to Missolonghi. The same day, the provisional government wrote to Byron formally requesting that he join Mavrokordatos there and provide financial support in the amount of £30,000 sterling. Only a week before, Mavrokordatos had written to Byron urging him once again to cross over to the mainland. The letter suggested that Byron take a leadership role in a military expedition to gain control of Lepanto, a place that held mythic power in Western culture as a site of the contest between Islam and Christianity. Mavrokordatos claimed that Byron's presence would "electrify the troops."[3] The autonomy of the Souliote bands and independent brigands had proved troublesome to Mavrokordatos' leadership, and he hoped that Byron's presence would unite these groups into a single body behind the provisional government.

Nationalism was still nascent in the country, and Mavrokordatos considered that the Greek forces had to present a united front if they were to attract the much-anticipated English loan to fund the war. On December 23, 1823, when Byron was about to sail to Missolonghi, Mavrokordatos spoke at a public meeting urging the combatant and civilian population to "bond together." He pointed out that no external body would provide loans without certainty as to how they would be repaid. Byron had told Hobhouse in a letter dated September 27, 1823 that his preference was to not become connected with any faction; the invitation from the provisional government allowed him to proceed with confidence to Missolonghi without affiliation to any political or social group.

Being a Philhellene, as Byron saw it, involved providing financial support for the soldiers to maintain stability among the Greek forces. He spelled this out to John Bowring of the London committee in October 1823. He was confounded by some of the items the committee had sent, including mathematical instruments and bugles. Byron had begun sending supplies for the wounded to Missolonghi while he was waiting on Cephalonia. As Stephen Minta has commented, "the fascination with the death of a famous man" has caused Byron's contribution to the war effort at Missolonghi to remain largely ignored.[4] Yet the fact that Byron forwarded money to Greece on his own initiative without reference to the London committee indicates a high level of commitment.

Byron continued to draw on his own funds during his time in Missolonghi. In a letter to his banker Douglas Kinnaird dated February 21, 1824, Byron anticipated the approval of an English loan to the Greek government and stated that he was supporting the government of western Greece with a combination of his own and committee funds: "I am maintaining the whole machinery nearly (in *this* place at least) at our own cost" (*BLJ* 11: 117). Receipts in the archive of the Committee signed by Missolonghi war council members show that these items included gunpowder, charcoal, oil for armoury, wages for carpenters, masons and blacksmiths, funeral expenses of people who died in action, as well as the general running of the War Office.[5]

A copy of a letter in the Greek State Archives provides evidence that Byron was an astute lender. He lent the western government £3,000 in February 1824 against the income of the saltpans at Missolonghi.[6] Pietro Gamba's journal provides insight into the reasons for this loan. In Cephalonia, Byron had engaged as his personal squadron a group of Souliotes, members of an eastern-orthodox ethnic community of north-western Greece known for their fierce resistance to Ottoman rule. Initially, he was confident that he wielded sufficient influence to keep them in peace with the other groups, but by February they had proved unruly; they were the main reason the Lepanto expedition was abandoned (*BLJ* 11: 111–12 and 145). On February 20, Gamba recalled that a group of Primates (respected citizens, or unofficial community leaders) came to visit Byron after a German officer had been killed in an altercation with a Souliote. They requested a loan of £3,000 to pay the rowdy Souliotes to leave the town. Byron had also experienced difficulties with the group's pay, and on February 15, 1824, he arrived at a decision: "Having tried in vain at every expence – considerable trouble – and some danger to unite the Suliotes for the good of Greece – and their own – I have come to the following resolution – I will have nothing more to do with the Suliotes – they may go to the Turks or – the devil" (*BLJ* 11: 111–12). Byron extended the loan provided that the Primates ensured the group left Missolonghi. This was political maneuvering on Byron's part, because it distanced him from the arrangement, and from exposing himself as financially malleable under pressure.

The Souliotes were not Byron's only source of concern at Missolonghi. There was an ideological divide between Byron and Leicester Stanhope, sent to Missolonghi as an administrator by the London Greek Committee. Stanhope's liberalism was influenced by Benthamite social theory, and he held firm ideas about Greece after the revolution, particularly the country's constitutional and educational systems, for which he favored reform based on Western models. Byron expressed his agitation with Stanhope's theorizing in a letter to the committee with the remark "I am tired of hearing nothing but talk – and Constitutions – and Sunday Schools – and what not" (*BLJ* 11: 102). Byron and Stanhope clashed over the latter's dissemination of Bentham's ideas in the *Greek Chronicle* newspaper. However, Vakalopoulos is one historian who has concluded that the publishing activities of Stanhope, along with the newspaper's editor Meyer, transformed Missolonghi into a "source of national enlightened and democratic consciousness."[7]

Byron's vexations in Missolonghi may have contributed to the despondency that characterizes his final poem, which was written there on his birthday, January 22, 1824. The tempestuous lagoon and the heavy rain that shrouds Missolonghi at that time of year may also have had a melancholic effect on Byron's psyche. Titled "On this day I complete my thirty sixth year," the poem begins with painful yearning for the sensation of love. This longing in the face of waning possibilities is made more tragic through the presence of unwavering desire. Consideration of a heroic death intersects this meditation on love because it also relates to validating life experiences. Byron fired up the Philhellene Romanticist associations between the Greek revolution and classical Greece with the lines

> The Sword – the Banner – and the Field,
>   Glory and Greece, around us see!
> The Spartan borne upon his shield,
>   Was not more free!
>   (st. 6, ll. 21–4 [*CPW* VII: 80])

Byron himself did not experience the heroic release from life that his poem praised, but there was no shortage of posthumous attempts to elevate him to that sphere. Byron's association with the Greek cause prompted solidarity from across the globe, as far away as the British colony of New South Wales in Australia. The poem titled "On the Death of Lord Byron," exemplifying Byron as a man of action, was published in the *Australian* newspaper seven months after his death on November 11, 1824. Simply signed "S." it strongly referenced *Childe Harold*, Byron's narrative poem about the travels of a jaded young man in foreign lands. Thus, Byron's verse "Where are thy men of might? thy grand in soul?" (*CPW* 11: 44, l. 11) is paraphrased as "WHERE art thou, man of might, thou grand soul."[8] This apostrophe of the deceased Byron, as well as the remark "Greece! Thou hast lost thy champion," promoted the poet as a warrior for the cause of

Greek liberation. The poem also features the Romantic image of the poet as a heroic solitary figure radiating positive qualities whose death has left *a twilight gloom* in its wake. Furthermore, the poem demonstrates that the Byronic legend contributed to the stability of the nineteenth-century Romantic view of Greece, one that coalesced the imagined with the real in the narrative of Greek independence.

In *The Reception of Lord Byron at Missolonghi* (Figure 9.1), Theodore Vryzakis confers upon Byron the status of messiah of the Greek nation. The insurgents' *esprit de corps* is the main political idea of the painting and is expressed by Vryzakis through the population's unified response to Byron's arrival on mainland Greece. The air of distinction conveyed by the mantle Byron wears is reinforced through his strong, offering stance with out-turned, open arms and widely planted feet. Vryzakis did not originate this pose; it was created by the French artist Tony Johannot during the 1850s as an illustration for the fourth line of stanza 30 of Alphonse De Lamartine's poem *Le dernier chant du Pèlerinage d'Harold* (see Figure 9.2). De Lamartine's poem has been interpreted as collapsing Byron and Childe Harold into a single persona to create a fictional account of Byron's final months. Also, Johannot's use of Thomas Phillips' well-known 1813 portrait of Byron at his literary acme as a model for the physiognomy of Childe Harold reinforces the connection between Byron and his heroic literary characters in the public imagination (see Figure I.1 in the Introduction).

Vryzakis' involvement in this process brings nation and imagination together to represent Byron at Missolonghi as a strong influence upon the creation of modern Greece. Byron's role in the regeneration of Greece is visualized by Vryzakis in a subtle yet extremely potent way. The Deacon standing to the left of the Archbishop amid a cloud of incense holds an icon representing the resurrection of Christ. The Icon of the Resurrection is an archetypal image of victory in the Orthodox faith, because it represents triumph over death. The golden-haired girl standing before the Icon reinforces the idea of Byron as the savior of the Greek insurrection. As she draws the attention of the person beside her to Byron, her raised pointed finger is before the Icon and directly below the figure of the resurrected and hovering Christ. The idea of Byron as the savior of Greece is ultimately delivered to the viewer by Vryzakis through the crimson lining of Byron's mantle, which is the same color as the shroud unraveling around Christ as he soars up to heaven and into divinity.

Byron's commitment to the Greek insurrection created enormous anticipation in Greece regarding Western aid and intervention into a war that did not officially have the sanction of Western governments, or

Tony Johannot pinxit.　　　　　　　　　　　　　　Gouttière sculpsit.

CHILDE HAROLD.

De chefs et de soldats Harold environné...

(Dernier Chant du Pèlerinage de Childe Harold XXX.)

Imp. d'Chardon A.ᵉ Soᵗ.1.Hautefeuille Paris.

Figure 9.2 Tony Johannot pinxit, Gouttière sculpsit, *Childe Harold*, c.1855. 23 × 14 cm, black and white copperplate. Demetriou Collection, Melbourne.

the resources for decisive military engagements. His financial resources supported the insurrection in Missolonghi during a volatile period and when the provisional government did not have any certain sources of income. A clue suggesting that Byron may have indeed sought a more invigorating role in the Greek War of Independence is that he did not actually wear the Hellenic-inspired military helmets he took to Greece. Military involvement or not, Vryzakis' use of the posture from Johannot's illustration, derived from a work of literary fiction based on the Byron–Childe Harold nexus, is a measure of the extent to which Romanticist depictions of Byron infiltrated Greek nationalist representations of his participation in the Greek War of Independence. Vryzakis' development of the post-Missolonghi Byronic legend has contributed significantly to the formation of Missolonghi into an emblem of Byronism.

NOTES

1 Byron to the Chairman of the Greek Committee, May 21, 1823, George Gordon Byron, Baron Byron Collection, New Haven, Yale University Library, GEN MSS 892 Box 1, Folder 14.

2 Doris Langley Moore, *Lord Byron: Accounts Rendered* (London: John Murray, 1974), 389.

3 E. Protopsaltes (ed.), Μνημεία της ελληνικής ιστορίας, Τόμ. Ε΄: ιστορικόν αρχείον Αλεξάνδρου Μαυροκορδάτου. Αθήνα: Γραφείον δημοσιευμάτον της Ακαδημίας Αθήνων (1963–86), vol. III, 545

4 Stephen Minta, "Byron and Missolonghi," *Literature Compass* 4.4 (2007), 1092–108 (1093).

5 Papers of the London Greek Committee. Athens, National Library of Greece, MSS K1–11 (1823–4): K8 A4, K8 B4, K8 C4, K8 D4, K8 M3, K8 O3, K8 P3, K8 Q3, K8 S3, K8 T3, K8 U3, K8 V3, K8 W3, K8 X3, K8 Y3 and K8 Z3.

6 General State Archives, Athens. (1834). Γενικά Αρχεία Κράτους. Αρχείο Περίοδου Όθωνος, Αρχείο Γραμματείας, Υπουργείο επί των Οικονομικών (1833–62), φακ. #266, Πληροφορίες για αλαταποθήκες – επισκευές αλυκών – Αρπαγή αλάτων – Μηνιαίοι λογαριασμοί άλατος – Δάνειο Λόρδου Βύρωνα στην ελληνική κυβέρνηση (1824) έναντι παροχής εισοδημάτων αλυκής Μεσολογγίου. Reference code: GRGSA-CSA_PAO005.00, Subseries: #002 – Salt pans [1833–41], file: GRGSA-CSA_PAO005.00.SFO01.SFO02.S02.SS02. SS02.F000266, items 1 -8, http://arxeiomnimon.gak.gr/search/resource.html? tab=tab02&id=4155&start=100.

7 A. E. Vakalopoulos, Ιστορ   ʹʹ ληνισμο΄, vols. I–VIII (1961–86), vol. VI: 603 Θεσσαλονίκη: s.n. [ιν.]   ιο...]

8 "On the Death of Lord Byron," *The Australian* (Sydney, N.S.W) (November 11, 1824), 3, http://nla.gov.au/nla.news-article37072527.

CHAPTER 10

Byron's Italy

Timothy Webb

Byron wrote numerous notes and letters in Italian to Teresa Guiccioli, yet, unlike his friend Percy Bysshe Shelley, he did not translate his own poetry into Italian, nor did he produce any independent work in Italian. At first sight, this may seem surprising, not least because of Byron's intense interest in the Italian language and specifically Venetian, which, by his own account, he spoke with ease and vivacity (and, according to others, as if he were talking with a brogue or a Somersetshire accent). He was amusingly critical of those who lacked his linguistic competence, such as John Murray (his publisher), Henry Brougham (the lawyer) and William Sotheby (the translator). His correspondence from Italy is rich in Italian usages, some of which he did not bother to explain. His poetic ambitions were even more closely connected with the language. On April 6, 1819, he informed Murray: "I mean to write my best work in *Italian* – & it will take me nine years more thoroughly to master the language – & then if my fancy exists & I exist too – I will try what I *can* do *really*" (*BLJ* 6: 105). Unfortunately, Byron did not exist nine years later, but his commitment to an extended discipline is hard to ignore. For a variety of reasons, he sent his young daughter by Claire Clairmont to a convent, where, as Shelley's report of his own visit indicates, she conversed in Italian. Over two years later, Byron instructed Lady Byron that their daughter Ada should learn Italian and proceeded to an extraordinary imagining: "[P]erhaps by the time that she and I may meet (if ever we meet) it will be nearly necessary to converse with me – for I write English now with more facility than I speak it – from hearing it but seldom." He continued: "It is the reverse with my Italian which I can speak fluently – but write incorrectly – having never studied it & only acquired it by ear" (*BLJ* 8: 210).

Not many writers of note have managed to write effectively, consistently and with originality in a language that is not their own. Joseph Conrad and Samuel Beckett have few if any successors. Whether Byron would have achieved such linguistic distinction and composed *Don Juan* or its sequel in Italian, it will never be possible to say. But Byron's apparent seriousness in the matter is in keeping with his unusually strict approach to translating Luigi Pulci's *Morgante Maggiore* (published in the *Liberal* in 1823), and with the appreciation and emotional commitment that characterized his attitude to the Italian language. These attitudes can be clearly identified in two letters (*BLJ* 6: 147, 149) where he scrutinizes two epitaphs he had observed in a cemetery in Ferrara ("Martini Luigi / Implora pace" and "Lucrezia Picini / Implora eterna quiete"). He considers both epitaphs in detail and applies them to his own imagined funeral at "the foreigners' burying-Ground at the Lido" in Venice. In Byron's opinion, these simple words "comprize and compress all that can be said on the subject – and then in Italian they are absolute Music." This loyalty to the Italian way of doing things necessarily implies a rejection of the English alternative: Byron's "allegiance to the 'few words' of the Italian inscriptions is driven by a fierce resistance to the thought of an English cemetery and a considered preference for the unassuming and dignified grace of the Italian alternative."[1] Byron must have been aware of the Latin roots of this kind of funerary expression, since one of his notes to *Childe Harold's Pilgrimage* also celebrates a Latin inscription to Julia Alpinula ("I know of no human composition so affecting as this, nor a history of deeper interest" [*CPW* II: 308, n. 634])." His commitment to the "beautiful" Italian language is given more public expression in his preface to the fourth and final canto of *Childe Harold*, where he also celebrates the capabilities of the Italian people, markedly contrasted with the drunken roars of his English contemporaries.

Byron's writing, both in his detailed letters and in *Childe Harold*, and the meticulous record of Hobhouse's journals, indicate that, whatever his scorn for tourists, Byron himself visited many sites popular with visitors. Not least among these was the Ferrara prison cell of the Renaissance poet Torquato Tasso, also visited by Shelley, who sent part of its door to Thomas Love Peacock in England. Like Shelley, Byron identified with Tasso, the subject of his *The Lament of Tasso* (1817), who was imprisoned for loving the wrong woman and served as a figure of the misunderstood poet for many of his European contemporaries. Perhaps, though, his most extensive engagement with the Italian way of life can be found in *Beppo* (1818), which is freighted with his excitement at discovering Venice and encountering many of the contexts of Italian literature.

Ostensibly, this "Venetian Story" does not record the views of George Gordon, Lord Byron, himself but those of "A broken Dandy lately on my travels," who reveals that he is an incompetent narrator, one "who speaks as a spectator, not officially" and is anxious to avoid causing offence. Yet, in spite of the inescapable presence of this *persona*, the device is little more protective than the masks of a carnival (one of the central metaphors of the poem) since *Beppo* is obviously informed by Byron's own views, attitudes and impressions of Italy, seen through the prism of Venice, which (like Italy itself) he had encountered only recently. Here, for the first time, Byron employs the eight-line stanzas of *ottava rima*, allowing him to engage with the features of Venetian (or Italian) life in a verse form that is quintessentially Italian while also giving voice to the attitudes of the narrator and especially Byron himself. The following year *The Prophecy of Dante* (published 1821) expressed his allegiance to the exiled Dante by employing *terza rima*, with which Dante was always identified, giving his verse a strangely haunted ventriloquial quality not evident in his later letters from Ravenna.

The perspective of *Beppo* may be revealingly compared to that of Leigh Hunt, who stayed in Byron's *palazzo* in Pisa. For Hunt, the social feature strangest to English readers was *Cicisbeismo* – in effect, second marriage – by which women were seen to be permitted to have two men. The *Cavalier Servente* is, as Byron writes in *Beppo*, "a vice-husband, *chiefly* to *protect her*" (*CPW* IV: 138, l. 232), or, viewed from a different angle, a "supernumerary slave, who stays / Close to the lady as a part of dress, / Her word the only law which he obeys" (*CPW* IV: 141, ll. 315–17). Expressing mock horror at such permissiveness, the poem also reveals the implications of a more seemingly "moral" system, exclaiming, "But Heaven preserve Old England from such courses! / Or what becomes of damage and divorces?" (*CPW* IV: 140, ll. 295–6). Hunt condemned this "stupid system" as "almost as gross, more formal, and quite as hypocritical as what it displaces" (*Liberal* 2 [April 1823], second edition, 57). Byron's view was a shifting one, based on his relationship with Teresa Guiccioli. Unlike Hunt, he had direct experience of what he once resentfully called "this Cicisbean existence" (*BLJ* 6: 214), and on October 3, 1819 he complained:

> I am not tired of Italy – but a man must be a Cicisbeo and a singer in duets and a Connoisseur of operas – or nothing here – I have made some progress in all these accomplishments – but I can't say that I don't feel the degradation … I have been an intriguer, a husband, and now I am a Cavalier Servente. (*BLJ* 6: 226)

Within five months, he could report a change of attitude: "I have settled into regular Serventismo – and find it the happiest state of all" (*BLJ* 7: 51).

Beppo's emphasis on masquerade is crucial to its social analysis, and its implications were political as well as sociological: "Perhaps, the Italians would but ill exchange their Carnival for a Parliament, – but they long for the latter – and if England would barter with them – there might be no great loss to either." Byron's poem devotes some attention to the gaiety of Lent (vividly evoked by a succession of plurals in the opening stanzas); the Carnival (also the topic of an acid unfinished essay describing it as "a drama without the fiction" and "that universal Harlequinade in Catholic Countries – but more especially in Italy" where all is "Music – and Masque – and 'Christian fools with varnished faces' "; gondolas and gondoliers (here compared to London coachmen, not least because of their expertise in swearing), who were the subject of a long, memorable foot-note by Hobhouse to the fourth canto of *Childe Harold*, including Byron's recollection of hearing gondoliers singing alternate stanzas from Tasso's *Gerusalemme Liberata*; the social politics of the Ridotto with its "mix'd company" (compared in some ways to London's Vauxhall, "Excepting that it can't be spoilt by rain," says the narrator, who is acutely conscious of contrasts in weather); the Italian language ("that soft bastard Latin / Which melts like kisses from a female mouth"), which is favorably contrasted to "our harsh northern whistling grunting guttural"; Italian women's com-posure when faced by a sudden crisis as compared with English women's cultural practice of fainting.

As these examples suggest, much of the strength of the poem, like that of the essay, is comparative; *Beppo* is concerned with Italy, especially with Venice, but that necessarily involves an engagement not only with Italian practices but also with the routines of English life. It is no acci-dent that, near the middle of the poem (ll. 321–92), it explicitly debates the rival claims of Italy and England. Italy attracts the narrator, as it attracted Byron himself, because it offers experiences not available in England, especially of a sensual nature; but England has its virtues, espe-cially freedom of speech, "freedom of the press and quill," parliamentary debates (Byron himself had addressed the House of Lords), in spite of "Our cloudy climate, and our chilly women." In leaving England for Italy, Byron changed some aspects of his life: although he continued to ride and swim, he seems to have abandoned boxing, and although he attended the theater, he did not maintain the closeness to plays and actors that left its impress on so many of his letters. The Italian *conversaz-ione* was very different from the English party where Byron had recently cut so glamorous a figure.

There were compensations. Byron often recorded his engagement with Italian customs in his prose, especially his letters, which were not primarily intended for public consumption. A letter of May 30, 1817 to John Murray provides a striking example, describing what Romans might expect from an execution:

> The day before I left Rome I saw three robbers guillotined – the ceremony – including the *masqued* priests – the half-naked executioners – the bandaged criminals – the black Christ & his banner – the scaffold – the soldiery – the slow procession – & the quick rattle and heavy fall of the axe – the splash of the blood – & the ghastliness of the exposed heads – is altogether more impressive than the vulgar and ungentlemanly dirty "new drop" & dog-like agony of infliction upon the sufferers of the English sentence. Two of these men – behaved calmly enough – but the first of the three – died with great terror and reluctance – which was very horrible – he would not lie down – then his neck was too large for the aperture – and the priest was obliged to drown his exclamations by still louder exhortations – the head was off before the eye could trace the blow – but from an attempt to draw back the head – notwithstanding it was held forward by the hair – the first head was off cut close to the ears – the other two were taken off more cleanly; – it is better than the Oriental way – & (I should think) than the axe of our ancestors. – The pain seems little – & yet the effect to the spectator – & the preparation to the criminal – is very striking & chilling. – The first turned me quite hot and thirsty – & made me shake so that I could hardly hold the opera-glass (I was close – but was determined to see – as one should see every thing once – with attention) the second and third (which shows how dreadfully soon things grow indifferent) I am ashamed to say had no effect on me – as a horror – though I would have saved them if I could. (*BLJ* 5: 229–30)

This unforgettable description is surely one of Byron's major contributions to an understanding of Italian culture. For all his radicalism and revolutionary spirit, his poetry of this period prefers to avoid "the splash of the blood" or the vivid and at times grotesque details of this letter to his publisher.

In some ways, Byron's reluctance to introduce tangible contemporary realities into his poetic version of Italy has something in common with the popular but misleading treatment by his friend Samuel Rogers in *Italy* (later illustrated by Turner), which carefully transfers any signs of violence and bloodshed to the past, even though Rogers' own diary demonstrates that he was in the middle of a violent political situation. The nature of Byron's approach, and its deliberate limitations, can be clarified by comparing his prose account to the stanzas in the final canto of *Childe Harold* devoted to the dying Gladiator, "Butcher'd to make a Roman holiday" (*CPW* 11: 171, l. 1267). Although Byron focuses on the flow of blood, poetic decorum requires that he soften its impact by introducing a simile: "through his side the last drops, ebbing slow / From the red gash, fall heavy, one by one, / Like the first of a thunder-shower." The effect of this description is to engage our emotions while presenting the scene in a way that is memorable but curiously distanced. The comparison indicates that there were still important generic distinctions between what was considered possible in poetry and in prose.

Not surprisingly, most travel writers avoided the kind of disturbing and violent spectacle presented in Byron's description of the execution, preferring to concentrate on the measurement of architecture or the intricacies of history. One exception was Charles Dickens, who includes a vivid account of a Roman execution in his much later *Pictures from Italy*. The connection between Byron and Dickens should not be surprising, since both writers display an affinity for the violent and the grotesque. Although Dickens shared Byron's fascination with the shedding of blood ("There was," he says, "a great deal of blood"), both his sense of revulsion and his judgmental morality ("It was an ugly, filthy, careless, sickening spectacle") are strikingly absent from Byron's account.

What makes Byron's description even more arresting is the final sentence in which it observes the trembling voyeur with unsentimental clarity. Unlike the egoistic self-focus of *Childe Harold* (where Harold/Byron is "a ruin amidst ruins"), Byron presents here an almost clinical focus on his own reactions ("The first turned me quite hot and thirsty – & made me shake so that I could hardly hold the opera-glass"), combined with a wider interest in human behavior ("how dreadfully soon things grow indifferent"). The same curiosity marked his experiences in Italy, as it did elsewhere ("one should see everything once – with attention"). This greed to observe everything possible leaves a strong impress on his writings from Italy: consider, for example, his account of the political assassination and eventual death of the military commandant of Ravenna, which the poet "gazed" on uncomprehendingly, that also forms the central subject of three detailed letters (*BLJ* 7: 245–51) and of seven stanzas in *Don Juan* (Canto v, st. 33–9).

Like the disturbing conjunctions of *Beppo*, this description of the execution is also marked by a comparative perspective. Byron witnesses an execution not only with the attention of a fellow human being but with the unblinking eye of a sociologist. The zest and exactitude in his recording of customs and practices is almost anthropological, as in his treatment of the system of cicisbeism, both in his letters and, more publicly, in *Beppo*. The procedures of Roman executions are of interest because they can be compared with "the Oriental way," the ancestors' axe and the procedures by which such things were currently ordered in Britain. The solemnity of the occasion, and its vividly itemized impressiveness as a spectacle, is pointedly contrasted to the infelicities of the Newgate drop and its "dog-like agony of infliction." As an observer, Byron's assessment is pragmatic or aesthetic rather than moral. Unlike Shelley, who was initially shocked when young ladies of rank smelt of garlic, Byron is excited and stimulated by the *otherness* of Italian life, as he is charmed and impressed by the character of its language. Above all, he is open to difference and records what he experiences, sometimes with dramatic emphasis but without embarrassment or shock. Byron prided himself on an intimate understanding of the customs, practices and traditions of Italian life, which, he insisted, separated him from the superficial or even mercenary engagements of those who were merely tourists. Writing from Ravenna in 1820, he claimed that he had been protected from this superficiality because he had lived in "parts of Italy freshest and least influenced by strangers," where he had become "a portion of their hopes, and fears, and passions" and, by a mysterious but constructive process, was "almost inoculated into a family" (*BLJ* 7: 170–1). The hint of reservation in "almost" claims our attention; Byron was aware that, however convincing his mastery of the language or his ability to identify with the Italian people or their customs, he would always be merely a captivated outsider.

NOTE

1 Timothy Webb, "'Soft Bastard Latin': Byron and the Attractions of Italian," *Journal of Anglo-Italian Studies* 10 (2009), 77–8.

CHAPTER II

Orientalism

Gerard Cohen-Vrignaud

Ever since the appearance of Edward Said's postcolonial tour de force, *Orientalism* (1978), Byron's taste for Eastern characters and settings has provoked much commentary from scholars. Byron, after all, spent a large part of his poetic career depicting the contemporary and historical Middle East, starting with Canto II of *Childe Harold's Pilgrimage* (1812), through the Turkish tales of 1813–14 (*The Giaour, The Bride of Abydos, The Corsair, Lara*) to his Assyrian historical drama *Sardanapalus* (1821) and *Don Juan's* Greek and Turkish cantos (1819–23). He also famously donned Albanian dress for one of his most iconic portraits, an image frequently used to adorn biographies, scholarly treatments and collections of his works (see Figure 16.1 in Chapter 16) He may therefore be considered the foremost exoticist in the English literary canon, a writer whose writing and personal mystique are fundamentally defined by his mobilization of cultural difference.

How to politically parse this literary use of the East is one crucial interpretive issue that has preoccupied scholars writing after Said. The overriding question has been to what extent, to deploy the language developed by postcolonial criticism, Byron's "cultural appropriation" of Eastern peoples, habits and settings mirrored or contributed to British imperialism, which reached its ideological and territorial peak in the long nineteenth century. That Byron gave aesthetic cachet to the commercialization and exoticization of non-Western cultures is beyond doubt, though he was far from the first or the last to do so. That he was simultaneously and passionately opposed to imperial domination is also largely incontrovertible, in part because he gave his life in support of the Greek revolution against Ottoman rule. How, then, to reconcile the ease with which Byron "borrowed" from and impersonated cultures not his own with his well-documented passion for the liberty of individuals and of peoples?

One part of the answer lies in recognizing that the literary "Orient" was a set of ritualized figures and tropes through which Western writers worked out issues of interest to them and their audiences. After the French Revolution and the advance of liberal political rights, for instance, Orientalism redounded with themes of freedom and bondage, as the causes of juridical equality and economic solidarity raged across Europe and the world. To depict Eastern characters struggling against social and institutional oppression was a pleasurable and safe way to allegorize the condition of downtrodden Europeans. Hence, Selim, the protagonist of *The Bride of Abydos* (1813), embarks on a career of piracy and holds up the economic deprivation of common folk to justify his rebellion against his kin, the pasha: "Survey the waste – / And ask the squalid peasant how / His gains repay his broiling brow!" (*CPW* III: 131, ll. 257–9). A poem like *Lara* (1814) literalizes and reverses this type of allegorical translation by having its eponymous hero return from the East to his unspecified European country and start a plebeian revolution. In this way, Byron's Orientalism resembles that of his contemporary Percy Bysshe Shelley, whose epic *The Revolt of Islam* (1817), though set in the Ottoman Empire, is explicitly framed from the beginning as a "beau ideal" rewriting of the French Revolution.[1]

At the same time, Byron's Orientalism not only refracts contemporary concerns but also participates in a long European tradition of representing the Muslim world. Especially after the translation of *1001 Nights* in French and then into English in the early eighteenth century, Western audiences became fascinated by Arab, Persian and Turkish cultures and literatures. The eighteenth century witnessed an efflorescence of pseudo-Eastern stories written by Europeans, from Montesquieu's *Persian Letters* (1721) to Samuel Johnson's *Rasselas* (1759) and, most influentially for Byron, William Beckford's Gothic-Orientalist novella *Vathek* (1786). Due to the nature of *1001 Nights*, much of the Orientalist literature in its wake played up the fantastic elements that reflected the Arabian tales' origins in folk culture. Like most of his contemporaries, Byron read with enchantment this diverse array of texts; and like a number of his Romantic peers, he wrote his own, though with the significant difference that his poems, in a more realistic vein, discarded the supernatural apparatus. In turn, he would inspire others to produce their own Orientalist set-pieces, not only Shelley with his *Revolt of Islam* and *Hellas* (1822), but also the most commercially successful poem of the lot, Thomas Moore's *Lalla Rookh*, which found an immense readership upon its publication in 1817.

In addition to works of fancy, the eighteenth-century gusto for the exotic stimulated the academic study of various Eastern lands, anthropological research that Byron also read enthusiastically and cited liberally in the footnotes to his Orientalist poems. Raymond Schwab dubbed this European effusion of scholarship "the Oriental Renaissance."² Part of the interest clearly stemmed from imperial conquest; Britain's territorial expansion in India and elsewhere prompted investigation of those places and peoples whose lives were increasingly administered in London. A renowned public figure like William Jones, the Orientalist scholar, poet and colonial bureaucrat of the late eighteenth century, emblematizes this nexus of creative, scholarly and imperial energies. Even when written by Western writers not generally supportive of empire, Orientalist scholarship could still serve the purposes of foreign occupation. Hence, the French scholar Volney's ethnography *Travels to Syria and Egypt* (1787) was useful to Napoleon when France invaded and briefly ruled Egypt, formerly under the nominal control of Turkey. By contrast, Byron's Orientalism focused on regions (Turkey, Greece and the Levant) that were not governed by the West, which makes accusations of colonial complicity less germane.

A harder charge to answer has been the uninformed basis of Western Orientalism and the many stereotypes that pervade it. Much of the writing on the East was written without personal experience of those places depicted, meaning that writers mostly relied on their readings to substantiate their accounts of regions they knew only by hearsay. However, like Jones and unlike many writers who dabbled in literary Orientalism, Byron had actually traveled to some of those territories he depicted in his poetry. He famously left England from 1809 to 1811 for the nobleman's customary grand tour, a tour that took him through Greece, Albania and Turkey, in a departure from the usual French–German–Italian route, then rendered difficult by the ongoing Napoleonic Wars. Upon his return, he composed the crypto-autobiographical *Childe Harold*, which drew upon this foreign experience and was received to critical and commercial acclaim. He then returned to his Eastern theme over the next few years with four so-called "Turkish tales," works that exemplify his brand of populist Orientalism and feature the type of protagonist that came to be known as the "Byronic hero."

The Corsair (1814), for instance, concerns Conrad, a mysterious pirate of ambiguous European origin living on a Greek island and competing for spoils with the neighboring pasha, an Ottoman governor. The moody protagonist is an outlaw fundamentally at odds with society, both his place of birth and the one he has chosen. Though he displays fondness for companionate marriage (his partner Medora lives with him in domestic bliss on the island), he also becomes attached to Gulnare, a harem slave he rescues from fire after his attack on the pasha goes awry. *The Corsair* epitomizes how exoticist fantasies could serve Western writers to explore questions of personal identity and cultural belonging, all the while trading on a hoary set of Orientalist commonplaces and stereotypes (the cruel and insecure Eastern despot, the beautiful and sexually available harem slave, the brutality of Ottoman life, to name the most obvious). The poem's popularity (selling 25,000 copies in nine editions published within two years) underscores the commercial standing of this literary East as well as Byron's knack for profiting from the Other.

In this regard, Byron's exoticist work is of a piece with much of the travel writing in the eighteenth and nineteenth centuries. Accounts of far-away places met with much success in Europe, as the aims of education and pleasure became intertwined. One could be entertained about the curious customs of other lands while also fulfilling one's obligation to be an informed citizen of the world. Of course, this educational function does not fully account for Orientalism's resonance, and, certainly, the amount of actual learning imparted by exoticist writing is often minimal. But the authorial aspiration to document the sources for the facts depicted in Orientalist works – indicated by the copious footnotes to Southey's *Thalaba the Destroyer* (1801), Moore's *Lalla Rookh* or Byron's Turkish tales – reveals that these poems were conceived not only as escapist frivolity but also as informational and culturally accurate.

Still, spreading knowledge is far from the goal in one of the most performed ballets in the canon, "Le Corsaire" (1856, libretto by Jules-Henri de St. Georges, choreography by Joseph Mazilier, significantly revised in subsequent adaptations). This nineteenth-century adaptation of *The Corsair*, with its ridiculous pasha, lavish costuming and fantasy scenes of dancing harem girls, speaks to the international and cross-media appeal of Byron's poetry. Unlike the other Romantic poets, he was immediately admired and read both at home and abroad. Byron's Orientalism probably contributed to this transcultural popularity, as it was one aesthetic fashion that had united Europeans since *1001 Nights*. The adaptation of Byron's work by painters like Eugène Delacroix and composers such as Hector Berlioz and Giuseppe Verdi speaks not only to his poetry's translatability but also to his focus on narrative verse, more open to dramatic reworkings than the lyric volubility of his Romantic contemporaries. With Walter Scott, Byron can be considered one of the preeminent storytellers of his generation, and his plots and characters – many of them Orientalist – inspired both his audience and the artists across Europe who reimagined them.

But beyond stories about exotic characters and customs far from European routine, the aesthetic profit of Orientalism was also decorative, as we sense in Byron's famous (and, of course, ironic) description of himself, in *Beppo* (1817), as offering "samples of the finest Orientalism," titillating pieces of descriptive Otherness that he "mix'd with western sentimentalism," the moralizing concoction with which Britons were intimately familiar (*CPW* IV: 145, ll. 408, 407). His awareness that this Orientalist sampling was designed to "sell" – and the suggestion here of dealing in patches of cloth is not incidental – places Byron, again, squarely in the company of Scott, whose historical novels similarly exploit the nineteenth-century fascination with foreign and past practices. Both types of art – historicist and exoticist – allowed readers to be transported far away from the mundane realities of their contemporary moment. The same market demand led to the nineteenth-century revival of culturally distinct styles across various artistic domains, most concretely in the architecture that sought to recapture the feel of the Gothic, Moorish or Byzantine built environment. This materialist stress on what would come to be known as "local color" is a less emphasized feature of Romanticism, which has tended to be described in psychological, philosophical and transcendental terms.

At the same time, Romantic Orientalism lived up to its lineal descent from the romance tradition, continuing to offer the desired entertainment and escape, even as sociologically situated realism became more and more canonical, as in the case of William Wordsworth's ballads of common life and Jane Austen's ironic depictions of the contemporary marriage market. One difference in degree from past romance is that Romanticism fleshed out cultural difference to a much greater extent: hence the sensualist appreciation in Byron's stress on the "finery" of his Orientalism. From the philosophical musings of Johnson's *Rasselas* to Byron's own Oriental tales, we notice an appreciable gain in exoticist detailing, terms and imaging, an advance that might be said to derive in part from the hedonistic collecting instinct that animates Beckford's sumptuous *Vathek*. The latter work revealed the readerly benefits of dwelling on Middle Eastern practices, costumes and other material customs. This elaboration of an embodied East is one that Byron took to heart, though it was not necessarily the only way to write Orientalist poetry, as evidenced by Shelley's *Revolt of Islam*, which sheds most of its setting's "Mahometan manners" in order to tell a transcendental tale of revolution and liberation.[3]

This accumulation of cultural "manners" also reflects the rise of nationalism in the Romantic period, a trend manifested by the scholarly publication of traditional English, Scottish and Irish ballads. Romantic Orientalism departs from eighteenth-century Orientalism in the growing sense that different places and moments have their own particularities, in contrast to the universalism of Enlightenment views on humanity. This faith in and attachment to a national spirit and body help to account for Byron's Orientalism being entangled with his philhellenic support for the Greek cause of independence, a postcolonial revolt much like those taking place simultaneously in South America. *The Corsair*, for instance, features a lengthy apostrophe to degraded Greece between its second and third cantos; similar moments punctuate Byron's other Orientalist poems. While his contemporaries often couched the strife between Christian Greeks and Muslim Turks as a civilizational and religious chasm, Byron did not paint the conflict in such simplistic binaries, even as he dwelt on cultural differences. Hence, *Beppo* classifies "a Grecian, Syrian, or *As*syrian tale" (*CPW* IV: 145, l. 406) as interchangeable elements of the same "finest Orientalism," suggesting how syncretic and international was Byron's "Orient."

One dimension to this broadly imagined East that appealed to Europeans generally and to Byron in particular was the erotic multifarious-ness thought to prevail beyond Britain. Byron's *Lara* (1814), for instance, can be read as a homoerotic fable if we bear in mind the page-boy Kaled's status as a representative figure of a Middle East where same- and opposite-sex relations were equally permissible. Moreover, the possibility of licit polygamous relations clearly fascinated Byron, who would, for instance, dedicate an entire canto of *Don Juan* to his protagonist's adventures in the overstuffed harem of the Ottoman Sultan in Istanbul. In this regard, Don Juan's harem adventures play into a longer, especially theatrical tradition of Orientalism, where the comic possibilities of romance and marriage could be multiplied through the more numerous and varied partners available to Eastern men of status.[4]

Byron's Orientalism, then, might be thought of as an extension of his libertinism. In 1810, during his voyage through Turkey, he would write home denying the essential difference between cultures, even as he detailed some telling divergences: "In England the vices in fashion are whoring & drinking, in Turkey, Sodomy & smoking, we prefer a girl and a bottle, they a pipe and pathic" (*BLJ* I: 238). The easy reference to the receptive male partner reveals Byron's particular interest in a world of sexual possibility beyond Britain and its contractual, heterosexual monogamy, while at the same time, the "we" constituted here is clearly grounded in aristocratic privilege and sexual license. Byron mixed his romantic "sentimentalism" – epitomized by the scenes with Haidée in *Don Juan* – with the wandering fancy of a polyamorous Orientalism that erred from shore to shore and partner to partner. This dialectic endured throughout his career, from the contrast between Gulnare and Medora in *The Corsair* to the rivalry between Myrrha and Zarina in *Sardanapalus* (1821).

If Orientalism enabled Byron's thematic exploration of sexual pluralism, it also wrote it larger as a cosmopolitan openness to other cultures. Thus, even as nationalism was heightened by the Napoleonic Wars, and writers like Edmund Burke, Wordsworth and Austen comforted the English on the supremacy of their own country and its traditions, other writers took to Orientalist subjects as a way of performing their broad-minded views and subjecting British nationalism to critique. In this way, Byron's passion for Orientalist "infidelity" – his "Giaour" is the Turkish name for "infidel" – appears as an invitation to refuse not only the chains of marital monogamy but also nationalist fidelity to British traditions and superiority, a belief system that underwrote the foreign wars that resulted in hundreds of thousands of deaths across Europe.

Byron's association with the East he depicted so frequently in his poetry meant that the poet and the exotic would become inextricably linked in the British imagination from this moment onward. Thus, Mary Shelley would depict Byron in *The Last Man* (1826) as Lord Raymond, an Orientalized nobleman who dies before his time in Turkey. In her *Felix Holt, the Radical* (1866), George Eliot featured a Byronic character named Harold Transome with an appropriately Eastern background, enticing her female protagonist, only to be repudiated later on. Anthony Trollope would telegraph the perfidy of Lady Eustace in *The Eustace Diamonds* (1871) by repeatedly adverting to her taste for the transports of Byronic exoticism. These intertextual returns suggest the degree to which Byron and Orientalist romance were connected for British audiences, an association that would sink Byron into disrepute as the racialist exceptionalism of mainstream Victorian thinking progressed in the nineteenth century.

This turn away from Byron's brand of hedonistic Orientalism was officialized by Queen Victoria's abandonment of the Brighton Pavilion, built by her uncle, George IV, in the style of Mughal architecture with Chinese-inspired interiors. Such an over-the-top piece of exoticist fantasy architecture, much like Byron's Orientalist extravaganzas, might have thrilled Victorians as much as it did their Georgian predecessors, but it no longer commanded the cultural cachet it once did. Though the escapism of romance had always made it a "genre" pleasure of sorts, the Romantic period witnessed the only moment when Orientalism, briefly and evanescently, rose to the status of high art, as the simultaneously populist and prestigious figure of Lord Byron managed to elevate and sanction the oft-depreciated taste for outlandish excess.

Notes

1 Letter by Shelley to his publisher, cited in Donald H. Reiman, Neil Fraistat and
  Nora Crook (eds.), *The Complete Poetry of Percy Bysshe Shelley* (Baltimore: Johns
  Hopkins University Press, 2012), vol. iii, 552.
2 Raymond Schwab, *The Oriental Renaissance: Europe's Rediscovery of India
  and the East, 1680–1880*, trans. Gene Patterson-King and Victor Reinking
  (New York: Columbia University Press, 1984).
3 Ibid., 552.
4 On this exoticist genre, see Daniel O'Quinn, *Staging Governance: Theatrical
  Imperialism in London, 1770–1800* (Baltimore: Johns Hopkins University Press,
  2005) 17–18.

CHAPTER 12

Religion

Christine Kenyon Jones

"I deny nothing, but doubt everything," Byron wrote of his religious views in 1811 (*BLJ* 2: 136). The complexity of Byron's religious thought, with its apparent contradictions, its changing nature over time and the deliberate facetiousness with which he often addressed such topics, all make it difficult for commentators to categorize his views. Similarly, the modern loss of sensitivity to questions of theological detail that to Byron were clear and self-evident has meant that many conflicting labels have been applied to Byron's references to religion in his verse and prose. This chapter considers Byron's shifting and multiple religious identifications and sympathies, from his engagement with Calvinism to his deism, agnosticism, skepticism and sympathies with Catholicism and Islam, not only in relation to his biography but also within the complex landscape of religious belief and the politics of religion in the Romantic period.

As Byron pointed out, he was "half a Scot by birth, and bred / A whole one," adding that he was "bred a moderate Presbyterian" (*CPW* v: 442, ll. 135–6 and 615, l. 728]). Brought up "among Calvinists in the first part of my life – which gave me a dislike to that persuasion," he was "early disgusted with a Calvinistic Scotch School where I was cudgelled to Church for the first ten years of my life" (*BLJ* 3: 119, 64). Byron's nurse seems to have tried to instill in him the dogmas of her own Calvinistic creed, and he was taught by at least two different Presbyterian ministers (see Marchand 1: 33; *BLJ* 8: 108). He was therefore aware from a young age of the bitter divide among Scottish Presbyterians in this period concerning the doctrines of predestination and universal atonement: whether only God's elect could be saved, or whether Christ's sacrifice was available to all.

The boy's Bible-reading was early and intensive: "I am a great reader and admirer of those books – and had read them through & through before I was eight years old – that is to say, the *old* Testament, for the New struck me as a task – but the other as a pleasure" (*BLJ* 8: 238). Of the 1,704 quotations and allusions to the Bible in Byron's poetry, approximately two-thirds are from the Old Testament.

These experiences "among Calvinists" in Aberdeen were not the only religious influences Byron encountered as a child. His mother's family, the Gordons of Gight, had once been Catholic, and Byron was formally an Anglican: his parents were married in a Church of England service and he was christened at St. Marylebone Parish Church in London on February 29, 1788. While the services he was "cudgelled to" at Aberdeen Grammar School were those of the Church of Scotland, he and his mother regularly attended St. Paul's Chapel in Gallowgate, Aberdeen, which was not Presbyterian or even Episcopalian but actually an offshoot of the Church of England. Here the Anglican liturgy was chanted as in English cathedrals, accompanied by an organ (in 1754, apparently the only one in Scotland).

Far from being the recipient of a monocultural Calvinism, Byron was therefore exposed to many different types of religious teaching and vocabulary. At the age of ten, moreover, he was uprooted from Scotland and brought south to claim his English baronial inheritance, giving him exposure to further levels of distinction in religious creeds, social classes and national consciousnesses. Byron was, as it were, multilingual in religious matters from an early age, and this gave him an acute sensitivity to nuances of doctrinal argument; an intense and lifelong interest in religious and theological matters and their effect upon psychology and motivation; a delight in the cut and thrust of theological debate; and a notably tolerant attitude to different faiths combined with a deep distrust of religious cant and hypocrisy.

In England, Byron's Anglican religious instruction continued at Harrow and then at Cambridge, where his reading included the "Natural Theology" of Archdeacon William Paley (*CMP* 5). Paley's popular work, *Natural Theology: or Evidences of the Existence and Attributes of the Deity. Collected from the Appearances of Nature* (1802), showed how God's goodness to humankind could be demonstrated by the design of the natural world and "the order and beauty of the universe."[1] But Paley's insistence that "happiness is the rule; misery the exception" is constantly challenged by the protagonists in Byron's "metaphysical" dramas.[2] *Cain* (1821), *Heaven and Earth* (1823) and *The Deformed Transformed* (1824) all argue that the God represented by nature may be a vindictive destroyer rather than a benevolent creator. Byron refutes Paley's claim that the universe was made for man by downgrading the status of humankind, deploying Georges Cuvier's geological and paleontological theories of "Catastrophism" to demonstrate that "the pre-adamite world was … peopled by rational beings much more intelligent than man" (Preface to *Cain*, *CPW* VI: 229). In an 1813 letter to William Gifford, and in Cain's journeys through the stars, astronomy is deployed to undermine the same belief: "It was the comparative insignificance of ourselves & *our world* when placed in competition with the mighty whole of which it is an atom that first led me to imagine that our pretensions to eternity might be overrated" (*BLJ* 3: 64). Paley presented pain as a necessary part of God's plan, but Byron vehemently opposed the idea of suffering being meted out by a benevolent creator: "[T]he basis of your religion is *injustice*; the *Son of God*, the *pure*, the *immaculate*, the *innocent*, is sacrificed for the *guilty*. This proves *His* heroism; but no more does away with *man's* guilt than a schoolboy's volunteering to be flogged for another would exculpate the dunce" (*BLJ* 2: 97). Lucifer in *Cain* similarly excoriates God for his "Molochism" (Moloch was the god of the Ammonites, to whom children were sacrificed in II *Kings* 22:10). These notorious lines were removed from the published drama by John Murray and never printed in Byron's lifetime:

> perhaps he'll make
> One day a Son unto himself – as he
> Gave you a father – and if he so doth
> Mark me! – that Son will be a Sacrifice.
> (*Cain* I, i, ll. 163–6 [*CPW* VI: 237])

This issue of theodicy – the question of why a good god permits the manifestation of evil – is discussed at length by Cain and Lucifer in terms of dualism and Zoroastrianism, and Byron's knowledge of such now little-known belief systems as the "Paulician, Manichean, Spinozoist, Gentile, [and] Pyrrhonian" heresies is evident in many places in his writings (*BLJ* 2: 89).

Byron's wide reading in theological criticism is attested by his own lists of books read; by references in his letters and diaries; by the notes to *Childe Harold's Pilgrimage* and other works, and by the titles of books from his library sold in auctions in 1816 and 1827 (*CMP* 231–45, 245–54). Particularly significant sources were Barthélemy d'Herbelot's *Bibliothèque orientale* (1697); Voltaire's *Essai sur les mœurs et l'esprit des nations* (1756) and *Dictionnaire philosophique* (1764); Edward Gibbon's *History of the Decline and Fall of the Roman Empire* (1776–89); and, above all, Pierre Bayle's *Dictionnaire historique et critique* (1697). As Peter Thorslev points out, Byron felt a special affinity with Bayle: as a "corollary of their ironic skepticism," they both had "respect for the individual conscience, for a universal intellectual freedom, for all beliefs sincerely held."[3]

Byron encountered (Roman) Catholicism in two very different contexts. Growing up during a time of widespread unrest in Ireland, leading to the Rebellion of 1798 and the imposition of the Act of Union of 1801, Byron as a young man perceived Catholicism as the religion of the downtrodden: an important element of Irish freedom and a rallying point for Irish identity. Catholics were disenfranchised throughout the United Kingdom both before and after the Act of Union; and one of Byron's three speeches in the House of Lords was a stirring appeal for Catholic liberties (see *CMP* 32–43) – reforms that, when eventually enacted in 1829, would at last give Catholics the right to worship freely and participate in British civil life.

Like the *Irish Melodies* (1807–8) of his good friend Thomas Moore, which lyrically and musically wooed listeners to sympathize with the cause of an oppressed people, Byron's *Hebrew Melodies* (1815) appealed to the contemporary enthusiasm for national lyrics, and also to the sympathy for Judaism expressed during the French Revolution and in Napoleonic France. The collection also drew on Bishop Robert Lowth's *Lectures on the Sacred Poetry of the Hebrews* (1749–50), which for the first time treated the Bible in secular fashion as literature. Only some of Byron's "Hebrew" poems were actually based on Jewish material, and the music by Isaac Nathan was not all from Jewish sources such as the synagogue and Jewish folk tradition. Nevertheless, the collection was clearly offered in the context of the parallels Byron saw between the oppression of Catholics and Jews, and that of the Greeks under Ottoman rule: "At present, like the Catholics of Ireland and the Jews throughout the world, and other such cudgelled and heterodox people [the Greeks] suffer all the moral and physical ills that can afflict humanity" (Byron's note to *CHP* I, st. 73 [*CPW* II: 201]). Byron also encountered Catholicism as the dominant Christian faith of southwestern Europe. At first he was shocked by some aspects of this culture, such as (in Spain) its apparent tolerance of sexual promiscuity and Sunday bullfights and (in Antwerp) the high counter-Reformation religious paintings of Rubens, whom he denominated "the most glaring – flaring – staring – harlotry impostor that ever passed a trick upon the senses of mankind" (*BLJ* 5: 73). It was not long, however, before he learnt a greater appreciation of Catholic (particularly Italian) art and culture, and began to find the Catholic way of life attractive and comfortable. In his half-flippant, half-serious letters of 1822 to Moore, he describes how he is raising his daughter Allegra as a Catholic, "that she may have her hands full": "What with incense, pictures, statues, altars, shrines, relics, and the real presence, confession, absolution, – there is something sensible to grasp at. Besides, it leaves no possibility of doubt; for those who swallow their Deity, really and truly, in transubstantiation, can hardly find any thing else otherwise than easy of digestion" (*BLJ* 9: 123). According to Thomas Medwin, Byron maintained that he had often wished he had been born a Catholic, citing "[t]hat purgatory of theirs" as "a comfortable doctrine" (Medwin 80). Walter Scott predicted that Byron would "retreat upon the Catholic faith" (Marchand 11: 259). "Insofar as religion appealed, Catholicism appealed," concludes William Donnelly, pointing out that the appeal lay as much in the ambience of Catholic Europe, where Byron found a welcome absence of the hypocrisy and cant of northern morality, as in the religion itself.[4]

The extent of Byron's familiarity with, and attraction to, Islam has been widely discussed, including within the Orientalist and cultural imperialist agenda outlined by Edward Said. Byron himself was anxious to emphasize the first-hand nature of his experience of the East, and Naji B. Oueijan claims that Byron was "the only Englishman who truly experienced the Orient by assimilating himself into the culture."[5]

Nevertheless, many of the details Byron gives of Islamic life and customs are drawn from Western literary sources such as Lady Mary Wortley Montagu's *Turkish Embassy Letters* (1763); the work of the Oriental scholar and linguist Sir William Jones, and, in particular, one of Byron's favorite works, William Beckford's 1786 Orientalist novel *Vathek*. In spite of Byron's comment in his 1807 reading list that the "Koran contains most sublime poetical passages far surpassing European Poetry" (*CMP* 1), Peter Cochran is skeptical about whether he actually read the Quran, either in Arabic or in English translation. Cochran gives nineteen examples of concepts mentioned in the "Oriental tales" that Byron could have found in *Vathek* and its accompanying notes, including the word "Giaour" itself, and religious details such as the order of Muslim prayers; peris; ghouls; the "black angel" Monkir; Al-Sirat, the bridge to paradise, and Eblis.[6] Seyed Mohammed Marandi points out that in *The Bride of Abydos* Byron treats Islam as monolithic (ignoring the schism between Sunni and Shia, for example), and that he speaks of Ottoman society as if it were the only kind of Islamic culture.[7] Byron's description in *The Giaour* of Hassan's belief that Leila could not, as a woman, enter heaven, as "[a] vulgar error; [since] the Koran allots at least a third of Paradise to well-behaved women" is, Cochran says, itself a "vulgar error," because the Quran puts no limit on the proportion of women who may enter Paradise.[8]

Despite these limitations, Byron's attitude to Islam is notable overall for its respect. His "Additional Note, on the Turks" to *Childe Harold* Canto 11 describes their hospitality, conviviality, honesty, generosity and friendliness, and compares the Turks' attitude to the Greeks favorably with that of the English to the Irish (*CPW* II: 209–11). In 1813 Byron wrote to his future wife that "ye Moslem ... is the only believer who practices the precepts of his Prophet to the last chapter of his creed" (*BLJ* 3: 119–20). After their marriage was over, she reported that he "preferred the Turkish opinions, manners & dress in all respects to ours," adding that Byron had claimed that he "was very *near* to becoming a Mussulman."[9]

Byron's broadly respectful attitude to Islam contrasts markedly with that of his *bête noir* Robert Southey, who professed contempt for the "dull tautology" of the Quran and opined that "A waste of ornament and labour characterizes all the works of the Orientalists" (Southey IV: 28, 29). As Marilyn Butler has pointed out, the two poets' presentations of Oriental material were influenced by their opposing attitudes to the contemporary controversy over the introduction of Christian missionaries to India. Whereas it had previously been a cornerstone of British East India Company policy to respect the spheres of influence of Hindu and Moslem religious leaders, and tolerate the indigenous practices of the subcontinent, from the 1790s a campaign among Evangelicals and other British Christians sought to promote the spread of Christianity in India, alleging that the local religious laws were chaotic, barbarous and despotic. From 1802 Southey took up this imperialistic cause, and his 1805 epic *Madoc*, set in pre-conquest Mexico, made a forceful case for the mass conversion of native peoples where, he averred, their own religions were cruel and oppressive: "Except the system of Mexican priestcraft, no fabric of human fraud has ever been discovered so deadly as the Braminical."[10]

In 1813, in a campaign led by William Wilberforce, Anglican and Dissenting congregations deluged Parliament with petitions requesting that Protestant Christian missionaries should be sent to India, and in fact the *Morning Chronicle* on June 2, 1813 mistakenly identified Byron as having presented "several petitions facilitating the introduction of Christian Knowledge into India" (in reality, he presented a petition on behalf of Major John Cartwright complaining of harassment by military and civil forces in connection with his campaign for parliamentary reform) (*CMP* 43–5). Byron was particularly irked by this evidence of the British public's wish to impose its own values on another people; as Butler points out, Southey's influence, and that of this campaign was reflected in *The Giaour*, where Byron countered Southey's disrespect for religions other than Christianity by presenting Islam as "the religion of leaders as well as followers ... [which] can be illustrated from elegant courtly literature, while Christianity has no spokesmen in the poem but ignorant zealots."[11]

Despite such apparent privileging of Islam, however, ultimately *The Giaour* presents love between individual human beings as superior to and perhaps incompatible with belief in either of these two great monotheistic religions, portraying both Christianity and Islam as instruments of personal control over the lives of men and women, and potentially of political control by great powers over the destiny of small nations. "Religions take their turn," observes *Childe Harold* Canto II, contemplating the Acropolis:

> 'Twas Jove's – 'tis Mahomet's – and other creeds
> Will rise with other years, till man shall learn
> Vainly his incense soars, his victim bleeds;
> Poor child of Doubt and Death, whose hope is built on reeds.
>
> (st. 3, ll. 24–7 [*CPW* II: 45])

Human qualities (both good and bad) are not unique to any particular creed or nationality:

> With regard to morals, and the effect of religion on mankind, it appears, from all historical testimony, to have had less effect in making them love their neighbours, than inducing that cordial christian abhorrence between sectaries and schismatics. The Turks and Quakers are the most tolerant; if an Infidel pays heratch to the former, he may pray how, when, and where he pleases; and the mild tenets, and devout demeanour of the latter, make their lives the truest commentary on the Sermon of the Mount. (Deleted note to *CHP* II, st. 3–9 [*CPW* II: 283])

This skepticism was, however, hard to maintain in the predominantly religious societies where Byron lived. The personal strain and tension caused by such a stance is reflected in his 1817 comment to Hobhouse: "I do not know what to believe – or what to disbelieve – which is the devil – to have no religion at all – all sense & senses are against it – but all belief & much evidence is for it – it is walking in the dark over a rabbit warren – or a garden with steel traps and spring guns" (*BLJ* 5: 216).

NOTES

1 William Paley, *Natural Theology: Or Evidences of the Existence and Attributes of the Deity. Collected from the Appearances of Nature* (1802) (London: Faulder, 1803), 42

2 Ibid., 497.

3 Peter L. Thorslev Jr., "Byron and Bayle: Biblical Skepticism and Romantic Irony," in Wolf Z. Hirst (ed.), *Byron, The Bible and Religion* (Newark: University of Delaware Press, 1991), 69–70.

4 William J. Donnelly, "Byron and Catholicism," in Angus Calder (ed.), *Byron and Scotland: Radical or Dandy?* (Edinburgh: Edinburgh University Press, 1989), 48.

5 Naji B. Oueijan, *A Compendium of Eastern Elements in Byron's Oriental Tales* (New York: Peter Lang, 1999), 18.
6 Peter Cochran, "Byron's Orientalism," in *Byron and Orientalism* (Newcastle upon Tyne, UK: Cambridge Scholars Press, 2006), 18, and Cochran, *Byron's "Turkish Tales": An Introduction*, 4, petercochran.files.wordpress.com/2009/03/turkish_tales_introduction.pdf.
7 Seyed Mohammed Marandi, "The Bride of the East," in Peter Cochran (ed.), *Byron and Orientalism* (Newcastle upon Tyne, UK: Cambridge Scholars Press, 2006), 215–31.
8 Cochran, "Byron's Orientalism," 13.
9 Malcolm Elwin, *Lord Byron's Wife* (London: Macdonald, 1962), 270–1.
10 Southey in "Periodical Accounts, Relative to the Baptist Ministry Society, &c," *Quarterly Review* 1 (1809), 194, quoted in Marilyn Butler, "The Orientalism of Byron's *Giaour*," in Bernard Beatty and Vincent Newey (eds.), *Byron and the Limits of Fiction* (Liverpool: Liverpool University Press, 1988), 78–96 (81).
11 Cited in Butler, "Orientalism," 86.

CHAPTER 13

Natural Philosophy

Thomas H. Ford

Byron's scientific context was no longer natural philosophy, but was not yet modern science. Through the eighteenth century, "natural philosophy" – traceable back to classical *philosophia naturalis* – had been the primary rubric organizing the investigation of natural phenomena. It was one of a set of English terms, including "natural religion" and "natural history," that together positioned the study of nature as continuous with Anglican orthodoxy. "Science," meanwhile, had a much wider field of reference than it does today. It named literate knowledge generally, and was often used synonymously with "literature," which, prior to its Romantic-period redefinition as imaginative writing, likewise referred to all forms of knowledge communicated through the medium of letters. But from the late eighteenth century, just as "literature" was taking on a newly specialized meaning, "science" too was being redefined as the collective term for an emergent series of specialized disciplinary fields of research.

These developments culminated in the 1830s with William Whewell's neologism "scientist," the "name by which we can designate the students of the knowledge of the material world collectively."[1] "Scientist," by contrast with earlier labels, registered a role distinct from theology, metaphysics and literature. Whewell noted that while mathematicians had once also been philologists, the modern "separation of sympathies and intellectual habits" meant that science and literature had become mutually exclusive. But even as the introduction of "scientist" reflected this new division between "students of books and of things," it also responded to the absence, on the side of the sciences, of any unifying principle that might link the disparate new scientific disciplines together into a common enterprise: "the disintegration goes on, like that of a great empire falling to pieces; physical science itself is endlessly subdivided, and subdivisions insulated ... And thus science, even mere physical science, loses all traces of unity."[2]

Byron's death preceded Whewell's new word by a decade. Nonetheless, the discursive realignments Whewell sought to resolve with the word "scientist" were already powerfully at work during Byron's lifetime. While remaining deeply informed by the classical traditions of his aristocratic education, Byron's expansive poetic vocabulary was also acutely calibrated to new semantic undercurrents. As such, his poetry possesses an uncommon capacity to present this transformation in the cultures of natural knowledge as layered and multiform, tracing connections across what can now appear as a sharp epistemic break and linking together apparently distant fields of meaning. Take the term "science" in *Don Juan*, for example. Byron uses it to refer to Socratic ignorance and as synonymous with philosophy – the ancient meaning of the word (*CPW* v: 338, l. 31; 594, ll. 133–4). But the sciences are also contrasted with the languages and arts to mark the two broad divisions of Juan's education – the word's modern meaning (*CPW* v: 12, l. 74; 21, l. 314). And beyond these ancient and modern fields of reference, Byron further uses "science" to refer to a series of much less intellectually respectable practices, including cookery, dancing, opera-singing and boxing (*CPW* v: 609, l. 551; 486, l. 560; 231, l. 707; *DJ*, note to XI, st. 19 [*CPW* v: 747]).

Byron's wordplays on the shifting vocabularies of natural philosophy present sudden and satiric juxtapositions of incongruous social worlds. For Whewell, the sciences advanced into disunity. Byron takes that fragmentation of natural philosophy into the sciences as a figure for a much wider set of discursive fractures in Regency society. The speculative materialism of Byron's poetry from the late 1810s drew increasingly direct inspiration from contemporary scientific ideas, particularly those he could mobilize against traditional religious conceptions of divine benevolence and official morality. But throughout his poetry his engagement with science was materialist in this second sense too: that of the sometimes startling links it drew between scientific concepts and the wider cultural and linguistic practices that generated them – between diverse modes of knowledge and the increasingly distant discursive communities in which they emerged and circulated.

Those materialist links were often gendered. In Canto 1 of *Don Juan*, Donna Inez effects a notable exclusion in Don Juan's otherwise comprehensive education: "no branch was made a mystery / To Juan's eyes, excepting natural history" (*CPW* v: 21, ll. 311–12). Some stanzas earlier, Donna Inez had been classed among those "ladies intellectual" who tire their husbands with "scientific conversation" (*CPW* v: 15, ll. 172, 175). The meaning of "conversation" was still shadowed in this period by its potential reference to sex, as in "*crim. con.*" (*CPW* v: 613, l. 667). Donna

Inez's "scientific conversation" is a dialogic relationship in which sex has been displaced by science, bodily intimacy abstracted away into pure intellect. But like conversation, science too was often associated with sexuality – which, after all, is why Donna Inez expurgates natural history from Don Juan's curriculum. Erasmus Darwin's *The Loves of the Plants* of 1789, for example, had influentially celebrated sexual desire as the basic principle of botanical life. But by the late 1790s, Darwin's poetry had become the subject of conservative attacks that saw its declared aim of opening botanical knowledge to a wider and mixed-gender public as merely a subterfuge for the sexual corruption of middle-class women to republican ends. "How the study of the sexual system of plants can accord with female modesty," Richard Polwhele commented, "I am not able to comprehend."[3]

Byron takes up this 1790s gendering of scientific knowledge in a text of his juvenilia, his "Reply" to "A Petition, Addressed to 'Doctor Moyes, a celebrated lecturer on Natural Philosophy' by 300 Ladies of Edinborough."[4] Dr. Moyes – a notable tourer of the provincial lecture circuit of Scotland and Northern England in the 1780s and 1790s – is praised in "A Petition" for his explanations of electrical, meteorological and geological phenomena "besides a hundred wonders more, / Of which we never heard before."[5] But the ladies censure him for eliding "a most important matter," namely "the natural history of love."[6] Don Juan will later suffer the same feminizing exclusion. His bowdlerized scientific education corresponds precisely to that described by the "Ladies of Edinborough," who themselves reappear in *Don Juan*'s "ladies intellectual."

Byron's "Reply" – ambiguously voiced as if by Moyes himself – locates scientific lecturing within an eclectic list in which fashionable public distractions appear alongside specialized schools of knowledge. The astronomy of William Herschel and the physiognomy of Johann Kaspar Lavater, for instance, are juxtaposed with performances of the soprano Brigida Banti and the child actor William Betty (*CPW* 1: 195–6). Byron even includes his own first volume, *Hours of Idleness*, in his survey of the "morbid symptoms" and "daily wonder[s]" of the present age (*CPW* 1: 195, l. 3; 196, l. 22). Answering the question "What is Enlightenment?" in 1784, Immanuel Kant defined it as humanity's exit from self-imposed immaturity. Byron's assertively juvenile "Reply" reverses such associations of public enlightenment with cultural adulthood. Like poetry, scientific lecturing is a performative medium for the extension of enlightenment knowledge to a mixed-gender audience. But as such, both science and poetry are also rendered legible in the terms of an infantilizing and phantasmagoric theatrical culture, a Romantic-period society of the spectacle:

> Religion split in many a Schism,
> Lectures commence on Galvanism,
> The marvellous phantasmagoria,
> Work on the optics, and *Sensoria* …
> And last though not the least in Crime,
> A sucking *Peer* pretends to rhyme …
> Such Trifles now amuse the Age,
> Infant Attempts are all the Rage,
> Knowledge is daily more prolific,
> Babes will soon be scientific.
>
> (*The Edinburgh Ladies' Petition to Doctor Moyes, and his
> Reply*, ll. 17–20, 31–2, 37–40 [*CPW* I: 195–6])

Byron's poem locates the natural history of love at once inside and outside these proliferating forms of modern juvenile sociability. It is officially excluded: "Yet in the midst of general Science / *One theme* to *Sophists* bids defiance" (*CPW* I: 196, ll. 41–2). It is even said to be literally unspeakable, "Because the best detailed Narration / Falls very short of Demonstration" (*CPW* I: 197, ll. 61–2). But the natural history of love also turns out to be something like the principle generating the kaleidoscopic practices of Regency publicity reviewed in the poem. Byron's "Reply" is a conversation poem, but one differing sharply from Coleridge's model in its insistence on the sexual double meaning of "conversation" – both as a masculine "Reply" to the "Petition" of the "300 Ladies," and as a theatrically ventriloquized textual seduction. Love is elusively mobile in this text, bridging oppositions and canceling such distinctions as those between pleasure and pain, young and old, "*Alpha* and *Omega*" (*CPW* I: 197, l. 78). "The Loves of plants are all the Fashion," Byron notes with reference to the Darwin controversy of the 1790s, which had gendered scientific knowledge in the service of a repressive anti-Jacobin sexual politics (*CPW* I: 197, l. 69). In response, Byron's "Reply" enacts a copulatory epistemology, in which the gendering of science provokes ever further acts of discursive hybridization, perversion and "conversation."

From the late 1810s, Byron drew increasingly on the new scientific discipline of geology, which in the Romantic period was redescribing the knowable dimensions of earth history. For Georges Cuvier – Byron's main geological source – fossils and geological strata documented a prehuman history of the planet that stretched across vastly expanded chronological scales, challenging Scriptural accounts of creation and offering the destabilizing perspective of an immense material temporality indifferent to human existence. Marilyn Butler has shown how this shift from natural history to geology offered Byron and other Romantic poets "a systematic totalizing history of the universe as the site of perpetual change."[7] Paradoxically, modern science's cosmic decentering of the human world also presented a potentially unificatory view on history and humanity's place within it. Following Butler, this complex conceptual shift has been subject to renewed critical attention from historians of Romantic science and literature in the Anthropocene, the proposed new anthropogenic geological epoch of the present. The case of Byron suggests that this earlier geological rupture also involved an implicit regendering of scientific knowledge. The strongly gendered terms of Byron's juvenile poetry are largely suppressed in his reception of the new geology. But in taking Cuvier's geology as a figure for print culture as a whole – for the totality of public discourse – he allows us to glimpse elements of a new relationship being established between gender and the knowledge of nature.

In the "Preface" to *Cain*, Byron calls the reader's attention to the poem's adoption of "the notion of Cuvier, that the world had been destroyed several times before the creation of man" (*CPW* vi: Preface, ll. 49–50). In Act ii, Lucifer transports Cain through the universe to view the cosmic insignificance of our world and to Hades – in effect, back in geological time – to visit the extinct species described by Cuvier. Upon returning to earth, Cain tells Lucifer

> Thou hast shown me wonders; thou hast shown me those
> Mighty Pre-Adamites who walk'd the earth
> Of which ours is the wreck; thou hast pointed out
> Myriads of starry worlds, of which our own
> Is the dim and remote companion, in
> Infinity of life.
>
> (*Cain*, ii, ii, ll. 358–63 [*CPW* vi: 271])

Cain dramatizes the acquisition of scientific knowledge. But it does so via a sustained rhetoric of diminishment. In the parallel syntactic turns of these clauses, the conceptual vistas opened by geology and astronomy rebound back on our world to reveal it as a "wreck," "dim and remote." Here and elsewhere, Byron drew on Cuvier's radical deepening of time to effect a pessimistic and materialist decentralization of human perspectives on historical meaning.

That depressive poetics linked geology to a complex and polyphonic array of ideas and discursive modes, including to elements of earlier natural philosophy, to libertine traditions of free thought and the eighteenth-century revival of Lucretian atomism, and to Georgic forms and classical mythologies of decline. When Cain tells Lucifer "Thou hast shown me wonders," his response to Lucifer's representation of scientific knowledge invokes a further interpretative frame – one of particular importance for a closet drama – that of the theater. For not only is Lucifer identified with the geohistorical imagination in *Cain*, he also acts out, more specifically, a key Romantic-period role for the institutional performance of scientific know-ledge, that of the lecturer in natural philosophy. The "wonders" curated by Lucifer in *Cain* recall the "daily wonder[s]" of Regency theatricality in Byron's early "Reply," which in turn echo the "hundred wonders" the ladies of Edinburgh discovered in Dr. Moyes' lectures. Theatricality was central to Romantic-period scientists' assertions of epistemological authority, for scientific communication was theatrical in multiple forms, ranging from literary practices of virtual witnessing to the staging of experiments for mixed-gender publics by such figures as Humphry Davy and Dr. Moyes. Reading *Cain* then involves a doubled act of imaginative transport. The reader, like Cain, is presented with a series of depressing scientific shows. But the text also enfolds that presentation within an imagined theater of the mind that is at once scientific and literary, at once a lecture theater of Romantic geology and a modern print revival of the medieval mystery play. For the reader of his words, Cain's descriptions of his encounter with the new geology bear this further and ironic layer of reference to the worlds of print and performance that the new geology shared with literature.

Byron's references to Cuvier in Canto ix of *Don Juan* are similarly oriented by print culture. Byron invokes writers:

> Oh ye great Authors luminous, voluminous!
> Ye twice ten hundred thousand daily scribes,
> Whose pamphlets, volumes, newspapers illumine us!
> (*DJ* ix, st. 36, ll. 273–5 [*CPW* v: 419])

But he does so only to forget what he was going to say. Modern print culture is presented as a condition of generalized historical amnesia, for what motivates the poet's act of forgetting is precisely the scale of the print universe that has been invoked. Two stanzas later, Byron consigns his lost thought to the revolutions of Cuvier's geohistory, drawing a parallel between the dizzying immensity of contemporary print production and the geological vistas of deep time:

> But let it go. It will one day be found
> With other relics of a former world,

When this world shall be former, underground,
  Thrown topsy-turvy, twisted, crisped, and curled,
Baked, fired, or burnt, turned inside out, or drowned,
  Like all the worlds before, which have been hurled
First out of and then back again to chaos,
  The superstratum which will overlay us.

  So Cuvier says.
                    (*DJ* IX, st. 37, ll. 289–97 [*CPW* v: 420])

The innumerable "pamphlets, volumes, newspapers" summoned two stanzas earlier are imagined here as being compacted, stratified, folded and transfigured – twisted, curled, burnt and, like Prospero's book, drowned. Present-day print culture is relocated materially into the fractured geology of a future earth. Even what seems to disappear entirely without textual trace will be preserved through these future geological revolutions. Both the unremembered thoughts of the poet and what "Cuvier says" are to be found among the "relics" that will, to the future inhabitants of the earth, "when they see 'em / Look like the monsters of a new Museum" (*CPW* v: 421, ll. 319–20).

Whewell first introduced the word "scientist" in his review of Mary Somerville's 1834 *On the Connexion of the Physical Sciences*. In her prefatory dedication of that book, Somerville stated her aim as being "to make the laws by which the material world is governed more familiar to my countrywomen."[8] Her text then belongs within a Romantic-period tradition of female scientific education in which we might now also position Byron alongside such figures as Darwin, Moyes and Davy. In her section on astronomical parallax, Somerville ventures a sublime speculation, in which "man, the inhabitant of the earth, soars beyond the vast dimensions of the system to which his planet belongs, and assumes the diameter of its orbit as the base of a triangle, whose apex extends to the stars."[9] But she dismisses this sublime vision in the next sentence: the interstellar distances involved are simply too great, the orbit of man too small, to allow the measurement of any parallax. Somerville instead turns to an alternative aesthetic of the sublime, one in which scientific knowledge, rather than affirming the prestige of the knowing human subject, decenters that subject. To communicate the magnitude of interstellar distance, Somerville invokes the impossibility of cosmic communication – a negatively troped sublimity that she derives from Byron. It would take many thousands of years, Somerville writes, for light "to come to the earth from those myriads of suns, of which our own is but 'the dim and remote companion.' "[10]

The gendered terms of scientific knowledge, which were largely under erasure in Byron's *Cain*, are strongly reasserted in Whewell's review of Somerville. Indeed, alongside science's conceptual disunity, its gendering is Whewell's other main theme. Science, as it advances into plural sciences, fragments into increasingly isolated discursive contexts. But "there is a sex in minds," Whewell states, which equips women with specific intellectual capacities to synthesize and totalize these fractured knowledges.[11] Somerville's book, Whewell concludes, should then be read by all students of the sciences – not just by her "countrywomen" – because, as a woman, Somerville possesses a peculiar power of revealing the sciences' "connexion." Whewell's new word was motivated by the same project of epistemological connection, suggesting that, when first conceived, "scientist" was implicitly gendered female. It was "the dim and remote companion," in a phrase Somerville borrowed from Byron, of the public totality of communicative acts; it offered an impossible vision, at once from inside and outside, of the modern universe of knowledge.

NOTES

1 William Whewell, "*On the Connexion of the Physical Sciences* by Mrs. Somerville," *Quarterly Review* 54 (1834): 54–68 (59).
2 Ibid., 59.
3 Richard Polwhele, *The Unsex'd Females* (London: Cadell & Davies, 1798), 9.
4 R. D. [Robert Charles Dallas?], "A Petition, Addressed to 'Doctor Moyes, a Celebrated Lecturer on Natural Philosophy' by 300 Ladies of Edinborough," *The Babbler: Or, Weekly Literary, and Scientific Intelligencer* 1 (1821): 234–5. See *CPW* 1: 193, 200, 386.
5 R. D., "A Petition," ll. 11–12.
6 Ibid., ll. 14, 16.
7 Marilyn Butler, "Revolving in Deep Time: The French Revolution as Narrative," in Keith Hanley and Raman Selden (eds.), *Revolution and English Romanticism: Politics and Rhetoric* (New York: St. Martin's Press, 1990), 1–22, 17.
8 Mary Somerville, *On the Connexion of the Physical Sciences* (London: John Murray, 1834), n.p.
9 Ibid., 65.
10 Ibid., 66.
11 Whewell, "*On the Connexion*," 65–6.

CHAPTER 14

Sexuality

Richard C. Sha

"Sexuality" refers to "a person's sexual identity in relation to the gender to which he or she is typically attracted" (*OED* def. 3). When considering Byron's sexual identity, several interpretative problems arise. Although sexuality is now seen as a container for identity, it did not always have such powers. Philosopher Michel Foucault alleged a turn from sex to sexuality, which he suggests does not happen until the term "homosexuality" was coined in 1869, when as he put it, "the homosexual became a personage."[1] Before the homosexual, there was the sodomite, whose identity consolidated around the performance of nonnormative sex acts (acts outside of reproductive intercourse). In this view, these acts were not yet part of identity because the discipline of psychology had not yet provided concepts like dispositions and preferences to stitch acts to identity.

The strength of the Foucauldian approach is that it distinguishes between sexual behavior, which is universal and timeless, and sexual identity, which is historically specific. Its weakness is that it presumes a clear-cut radical 180-degree shift in discourses from sex-as-acts to sexuality-as-identity, which some have dubbed history with a saw. That saw acquires sharper teeth because of the demand that sex in the past be understood in terms of alterity, its otherness. The logic goes like this: homosexuality is not a transhistorical essence but rather a set of discrete historical practices. But does it make sense that, all of a sudden, folks thought completely differently about their sexual practices? Eve Kosofsky Sedgwick cautions that competing models of sex and sexuality do not so much replace each other as operate simultaneously, inhabiting what she refers to as "the relations enabled by the unrationalized coexistence of different models."[2]

What makes the question of Byron's sexuality so vexed is that he is clearly thinking about the relation of sex to identity, well before that shift is thought historically to have taken place, and, at the same time, is framing identity in terms of mobility. Take Byron's famous letter to Charles Skinner Matthews of June 22, 1809, where he writes, "we are surrounded by Hyacinths & other flowers of the most fragrant [na]ture, & I have some intention of culling a handsome Bouquet to compare with the exotics we expect to meet in Asia" (*BLJ* 1: 207). Sexual identity is collective and coded in terms of plants; indeed, the *OED* cites one of the first uses of the term "sexuality" as referring to plant sexuality. The definition implies that plants had sexuality before human beings did. But plants allegorized human sexuality. Nowhere is this clearer than with all the talk within Linnaean botany of the "marriages" of the plants – marriages being a euphemism for sexual intercourse. Because Linnaean botany organized its taxonomy around the sexual organs of plants, with pistils being the female organs and stamens being the male ones, plant sexuality was allegedly transparent and conformed to an unambiguous taxonomy. Hyacinths, of course, refer to the legend of Apollo's love for a beautiful boy. Yet to see Linnaean botany as a secure taxonomy was to ignore all the proliferating categories, along with the patent anthropomorphizing of the plants. The figure of plants further denies human mobility even as Byron's framing of Falmouth as a sexual niche suggests that sexuality operates according to its local contexts; but this is to forget the poet's movements in and out of Falmouth, which contained an important English harbor. In this very harbor, Byron jokes that he will write a treatise, "Sodomy simplified or Paederasty proved to be praiseworthy from ancient authors and modern practice" (*BLJ* 1: 208).

Linnaean botany seems to uphold the break between sex-as-acts and sexuality-as-identity because plant sexuality is categorized by the numbers of stamens and pistils their flowers have, as if numbers of sexual organs are the sole determinants of the "sexuality" of plants. Nonetheless, Linnaean botany proliferates the kinds of sexuality that are possible – Linneaus depicts multiple wives consorting with any number of husbands – showing that heternormativity has multiple forms that strain normativity into plurality. If normality is plural, we might ask, then, can there even be perversions, since there is no one unambiguous standard against which to measure a perversion? The allusions to plant location further render natural what is in the West normally understood as Eastern sexuality; and geography reminds us that although the official Western line is that the perversions originate in the East with the "exotics," here Byron has found Eastern exotics in Falmouth of all places. Byron's choice of verb, "culling," with its oblique reference to the cull or arse, collapses the harvesting of nature with sodomy, and natural history is revealed to have been unnaturally shaped by the demands of Empire. On the one hand, sexual otherness is Orientalized and thereby racialized. On the other hand, because the Orient is, as Edward Said has shown, the West's most persistent fantasy, the Orientalizing denies the possibility of Western perversion. Byron, by contrast, insists upon traffic between East and West, the unnatural and the natural. Seeing how race and sex intersect, then, calls into question the degree to which sexuality alone can consolidate identity. It further suggests that the act of looking shapes how one thinks about sexuality, leading to a sexuality that only becomes visible at the intersections between identity categories, of which sexuality can only be one. Finally, the poet's reference to "intention" psychologizes sex, and gives it an interiority, a kind of mental existence.

In *Manfred, A Dramatic Poem* (1817), Manfred's identity is indelibly marked by his sexual transgressions, even if the actual transgression is ambiguous. In *Don Juan* our hero is "a broth of a boy" (*CPW* v: 372, l. 185) subject to the ogling of both male and female characters, and presents himself as intergender (between the genders). "Broth" refers to boiling down or liquefying, and so the trope both concentrates and dissipates boyhood. Boyhood as distinct from manhood hints at the sexualization of gender that occurs with puberty. There is also no question that Byron was bisexual, as he had erotic relations with both men and women, and that he coded his bisexuality on the model of Horace, who had lovers of both sexes. Bisexuality threatens the either/or binary of homo-/heterosexuality, with its insistence upon both/and. And as Stephen Angelides has theorized, the reason why bisexuality has not been given enough attention within sexuality studies is that it both represents a crisis in the knowability of sexuality and a surprising "occlusion" between what should be the relation of "gay and lesbian history to queer theory."[3] The *OED* definition above assumes that one is only typically attracted to one gender. If we cannot distinguish between heterosexuals and homosexuals – if these are not mutually exclusive categories – then what do we actually know about sexuality?

How, then, to frame Byron's sexual identity so as to capture its simultaneous mobility and fixity, without assuming in advance political implications of both? Perhaps it is fruitful to consider his simultaneous construction and deconstruction of his sexual identity: the ways in which, for instance, his homoeroticism seems to nullify his heterosexuality. We might also ask what roles do gender, class and race play in the making and unmaking of sexual identity? We should not forget the role of Byron's aristocracy, and how class at once made it possible for him to pursue his nonnormative desires, but also threatened his undoing.

Jonathan Dollimore has rebuked queer theorists for the "tendentious posturing" entailed in the celebration of the disruptiveness of sexual desire while never acknowledging themselves disrupted by desire.[4] Dollimore prompts us to ask are there forms of disruptiveness, like bisexuality, that are too disruptive for even queer theory to accommodate? Although queer theory can be described as a coalition of practices that demonstrate the incoherence of a concept of normative identity, if such incoherence facilitates the coherence of queer theory, then is it possible to value incoherence over this coherence?

To the extent that the official *OED* definition of sexuality foregrounds the issue of the gender identification of one's primary erotic partners, gender identification was likewise hardly transparent; and it, too, was quite mobile in the Romantic period. Randolph Trumbach has argued that there were three genders in Europe during the eighteenth century: men, women and a third gender of "effeminate adult sodomites."[5] In the same way that bisexuality undermines any clear dualism between hetero- and homosexuality, male effeminacy complicates the intelligibility of a gender binary, and further makes it possible to see desire as being about similarity as opposed to difference. The discourse of puberty in this period further destabilized both gender and sex, because before puberty, which was thought to last twenty years or more, there was, according to Galenic models of the body, basically one effeminate male sex, making desire necessarily homoerotic. As Thomas Laqueur submits in *Making Sex*, up until 1800, the Galenic model of bodies insisted upon the existence of only one sex: in this view, "women were essentially men," with their genitals on the inside.[6] In Byron's case, Don Juan's prolonged puberty provides a kind of erotic limbo where partners can be of any gender, at least in the East. In accounting for why Byron was so demonized by his readers, Andrew Elfenbein argues that he "jolted his audience by cutting off masculinity from morality," rendering his heroes bankrupt of moral instruction, but also sexually dubious, and in this way, Byron renders conventional masculinity into a kind of death.[7]

At this point, one might despair of ever getting to any truth of Byron's sexuality. But things get even murkier. Byron also coded his homosexual practices in terms of Ancient Greek pederasty, a sexual regime in which an older male lover could anally penetrate a younger male, provided this could be coded as an exchange of wisdom for beauty. If the younger male was bearded, however, he was beyond approaching, because his desire to be penetrated could never be excused insofar as it meant giving up his male gender identity. Now we have mobile Romantic sexual behavior that is coded in terms of the pederasty of ancient Greece. In 1809, Byron was twenty, which meant that he already had the ability to grow a beard. Yet perhaps the ancient Greek model was comforting because it gave this desire a genealogy, and a set of rules by which one's choices could be evaluated. For the Greeks, the problem was not so much heterosexual or homosexual acts, but the quantity of those acts and the ways in which those acts performed the right gender identity. What then did the two models have to say to one another? If perversions granted Byron an individuality all his own – Byron's Manfred never states his sexual crimes explicitly, but clearly sees himself outside of human community – a genealogy of such alternative sexual practices fostered the possibility of human if perverse community. Manfred insists he is his "own destroyer" and promises that he will remain so into the future. His "Dramatic Poem" tenses drama against a kind of lyric poetry that underscores individual consciousness, and Byron turns to drama to measure the costs of lyric interiority. Nowhere is this clearer than when the Chamois Hunter addresses Manfred twice, only to have not been heard. Yet, as Gary Dyer has argued, Byron's overt allusions to sodomitical behavior within *Don Juan* were hostile. The poet's hostility is geared toward the fact that the male gender of the actor was undone by the sexual act because he allowed himself to be penetrated, "taken by the tail."[8] Byron alludes to the fact that the Bishop of Clogher was put on trial in 1822 for sodomy and fled the country after having paid his fines. The act of penetrating, then, was an act of gender performance, but what was it about Romanticism that allowed the ancient Greek model of pederasty to preside over meaning?

We might attain firmer ground if we ask what resources poetry has for helping us to grapple with the topic of sexuality. Given the mobility of Byron's sexual identities, what can Byron's poetry tell us about these issues, and how might formal concerns help us rethink or reconfigure these historiographical problems? Forbidden desire has an inverse relation to explicitness, so that the reader must become more active to intuit what the text does not say; thus any essay into the poet's sexuality must confront the limits of what is made explicit, and what can be made so. In this view, the indirections of figuration, such as Byron's allusions to plants, allow sexuality to be a code to be deciphered only by those in the know. That repetition makes desire into a pattern that can be recognized and allows formal analysis to provide insights into sexuality. We might add to this the insight that the Orient becomes so powerful for Byron because it allows him to write cultural antagonisms in gendered terms. Paradox, then, might be a better container for sexuality than identity.

Rhyme for Byron was a way of thinking about agency as a form of picking the contingencies by which one allows oneself to be defined. Certain identities are thus deconstructed, while others are tried on for size. In *Don Juan*, the *ottava rima* form demands that the poem obey the rhyme scheme, but because the choice of rhyme is always contingent, one can consider how the poet is forced to choose one contingency over another and agency thereby becomes a form of contingency. So too for sexual agency: as Canto IV draws to a close, Byron surveys the world's slavery market, and Juan's fate depends on the national identity of his purchaser. In Canto V, stanza 17, the narrator fittingly comments, "Men are the sport of circumstances, when / The circumstances seem the sport of man." Here the inversion between men the subject and man the object comes at just the moment when Juan as Juanna is about to be sold into a harem. Of course, this inversion implies that even gender identity can be inverted. Slavery here becomes a metaphor for sexual agency in a world where the tyranny of markets, like the tyranny of sultans and sultanas, defines agency. When Juan is sold as a slave to a sultana, he refuses to submit to her sexual desires. Her immediate reaction is rage: "And the deep passions flashing through her form / Made her a beautiful embodied storm" (*CPW* v: 284, ll. 1079–80). Gary Dyer has argued that "flash" means to be "clued in," and that it hints of a submerged sodomitical code, which her Eastern sexuality already insinuates; and yet what kind of stable embodiment does a storm provide?[9] Body here is a structure, but also a dynamic one that threatens to engulf this structure into chaos. Byron fittingly enjambs the storm ("And the deep passions flashing through her form / Made her a beautiful embodied storm"). While the a and b rhymes before this couplet insist upon polarity, the c rhyme form/ storm allows fluidity to supervene upon form.

Formally, there are also the multiple roles that Byron plays: sometimes character, sometimes narrator, sometimes actor and sometimes acted upon. With this proliferation of roles, the poet suggests that sexuality is itself a form of positionality, merely a role to be played rather than an identity to be embodied. Supporting this are his references to hot climes: the hotter the place, the more the vice, but again this does not prevent Britain from having vices.

It may be time, then, to consider the politics of Byron's fluid and fixed identities, and the ways in which both sexual acts and identities can shape being. If mobility now works to render heterosexuality suspect, Romantic mobility was also a sign of class and gender privilege. It functioned ambiguously both to shore up Byron's social position and to allow him the privilege of questioning societal mores. Aristocratic Byron can afford to project a mobile identity. Jerome Christensen argues in *Lord Byron's Strength* that it is precisely privilege that enables him to confound reference, to allow "[his] style [to] perform lordship."[10] In *Romantic Genius*, Andrew Elfenbein has further shown how genius came to be embodied in "transgressive sexual representations, especially those of same-sex eroticism, to mark their perceived superiority" even as he finesses the issue of sexual identity by highlighting homosexuality as a "prehistory" and a "role."[11]

If both the fixity and fluidity of identity can be useful politically, the basic question, then, surrounding Byron's sexuality is when are mobilities meaningfully transgressive of heteronormativity, and when do they merely enable the consolidation of societal organization and discipline? Leo Bersani raises this precise issue in *Homos*, and warns that "suspicions of identity are necessary, [but] are not necessarily liberating."[12] Bersani, moreover, argues that in its insistence upon sameness, homosexuality takes sexuality outside of relationality and outside society. Because of its antisocial nature, homosexuality refuses all forms of redemption that might be ascribed to it. Homosexuality in this view is meaningfully transgressive because it will not allow itself to be consolidated within heterosexual society. For Byron, who exiled himself from England, the costs of his sexual transgressions were perhaps too high.

NOTES

1 Michel Foucault, *The History of Sexuality*, trans. Robert Hurley (New York: Pantheon, 1978), vol. 1, 140–7.
2 Eve Kosofsky Sedgwick, *Epistemology of the Closet* (Berkeley: University of California Press, 1990), 47.
3 Stephen Angelides, *A History of Bisexuality* (Chicago: University of Chicago Press, 2001), 8–10.
4 Jonathan Dollimore, *Sex, Literature and Censorship* (Cambridge, UK: Polity Press, 2001), 5.
5 Randolph Trumbach, *Sex and the Gender Revolution* (Chicago: University of Chicago Press, 1988), vol. 1, 6.
6 Thomas Laqueur, *Making Sex* (Cambridge, MA: Harvard University Press, 1990), 4.
7 Andrew Elfenbein, "Byron: Gender and Sexuality," in Drummond Bone (ed.), *The Cambridge Companion to Byron* (Cambridge, UK: Cambridge University Press, 2004), 59.
8 Gary Dyer, "Thieves, Boxers, Sodomites: Being Flash to Byron's Don Juan," *PMLA* 116.3 (May 2001), 573.
9 Ibid., 562–5.
10 Jerome Christensen, *Lord Byron's Strength: Romantic Writing and Commercial Society* (Baltimore: Johns Hopkins University Press, 1993), 22.
11 Andrew Elfenbein, *Romantic Genius: Towards a Prehistory of a Homosexual Role* (New York: Columbia University Press, 1999), 14.
12 Leo Bersani, *Homos* (Cambridge, MA: Harvard University Press, 1995), 4.

CHAPTER 15

Libertinism

Adam Komisaruk

In the biographical foreword to his ten-volume edition of Pope (1806), the Rev. William Lisle Bowles observed that the poet often "appears to have felt a sort of libertine love, which his passions continually prompted him to declare; but which the consciousness of his infirmities, and we ought to add his moral feelings, corrected and restrained."[1] Byron seized indignantly on the first phrase, asking:

> to what does this amount? – that Pope when very young was *once* decoyed by some Nobleman and the player to a house of Carnal recreation. – – Mr. Bowles was not always a Clergyman – & when he was a very young man was he never seduced into as much? … But should I, for a youthful frolic – brand Mr. B. with "a libertine sort of love" – or with "licentiousness"? … The truth is that in these days the grand "primum mobile" of England is *Cant.* (*CMP* 127–8)

Byron alludes to a story about Bowles told by Thomas Moore, which Byron repeats in a letter to Murray of May 10, 1821. Apparently the young Bowles, in Paris, had tried unsuccessfully to pick up local girls.

> At last wound up to a pitch of amatory desperation, I rushed forth determined to bring the question to a point with the first fair one of whatever quality I met with. – – I had not gone far before I met with a lady-like modest-looking female – whom I accosted as follows – "Madame – voulez vous *foutre?*" she replied "*Si vous plaît Monsieur*" in the softest accents – I did so, caught a rousing p[ox] – was laid up for two months – & returned perfectly persuaded that there were the finest women in the world at Paris. (*BLJ* 8: 112)

Whatever the truth of the anecdote, Bowles replied to Byron by insisting – accurately – that he had referred only to the "general tone" of Pope's correspondence with women, and hoping to be acquitted of any "tincture … of hypocrisy, or fanaticism."[2]

It is strange that Byron would repudiate the very word – libertine – with which his own life and work would seem most naturally to be associated.

Yet in accusing Bowles of hypocritical "cant," he may expose what several
commentators have since recognized about libertinism itself: that the very
"attempt at a definition [of it] is basically an *a posteriori* rationalization
of a category that was originally established on disputable grounds."[3] It
is no easy matter to sort out what "libertinism" may have meant contemporaneously as opposed to retrospectively; what it may have meant
to its supposed adherents as opposed to its detractors; what its disputants
may have espoused in theory as opposed to what they may have done, or
been rumored to have done, in practice; what it looked like in England
as opposed to France, Italy, America or elsewhere; whether it changed or
stayed the same throughout modernity; how its variously spiritual, philosophical, political and sexual contexts did and did not intersect; whether,
in any one of these spheres, its propensities may be more fairly classified as
progressive or as conservative, even reactionary; or where it positions itself
relative to the levers of power – let alone where Byron, with his myriad
fictions, stands on any of these matters. In what follows, rather than
explore to what extent Byron "is" a libertine, I shall try to suggest how he
dramatizes, without resolving, the problem of what libertinism – and, by
extension, he himself – "is."

The word *libertinus* originally referred to a freed Roman slave or,
as in Acts 6.9, a member of a Jewish sect comprising the sons of such.
Accordingly, the link to manumission of various kinds is traditionally
stressed. By the sixteenth century, *libertin* came to signify a religious nonconformist, especially an Anabaptist of northwest Europe. Within this
definition, however, a paradox emerged. On the one hand, libertinism
could connote hostility to religion itself on rational-materialist grounds,
a "mocking denial of the truth and relevance of Scripture"; on the other,
an "intensification of spirituality among radical Protestants," a highly sect-
arian form of dissent associated with antinomianism or rejection of the
moral law.[4] Complicating matters further, these two meanings tended to
converge, as Puritan fervor approached materialism in its adoration of the
living God.

None of these traditions prevented the frequently derogatory use of the
term "libertine," as in Calvin's *Contre la secte phantastique et furieuse des
libertins qui se nomment spirituels* (1545). Since accusations of moral turpi-
tude predictably took a sexual form, religious partisanship was conflated
with hedonism, and the libertine was irrevocably associated with the
carnal. In the puritan/republican alliance of the 1640s, bodily freedom was
sometimes brandished as a badge of honor: if "sin was finished and ended,"
only the "supremacy of the individual conscience" governed sexual and

other conduct.[5] At other times, imagery of sexual license could be deployed to discredit political foes, as it was variously in anti-Parliamentary, anti-Cromwellian and anti-royalist satire. The debauchery of the restored Charles II, often reputed to have superintended a golden age of libertinism, not only antagonized the orthodox right but provided the symbolism in which a revitalized left couched its critique of his crackdown on religious nonconformists. So equivocal were attitudes toward sexuality itself that a seventeenth-century *"libertinage érudit,"* defined by its philosophical, theological and political commitments, has sometimes been differentiated from a more strictly erotic variety developing later. Byron's intervention in the Pope–Bowles controversy suggests some of this terminological squeamishness, as does Hobhouse's note to *Childe Harold's Pilgrimage* describing Machiavelli as "put to the torture for being a *'libertine,'* that is, for wishing to restore the republic of Florence … [W]hat was once *patriotism*, has by degrees come to signify *debauch*" (*CPW* II: 237).

In sexual as in other matters, we can certainly discern a libertine ambivalence toward freedom and restraint. Some commentators suggest that repression could furnish libertine writers with notoriety or new creative outlets, as when the wits kicked out of the English court in the 1670s began writing for the theater. Others point out that the libertines could arrogate the regulatory power to themselves: in their pastoral affectations, for instance, the Earl of Rochester (John Wilmot) and Aphra Behn flaunt an intellectual and socioeconomic gentility that differentiates them from the uncouth masses. Most crucially, however, restraint is constitutive. The libertines must acknowledge the regulatory systems that they reject, or else their transgression would not mean very much. Theirs is not "a democratic idea gone mad … Everyone cannot do a certain number of things … '[F]ree love' … would be the opposite of libertinage. In fact, that is catechism."[6] Conversely, a catechistic or what James Grantham Turner calls "Pornodidascalian" rhetoric enables the young initiates of early libertine literature to discover new frontiers of pleasure; the "University of Love trope" is *de rigueur*.[7] By the Georgian age, sentimentalism would impose its own normative structures on libertinism. Yet one might say that, with the writings of the Marquis de Sade, the old pedagogical paradigm survives in extreme form. Birthed in the transition from the absolutism of the *ancien régime* to the absolutism of the French Revolution, Sade's erotics imposes an escalating series of requirements on its protagonists and, arguably, on its readers.

"Everyone cannot do a certain number of things": Phillippe Sollers' libertine precept is worth bearing in mind for Byron, where the axes of sexual and political freedom rarely align in predictable ways. *The Vision of Judgment* (1822), for example, features an appearance by the archetypal late-eighteenth-century libertine, John Wilkes. Wilkes' career in government (variously as MP for Aylesbury and Middlesex; and as alderman, sheriff and Lord Mayor of London) was interspersed with periods of exile. Most notoriously, he was outlawed in 1764 in connection with twin libels – his obscene poem "An Essay on Woman" (1754) and his anti-ministerial newspaper the *North Briton* no. 45 (1763) – in which his reputations for sexual and political freewheeling converged. In both Byron's *Vision* and Southey's, he therefore makes an appropriate witness for Sathan/Satan; in neither can he bring himself to accuse George III. Yet while Southey uses this hesitation to suggest the shaming power of the majestic presence, Byron uses it to question the radical commitment itself. Wilkes proves a thoroughgoing politician even in the afterlife, trawling for votes, shifting his loyalties as the occasion suits, and excusing similar foibles in his erstwhile opponent: "in the sky / I don't like ripping up old stories, since / His conduct was but natural in a prince" (*CPW* VI: 334, ll. 558–60). Withal, the storied civil libertarian "vote[s George's] 'habeas corpus' up to heaven" (*CPW* VI: 334, l. 568). Wilkes may not have "turn'd to half a courtier ere [he] died" (*CPW* VI: 334, l. 570), as Sathan puts it, but Byron's portrait is a fair one. Wilkes was a moderate on many questions of political power – even "No. 45" attacked not the king but his counselors – and disavowed the mob actions perpetrated in his name. His saving grace for Byron is that he is consistent in his opportunism or, at least, honest about his inconsistency; Satan, in whose school Southey classes both Wilkes and Byron, is pitifully consistent (Coleridge famously called him a "*systematic criminal*"[8]); Southey, who for Hazlitt was a "poetic libertine" himself, is a hypocrite pretending to consistency and therefore proves too rotten for either heaven or hell.[9]

In *Marino Faliero* (1821), Byron would seem to give us something like an anti-Wilkes but reenacts, from a different vantage point, the contradictions inherent in libertinism. The titular Doge of fourteenth-century Venice has always been straitlaced to a fault: "love, romantic love, which in my youth / I knew to be illusion, and ne'er saw / Lasting, but often fatal, it had been / No lure for me, in my most passionate days" (*CPW* IV: 346, ll. 349–52). When his ducal throne is defaced with a lewd insinuation against his wife, Angiolina – and the Council of Forty delivers a lenient sentence against the perpetrator, Michel Steno – he takes it as an assault on the social order. Although Angiolina herself thinks he is overreacting to an "absurd lampoon," the Doge sets a coup in motion that will end in failure and his execution (*CPW* IV: 343, l. 241). He justifies his extremism on progressive grounds, however, styling himself a reluctant sovereign who would slay the "o'ergrown aristocratic Hydra" (*CPW* IV: 326, l. 421). In the Forty, prurience thus appears linked to authoritarianism; in the Doge, prudery to reformism. Yet the Doge's "fair free commonwealth" is to forestall a "rash equality" (*CPW* IV: 362, ll. 169–70); his progressive protestations cannot conceal his wounded sense of chivalric honor or his distrust of democracy. We could therefore envision a true libertinism that would be emancipated in all the ways that the Doge is repressed; but Byron neither suggests a viable alternative in Michel Steno with his adolescent sexual attitudes (and nine lines of dialogue), nor absolutely rejects the Doge despite his senescent political ones. Indeed, Byron invests the Doge with much of the "power" that Percy Bysshe Shelley detected in a flawed hero like William Godwin's Falkland or that characterizes Byron's own Manfred, among others (*LPBS* I: 573).

"Everyone cannot do a certain number of things." Thus far, I have tried to focus on one meaning of this axiom – libertinism as proscription – which corresponds to the qualified liberalism portrayed sympathetically by Byron the Whig aristocrat. There is, however, a second meaning – libertinism as incapacity – which is more fundamental and more Byronic. It is no accident that the rise of libertinism coincides with the rise of modern materialism, for the libertine knows especially well what is true of all bodies: they malfunction, decay and die. Embodiment exposes the stable self as a fantasy, especially of the male. Indeed, we may trace a direct line from the Restoration rake, with his litany of premature ejaculation, onanism and impotence; to Byron's Don Juan, whose own agency pales before the oceanic appetites of Semiramis-figures like Catherine the Great; and even to Byron himself, whom the forwardness of a "demirep" like Harriette Wilson seems to have thrown off his game.

Sexual anxieties are existential. The libertines' "consistent privileging of the moment" comes with an "awareness of the moment as a temporality revealing the always arbitrary foundations of any cultural narrative."[10] Surely they would not accept wholesale what Martin Heidegger calls the "vulgar identification of time as an endless, irreversible succession of nows."[11] It would be equally misleading, however, to ascribe to the libertine an absolute repudiation of idealism. The libertine's condition is rather a liminal one that can neither attain its goal, nor give up trying to do so, nor forget either fact. When the narrator of *Don Juan* wishes "That Womankind had but one rosy mouth, / To kiss them all at once from North to South" (*CPW* V: 307, ll. 215–16), he explains why the libertine is under a repetition compulsion: he is chasing the fantasy of a *jouissance* in which all will be one.

The pilgrimage of Childe Harold epitomizes the perpetual motion to which the libertine is destined. World-weary, "he through Sin's long labyrinth had run" (*CPW* II: 9, l. 37); both in spite of and because of this fatigue, he goes on the run again, seeking to escape from brokenness into wholeness. At every step he recalls the ideal that he can neither attain nor abandon:

> Oh Love! no habitant of earth thou art –
> An unseen seraph, we believe in thee,
> A faith whose martyrs are the broken heart,
> But never yet hath seen, nor e'er shall see
> The naked eye, thy form, as it should be;
> The mind hath made thee, as it peopled heaven,
> Even with its own desiring phantasy,
> And to a thought such shape and image given,
> As haunts the unquench'd soul – parch'd – wearied – wrung – and riven.
> (*CHP* IV, st. 121, ll. 1081–9 [*CPW* II: 164])

This haunting, of course, defines Harold's physical as well as psychical ports of call. The ruins of empire are within him and around. Particularly acute is the case of Greece: a temporalized space, both east and west, dead and alive, the graveyard of antiquity and a modern power, a state Byron called unworthy of the independence for which he made his last stand, it proves a fitting site to interrogate the prospects of any certain knowledge.

"I hate inconstancy," proclaims the narrator of *Don Juan* (*CPW* V: 154, l. 1665). Prematurely exhausted at thirty but with life yet in him, he attempts to reconcile sober philosophy with the stirrings of passion before concluding, in characteristic libertine fashion, that they are one and the same. The "Platonic" is everywhere "filter'd through the skies" (*CPW* V: 155, ll. 1691–2); though it is unknowable as such, we can approximate it by embracing those phenomena in which it becomes incarnate. Thus, the "adoration of the real / Is but a heightening of the 'beau ideal'" (*CPW* V: 155, ll. 1687–8). Byron's recognition "that flesh is form'd of fiery dust" is proverbial (*CPW* V: 155, l. 1696). His context emphasizes the adjective, not the noun: what seems dust is in fact fiery. Immediately afterwards, however, he reminds us that the reverse is also true: what seems fiery is in fact dust. What filters down to us may be the best we have, but it must never be mistaken for the thing itself that it intimates, or as anything other than provisional. There is no greater reminder of this temporality than love: "The heart is like the sky, a part of heaven, / But changes night and day too, like the sky" (*CPW* v: 156, ll. 1705–6). In this light, the turncoatery that Byron deplores in the Lake poets might be viewed as the effluvium of a noble if misguided idealism. Might one make room to forgive even Southey by virtue of his being just what Hazlitt calls him – a poetic libertine?

NOTES

1 William Lisle Bowles, "Memoirs of the Life and Writings of Pope," in *The Works of Alexander Pope, Esq., in Verse and Prose*, 10 vols. (London, 1806), vol. I, cxxx. Emphases in originals throughout.

2 William Lisle Bowles, "Observations on the Poetical Character of Pope," *Pamphleteer* 18.36 (1821), 335.

3 Jean-Pierre Cavaillé, "*Libertine* and *Libertinism*: Polemic Uses of the Term in Sixteenth- and Seventeenth-Century English and Scottish Literature," *Journal for Early Modern Cultural Studies* 12.2 (2012), 13.

4 James Grantham Turner, "The Properties of Libertinism," *Eighteenth-Century Life* 9.3 (1985), 78.

5 Christopher Hill, "Freethinking and Libertinism: The Legacy of the English Revolution," in Roger Lund (ed.), *The Margins of Orthodoxy: Heterodox Writing and Cultural Response 1660–1750* (New York: Cambridge University Press, 1995), 61–2.

6 Philippe Sollers, "What Is Libertinism?" *Yale French Studies* 94 (1998), 205–6.

7 James Grantham Turner, *Schooling Sex: Libertine Literature and Erotic Education in Italy, France and England 1534–1685* (New York: Oxford University Press, 2003), 45, 54, 56.

8 Samuel Taylor Coleridge, *The Statesman's Manual: Lay Sermons*, vol. VI, *The Collected Works of Samuel Taylor Coleridge*, ed. R. J. White (Princeton: Princeton University Press, 1972), 66.

9 William Hazlitt, *The Spirit of the Age*, vol. XI, *The Complete Works of William Hazlitt*, ed. P. P. Howe (Toronto: J. M. Dent, 1930–4), 82.

10 Thomas Kavanaugh, "The Libertine Moment," *Yale French Studies* 94 (1998), 80, 81.

11 Martin Heidegger, *Being and Time*, trans. Joan Stambaugh (Albany: State University of New York Press, 2010), §81, 405.

CHAPTER 16

Fashion, Self-Fashioning and the Body

Laura J. George

Throughout his brief life Lord Byron attracted the gazes of others – because he was disabled, because he was a lord, because he was a literary idol, because "at least a third part of the day, [he] was a dandy" (Stendhal quoted in *HVSV* 201), because he was fat, because he was thin, because of his beauty or because his appearance disappointed. Byron was surveyed, prepared himself to be surveyed and surveyed himself internally. His own self-fashioning, as author, as part-time dandy and as athlete (pugilist and swimmer especially), took place in the context of his experiences in his own body, but his self-fashioning takes place for us, above all, in his words.

There are three significant scenes in Byron's poetry where a male figure surveys himself in a mirror. European culture had for centuries typically placed women and effeminate men in relationship to mirrors, but the dandies of Byron's time challenged their culture's derogation of men at mirrors, and so does Byron. The first of these three mirrors appears in his play *Sardanapalus* (1821). In Act 3, Sardanapalus appears to transform himself from an effeminate sybarite into a man of action, but at the same time that he dons his armor he insists on sending for a mirror so he can survey how well he looks arrayed for battle. By the end of *Don Juan* (1819–24), Juan is a British-style dandy, revealing his distress one morning when he uncharacteristically puts his mirror away quickly. Arnold, from *The Deformed Transformed* (1824), views his disabled body in a stream and recoils with a distaste that the play may later suggest is wrong-headed. Taken together, these three scenes of masculine self-surveillance suggest the extent to which questions of fashion, self-fashioning and the body were tightly interlinked for Byron.

Byron's relationship to his own to-be-looked-at-ness was shaped in part by cultural transformations in masculine dress. Relationships between masculine style, specularity and power shifted dramatically in Britain between the 1780s and the 1820s. Bright colors, shiny fabrics and glittering ornaments were increasingly repudiated by men (except in specific zones, such as the military), and the clothing of men's legs changed quite a bit (again, outside of restricted zones like court appearances): breeches became passé and what we might now call trousers (once primarily the attire of physical laborers) went through different styles and shapes, including very tight pantaloons and very wide Cossacks, before settling into the relatively columnar shapes familiar today. As styles for dressing modern masculinity shifted, styles of masculine sartorial resistance shifted as well, as was particularly marked in this period by a new term (one that was important to Byron): "dandy."

Byron would have experienced these stylistic changes at least in part in the context of his disability. Form-fitting styles for clothing male legs would have made his disability (most likely a club foot) more visible, while extremely loose trousers like Cossacks would have hidden it almost entirely until he moved. There is good reason to suspect that Byron experienced anxieties about his masculinity in response to his disability; as Andrew Elfenbein has remarked, Byron "strenuously combated his lameness with his athleticism, restless travel, prodigious literary output, and exhausting sex life."[1] Christine Kenyon Jones has drawn on research detailing shifts in attitudes toward disability from a frankly disparaging eighteenth-century discourse to a sentimentalized Victorian one, in order to argue that Byron's early defenders drew on sentimentalized languages of disability specifically to soften attitudes toward his (perceived) diabolical behaviors and poetry. Byron's own identification with *le diable boiteux* ("the crooked devil," from Le Sage's 1707 novel of that name) is clear in his letters and journals. It informs what Kenyon Jones describes as his "defiantly iconoclastic response" to his disability, one rich with "the self-scrutiny, irony, *sang froid*, humor, and ribaldry which are readily identifiable with Byron's writing on other subjects."[2]

Many commentators have argued that the gaze is structured around gender and that women in particular are trained to experience themselves as objects for the male gaze and learn to prepare themselves to be surveyed and to survey themselves internally. While the force of this gendering of the gaze is certainly powerful, standard biographical accounts of Byron's life make clear the extent to which Byron experienced himself and his body as closely observed and performative. One of the earliest anecdotes Thomas Moore relates involves someone saying to Byron's nurse when he was about five: "What a pretty boy Byron is! What a pity he has such a leg!" upon which Byron is reported to have cried, "Dinna speak of it!" (Moore 1: 10). Just a few pages later we read, "it is said that the day after little Byron's accession to the title, he ran up to his mother and asked her 'whether she perceived any difference in him since he had been made a Lord'" (Moore 1: 20). That is, between his disability and his title, accounts of the young Byron, including his own, repeatedly stress his consciousness of how he appears in the eyes of others.

Other anecdotes from throughout Byron's life refer to Byron's anxieties about his weight – anxieties that seem to pass at points into what might today be diagnosed as anorexia or another eating disorder. Byron was aware that his own contemporaries were attentive to changes in his weight. For example, when Thomas Moore visited Byron in Venice in 1819 he noted that: "I was a good deal struck, however, by the alteration that had taken place in his personal appearance. He had grown fatter both in person and face, and the latter had most suffered by the change, – having lost, by the enlargement of the features, some of that refined and spiritualized look that had, in other times, distinguished it" (Moore 2: 248). In Byron's years of fame at the glittering center of Regency high society, he had maintained this "refined and spiritualized look" by extremely abstemious eating and frequent chewing of mastic gum, a pine-flavored substance made from the resin of the mastic tree. Both Thomas Moore and Robert Dallas comment on Lord Byron's habit of chewing "mastic" in a quest to suppress his appetite for food, a habit he had likely picked up during his travels around the eastern Mediterranean, where mastic gum was used as an ancient remedy for colds, bad breath and digestive problems.

Byron's self-consciousness about his body shows up clearly in his responses to his disability and to his weight. Self-consciousness in another form is evident in his love of sartorial finery. In addition to picking up the habit of mastic chewing in the East, he acquired the Albanian costume he wore in the famous Thomas Phillips portrait of *c*.1814 (see Figure 16.1). In a November 12, 1809 letter to his mother, Byron appreciatively described Albanian costume as "the most magnificent in the world, consisting of a long *white kilt*, gold worked cloak, crimson velvet gold laced jacket & waistcoat, silver mounted pistols & daggers" (*BLJ* 1: 227), suggesting a love of finery that did not at all abate once he found himself back in London and famous, although the colors he selected to wear there had to be rather more restrained. Marchand notes that

> Byron's tailors' and jewelers' bills in 1812 are an index to his aspirations to dandyism. On June 20 he bought "20 Fine white Quilting Waistcoats"; on July 1 "A spfine [superfine] Olive Court dress Coat lined Completely thro wh White Silk, 20 Elegantly Cut & Highly Polished Steele buttons, A very rich Embroidered Court Dress Waistcoat, [and] A pair rich black

Silk Breeches." In August and September he added dozens of other items. (Marchand 1: 351 n. 5)

In his attraction to fine costuming, whether Oriental brilliance or the more subdued but still fine style of the dandies, as well as in his persistent fretting about his weight, Byron demonstrated his keen awareness that he was the object of the gazes of others. With his finery, at least, he clearly courted those gazes.

There is a rich and complex history of English terms for men who in different ways court the gazes of others for their clothing or their bodies. When Byron was born, in the 1780s, the dominant term for men who dressed to attract attention was "fop," a term that dates back at least to Shakespeare and originally meant something like "fool," but that in the Restoration period had narrowed to a focus on men who dressed for attention. The new meaning of "fop" was culturally foregrounded during the crisis in masculine authority of the reign of Charles II. Throughout the eighteenth century the term "fop" circulated in a fuzzy cloud – not a clear taxonomy – of inter-related terms like "beau," "macaroni" and "coxcomb." Byron's lifetime, however, coincides with the rise to prominence of a new term, "dandy," which, over the course of the nineteenth century, came to dominate. The term "dandy" moved into circulation during another period of crisis in masculinity and authority in the wake of the French Revolution and the Industrial Revolution with their unstable shifts in the social configurations of land, money, power and labor. Byron certainly knew that "dandy" was a newly popular term in his lifetime (in his "Detached Thoughts," Byron remembers tales that circulated before he was of age and reflects that "*dandies* were not then christened" [*BLJ* 9: 29]).

By far the most famous dandy during Byron's time in London was George Brummell, called "Beau" (1778–1840). Dandies after Brummell, like Count Alfred D'Orsay (the so-called "Butterfly Dandy") and Oscar Wilde were gorgeously and performatively resistant to dominant ideas about the severe masculine style of their periods; but unlike these later and more flamboyant dandies, Brummell dressed simply. Writing at the end of the century, Max Beerbohm happily recalled "that bright morning when Mr. Brummell, at his mirror, conceived the notion of trousers and simple coats."[3] Brummell's dress and conduct were received as revolutionary and startling because, unlike the fops who were consistently trivialized in Restoration and eighteenth-century literature and come to us largely through fictional representations in plays and novels, Brummell was a historical figure who had significant social power for a time through his close connection to the Prince Regent. Even

Figure 16.1 Thomas Phillips, *Portrait of a Nobleman in the Dress of an Albanian*, 1814. 127.5 × 102 cm, oil on canvas. UK Government Art Collection, HM Embassy, Athens.

more startling, Brummell used that power to carefully wear, observe and discuss men's clothing and style. In aspects of his restrained dress, Brummell was a harbinger of modern male style; in his publicly performed attentiveness to his own dress and the dress of other men, Brummell was a decisively resistant figure. Although his nickname contained the lovely alliteration with the older term "beau," he and his cohort were always referred to as dandies. As Byron recalled in his "Detached Thoughts," "I liked the Dandies – they were always very civil to *me* ... Our Masquerade was a grand one – as was the Dandy Ball" (*BLJ* 9: 22). Stendhal recorded that "In his moments of dandyism, he always pronounced the name of Brummell with a mingled emotion of respect and jealousy" (*HVSV* 201).

Byron's literary engagement with the figure of the dandy began to blossom in earnest after he left England in 1816. In fact, the dandy can be understood as central to Byron's revisionary stance toward his early fame and as a productive, germinal figure for his new experiments in poetics. Byron's first extended engagement with the dandy appeared in *Beppo* in 1818. *Beppo* can also be seen as a happy travesty of the writing that had made Byron famous, with Beppo a version of one of Byron's tortured outlaw heroes returned from beyond the horizon to settle into marital irritations and friendship with the man who slavishly adores his wife. Beppo and his wife's lover effectively mark their new friendship by exchanging underpants. The narrator of this silly tale is "a nameless sort of person, (A broken Dandy lately on my travels)" (*CPW* IV: 145, ll. 409–10). When Byron begins to rewrite the very poetry that brought him fame, he does so under the sign of a "nameless, broken dandy."

Dandyism per se seldom gets explicit attention in *Don Juan*; however, the dandies around Brummell were known for their wit and their wordplay. In his "Detached Thoughts," for instance, after remarking that he liked the dandies, Byron remembers that they "persuaded Me. de Stael" that Lord Alvanley, one of their number, "had a hundred thousand a year &c. &c. till she praised him to his *face* for his *beauty*! – and made a set at him for [her daughter] Albertine (*Libertine* as Brummell baptized her – though the poor girl was – & is as correct as maid or wife can be)" (*BLJ* 9: 22). Anecdotes that circulated about dandy wit during the Regency and after often revolved around puns and language play as well as dress – features of *Don Juan* throughout, where the density of language games increases in the later cantos and especially in the English cantos.

At the end of 1820, Byron completed Canto V, which features Don Juan cross-dressing in a harem. On January 13, 1821 he began work on *Sardanapalus*, a play about the fall of the last Assyrian king, who is first seen in Act I coming out of the harem. Sardanapalus does transform into a man of action before the play is over, but throughout he acts in many ways like a Regency dandy. In an initial confrontation with courtiers planning treason, he burlesques conventional martial manhood. He complains that a sword he borrows is "A heavy one; the hilt, too, hurts my hand" (*CPW* VI: 53, l. 194). When he finally prepares to fight, he notoriously sends for a mirror first, to examine how he looks with a diadem (he refuses to wear a helmet because it is too heavy), baldric and cuirass. When his loyal second-in-command Salamenes praises his fighting as "The brightest and most glorious [hour] of your life," Sardanapalus responds "And the most tiresome" (*CPW* VI: 83, ll. 343–4). Such poses of boredom and play with the conventions of masculinity were prominent aspects of the legends that swirled around the dandies. Byron situates his Sardanapalus at the point of a heterosexual love triangle, but his sources for the play highlighted Sardanapalus' homoeroticism as well as his effeminacy in ways that Byron would have expected many of his readers to know. In classical accounts, Sardanapalus is associated with harem and distaff and homoeroticism, but not with a mirror. Byron's invented mirror scene subversively has Sardanapalus survey himself at the very point of his transition into a military hero, and links Sardanapalus to the dandies whose specular form of masculinity Byron reflected on a great deal during this period, in his "Detached Thoughts" as well as in *Sardanapalus*.

Byron resumed work on *Don Juan* in July 1822 and was working on the English cantos by September of that year. In these cantos, in addition to some reminiscing on the part of the narrator about the heyday of the Regency dandies, we find that Don Juan himself has become a young dandy of the Brummellian variety, as signified by his relationship with his mirror. The morning after Juan sees the specter at Norman Abbey, he inadvertently displays his distress by making the very slightest of errors in his dress:

> In the mean time, his valet, whose precision
> Was great, because his master brooked no less,
> Knocked to inform him it was time to dress.
>
> He dressed; and like young people, he was wont
>   To take some trouble with his toilet, but
> This morning rather spent less time upon't;
>   Aside his very mirror soon was put;
> His curls fell negligently o'er his front,
>   His clothes were not curb'd to their usual cut,
> His very neckcloth's Gordian knot was tied
> Almost a hair's breadth too much on one side.
>   (*DJ* XVI, st. 28–9, ll. 222–32 [*CPW* V: 627])

The repetition of "very" here – "very mirror" and "very neckcloth" – implies that Juan would normally take much more time with his toilette. The mirror, the neckcloth, the value placed on extraordinary precision – all are central to the legends surrounding Brummell. Byron's second mirror, then, reinforces the oppositional poetics of masculinity he has been experimenting with since *Beppo*.

The Deformed Transformed contains the third and final man at a mirror scene that Byron was able to compose before his death. In his attempts to renovate the dandy as hero, Byron taught himself a great deal about oppositional poetics; in the incomplete *The Deformed Transformed*, Byron uses the Faust legend to challenge the abjection of disability. Arnold, the main character, is born hunchbacked and "crooked"; he is convinced that he will never be able to find love because of his disability. Arnold already sees himself as a devil before he views his image in a stream: "Nature's mirror shows me / What she hath made me … The very waters mock me with / My horrid shadow – like a daemon" (*CPW* vi: 521, ll. 46–50). Sardanapalus is quite satisfied as he surveys himself in his mirror, in all his battle array; Don Juan's failure to carefully survey himself and his dress in a mirror reveals his typical careful attention to both. Arnold, here, finds his sense of daemonism confirmed by his reflection. But what we have of the play suggests that Byron was experimenting with the idea that Arnold is wrong. When he is approached by what seems to be an actual devil known only as the Stranger, he is offered the opportunity to shop for a new and gorgeous masculine body, eventually selecting that of Achilles. Once Arnold is wearing his beautiful new body, however, the Stranger inhabits his old disabled body and promises to follow him around perpetually. That is, Arnold assumes that his crooked body deserves to be discarded, but learns that it cannot be discarded, and perhaps even that it had the potential to be loveable as well. While the play is unfinished, a note from Byron suggests that he intended to set up a love triangle, with Arnold's beloved loving the Stranger instead of him, despite or because of the Stranger's disabled body.

Byron died less than a year after sending parts one and two of *The Deformed Transformed* to Douglas Kinnaird, so we can only speculate about how the play might have ended, just as we can only speculate about whether or how *Don Juan* might have concluded. In the years immediately preceding his untimely death, Byron became increasingly explicit about challenging his culture's dominant ideals of masculinity. Sadly, we can also only speculate about where Lord Byron's oppositional explorations of masculinity might have taken him.

NOTES

1 Andrew Elfenbein, "Byron and the Fantasy of Compensation," *European Romantic Review* 12.3 (Summer 2001), 269.

2 Christine Kenyon Jones, "Deformity Transformed: Byron and his Biographers on the Subject of His Lameness," *European Romantic Review* 12.3 (Summer 2001), 252.

3 Max Beerbohm, "Dandies and Dandies," in Phillip Lopate (ed.), *The Prince of Minor Writers: The Selected Essays of Max Beerbohm* (New York Review Books, 2015), 150.

PART III

Literary Cultures

CHAPTER 17

Classicism and Neoclassicism

Bernard Beatty

"Neoclassical" is a tricky term in literature. It was not used until the 1870s but is readily applied to some paintings, sculpture and architecture in the late eighteenth and early nineteenth centuries and to some music in the early twentieth century. I will use it here to mean a self-conscious defense or adoption of classicism. In this regard, Byron's life witnesses a singular change of context. Born into a classically based culture, but forced to defend it with increasing explicitness, he recognized himself, in effect, as neoclassical. The classical was customarily distinguished from the "barbaric," "uncivilized" and "unpolished." Byron uses terms like this, as we shall see, but eventually finds it harder to do so since the term is increasingly used in contrast with other styles – especially the Elizabethan and the "Romantic."

Byron was introduced into this classically based culture by his reading of Pope, especially Pope's translation of the *Iliad*, which, together with the Scriptures, were almost certainly the most important early literary influences on him. Here he encounters the high style of epic heroism. His later reading of Pope introduced him to satire, urbane conversational idiom and mock epic. Much of Byron's writing can be classified through these four terms, especially if we recognize the epic scale of *Don Juan* and the Achillean strain, however startlingly refashioned, in the Byronic hero who is, after all, always skilled in fighting, concerned with his own honor, and charismatically haughty.

"Classical" primarily referred to Greek and Roman models, but Byron's introduction to these was mediated through Pope and Dryden, themselves now accepted as classical writers who, together with Milton's high Latinate style of *Paradise Lost* (1667), were understood as having instated as permanent a revolution in English literary and speech idiom as the political revolution of 1688. Nevertheless, Byron's injunction in the first canto of *Don Juan*,

Thou shalt believe in Milton, Dryden, Pope;
Thou shalt not set up Wordsworth, Coleridge, Southey
(st. 205, ll. 1633–4 [*CPW* v: 74])

shocked its readers because it blasphemously parodied the Ten
Commandments; and, by 1819, the conjunction of Milton with Dryden
and Pope was no longer incontestable, in part because Wordsworth,
Coleridge and Southey had undermined it. Their reputation now stood
much higher than a decade ago. *English Bards and Scotch Reviewers* (1809)
makes the same point but without the cockily defiant tone Byron thinks
necessary ten years later:

These are the Bards to whom the Muse must bow:
While MILTON, DRYDEN, POPE, alike forgot,
Resign their hallow'd Bays to WALTER SCOTT.
(ll. 186–8 [*CPW* i: 235])

The conjunction of Milton, Dryden and Pope, and the confident use of
the heroic couplet to defend them, was a commonplace. Richard Mant's
The Simpliciad, published the year before, praises Milton, Thomson,
Cowper, Pope, Gray and Dryden as a group. Byron was writing in the
confident stance and idiom (modified by Charles Churchill's freer style)
of William Gifford, whose *The Baviad* (1791) was widely accepted as
having demolished the Della Cruscan poets, who emphasized sensibility
and sought for different earlier authorizing models of poetry than the
Augustans. Byron rejoiced that Gifford had used the style of poetry they
disliked in order to ridicule them. The success of *English Bards*, which
critiques a wide range of living authors, suggests that Byron was right that
his audience still largely shared his assumptions. An unsigned review in the
Gentleman's Magazine for March 1809 praises its "impassioned yet diligent
study of the best masters, grounded on a fine taste" (248) and aligns it with
Pope's *Essay on Criticism* (1711).

   A decade later there would not be this kind of shared assurance as to
who "the best masters" were. No one was clearer than Byron about this
change. Writing to Octavius Gilchrist (September 5, 1821), he formulates
"the present question" thus: "Indeed I look upon a proper appreciation
of Pope as a touchstone of taste – and the present question as not only
whether Pope is or is not in the first rank of our literature – but whether
that literature shall or shall not relapse into the Barbarism from which it
has scarcely emerged for above a century and a half" (*BLJ* 8: 200). What
is striking here is Byron's adoption of the vocabulary and assumptions of
those contesting Pope's position in "the first rank of our literature." Their

whole endeavor was precisely to remove Pope to the second rank of poets. Byron attacks them openly in the collection of material that has come to be known as "The Bowles Controversy" (1821). Bowles had produced his edition of Pope's *Works* in 1806 with an introduction patronizing Pope and asserting the superiority of imagery drawn from Nature rather than social ("artificial") life. It was not well reviewed at the time of publication, but the situation had changed by 1819, when Bowles reasserted the same views in his essay on "The Invariable Principles of Poetry." Byron had once assumed that the revolution at the time of Milton and Dryden was permanent, but now he shares his opponents' imagination, though not their evaluation, that it was only the passing style of a particular time. He accepts that his own poetry has played some part in this. Leigh Hunt had praised *Childe Harold's Pilgrimage* III in the opening paragraphs of his "Young Poets" as though Byron belongs with them. In this sense, and against his will, Byron is forced to relinquish his unformulated classical assumptions and embrace a neoclassical stance. In Gavin Sorgen's phrase, Byron is now primarily engaged in "salvaging" Pope.[1]

A key indicator here is Francis Jeffrey's 1816 review of Scott's edition of Swift's *Works*, which became notorious not only for its violent personal attack on Swift, but also for its opening paragraphs, in which Jeffrey notes that "some twenty-five years ago … every young man was set to read Pope, Swift, and Addison as regularly as Virgil, Cicero and Horace … All this is now pretty well altered … In this decay of their reputation they have few advocates and no imitators" (*ER* 53, September 1816, 1). These words from the influential Jeffrey must have appalled Byron, who was advocate and imitator of all things Augustan. The two grounds of Jeffrey's argument would have disturbed him still more. Jeffrey takes for granted that the Augustan writers have "been eclipsed by those of our own time" and that the literature of the reign of James I "reached the greatest perfection to which it has at yet attained" (*ER* 53, September 1816, 2, 4). If Byron was appalled, Leigh Hunt was delighted. In "The Young Poets" (*Examiner*, 1816) Hunt refers to Jeffrey's article with approval and links it with the three "young poets," Shelley, Reynolds and Keats, to whom he is introducing his readers. Worse still, he associates the recently published *Childe Harold* III with this shift in taste. The sequence here is important. Jeffrey now thinks that contemporary literature is greater than that of the previous century. This is presented as a matter of judgment but it is really the displacement of one set of assumptions by another, which depends upon the revaluation of Elizabethan and Jacobean literature as being not only greater than that of the Augustans but a possible model to imitate.

The ready acceptance of this view by 1816, which had been novel in the eighteenth century, has as much to do with politics as literary taste. Jeffrey associates the changed cultural situation with "the agitations of the French Revolution," which have produced a new world. "French" has become a nasty word for him. He presents Dryden as struggling between "the genius of the English and the French school of literature" with "the evil principle [having] prevailed" (*ER* 53, September 1816, 8 and 5). The casual use of "evil" was surely influenced by England's new self-assertion after 1815. David Duff has observed that after the French Revolution in 1789:

> British sensitivity to the foreignness of neoclassicism became even more marked ... "French Theory" of all kinds came to seem suspect and threatening, despite the fact that neoclassicism was, in essence, an international code, the intellectual attraction of which lay precisely in its cosmopolitan character, its transcendence of national boundaries, and its ability to bridge the temporal gap between ancient and modern cultures.[2]

When Byron talks about "emerging from barbarism" he means acclimatizing this "international code." His extraordinary statement that Pope is "the moral poet of all Civilization" (*CMP* 150) can only be understood in this way, for Pope represents England's acceptance by the company of civilized Classical Europe. He was the first major English writer to be translated into and widely read in French. Correspondingly, Milton, Dryden and Pope, like Byron himself, were translators or imitators of major classical texts. But the increasingly accepted endorsement of pre-Augustan poetry as primary implied that English literature should repudiate this "international code" as that of a French school and find renewal in its own pristine origins. This would have a whiff of triumphalist patriotism about it, for 1816 was the first year of peace after a long conflict with France that England had won. It was also the year when Byron went abroad permanently and immersed himself in Italian culture. The following year, he writes *Beppo* and visits Rome, which, rather than the "Nature" of *Childe Harold* III, is to dominate Canto IV. In 1818, he writes, in "E Nihilo Nihil; or an Epigram Bewitched": "Whate'er I was – I'm classic now –" (*CPW* IV: 209).

Rémi Brague's *Eccentric Culture: A Theory of Western Civilization*,[3] in which Rome figures very largely, helps us here. Brague argues that Europe is an eccentric culture, i.e. one that knows that it does not have its origin in itself. Rome, its forerunner, recognizes Greek culture as its informing superior, whereas the Greeks contrasted their self-originated culture with that of "barbarians." Europe derives directly from Rome and knows this.

England had as much sense of its mediated culture as any country in Europe, but, through the peculiarity of its Elizabethan religious settlement and a new kind of patriotism after the defeat of the Armada's threatened invasion, it developed an outsider mentality. Byron's "above a century and a half ago" fixes the moment when the country largely loses this outsider mentality. Jeffrey notes that "some twenty-five years ago" (in 1791, before England went to war with France) everyone read "Pope, Swift, and Addison as regularly as Virgil, Cicero and Horace." In doing so, they recognized English as a mediated, "eccentric," European culture. Jeffrey's sense that the power of both pre-Augustan and contemporary literature, connected as model and imitator, was greater than that of Dryden and Pope, undoes this sense of mediation upon which the "classical" rests. Milton is now conceived of as an instance of English genius understood in relation to his Elizabethan predecessors and contemporary criticism and poetry rather than sharing a future with Dryden and Pope as European classical poets.

Byron strenuously resists this. The material that makes up the Bowles controversy is the only instance of Byron theorizing at length about poetry. It has magnificent phrases and passages but does not work as a whole. Byron disliked argument and was not very good at it; in this case, his argument was lost before it started. The classical had become acclimatized as a result of long-term cultural shifts, which produced virtually universal agreement on appropriate major forms. To use the argument of minor theorists in its defense is to turn it into the neoclassical, which is simply one preference among others, whereas the classical occupies the whole ground. Byron loses the prose argument, for he is forced into sustaining a single position, which is not his natural mode. On the other hand, *Don Juan* thrives in the space created by the tensions generated between Byron's genial occupancy of a broadly Classical mode of writing and the narrower sense in which this style is now being used "neoclassically" to satirize the different practice of those whom Hunt called "Young Poets." Byron, now, is quite clearly not one of them.

The best piece of writing to come out of the controversy is that of William Hazlitt, a natural arguer. Hazlitt's 1821 is not Byron's. He describes Byron's taste, despite his defense of the classical, as "wild, romantic, far-fetched, obsolete ... Oriental, Gothic, his Muse is not domesticated."[4] Cantos III–V of *Don Juan* were not published until two months later, but *Beppo* and *Don Juan*'s first two cantos were. They do not fit Hazlitt's adjectives. It would have been difficult for Hazlitt to take them into account, for, where it might be hard to find the classical principles of Byron's *Hints from Horace* exemplified in the Oriental tales or *Manfred*, it is not hard to do so in

Beppo and *Don Juan.* Hazlitt does not grasp the run of connection between classicism and Byron's *ottava rima* poems. His assumptions are shared by Hunt who insists that the only object of his "Young Poets" is "to restore the same love of Nature … which formerly rendered us real poets, and not merely versifying wits."⁵ Hazlitt assumes the new use of "Nature" as contrasted with Art, whereas Byron continues Pope's classical association of Art and Nature, as expounded in his *Essay on Criticism* ("*Nature* and *Homer* were, he found, the same").⁶

Byron enlists Pope as the defender not of the Book of Art but of "the Book of Life" (*CMP* 158), for "there is no poet – not Shakespeare himself – who can be so often quoted – with reference to Life" (*CMP* 182, ll. 10–12). We should link this with his famous defence of *Don Juan*, "is it not *life*"? (*BLJ* 6: 232). Nicholas Gayle is right: "Byron saw things in the man he called 'the best of poets' that were little valued by his contemporaries."⁷ Pope's classical world of heroism, domestic interiors, sex, politics, art, thought, landscape and vision is always a peopled, living world. Tillotson says that Pope "looked as long and as closely as any of our dramatists and novelists … at the 'glaring chaos and wild heap' of men, 'the field full of folk.' "⁸ Byron does the same and thus distinguishes himself from the "present literary world of mountebanks" who "have never lived either in *high life* nor in *solitude* – there is no medium for the knowledge of the *busy* or the *still* world" (*BLJ* 8: 207). Hazlitt, in his own way, knew both these worlds but took for granted that great poetry should neither concern itself with the busy world nor move between the two. *Don Juan* is Byron's witness to knowing and moving between busy and still worlds.

In this he is certainly like Pope, yet Sir Drummond Bone has pointed out that Byron's defense of Pope is itself "very unPopeian,"⁹ because Pope's poetics presuppose a stable cosmic and moral order, which Byron's cannot. There is obvious truth in this. Byron could not have written *An Essay on Man.* Pope could not have written *Manfred.* Both poems chime with their very different times. It may seem as odd for Byron to idolize Pope as for Tchaikovsky to idolize Mozart. We see the differences first. But it is not as clear-cut as this. There is something astonishing in the way that Byron, single-handed, maintains the substantiation of classical poetry in his three tragedies, *Beppo*, *The Vision of Judgment* and, especially, *Don Juan.* *Don Juan* does so as an openly mediated, epic-scale poem that is based on rhetoric, ethical in direction, using shared allusions with its audience, careful in its managements of diction, combining inherited formulas with urbane conversational language and addressed to the world and about the world. Its epigraph from Horace, *Difficile est proprie communia dicere* (*CPW* v: 1), is a calculated undermining of Wordsworth's theoretically demotic poetics. Byron attacks the present laureate as a sign of debased times, just as Pope did; the poem originally began with a preface parodying that of the *Lyrical Ballads* (*CPW* v: 662). It is of its time but, like Freedom's banner, "streams like the thunder-storm *against* the wind" (*CPW* ii: 157, l. 875).

Byron may not, as Sir Drummond insists, share the ideas that underpin Pope's poetry, but he does find a precedent for his stance in his avowed master. Hazlitt assumes that "the fashion of the day bore sway in his [Pope's] mind over the immutable laws of nature," and that Pope "basked in the favor of the great,"[10] but Byron knew better. Pope lived in opposition, especially between 1729 and 1743. Steven Shankman observes that Pope "unlike Horace, is not part of the establishment" and writes "from a position of self-righteous Achillean defiance of authority."[11] In *The Dunciad*, he presents himself as the single-handed defender of a civilization that has lost touch with its origins and is thus in creative free fall. Only the achieved art of the poem and the voice of its unsubdued poet maintain sanity by disclosing a creative energy still vivified by classical civilization and natural life. *Don Juan* makes and substantiates the same claim. Both Pope and Byron live, wittily and heroically, in Achillean opposition to established authority, rebuking current bad taste and cant, but they do not seek to celebrate their outsider stance; rather they wish to reconnect the dominant cultural world with perennial sources of renewal and they ridicule and deplore the movement away from them.

Byron often instances Thermopylae as a rallying cry for modern Greeks (see for example *CPW* ii: 68, l. 699). One of the many reasons that took Byron to Greece in 1823 was certainly the idea that he was defending the Greek springs of European civilization. The classical helmet that he commissioned is both part of his theatricality and his seriousness. He called Achilles "the bravest of the brave" (*CPW* v: 227, l. 603). Byron did not have time or opportunity to prove his own courage in Greece, but there are many kinds of bravery. Bowles saw Pope as a slightly ridiculous figure locked into an artificial social world. Byron saw Pope as a great Classical writer and a brave unsubdued man. He wished to copy him in both respects. He succeeded.

TE.

1 Gavin Sourgen, "'In a Manner That Is My Aversion': Byron's Objections to Romantic Blank Verse," *Byron Journal* 44.1 (2016), 1–14.
2 David Duff, *Romanticism and the Uses of Genre* (Oxford: Oxford University Press, 2009), 33.

3 Rémi Brague, *Eccentric Culture: A Theory of Western Civilisation* (South Bend, IN: St. Augustine's Press, 2002).

4 *London Magazine* 3 (June 18, 1821), 599.

5 Leigh Hunt, "Young Poets," *Examiner* (December 1, 1816), 761.

6 Alexander Pope, "An Essay on Criticism," in John Butt (ed.), *The Poems of Alexander Pope* (London: Methuen, 1963), 148.

7 Nicholas Gayle, *Byron and the Best of Poets* (Newcastle upon Tyne, UK: Cambridge Scholars Press, 2016), 250. This is the only full-length study of Pope and Byron.

8 Geoffrey Tillotson, *Pope and Human Nature* (Oxford: Clarendon Press, 1958), 135.

9 Private conversation, Keele University, September 30, 2016.

10 *London Magazine* 3 (June 18, 1821), 607.

11 Steven Shankman, "Pope's Homer," in Pat Rogers (ed.), *The Cambridge Companion to Alexander Pope* (Cambridge, UK: Cambridge University Press, 2007), 70.

CHAPTER 18

Epic (and Historiography)

Carla Pomarè

Ever since its inception, Western epic has been concerned with the narration of the past, be it human, cosmic or mythic. From Homer's siege of Troy and Virgil's foundation of Rome, down to Milton's "first disobedience," epic discourse has retraced key episodes in the historical memory of the West, generally shaping them around figures who have been cast into heroic relief. Recalling that "Mnemosyne, the rememberer, was the Muse of the epic art among the Greeks," Walter Benjamin wondered "whether historiography does not constitute the common ground of all forms of the epic,"[1] over and above the formal qualities traditionally associated with the genre – considerable length, elevated diction, supernatural machinery, rhetorical devices such as series and similes, set pieces like the invocation to the Muse and prophetic visions.

History was notoriously one of Byron's lifelong interests. As an avid book collector, he gathered in his library an impressive number of volumes that provided him with a variety of historiographical models, ranging from the classical historiography of Herodotus, Plutarch, Diodorus and Tacitus to Renaissance historians such as Francesco Guicciardini and Niccolò Machiavelli, to the philosophical history of Voltaire and Gibbon, to contemporaries versed in national histories such as William Mitford, Pierre Daru and Simonde de Sismondi. Historiography served for Byron a variety of purposes: it made him acquainted with characters and episodes that he reworked in his verses; exposed him to textual practices that were to become trademarks of his production, such as the massive use of footnotes, prefaces and appendixes; and helped him shape the historical frame through which he approached experience. Relevant as it was to almost all the genres he experimented with, historiography gave a specific contribution to the peculiar investment in the relationships between the worlds of fiction and fact that informs Byron's epic discourse.

Byron's involvement in the epic is a long-debated issue. Byron was apparently wary of epic pretensions, and resisted pressure from friends and associates to "undertake … a 'great work' an Epic poem … or some such pyramid," as he wrote in an 1819 letter to John Murray (*BLJ* 6: 105). Although he bluntly proclaimed, "I'll try no such thing – I hate tasks," Byron eventually styled his *Don Juan* as an "epic" ("If you must have an epic, there's 'Don Juan' for you," Medwin 164), complete with all the appurtenances of the form, as he advertised in the first of its seventeen cantos:

> My poem's epic, and is meant to be
>   Divided in twelve books; each book containing,
> With love, and war, a heavy gale at sea,
>   A list of ships, and captains, and kings reigning,
> New characters; the episodes are three:
>   A panorama view of hell's in training,
> After the style of Virgil and of Homer,
> So that my name of Epic's no misnomer.
>   (*DJ* 1, st. 200, ll. 1593–600 [*CPW* v: 73])

While paying lip service to the letter of the epic, Byron systematically reversed its spirit. His narrative is open-ended, trailing from Spain to Greece, Turkey, Russia, England, with no conclusion in view, and making free play with a series of fictional and historical materials ranging from Don Juan himself to Catherine of Russia, from a fabulous Orient to the 1790 siege of Ismail; all this, together with its ironic when not downright comic register, contradicts the closure, objectivity and seriousness traditionally associated with epic discourse. It does not come as a surprise, then, that critics have felt the need to qualify the peculiar turn of the epic in *Don Juan*, variously defining it as "mock epic," "comic epic," "epic satire," "modern epic," "epic of negation," "anti-epic," or simply "redefinition of epic,"[2] tracing its debts to a composite tradition that was being renegotiated during the Romantic period at the level of both theory and practice.

Drawing on Aristotle and Horace, the Renaissance poetics of Torquato Tasso's *Discorsi del poema eroico* (1594) and the neoclassical aesthetics of both the French and English traditions, exemplified respectively in René Le Bossu's *Traité du poème épique* (1675) and John Dryden's *Dedication* to his translation of the *Aeneid* (1697), placed the epic at the top of the generic hierarchy, stressing the value of the moral lessons it imparted. In Dryden's words, a heroic poem "raises the soul, and hardens it to virtue."[3] Theorists who set out to codify epic discourse focused on matters of poetic form, which they saw as universals embodied in the heroic strain of Homer and Virgil. Hence, they generally neglected nonheroic forms of the classical epic such as the philosophical (Lucretius' *De rerum natura*), the historical (Ennius' *Annales*), the mythological (Ovid's *Metamorphoses*) and the didactic (Manilius' *Astronomica*).

In the late eighteenth century, when the term "epic" was still used to confer an aura of poetic greatness, William Hayley published an *Essay on Epic Poetry* (1782) whose heroic couplets, accompanied by an apparatus of extensive notes, stressed the importance of freedom from generic constraints and opened up the canon of epic poems both chronologically and geographically to include Lucan's *Pharsalia* (61–65 AD), Dante's *Divina Commedia* (1308–21) and Alonso de Ercilla's *La Araucana* (1569–89). At the same time, Hayley advocated the birth of a new "national Epic Poem," hailed as "the great desideratum in English literature," which would draw on "subjects from English History" and celebrate "the splendid fane of British Freedom."[4] In various ways, works as diverse as Joseph Cottle's *Alfred* (1800), John Ogilvie's *Britannia: A National Epic Poem, in Twenty Books* (1801) and Robert Southey's *Madoc* (1805) followed Hayley's precepts, contributing to the vogue of the national epic that marked the early years of the nineteenth century. Meanwhile, epic poetry was also taking a more libertarian turn in works such as Southey's *Joan of Arc* (1796) and Walter Savage Landor's *Gebir* (1798). It showed a more lyrical strain too in Wordsworth's *Prelude* (1805), which in the wake of Milton redefined heroism in spiritual and autobiographical terms, replacing the traditional figure of the warrior with that of the poet.

Byron viewed his contemporaries' manifold epic attempts with suspicion and was scathing about Southey's "unsaleables" (*BLJ* 3: 101). More generally, he perceived the anachronism of a genre mostly built on notions that were alien to him: the celebration of the martial ethos (whose paradoxes and ultimate destructiveness he had exposed in the Oriental tales); the ideology of imperial conquest, with the attendant view of a teleological design governing the flow of history; and the narrative linearity that conveyed single-minded versions of events, usually described from the victors' point of view. But the generic instability of the epic in the Romantic period allowed Byron to appropriate it on his own terms, doing away with both the providentially ordained design of Virgil's *Aeneid* and the allegorical frame of later epics such as Dante's *Commedia*. Exploiting the traditional inclusiveness of epic discourse and its typical tendency to operate through "imitative devices,"[5] Byron cross-fertilized strands as varied as epic, romance and the new cognitive protocols being developed in the historiographical field.

The contamination of epic with romance was almost as old as the epic itself. The earliest example can be traced as far back as the third century

BC, in Apollonius of Rhodes' *Argonautica*, which introduced the motif of the passion of Jason and Medea into the epic narrative of the recovery of the Golden Fleece. In the Italian Renaissance, both Boiardo's *Orlando Innamorato* (1495) and Ariosto's *Orlando Furioso* (1516–32) revisited the theme of the antagonism between Christian and Muslim cultures recounted in the Carolingian *Chanson de Roland* by grafting onto the traditional epic focus on war a labyrinthine series of love adventures, which explored the domain of fantasy, magic and illusion. Initiated by Giuseppe Baretti's *Dissertation Upon the Italian Poetry* (1753), Ariosto's vogue ran high in eighteenth-century England, with two new translations of the *Furioso* in less than thirty years, by William Huggins in 1755 and John Hoole in 1783. The same interest surrounded the works of Torquato Tasso, who similarly included romantic episodes in his *Gerusalemme Liberata* (1581), although subscribing to a more orthodox and Christianized notion of the epic, strictly dependent on historical and religious truth and informed by the respect of the Aristotelian unities.

Byron was well aware that Ariosto and Tasso were "not of the same genus" (*BLJ* 8: 210). Ever since the sixteenth century their stylistic, structural and thematic choices had been hotly debated in Italy, with Ariosto's supporters criticizing Tasso's lack of invention and his broken style, while Tasso's admirers censured Ariosto's variety of plots and penchant for sensuality. Steering clear of the *querelle* between the *ariostisti* and *tassisti* camps, Byron put Ariosto and Tasso to different uses in his epic discourse. While Tasso's tormented and much fictionalized biography, revolving around the seven years he spent as captive of duke Alfonso d'Este in a Ferrara madhouse, provided Byron with a model of an epic writer with whom he could identify – colliding with and succumbing to hostile political power, but capable of making his voice heard across the centuries (like the Dante he would celebrate in his *Prophecy of Dante*) – Ariosto taught him a lesson of form. The episodic structure and multiple story lines of the *Furioso*, punctuated by ironic commentary often based on the juxtaposition of different points of view, represent a radical alternative to the narrative order of orthodox epic discourse and to its implied notion of a unified meaning of history.

To Byron's notorious skepticism, this was a strong inducement to try his hand at an Ariostesque narrative, rambling and nonhierarchical, which would accommodate his a-teleological and contingent approach to reality. "You ask me for the plan of Donny Johnny," he wrote to Murray in 1819, adding, "I *have* no plan – I *had* no plan – but I had or have materials" (*BLJ* 6: 207). Jerome McGann has aptly remarked that "*Don Juan* is not a poem that develops, it is a poem that is added to."[6] Byron had been experimenting with this accretive model before: witness the composition of *The Giaour* and his letter to William Miller explaining that the first two cantos of *Childe Harold's Pilgrimage* were "intended to be a poem on *Ariosto's plan* that *is to say* on *no plan* at all" (*BLJ* 2: 63). By opposing "plan" and "materials," Byron hints at the all-encompassing flavor of his personal idea of epic – a trait reinforced by his apparently contradictory claim later, when Murray was shying away from the controversial publication of *Don Juan*, that he "had all the plan for several cantos – and different countries & climes" (*BLJ* 8: 198). Incorporating the most diverse materials, from newspaper reports to pre-existing literature and historiographical sources, spanning a variety of "countries & climes," *Don Juan* qualifies as one of the encyclopaedic, supranational narratives that Franco Moretti calls "world texts,"[7] retracing in them the modern form of the epic – culturally and linguistically heterogeneous, incomplete, ironic and self-conscious.

Self-consciousness in *Don Juan* takes the form of the innumerable digressions that interrupt the narrative line, providing a run-on commentary on its contents, mode and above all departure from the heroic epic ("as I have a high sense / Of Aristotle and the Rules, 'tis fit / To beg his pardon when I err a bit" [*CPW* v: 47, ll. 958–60]), often producing effects of comic deflation that harken back to the classical examples of epic pastiche, from the anonymous *Batrachomyomachia, or The Battle of the Frogs and Mice*, probably dating to the first century BC and for a long time attributed to Homer, to Petronius' *Satyricon*, written in the first century AD. In England this model had left traces in the mock-heroic tradition of Dryden's *Mac Flecknoe* (1682) and Pope's *Rape of the Lock* (1714), whose ironic target was not the epic (which Dryden and Pope highly esteemed, having translated, respectively, the *Aeneid* and the Homeric poems), but the social and cultural conditions that made the contemporary world inhospitable to it. Although Byron nourished a true admiration for Pope and Dryden, his *Don Juan* departs from their "loyalist parodies"[8] in its radical assault on the epic, which owes much of its piquancy to an Italian burlesque reworking of the epic model: Luigi Pulci's *Morgante Maggiore* (1483), which Byron first met through John Hookham Frere's adaptation and then himself partially translated in 1820. Frere's *Prospectus and Specimen of an Intended National Work* (1817), also known as *The Monks and the Giants*, imported into English Pulci's fantastic meeting of Charlemagne's paladins with the giant Morgante, and developed it into a series of rambling adventures involving King Arthur's knights, the rescue of damsels in distress and the defeat of a race of wicked giants. More significantly, Frere imported into

English Pulci's prosodic model of *ottava rima*, which he used to develop a markedly self-reflexive strain very much like Byron's, which punctuates the *fabula* of the poem with considerations about the details of its composition ("I've finished now three hundred lines and more, / And therefore I begin Canto the Second, / Just like those wand'ring ancient Bards of Yore; / They never laid a plan, nor ever reckon'd / What turning they should take the day before.")[9]

Originating in the oral tradition of *cantastorie* and *improvvisatori*, *ottava rima* was the Italian standard form for narrative verse, shared among others by Ariosto and Tasso. It was characterized by extreme flexibility, with three alternating pairs of rhymes (ABABAB) that provided scope for the narrative or descriptive moment, while the final couplet (CC) allowed the shift to commentary, bathos and wit. Having first experimented with *ottava rima* in *Beppo* (1818), in *Don Juan* Byron exploded the digressive potential of its stanzaic structure, with its sudden transitions in tone, subject, point of view and register, often enhanced by odd or dissonant rhyming. The result was the flexibility that Virginia Woolf pointed out in admiration when she described Byron's *ottava rima* as an "elastic shape which will hold whatever you choose to put into it."[10]

In addition to the social, cultural and political criticism that Byron chose to put into his epic, *ottava rima* proved congenial to the epistemological concerns about the value of facts that followed from his investment in the historiographical field. "There's only one slight difference between / Me and my epic brethren gone before," Byron writes, explaining that "They so embellish, that 'tis quite a bore / Their labyrinth of fables to thread through, / Whereas this story's actually true" (*CPW* v: 74, ll. 1609–16). The authenticity that Byron flaunts throughout *Don Juan* – setting it up against the "outrageous fictions" (*BLJ* 3: 101) of Southey's epic – is a value typical of the new historiography that he enjoyed referencing, from Gibbon's *Decline and Fall* (1776) to Mitford's *History of Greece* (1784–1810), Sismondi's *Histoire des républiques italiennes du Moyen-âge* (1807–8) and Daru's *Histoire de la République de Venise* (1819–22). The historical discipline that developed across the eighteenth and nineteenth centuries turned away from teleological readings and increasingly relied on "scientific" procedures for the study of the past, priding itself on its accurate recovery of sources through methodical archival research, while also broadening its horizons well beyond historiography's traditional concerns with martial feats. As such, historiography entered a complex interplay with the literary field, influencing and being in turn influenced by similar developments in the realistic novel, with its claim to be reporting the "real" adventures of "real" people. That Byron repeatedly experimented with the form of the novel, most notably in late 1817, when he wrote an aborted prose narrative whose protagonist was a young Spanish nobleman called "Don Julian,"[11] is indicative of how novelistic, historical and epic categories overlapped in his production. But if the distinctive quality of Byron's epic is to be found in the repeated claims about its factual truth, such claims rarely escape ironic deflation. After averring that his epic is "really true," Byron appeals "To history, tradition, and to facts" to corroborate his statement, only to conclude that the best proof "Is, that myself, and several now in Seville, / Saw Juan's last elopement with the devil" (*CPW* v: 74, ll. 1618–24).

Don Juan is indeed an "audaciously false claim to be telling a true story,"[12] and Byron manifestly relishes such incongruence, debunking with often hilarious effects his own insistence on factual accuracy and ultimately destabilizing the very notion of a single "truth" – historical or otherwise – hailing "Doubt" as "sole prism / Of the Truth's rays" (*CPW* v: 465, ll. 13–15). Subverting any simplistic views of the relationship between literary and historical discourses, Byron's epic no longer celebrates the heroic past. Rather, it acts upon history by forcing readers to acknowledge the multiple perspectives through which the past, as well as the present, can be viewed and judged.

NOTES

1 Walter Benjamin, "The Storyteller," in *Illuminations: Essays and Reflections* (New York: Shocken Books, 2007), 97, 95.
2 See Nicholas Halmi, "The Very Model of a Modern Epic Poem," *European Romantic Review* 21 (2010), 589, 592.
3 Vergil, *Æneid*, trans. J. Dryden, in C. W. Eliot (ed.), *The Harvard Classics* (New York: P. F. Collier & Son, 1909–49), vol. XIII, 5.
4 William Hayley, *An Essay on Epic Poetry* (London: J. Dodsley, 1782), 96, 111.
5 Brian Wilkie, *Romantic Poets and the Epic Tradition* (Madison and Milwaukee: University of Wisconsin Press, 1965), 14.
6 Jerome J. McGann, *"Don Juan" in Context* (London: John Murray, 1976), 60.
7 Franco Moretti, *Modern Epic: The World-System from Goethe to García Márquez*, trans. Q. Hoare (London and New York: Verso, 1996), 2.
8 Claude Rawson, "Mock-Heroic and English Poetry," in C. Bates (ed.), *The Cambridge Companion to the Epic* (Cambridge, UK: Cambridge University Press, 2010), 169.
9 John Hookham Frere, *Prospectus and Specimen of an Intended National Work, by William and Robert Whistlecraft*, 2nd ed. (London: Murray, 1818), 25.

10 *The Diary of Virginia Woolf. Vol. I: 1915–1919*, ed. A. Olivier Bell (New York: Harcourt Brace Jovanovich, 1977), 180.

11 E. F. Boyd, *Byron's "Don Juan": A Critical Study* (New Brunswick: Rutgers University Press, 1945), 11.

12 Wilkie, *Romantic Poets*, 196.

CHAPTER 19

Romance

Omar F. Miranda

The literary romance – the medieval genre involving questing knights, courtly love, codes of chivalry and exotic, enchanted settings – rose again to high fashion during Lord Byron's time. The form became one of the hallmarks of Romanticism, a period whose very etymology captures the cultural obsession with the glories of the Middle Ages. Several factors contributed to the revival, including interest in the power of the imagination and the desire to consolidate national literary histories during the rise of the modern nation-state. In general, the romance differs from the epic, the genre out of which it grew, because it prioritizes chivalric values such as honor and justice and centers on the rewards of courtly love obtained following combat in foreign lands.

Byron was one of the great innovators of the romance genre. He sustained his attention to it throughout his career, from his early poems in *Hours of Idleness* (1807) to *Don Juan* (1819–24). In his hands, a genre that had once been confined to the courts of medieval Europe developed into a global form with a diversity of subject matter and settings across Europe and Asia. Byronic romance employed a variety of literary registers that enabled its author to tell a story or joke, comment on social, political and historical topics, and foreground the novelty of cultural encounter. Through it, Byron deployed many iterations of what we now call the Byronic hero – the enigmatic aristocrat in exile inhibited by a dark, secret past – which became the literary sensation based on Byron's self-fashioned public persona. Byron's multiple versions of this character produced the phenomenon of Byronism, a craze that enjoyed transnational appeal and encompassed a range of cultural products associated with the Byronic hero. With the help of John Murray, Byron's publisher in London, this market phenomenon sprang fully into existence in 1812 with the publication of Byron's first major experiment in the romance genre: the first two cantos of *Childe Harold's Pilgrimage, a Romaunt* (the Middle English term for the genre). Beyond his published work, what made Byron's relation to the romance extraordinary is that he sought to epitomize and live out a romance himself. As recounted by journalists and biographers, Byron's own life of celebrity, which included dramatic love plots, episodic adventure and an anti-imperial campaign in support of liberating Ottoman-occupied Greece, also embodied romantic conventions.

Like many of his contemporaries, Byron was disillusioned by the violence of the French Revolution and the bleak, turbulent milieu of the Napoleonic Wars across Europe. This disenchantment made any attempt at recapturing the chivalric ideals of honor and justice appear disingenuous and vain. In *Reflections on the Revolution in France* (1790), Edmund Burke argued that the disorder and bloodshed caused by the revolution had brought chivalry to its demise. For many critics, Byron's writings – with their quintessential irony, skepticism, satire and narrative digression – offered a distinctive (albeit parodic) reiteration of the Burkean view that chivalry was no longer possible in the present day. In his "Addition" to *Childe Harold*'s preface (1813), Byron criticized the medieval epoch for being "the most profligate of all possible centuries" and a time of "monstrous mummeries" (*CPW* II: 5–6).

Nevertheless, Byron's censure of the era that gave birth to the romance did not signify that either romance or chivalry had run its course. Rather, each demanded reinvention. In his writings, Byron sought to challenge the Burkean idea of chivalry itself: the tendency to regard chivalry in uncritical terms. In his response to such prescriptive notions of the chivalric age, Byron cultivated a series of personae and speaking voices that balanced romantic idealisms with the irony and stoicism needed to survive in the post-revolutionary world. Instead of suspending reality, portraying fantastical realms or advancing toward some religious objective, his poetry would bring myth, fact and reason into coexistence within a reconfigured version of the genre.

Perhaps the oldest influence on romance can be traced back to the Homeric and Virgilian epic. Homer's *Odyssey* details the multiple adventures of its exiled hero, Odysseus, in his attempt to return home. In *The Progress of Romance* (1785), Clara Reeve contended that Homer was not only the "Prince of Epic poetry" but also "the parent of Romance" who inspired Virgil's writings.[1] In addition to the popular romances that circulated during the Middle Ages, including *Song of Roland* (eighth century), works by Chrétien de Troyes (twelfth century), *Sir Gawain and the Greene*

Knight (late fourteenth century) and Thomas Malory's *Le Morte D'Arthur* (1485), the later verse romances of Edmund Spenser, Ludovico Ariosto and Torquato Tasso from the sixteenth century served as inspiration to Byron, as he noted in his writings. To this list must be added Miguel de Cervantes' famous prose parody of the form, *Don Quixote* (1605). According to Byron, "Cervantes smiled Spain's Chivalry away" with his publication, and proclaimed the birth of the modern era (*CPW* v: 528, l. 81).

The romance revival associated with Romanticism began earlier in the eighteenth century. One could trace these origins to 1760 when James Macpherson supposedly translated an ancient Scottish epic composed by Ossian, a third-century Scottish bard. Although charges were raised that Macpherson falsified his "discovery" and composed the poems himself, the publication provoked a widespread fascination with recovering the aesthetic treasures of bygone epochs. The publication of Thomas Percy's *Reliques of Ancient English Poetry* (1765), a three-volume collection of popular folk ballads and songs obtained from a variety of sources, contributed to this antiquarian trend. In his *Rowley Poems*, Thomas Chatterton famously forged several manuscripts by adopting the authorial persona of Thomas Rowley, a fifteenth-century monk, and inserting archaic spellings and diction into his own compositions.

Allegorical romances in the style of Spenser's *The Faerie Queene* (1590–6) added to the vogue. With its Middle English archaisms, Spenser's poem became a model for reviving romance; it stood out with its signature nine-line stanzas (eight lines of iambic pentameter followed by one alexandrine, an iambic hexameter line). Other texts that influenced Byron were James Thomson's *The Castle of Indolence* (1748) and James Beattie's *The Minstrel: Or, the Progress of Genius* (1771–4), two didactic poems that highlight the supremacy of the quotidian world above that of fancy and imagination. In Beattie's text, a young medieval quester and minstrel in training, Edwin, fans "the flame of Industry and Genius" alike.[2] While the poem employs the Spenserian stanza as a platform for multiplicity and variety, as Byron himself noted, Beattie diverges from the romance tradition by integrating realistic elements from the everyday (*CPW* ii: 4).

William Jones, William Beckford, Walter Scott and Robert Southey were perhaps the greatest of all influences on Byronic romance. During an age of imperial expansion in which travel and trade increased dramatically, these writers embraced diverse cultural subjects in response to heightened appeal for the foreign and the exotic. A scholar of Persian and

Sanskrit who served on the Supreme Court in Bengal during the British occupation of India, Jones published *The Palace of Fortune, an Indian Tale* (1769), a visionary verse romance set in the Asian subcontinent. Beckford's *Vathek* (1786), an Arabian tale that fused Beckford's scholarly orientalist interests with homoerotic Gothic fantasy, influenced Byron's writing of *The Giaour* (and *Manfred*) explicitly; Byron highlighted this in a note to his tale in 1813. Following Jones' and Beckford's lead, Southey authored *Thalaba the Destroyer* (1801) and *The Curse of Kehama* (1810), whose respective Middle Eastern and Indian settings and themes added to the period fascination with cultures on the periphery of empire. Southey also turned his attention to the Hispanophone world – as Byron would do – with his translations of *The Chronicle of the Cid* (1808), publishing several accounts of Spain's eleventh-century legendary knight in exile. In addition to collecting border ballads and folk songs in *The Minstrelsy of the Scottish Border* (1802–3), Scott authored several verse romances between 1805 and 1811. Among them were the *Lay of the Last Minstrel* (1805), *Marmion; a Tale of Flodden Field* (1808) and *The Vision of Don Roderick* (1811). Scott manipulated the verse romance form in ways that would appeal to Byron, including shifting his settings from Anglo-Scottish to Spanish peninsular landscapes as well as characterizing Lord Marmion as a proto-Byronic hero – of "haughty demeanor and dark qualities."[3]

With the publication of the first two cantos of *Childe Harold*, Byron succeeded in radically altering the romance's functions and aims. On the surface, *Childe Harold* conforms to several romantic conventions and contains the "old ideals of justice, generosity and compassion for the distressed."[4] In addition to using the Spenserian stanza, it includes some of the Middle English archaisms used by Spenser in *The Faerie Queene* ("whilome," "hight," "Paynim" and "fytte"). Moreover, Byron's eponymous hero bears the title "childe," a medieval term for a young nobleman prior to being knighted. As the poem's title suggests, Harold ventures on a religious quest – a pilgrimage – that takes him across the Mediterranean world, where he visits several exotic places, including the court of the Ottoman ruler, Ali Pasha, in Albania.

Despite possessing such qualities, the poem fundamentally diverges from the romance tradition. It is not set in the distant past; nor does the pilgrimage culminate in any religious shrine. A cosmopolitan travelogue, the verse narrative takes place within Byron's contemporary world. Tracking the journey of the first iteration of the Byronic hero, the poem records Harold's (and Byron's) inner thoughts instead of describing acts of military or amorous conquest. These meditations range from observations on customs and manners to social and political commentary on recurring historical patterns or the ills of empires across time, including the Spanish colonial "wrongs" committed by "fell Pizarros" against the "once enchain'd" peoples of Central and South America (*CPW* II: 43, ll. 914–6). Given these features, *Childe Harold* offers a version of what Harold Bloom has called Romanticism's "Internalization of the Quest Romance," in which the landscape becomes a metaphor for the psyche and the journey the analogue for the road to enlightenment.[5]

Throughout Harold's travels, Byron identifies what appears antithetical to the spirit of medieval romance. In Canto I he observes that Portugal's "romantic hills" are devoid of "a freeborn race," while the "renown'd, romantic land" of Spain hears cries from "Chivalry, [its] ancient goddess" (*CPW* II: 22–4, ll. 342–406). Each landscape bears its country's chivalric legacy, but corrupt political systems and deleterious historical events have tarnished them. When Harold visits Cadiz at the end of his journey to the Iberian Peninsula, he notes the paradoxical state of "fallen Chivalry" in which the gentry no longer live out romantic ideals: "all were noble, save Nobility" (*CPW* II: 41, ll. 880–1). Later, in Canto IV, Byron muses about the "fall'n states and buried greatness" of Italy, "which *was* the mightiest in its old command" (*CPW* II: 132, ll. 220–1). His travels take him along a chain of disappointments, as Byron contemplates the futility of human endeavors and sacrifices.

And yet the ideals of medieval romance are not entirely lost; nor is Byron's account of the contemporary moment altogether bleak. Amid the decaying Italian landscape, Byron stresses that it still "*is* the loveliest": a land of "the heroic and the free, / The beautiful, [and] the brave" (*CPW* II: 132, ll. 222–5; Byron's emphasis). Earlier, in Canto I, Byron comments on his admiration for the "Kingless people" of Spain, these "vassals" who during the Peninsular Wars would "combat when their chieftains flee" – a reference to Napoleon's occupation of Spain and his removal of Ferdinand VII, their monarch (*CPW* II: 41, ll. 884–5). Here Byron champions an alternative chivalric mindset that, instead of reinscribing the traditions associated with monarchy or feudalism, is directed toward republican ideas. In addition to venerating the landscapes of former ages during the Moorish occupation of Spain, when "Moor and knight" coexisted along Spain's Guadiana river (*CPW* II: 23, l. 383), he turns more generally to nature in Canto III to alleviate his world-weariness. Byron reflects upon the majesty and restorative capacity of the natural scenes along his pilgrimage, which recall the chivalric landscapes from the first canto.

Based on a "redefined notion of chivalry," then, Byron's reformulated romance exposes political machinations and human faults, while also emphasizing beauty and beneficence wherever they may be found.[6] In his addendum to *Childe Harold*'s preface, Byron defends Harold against critics' charges that his hero appears "unknightly," insisting rather that Harold should be deemed "perfectly knightly in his attributes" and accepted "such as he is" (*CPW* II: 5–6). Instead of portraying Harold as an "agreeable" or "amiable" hero, Byron lays his flaws bare (*CPW* II: 6). In so doing, he suggests that his romance will also depict his contemporary world "such as it is." By Canto IV, the removal of Harold and any traces of linguistic archaism finalizes Byron's attempt to reimagine the romance by transforming it from the pure fiction of the medieval past to one inclusive of the vagaries of everyday modern life. Byron's poem offered his readers a secular and cosmopolitan pilgrimage that included the process of self-discovery and an array of meaningful encounters with other peoples and places. After all, the modern romantic hero lives not exclusively "in [him]self / but become[s] / Portion of that around [him]" (*CPW* II: 103, ll. 680–1).

Following the first installment of *Childe Harold*, Byron published his Turkish or Eastern tales: *The Giaour* (1813), *The Bride of Abydos* (1813), *The Corsair* (1813), *Lara* (1814), *The Siege of Corinth* (1814) and *Parisina* (1816). In these narrative verse romances, he created new versions of the Byronic hero that included all the necessary elements for maintaining Byron on his bestselling streak: precarious adventure, exotic settings and illicit (often triangular) love plots. Like his Orientalist predecessors, he fascinated his readers in both *Childe Harold* and his tales by inviting them into the unfamiliar Eastern world through descriptions of mosques and harems and the inclusion of fakirs and dervishes. Although Byron exposed the social and political hierarchy found in parts of the Islamic world, as well as its arbitrary, even violent, display of power, he is at least as critical of European and Christian traditions.

Following his Eastern tales, Byron continued to adapt the features of romance in two historical works, *Mazeppa* (1817) and *The Island* (1823), the latter of which retells William Bligh's account of the famous 1789 mutiny on *The Bounty* in the Southern Pacific Ocean. With the publication of *Don Juan* (1818–24), Byron returned to the Iberian setting with which he began *Childe Harold* in order to reconceive the classic Spanish seducer of women as a romantic exile on the run across Europe and parts of Asia. Like *Childe Harold*, *Don Juan* discriminates between the romantic and non-romantic elements in the places Juan visits. Unlike *Childe Harold*, however, *Don Juan* is a mock epic of seventeen cantos written in a comedic and satirical style. The poem extends the cultural and geographical limits as well as the range of styles found within the ambitious global scope of Byronic romance.

What remains to be addressed in this brief overview is the unfolding romance of Byron's own life and celebrity, which he actively incorporated into many of his works. In *Childe Harold*, Harold's travels across the Mediterranean mirror the route that Byron himself took on his grand tour of Portugal, Spain, Malta, Greece, Albania and Turkey from 1809 to 1811. In *Don Juan*, Byron reworked the themes of romance by representing the subject of his own celebrity. As I have argued elsewhere, Byron partly based the character and travels of his libertine Hispanic hero, Juan, on Francisco de Miranda (1750–1816), the Venezuelan exile, adventurer and revolutionary. Miranda dedicated several years in exile to liberating Spanish America from colonial rule, living out many of the adventures of which Juan would later partake in Byron's epic. Between 1786 and 1787, Miranda journeyed to Ottoman-occupied Greece, Turkey and Russia, where he stayed for about a year in Catherine the Great's court and allegedly became one of her lovers; he then turned back to London, where he resided for about fourteen years as a cultural diplomat (like Juan in the later cantos of *Don Juan*). In addition, Miranda anticipated Byron's celebrity in numerous ways. Both Byron and his South American predecessor distinguished themselves in part through a protean style of celebrity I call "exilic romance,"[7] which adopted the tropes and conventions of the medieval romance yet also undermined that image through a paradoxical series of poses and masks.

Toward the end of his life, Byron vacillated between aiding the South American and Greek anti-colonial resistance movements and contemplated moving to Venezuela, Miranda's homeland, with his daughter Allegra; ultimately, he chose the latter and died there as a hero of the Greek people. This final act was perhaps the most romantic event in Byron's life, sealing his place in history through his effort to both author and experience a distinctive form of romance in accordance with his own conception of heroism. For a world in which chivalry seemed untenable, he offered possibilities for what modern knighthood could look like.

Notes

1 Clara Reeve, *The Progress of Romance* (Colchester: W. Keymer, 1785), 1, 19.
2 James Beattie, *The Minstrel: Or, the Progress of Genius. A Poem. The Second Book* (London: Edward & Charles Dilly; Edinburgh: William Creech, 1774), 29.

3 Alison Lumsden and Ainsley McIntosh, "The Narrative Poems," in Fiona Robertson (ed.), *The Edinburgh Companion to Sir Walter Scott* (Edinburgh: Edinburgh University Press, 2012), 42.
4 David Duff, *Romance and Revolution: Shelley and the Politics of a Genre* (Cambridge, UK: Cambridge University Press, 1994), 124.
5 Harold Bloom, "The Internalization of Quest Romance," in *The Ringers in the Tower: Studies in Romantic Tradition* (Chicago: University of Chicago Press, 1971).
6 Duff, *Romance and Revolution*, 124.
7 Omar F. Miranda, "The Celebrity of Exilic Romance: Francisco de Miranda and Lord Byron," *European Romantic Review* 27 (2016), 207–31.

CHAPTER 20

Byron's Lyric Practice

Anna Camilleri

Byron's lyrics remain largely neglected by modern scholarship. The critical attention granted to them is commensurate with the room they take up on the page: a handful of essays and the odd book chapter are all that exists on the poet's engagement with the form. As James Soderholm quips, Byron's lyrics are "more unheard-of than overheard."[1] Yet lyric composition is of great importance not only for Byron's early poetic development, but for his whole creative life. It is the genre he returns to most consistently throughout his career. All four of his juvenilia collections – with the exception of various translations from Greek and Latin epic – consist exclusively of lyric poetry, while his final writings from Greece in 1824, including "On this day I complete my thirty sixth year," "A Song for the Suliotes" and "Love and Death," are all lyric poems. Why, given Byron's evident interest in the genre, are the lyrics overlooked? The answer is in part found in their contemporary reception: they sold less well than Byron's blockbuster narrative poems. Perhaps his best-known lyric collection, *Hebrew Melodies* (1815), had sold just 6,000 copies by 1819, compared with 20,000 copies of the first two cantos of *Childe Harold's Pilgrimage* (1812) and 25,000 copies of *The Corsair* (1814). Just as significant a factor is the ongoing legacy of M. H. Abrams' essay on what he terms "the greater Romantic lyric."[2] Although he does not claim that the greater Romantic lyric is the *only* lyric mode of the Romantic period, Abrams does contend that it stands as the period's one lyric innovation. Subsequently, despite his insistence to the contrary, it is difficult to avoid the insinuation that "greater" implies "a higher achievement than other Romantic lyrics."[3] With this in mind, Abrams' claim that "Only Byron, among the major poets, did not write in this mode at all,"[4] sounds rather a lot like "only Byron did not contribute to lyric innovation in the period."

As might be expected, the few who have written on Byron's lyrics have leapt to the poet's defense, the most popular apology being on the level of voice. Byron's lyric voice is performative, insincere, insouciant and playful.

Abrams' greater Romantic lyric (and lyric more generally) demands the exact opposite from the speaker. Another, perhaps more obvious, disqualifying factor is that of length. All the examples Abrams cites are substantial blank verse poems, for instance, Wordsworth's 160-line lyric meditation, "Lines Written a Few Miles Above Tintern Abbey." However, Byron's lyrics tend to be short. The shortest of his *Hebrew Melodies* is the eight-line "Sun of the Sleepless," and while at forty-eight lines, the longest poem in the collection, "The Vision of Belshazzar," can hardly be deemed short, it gives the impression of lyric economy, being arranged in six octave stanzas of iambic trimeter, which makes the poem appear rather more compact than a poem of equivalent length in blank verse. By the same token, meter reveals a third structural disqualifier from Abrams' definition of the greater Romantic lyric. Few of Byron's lyrics are in the more substantial iambic pentameter line of Keats' Odes or Coleridge's conversation poems, and none are in blank verse – a form we now associate with the solemnity of Wordsworthian introspection.

In style too, Byron's lyrics are rather different in character to Coleridge's, Wordsworth's or Keats'. While there *are* examples of loco-descriptive lyric meditation to be found embedded in *Childe Harold* (particularly Canto III), his autonomous lyrics more usually dwell on the traditional lyric subject of love or the less conventional lyric subjects of war and religion. The contents of his two lyric collections, *Hebrew Melodies* (1815) and the unassumingly titled *Poems* (1816), address either one of these subjects, while some, such as "Jeptha's Daughter," approach all three. These two collections reveal another feature of Byron's lyrics: they frequently resonate with tragic inflection. His love lyrics tend to be poems of separation, for instance, "I Speak Not – I Trace Not – I Breathe Not" (*Hebrew Melodies*), "When We Two Parted" (*Poems*), or "So, We'll Go No More a Roving" (1817). Meanwhile his warfare lyrics are either concerned with the demise of military heroes, as we find in "Saul" and its partner poem "The Song of Saul," or whole armies, as with the "Destruction of Sennacherib" (all in *Hebrew Melodies*).

Such striking differences between Byron's lyric practice and dominant classification of Romantic lyric reveal divergent models of literary influence. The greater Romantic lyric evolves from loco-descriptive meditative poems of the eighteenth century, Thomas Gray's *Ode on a Distant Prospect of Eton College* (1747) and William Lisle Bowles' *Sonnets* (1789) in particular. Its roots, however, are according to Abrams to be found in the mid-seventeenth-century topographical compositions of John Denham, for instance *Cooper's Hill* (1642), and devotional landscape poetry of Henry Vaughan, in particular *The Waterfall* (1655). Byron's lyrics are evidently written from a different lyric prospect. In terms of subject matter, Byron's lyrics are not so much *neoclassical* as *classical*, with his heart-wrenching poems of separation recalling the lovesick Sappho, while his military songs recall the soldierly compositions of the other lyric poet of Lesbos, Alcaeus. When Byron does look to eighteenth-century lyric, he appears less invested in the neoclassical tradition, being more closely aligned with the sentimental turn of the same period. Jerome McGann has persuasively argued that Byron's lyric mode looks back to Laurence Sterne and the Della Cruscans, along with the spontaneous artifice of other "proto-Baudelaireans."[5] Without wishing to downplay the evident importance of these eighteenth-century models for Byron's lyric practice, there are two major figures who stand somewhat closer to home: the Celtic songsters Thomas Moore and Robert Burns.

Byron produced fewer songs than Moore or Burns, yet he was equally insistent upon the idea of lyric as *song* or with the potential to be sung. Moore's songs, in particular, are evidently of great importance to Byron's creative development and Byron professes as much in a letter to the older poet: "I believe all the mischief I have ever done, or sung, has been owing to that confounded book of yours [*The Poetical Works of the Late Thomas Little* (1801)]" (*BLJ* 7: 117). Byron's lyric indebtedness to Moore is most clearly seen in the compositional circumstances surrounding *Hebrew Melodies*. Following the success of Moore's *Irish Melodies* (1815), the composer for that volume, Isaac Nathan, was keen to employ Byron's poetic talents for a volume of traditional Jewish songs. A handful of these lyrics, including "She Walks in Beauty," "Sun of the Sleepless," "Francisca," and "It Is the Hour," were sent to Nathan for use in his collection without Byron having heard the music. Nathan's settings pleased Byron so much that the remaining lyrics were produced through close collaboration between composer and poet, Nathan writing in a letter that "[Byron] felt anxious to facilitate my views in preserving as much as possible the original airs, for which purpose he would frequently consult me regarding the style and metre of his stanzas."[6] The resulting poems were, despite Byron's protestations, initially published without the music. How great a loss this was remains a matter of opinion, though Moore is uncompromising in his verdict, as he writes to his publisher: "Was there ever anything as bad as the Hebrew Melodies? Some of the words are of course good, tho' not so good as might have been expected – but the Music! 'Oh Lord God of Israel!' what stuff it is!"[7]

As with Moore, Byron's lyrical connection to Burns is through a shared interest in popular forms, which the drawing-room quality (and setting)

of many of Byron's lyrics belies. Byron's interest in Scots songs in particular can be observed in his secular love lyrics. For example, the source of
"So, We'll Go No More a Roving" is eighteenth-century Scots, the titular
refrain closely following the chorus of *The Jolly Beggar*, included in David
Herd's *Ancient and Modern Scottish Songs* (1776):

> And we'll gang nae mair a roving
> Sae late into the nicht;
> And we'll gang nae mair a roving,
> Let the moon shine near sae bricht.

Burns' own version of the song, "There Was a Lad," which revolves around
the erotic escapades of Burns himself, picks up on the association of sexual
adventurousness in the word "roving" in the refrain: "Robin was a rovin'
Boy, / Rantin' rovin', rantin' rovin.'"[8] Yet whereas Burns' poem thrives
on incorrigible laddishness, in Byron's version we get something rather
different:

> So, we'll go no more a roving
>   So late into the night,
> Though the heart be still as loving,
>   And the moon be still as bright.
>
> For the sword outwears its sheath,
>   And the soul wears out the breast,
> And the heart must pause to breathe,
>   And love itself have rest.
>
> Though the night was made for loving,
>   And the day returns too soon,
> Yet we'll go no more a roving
>   By the light of the moon.
>   (["So, We'll Go No More a Roving"]
>   ll. 1–12 [*CPW* iv: 109–10])

While Burns' Robin's rovin' is relentless and unstoppable, so integral to
his identity that it has become his epithet, Byron's use of *roving* suggests at
once the permanency of the act through the hallmarks of lyric commemoration – rhythm and rhyme – while simultaneously enacting a process of
erasure in "outwears" and "wears out." This uneasy negotiation between
permanence and transience is played out in both the subtle switching of
tense between past and present ("night was," "day returns"), and the repetition of the opening as closure in the final line of the poem. The very syntax
of the lyric's title and refrain, "we'll go no more," refuses to be sequestered
in the past, instead existing as a statement of expired potentiality, and so

becomes a symptom of the speaker's reluctance to acknowledge the pastness of erotic love.

The contrast between Burns' joyous bawdiness and Byron's lovelorn melancholy is one that usefully distinguishes the two poets' lyric *oeuvre*. Burns is not averse to writing despondent love lyrics: "Ae fond kiss," for example, whose closing refrain, "Fare thee weel, thou first and fairest! / Fare thee weel, thou best and dearest!" prefigures the language, if not the sentiment, of Byron's own *Fare Thee Well!* Yet while Burns' lyric poems vacillate between joy and tears, Byron's own lyric outpourings are almost exclusively elegiac laments for loss of love, loss of life, or both in the case of the late homoerotic lyric "Love and Death" (1824). Such reluctant nostalgia characterizes not only his autonomous lyrics, but the lyric incursions of his narrative poems. The first such example of digressive lyric lamentation can be found early in the first canto of Byron's lengthy narrative poem, *Childe Harold's Pilgrimage* (1812–16), which was drafted by the end of March 1810. In the following stanzas, the wandering Childe is moved to music as the sun sets over the seascape, which he views from his vessel bound for distant shores:

> But when the sun was sinking in the sea
> He seiz'd his harp, which he at times could string,
> And strike, albeit with untaught melody,
> When deem'd he no strange ear was listening:
> And now his fingers o'er it he did fling,
> And tun'd his farewell in the dim twilight.
> While flew the vessel on her snowy wing,
> And fleeting shores receded from his sight,
> Thus to the elements he pour'd his last "Good night."
>
> I.
> Adieu, adieu! my native shore
>   Fades o'er the waters blue;
> The Night-winds sigh, the breakers roar,
>   And shrieks the wild seamew.
> Yon Sun that sets upon the sea
>   We follow in his flight;
> Farewell awhile to him and thee,
>   My native Land – Good Night!
>
> (*CHP* i, st. 13, ll. 109–25 [*CPW* ii: 12–13])

The first of these three stanzas offers a near-textbook example of a Spenserian stanza. Though the third line demands the (rather clumsy) elision of "albeit" to ensure metrical cogency, the other eight lines provide rigorous decasyllabic consistency. The concluding alexandrine makes use

of trochaic inversion in the first foot to amplify the anticipated retard-
ation of the impulsive pentameter line, famously observed by Pope in his
Essay on Criticism (1711): "A needless alexandrine ends the song / That like
a wounded snake, drags its slow length along" (ll. 355–6). Shifting from
the newly adopted Spenserian stanza, Byron returns to the lyric forms
of his youth. This shift in generic gear is marked in two ways: first by a
change in narrative voice, the third-person narrative voice giving way to
the lyrical first person; second, and more strikingly, by a shift from the
iambic pentameter lines of the Spenserian stanza to the ballad form, its
alternating iambic tetrameter and trimeter lines appearing truncated in
contrast to the leggy alexandrine with which the Spenserian stanza closes.
These shortened lines create at once a visual differential, and an acoustic
one, with an escalated frequency of rhymes, i.e. every third or fourth foot
as opposed to every fifth or sixth.

In both *Childe Harold* and *Don Juan*, lyric interludes appear to be
deployed to complicate the boundary between the impartial epic narrator
and the subject of the poem: the hero. In the example cited above, this
behavioral shift – from the protagonist who undertakes epic action to the
poet he who sings about it – is accompanied by a shift in form. Later in
the poem, however, we can observe such radical shifts in voice and tone
within the boundaries of one stanza. The most overt example of this is the
opening stanza of the third canto, written while Byron was crossing the
channel in late April 1816, and finished in July the same year. The stanza
shares in the mood of the separation lyrics that Byron wrote throughout
1816 and 1817:

> Is thy face like thy mother's, my fair child!
> Ada! sole daughter of my house and heart?
> When last I saw thy young blue eyes they smiled,
> And then we parted, – not as now we part,
> But with a hope. –
>   Awaking with a start,
> The waters heave around me; and on high
> The winds lift up their voices: I depart,
> Whither I know not; but the hour's gone by,
> When Albion's lessening shores could grieve or glad mine eye.
>   (*CHP* iii, st. 1, ll. 1–9 [*CPW* ii: 76–7])

The apostrophic address of the opening lines of the above stanza retard
the progress of the poem's narrative, being, as Culler observes, resistant to
narrative progression: "Apostrophe resists narrative because its *now* is not a
moment in a temporal sequence but a *now* of discourse, of writing."[9] This

stanza offers a clear exemplification of the interruptive, digressive quality of lyric, which applies the breaks to overarching narrative impulse, in part because the lyric mode is one of static reflection. We might consider Wordsworth's "Elegiac Verses ['I only looked for pain and grief']": "Here did we stop, and here looked round/ While each into himself descends" (ll. 41–2). Byron's stanza inverts this Wordsworthian lyric manoeuvre by veering abruptly away from a descent into himself towards narrative action.

Writing a little later in the nineteenth century, John Stuart Mill contends that it is the quality of the "*over*heard" that distinguishes poetry from other kinds of formal speech.[10] The impression of being overheard is particularly significant for lyric address, as the above stanza exemplifies with the marked shift between private lyric and public narration. This embedded interaction between lyric reflection and epic narration has been deployed since antiquity. Both Homer's *Iliad* (Book 9) and *Odyssey* (Books 9–12) offer instances of the lyric disruption of epic, where the hero sings in his own voice, i.e. diegetically, which, if we follow Plato's categorization of genres, is characteristic of dithyrambic or lyric poetry.[11] Byron's lyric interludes are therefore nothing new, yet they cannot be solely read in the context of classical epic. They also engage closely with contemporary ideas on generic mixing. Wordsworth's categorization of genres in his "Preface" to his 1815 collection offers a theorization of such generic hybridity in its categorization of the "composite orders" of poems such as Edward Young's *Night Thoughts* (1742) and William Cowper's *The Task* (1785), which combine the lyric, the loco-descriptive and the didactic.[12] In their mixed use of narration and reflection, comedy and tragedy, both *Childe Harold* and *Don Juan* can be read as composite poems. All this should not tend to the inevitable conclusion that Byron's lyric practice is to be regarded as merely a rehearsal for his later success with the narrative poems. As I have shown, lyric is a remarkably dominant mode throughout Byron's writings. That said, one of the benefits of a greater comprehension of Byron's lyric practice is that it enables more astute readings of the generic complexity of his longer poems, particularly *Don Juan*, which frequently sidesteps from comic narrative to lyric sincerity as part of the poem's satirical strategy.

NOTES

1 James Soderholm, "Byron's Ludic Lyrics," *Studies in English Literature, 1500–1900* 34.4 (Autumn 1994), 749.
2 M. H. Abrams, "Structure and Style in the Greater Romantic Lyric," in *The Correspondent Breeze: Essays on English Romanticism* (New York: W. W. Norton, 1984), 76–108.

3 Ibid., 77.

4 Ibid., 76.

5 Jerome McGann, "Byron and the Lyric of Sensibility," *European Romantic Review* 4.1 (1993), 73. McGann also suggests the lyric pose of Charlotte Smith as an influence, see 77.

6 Isaac Nathan, *Fugitive Pieces and Reminiscences of Lord Byron* (London: Whittaker, Treacher & Co., 1829), 51.

7 Cited in Thomas Ashton, *Byron's Hebrew Melodies* (London: Routledge & Kegan Paul, 1972), 47. A twentieth-century recording of these melodies can be found on the Romantic Era Songs website, edited by Frederick Burwick and Paul Douglass, www.sjsu.edu/faculty/douglass/music/album-hebrew.html.

8 Robert Burns, "A Fragment [There Was a Lad]," in Robert Crawford and Christopher MacLaughlan (eds.), *The Best Laid Schemes: Selected Poetry and Prose of Robert Burns* (Princeton: Princeton University Press, 2009), 115.

9 Jonathan Culler, "Apostrophe," in *The Pursuit of Signs* (Abingdon, UK: Routledge, 2001), 149–71, 168.

10 John Stuart Mill, "What Is Poetry?" (1833), in *Collected Works of John Stuart Mill*, eds. J. M. Robson *et al.*, 33 vols. (1963–91); repr. London: Routledge & Kegan Paul, 1996), vol. 1, 348.

11 Plato, *Republic*, trans. Paul Shorey, in Edith Hamilton and Huntington Cairns (eds.), *Plato: The Collected Dialogues*, *Bollingen Series LXXI* (Princeton: Princeton University Press, 1961; repr. 2002), III.394^c, 639.

12 William Wordsworth, *The Major Works* (Oxford: Oxford University Press, 2000), 628.

CHAPTER 21

Satire

Mark Canuel

In *Natural Supernaturalism*, M. H. Abrams explains that he does not include a discussion of Lord Byron in his celebrated and influential book on the secular visionaries of the Romantic age because Byron's greatest work "speaks with an ironic counter-voice and deliberately opens a satiric perspective on the vatic stance of his contemporaries."[1] Recent criticism on the Romantic period complicates this view in two ways. First, the "satiric perspective" that Abrams deemed marginal to the Romantic age is now seen as central to Romantic literary culture, thanks to more inclusive studies of authors of the period. Second, Byron's ironization of his contemporaries' pieties is now appreciated as a particularly astute approach to the linguistic and political structures of his day. Rather than accept the ideas or categories of the Romantic imagination and literary integrity on its own "vatic" terms, critics from Jerome J. McGann to Susan Wolfson turn to Byron as a congenial exponent of the instability and fragility of Romantic selfhood and imagination. In this chapter, I take that argument a step further. Byron, I suggest, does not simply overturn the literary codes of his day. His satirical stance criticizes the production of normative aesthetic and political values while carving out an inclusive yet rigorously refined discourse that connects the satiric persona to his audience.

Byron's satire is fully aware of both its ancient and modern models, and (still more important) of satire's dependence on models in general. Satire, after all, is a form of pedagogy, offering laudable precepts and examples. The neoclassical writers whom Byron so admired insist that (in Alexander Pope's words) to "copy Nature" is to copy ancient models; Horace's gentle wit and Juvenal's righteous outrage exert a powerful influence on writers of the Augustan age, who craft their works as self-conscious imitations of them. Pope's Horatian Epistles and Swift's adaptations of Juvenal's Sixth Satire in his "Dressing Room" poems are two instances among many. Byron, in turn, has much to say in praise of classical satirists and their neoclassical admirers; although some critics today debate whether Horatian or

Juvenalian tradition is most visible in his work, it is more illuminating to see how he adapted both simultaneously for his own purposes.

Whether gently chiding the addressee and reader or overtly attacking them, classical writers and their later admirers demonstrate a long-standing truth about the genre of satire. By "diminishing" and "derogating" a subject, Abrams and Geoffrey Harpham point out, satire renders it ridiculous; its purpose is to "correct human vice and folly" by exhorting readers to adopt new actions or beliefs.[2] In order to make a satire work, the satirist must accept and enforce a legitimate point of view: satire engages in moral, political and aesthetic policing.

This begins to explain satire's continued prominence in the Romantic age. In the wake of the French Revolution, political, religious and aesthetic conventions were opened for outraged rebuttal or anxious defense. Radical satirists like Thomas Wooler and John Wolcot criticized court and party interests, while George Canning and Richard Polwhele lampooned radicals, feminists, atheists and religious dissenters. As Gary Dyer shows in his study of Romantic satire, both liberals and conservatives relied on the genre as a way of enforcing "pose[s] of orthodoxy" and tactics of intimidation.[3] The fact that radical satire risked charges of blasphemous or seditious libel chilled satirical expression without entirely silencing it.

Combining Juvenalian invective with Horatian wit, Byron's early forays into verse satire are overtly positioned as classical imitations; he pays homage to Roman satirists and English Augustans while openly acknowledging contemporary friends and foes. *English Bards and Scotch Reviewers*, published anonymously, writes defensively against criticism of Byron's first book of poems, *Hours of Idleness*. He also satirizes contemporary poetry, drama and popular taste. English audiences and critics display their lack of "taste and reason" by preferring "feebler Bards" to "Pope's pure strain" (*CPW* 1: 232–3, ll. 120, 118, 109).

In aesthetic preference and poetic style, Byron is also influenced by his contemporary William Gifford, whose *Baviad* (1791) and *Maeviad* (1795) rage against the shallow and oversentimental style of his competitors – particularly dramatists and Della Cruscan poets, from Hester Lynch Piozzi to Richard Brinsley Sheridan. Byron differs in remarkable ways from Gifford, however: he expands the objects of satiric attack while shrinking the number of available imitable models.

Indeed, the dynamics of blame and praise in *English Bards* lead to a considerable degree of complexity. On the one hand, Byron asserts fidelity to one lineage of poetry rather than another. Specifically, *English Bards* is written against current "wonders" in poetry (*CPW* 1: 233, l. 131) by poets like Robert Southey and Walter Scott. These leaders of "new schools" are merely "dull pretenders" for the "prize" of poetic fame (*CPW* I: 233, l. 136). Spurious arbiters of taste such as George Lambe and Francis Jeffrey are bold "tyrants" who lack learning or wit (*CPW* I: 231, l. 84). On the other hand, the preference for the line of poets including Milton, Dryden and Pope is clearly an artful, contentious pose that does not settle into a confident defense of traditional models (as it appears to do in Gifford). Byron's stance separates him from others; he derides not merely a particular group but a vast swath of his contemporaries. The fundamental paradox that emerges is that the "new" poets of the age are also old and tiresome. Scott foists his "stale romance" on a tired public (*CPW* I: 234, l. 172); Southey (later travestied in *The Vision of Judgment*) proves that "a bard may chaunt too often, and too long" (*CPW* I: 236, l. 226). Still others are condemned in this vein, from Wordsworth, Southey's "dull disciple," to the Bard of Sheffield (James Montgomery), whose poetry has fallen into an "early sleep" (*CPW* I: 236, l. 235; 242, l. 425).

Byron does praise some contemporaries: Gifford, Thomas Campbell, Samuel Rogers and Henry Kirk-White especially stand out. Even so, the praise is scant. *Juan* says that "Campbell's Hippocrene is somewhat drouthy," and Byron faults Campbell in the note for inaccuracy in his criticism (*CPW* v: 75, l. 1638). *English Bards* is still more underhanded: Kirk-White is praised elegiacally, admired because he is dead. Campbell and Rogers are urged to "rise" and "give ... scope" to their talents, as if they were not yet capable of providing the guidance that they appear to offer (*CPW* v: 254, ll. 801, 803). A similar sentiment is applied to Gifford; although he was alive and well when Byron was writing the poem (and Byron knew his 1800 translation of Juvenal), he is treated as voiceless.

Byron's appeal to the past, then, asserts his own aesthetic novelty and exceptionalism: he sets himself apart from his contemporaries in order to be new by being old. This point is repeated in the critique of novelty in *Hints from Horace*, the posthumously published sequel to *English Bards*. The politics associated with Byron's poetic lineage are worth some commentary here. James Chandler analyzes the contribution of poets from Wharton to Byron (and beyond) in the process of canon formation in the late eighteenth and early nineteenth centuries; Pope and his supporters became a popular target for those (like William Lisle Bowles) who wished to assert a distinctively nationalistic English canon against the classicizing (and thus Francophilic, anti-nativist) values of Pope. Byron attacks his contemporaries not only as degenerate or backward, but also as creatures of confined localities and limited perspectives. This limitation is a recurrent theme. *The*

Curse of Minerva depicts Lord Elgin as a lowbrow "plunderer" motivated by greed and self-interest (*CPW* I: 324, l. 128); in the *Vision*, Southey is a pathetic sycophant unceremoniously kicked away from the gates of heaven by St. Peter, tumbling to earth "into his lake" (*CPW* v: 344–5, ll. 827–9). And the "Dedication" to *Don Juan* declares that the "narrowness" of the Lake poets "makes me wish you'd change your lakes for ocean" (*CPW* v: 4, l. 40). Against the localizing bent of so many of his poetic and political contemporaries, Byron's satirical wit places the highest value on a more cosmopolitan or internationalist ethos and poetic style.

The aesthetic exceptionalism and political cosmopolitanism interrelated in Byron's early satire in turn inform the comic style of Byron's later works *Beppo* and *Don Juan*. As we have already seen, the poetic satires are not merely written against one camp in order to uphold another; they ridicule or demean nearly every extant poetic style. Similarly, Byron's later works, where the satire is more explicitly political, do not merely oppose one party in order to uphold another but oppose political, financial and religious interest in general. A comparison with Pope is instructive. Pope had few qualms about making his Tory political allegiances clear; he praises Queen Anne and attacks Whig adversaries such as Mary Wortley Montagu and Lord Hervey. Byron's multiple satiric barbs, in contrast, not only reflect but also construct a position of exile, opposition and detachment.

Beppo is a perfect example of this perspective, combining both direct and indirect satire. It is a brisk narrative in *ottava rima*, related by a speaker who is of English origin, living in Venice, but in a larger sense a citizen of the world. The poem tells the tale of a Venetian trader and his beautiful wife Laura. During one of his voyages, Beppo disappears and is captured and enslaved; he eventually joins a band of Turkish pirates. When Beppo returns from his adventures, his wife, who has taken a lover, gently chastises him, but he "reclaim[s] / His wife, religion, house, and Christian name" (*CPW* IV: 159, l. 776). Much is made of Beppo's conversion – he had become a "Musselman" among the Turks – and he is rebaptized as a Christian when he returns to Venice. Issues of religion and conversion are broached only to question their authority, though, for the narrator adopts a flagrantly casual perspective on religion, morality and nationality. The claim that "I like all and every thing" is the necessary accompaniment to the narrator's other truth, which is that he satirizes all and everything – or close to it (*CPW* IV: 144, l. 384).

The religious context for the poem, the Venetian carnival preceding Lent, is a subject for sustained and subversive humor. The most notable feature of the Lenten season, for instance, is the prevalence of bad food: "ill-dressed fishes, / Because they have no sauces to their stews" (*CPW* IV: 144, ll. 51–2). English travelers are warned to bring their own condiments and sauces (*CPW* IV: 144, l. 63). When Byron reveals the entire edifice of Catholicism as shallow and hypocritical, his purpose is not to criticize one religion in particular but to see Catholicism as a metaphor for established religion in all "Christian countries," which hypocritically imposes sanctions on urgent human desires (*CPW* IV: 144, l. 186). Muslims are satirical targets as well, but the satire is complex precisely because the normative ground for the satire is far from obvious. A brilliant stanza on Muslim women's lack of learning at first seems like an instance of Islamophobia:

> No chemistry for them unfold her gasses,
>   No metaphysics are let loose in lectures,
> No circulating library amasses
>   Religious novels, moral tales, and strictures
> Upon the living manners, as they pass us;
>   No exhibition glares with annual pictures;
> They stare not on the stars from out their attics,
> Nor deal (thank God for that!) in mathematics.
>   (*Beppo* st. 78, ll. 617–24 [*CPW* IV: 153])

But what may begin as an account of the knowledge lacking among Muslim women is hilariously complicated, rather than contradicted, by the ambiguous value of Western knowledge, which seems as prejudicial and flawed as any organized religion. Even beliefs and practices that seem remote from religion are satirized as versions of it: the fashionable "world" is run by its own "demagogues," and liberal politics draws on "homil[ies]" for its authority (ll. 478, 544). The poem ends on a note that is playful rather than punitive: Beppo is reconciled to Laura and even becomes friends with her "Cavalier Servente," as if the values of religion's carnivalesque inversion were finally those of the speaker and the subjects of his story (l. 313). Even the sanctity of marriage is shown to be a false construction, which the characters overcome and the narrator celebrates.

The fact that *Beppo*'s hero and the narrator are self-consciously shaped as exiles reminds us that satire has much in common with the more melancholy subject matter of works that range from the "Oriental tales" to *Manfred*. Just as comedy can be inhabited by a feeling of melancholic abjection, *Childe Harold's Pilgrimage* contains moments of satire amid its more pervasive contemplative mood. The same can be said of *Manfred*;

although it is a tragedy, its ironic critique of religion, family and patriarchal authority links it with more obviously satirical writing.

This critical power of the outcast is of signal importance to the hero
and narrator of Byron's *Don Juan*, the poem that occupied Byron for the
remainder of his career. *Juan*, like *Beppo*, adopts the form of *ottava rima*, a
stanza (first used by Boccaccio) whose six lines of a–b rhymes and closing
couplet combined comic repetition with epigrammatic wit. Of course,
neither *Beppo* nor *Juan* is a satire: the first is a comic romance and the
second – unfinished at the author's death – is explicitly designated in the
poem as an "epic" or "Epic Satire" (*CPW* v: 73, l. 1593; 587, l. 790). But the
jovial narrator repeatedly directs his attention critically toward the follies
of his world.

Epic genre itself, or more precisely mock epic, is crucial to Byron's satirical point, since the poem – snatching its hero from the low culture of
popular myth and pantomime – mocks the dubious heroes of his own day.
Political leaders from the conservatives Wellington and Castlereagh to the
liberals Romilly and Wilberforce are viewed with ridicule; the urgent political issues that absorb such so-called heroes – including the national debt,
continental warfare and slavery – are also wittily diminished, as if studied
positions on them were mere metaphysical posturing.

The digressive method of *Don Juan* permits the satire to diversify in
scope, directly or indirectly criticizing literature, modern science, philosophy, education and gender relations (among other things). The poem
continues Byron's literary satire, with the Lake Poets and the Bluestockings
among his favorite targets, and with Donna Inez in Canto i, he finds an
ingenious way to satirize the influence of religion on conventional systems
of education. Pieties about conventional gender roles and marriage are
gleefully dismissed throughout the poem; the truths that matter are the
body's attractions and the heart's affections, not the sanctity of vows. It can
hardly surprise us that idealist philosophies also come under fire. Platonic
love, one of the most pernicious of them, is a lie: the "sway" that Plato's
"system" attempts to hold over the "controlless core / Of human hearts" is
only "fancied" rather than real (*CPW* v: 45, ll. 924–5).

The tolerant perspective on humanity developed in *Beppo* and *Don
Juan* is often complicated by the problems that tend to haunt cosmopolitan discourse in our own day: in its effort to rise above local beliefs and
prejudices, it can sometimes sound elitist. In *Beppo*, despite the speaker's
(and author's) cosmopolitan ideals, the narrator critiques fashion but is
also a man of fashion: he can criticize structures of dependency and conventional ways of "*the World*" precisely because his means of support allow

it (*CPW* IV: 147, l. 471). And while Byron is often regarded as a prophet of material existence, with a digressive style that favors the ebb and flow of bodily experience, this is only part of the picture. Byron's nobility is a particular configuration (propertied, titled) of material and immaterial advantages that inform the cosmopolitan values endorsed by his satire. This is not simply a biographical fact. Aristocratic status figures in Byron's understanding of his identity as a poet throughout his works; it inflects the formation of his satirical personae, from his easy and casual displays of classical learning to his voluminous knowledge of foreign locales and luxury goods.

Still more, the multi-directional quality of Byron's mature satire – while it certainly relies on the weight of bodily experience against religion, metaphysics and multiple forms of political hypocrisy and "cant" – insists on the legitimate value of specific kinds of perceived matter to inspire his verse. Classical satire often takes the form of a critique of taste, and Byron follows in this tradition, in his appreciation not only of classical and neo-classical poetic forms, but also of bodies and practices that conform to that tradition. It is both comic and revealing that religion in *Beppo* is a problem of gustatory and aesthetic taste: the problem with Catholicism is bad food, and the problem with Muslim men (as Laura observes) is their strange clothes and long beards. The "Italian beauty!" praised by *Beppo's* narrator, in contrast, is a classical beauty that "inspire[d] / Raphael" (*CPW* IV: 143, ll. 362–3). This tradition of beauty links the ancient to the modern world: the greatest beauty of all is one who can show her "bloom" through the length of an entire ball (*CPW* IV: 143, l. 661). Ideal beauty in Byron is primarily fair skin, not too "pale," that sets off the mesmerizing attractions of eyes, lips and hair (*CPW* IV: 143, l. 656).

Don Juan raises aesthetic discrimination and "refinement" to an even more intense and consistent level of expression. The beauty that the poem's narrator observes in the world is Western, white and appreciated by a taste cultivated by a classical tradition: the beautiful bodies in *Juan* are "fair" and "smooth" and even likened to "alabaster" vases (*CPW* V: 394, l. 768). Byron's satire may be materialist, but matter becomes poetically mean-ingful when it is formed according to specific norms of beauty. Beauty has a moral and political meaning, too: implicitly rebutting Immanuel Kant's aesthetic formalism, *Juan* demonstrates how our actions in the world are motivated by attractions to beautiful things and people.

To make this point is not to criticize Byron for leaving a significant region of prejudice free from satire. It is rather to account for his explor-ation of satire's extent and limits. Having dispensed with the idea that satire embraces normative models for action, thought and representation in his early satires, Byron's later works nevertheless seek out the normative ground from which its iconoclastic satire can be aesthetically appreciated.

NOTES

1 M. H. Abrams, *Natural Supernaturalism: Tradition and Revolution in Romantic Literature* (New York: W. W. Norton, 1971), 13.
2 M. H. Abrams and Geoffrey Galt Harpham, "Satire," in *A Glossary of Literary Terms*, 9th ed. (Boston: Wadsworth Cengage Learning, 2009).
3 Gary Dyer, *British Satire and the Politics of Style, 1789–1832* (Cambridge, UK: Cambridge University Press, 1997), 30.

CHAPTER 22

The Satanic School

Mirka Horová

I am *Le Diable Boiteux* – a soubriquet, which I marvel that, amongst
their various *nominis umbrae*, the Orthodox have not hit upon.

(*BLJ* 10: 136)

The so-called Satanic school of poetry was a libel coined by the Poet
Laureate, Robert Southey, in the preface to his panegyric on George III's
ascension into heaven, *A Vision of Judgement* (1821). Its history is well
known, but its prodigious derogatory range less so. In part III, Southey
sets out to chastise readers, authors and critics alike for their perpetuation
of the "monstrous combinations of horrors and mockery, lewdness and
impiety with which English poetry has … been polluted," "intended as
furniture for the brothel" (Southey x: 203). With the causticity of a manic
street preacher, Southey deplores

> Men of diseased hearts and depraved imaginations, who, forming a system
> of opinions to suit their own unhappy course of conduct, have rebelled
> against the holiest ordinances of human society, and … labour to make
> others as miserable as themselves, by infecting them with a virus that eats
> into the soul! *The school which they have set up may properly be called the
> Satanic school*; for though their productions breathe the spirit of Belial in
> their lascivious parts, and the spirit of Moloch in those loathsome images
> of atrocities and horrors which they delight to represent, *they are more espe-
> cially characterised by a Satanic spirit of pride and audacious impiety, which
> still betrays the wretched feeling of hopelessness wherewith it is allied.* This evil
> is political as well as moral, for indeed moral and political evils are insep-
> arably connected. (Preface to *A Vision of Judgement* [Southey x: 205–6];
> my emphasis)

Decrying the "evil of this magnitude" where "the celebrity of an offender
serves as a privilege" (a thinly disguised attack on Byron; the gloves came
off in the ensuing letters to the press), Southey implicates "every person …
who purchases such books, or admits them into his house, promotes the
mischief and thereby … becomes an aider and abettor of the crime." He

deemed the "publication of a lascivious book" "one of the worst offences that can be committed against the well-being of society" (Southey x: 204). For Southey, then, the "Satanic" denotes a truly biblical scourge of anarchic personal tendencies that have the potential not only to "poison the waters of literature," but also to imperil "the well-being of society," thereby jeopardizing "the government." Indeed, he calls on "the rulers of the state" and "every one, whose opinion may have any influence" to "look to this, in time," and "to expose ... those writers" (Southey x: 206–7), warning that a collateral corrosive impact of the "Satanic" might indeed be imminent. This public denunciation remains one of the turncoat ironies marking Southey's life. In his liberal youth, he and Coleridge had penned the political satire "The Devil's Thoughts" and published it anonymously in the *Morning Post and Gazetteer* of September 1799.

Advocating his new-fangled "English hexameter," Southey's "'I first adventure, follow me who list!'" (Southey x: 202) quotes Joseph Hall's *Virgidemiarum* (1597–1602), which rhymes that line with: "And be the second English satirist." Southey, who had the good sense to anticipate a backlash against his "metrical innovation" (Southey x: 207), inadvertently set in motion a true "Harvest of Blows" (the subtitle of Hall's six-part satirical opus) that would entertain the literary scene for a considerable time and shape the legacy of both the Laureate and his rival. Southey's *Vision* became chiefly famous for "its accidental inspiration for one of the most concise and hilarious satires in English letters, Byron's *The Vision of Judgment*."[1] This ingenious refutation aside, the "Satanic school" proved a catchy, even "meritorious" critical term that continued to haunt Byron and erupted into orthodox outrage at the publication of *Cain* – "a most legitimate offspring of the Satanic School."[2]

There was nevertheless sympathy for the devil on the other side of the poetic–political spectrum. If the "Satanic" for Southey denotes moral perjury, inveterate corruption and profanity charged with political threat, for the poets implicated in this so-called "school" and their revolutionary predecessors such as William Blake, the term stands for a set of rather formidable traits – courage, dissent and an unassailable ethos of freedom, from Whig libertinism to radical freethinking; and it is precisely this "complexity, contradiction, and mobility" that was "feared by conservatives and orthodox believers."[3] Blake, and later Shelley and Byron, sought to recast and reposition the Satanic within the power narrative of the politics of paradise, introducing for the first time the potential "interchangeability" of "God" and "Devil" in terms of "evil."[4] In a letter to Hodgson discussing the ethics of tragedy, Byron answers the rhetorical question "Who is the hero of *Paradise Lost?*"⁵ symptomatically: "Why Satan" (*BLJ* 8: 115); in *Cain*, his Lucifer famously proclaims: "Evil and good are things in their own essence, / And not made good or evil by the giver" (*CPW* VI: 274, ll. 452–3). In his essay "On the Devil, and Devils," Shelley goes as far as seeing the "Omnipotent" as a tyrant responsible for Satan's transformation into a merciless, soul-hunting monster.

The paradigmatic revaluation of Milton's Satan as the hero of *Paradise Lost* (first advocated by Blake) gave rise, inter alia, to Gothic villains such as Radcliffe's Montoni and Schedoni, or indeed Lewis' Ambrosio, while also engendering Coleridge's critique of the Satanic leader whose definition fits the characters above rather organically: a predatory figure marked by "pride and sensual indulgence, finding in self the sole motive for action," replete with "restlessness, temerity and cunning."⁶ Finding perhaps its most lasting and influential permutation in the Byronic hero's bespoke sublime, the Satanic line reaches far and wide, from Pushkin and Lermontov to the Brontës, from the *poètes maudits* to the Beatniks and beyond.

Even this swift survey betrays the moral interpretive dichotomy of the Satanic. The Gothic villains are seductive yet irredeemably perverse, while Blake's take is poised between the warring principles of structure and chaos on a mythical scale, and Coleridge's reflections explore the political implications of "good" and "evil." For Shelley, Satan is both an aesthetic and political ideal and a problem: some tempering appears in the preface to *Prometheus Unbound* (1820), where he favors the titan, because the "character of Satan engenders in the mind a pernicious casuistry which leads us to weigh his faults with his wrongs, and to excuse the former because the latter exceed all measure."⁷ Later, however, "[n]othing can exceed the energy and magnificence of the character of Satan as expressed in *Paradise Lost*"; Shelley sees Satan as the model of a dissenting revolutionary and posits that "Milton … alleged no superiority of moral virtue to his God over his Devil," which he sees as "the most decisive proof" of his "genius."⁸ Shelley's radicalism is well attested here, and he shares with Byron the ambition "to dismantle Satanic myth and remake it into an instrument of controversial writing."⁹

The paternal path from Milton's Satan to Byron's heroes is well trodden. "Byron's significance" lies not in "authoring the Satanic myth or embodying it," however, but rather in "ingeniously adapting what many Romantics celebrated as Milton's heroic republican conception of Satan" into "a potent figure for cultural mediation and figuration itself."¹⁰ If Byron's "Satanic heroes, all 'errant on dark ways diverse,' are properly self-destroyed," and the Byronic hero tales are "records of guilt and suffering," they are also "actively intellectual works, whereas *The Monk* and *The Italian* ... rein in their questionings and set the reader's consciousness at rest."[11]

Across Byron's works, we can trace a unique evolution of scripting the Satanic: from the soul-capturing spirituality of *Manfred*, the cosmic casuistry of *Cain*, the doom-prophesying Satanic chorus in *Heaven and Earth*, to bureaucratic tedium in *The Vision of Judgment* and anarchic boredom in *The Deformed Transformed*. "In *Manfred* Byron presents his hero's refusal to be swayed, either by threats of damnation or promises of salvation," and "repentance is another form of the apostasy and time-serving";[12] for some, this Satanism "seems privately motivated, embodying the 'war with the world' [Byron] felt began when he left England in 1816."[13] If, for *Manfred*, the Satanic models were Milton and Faust (the mind its own place, the tree of knowledge not that of life), in *Cain*'s defiant Byronic bravado we can trace the "temerity" and "perniciousness" of the Satanic model that Coleridge and Shelley came to criticize. However, Byron's *coup de théâtre* at the end of the biblical drama – an interpolation of God's own lines in Cain's "That which I am, I am" (*CPW* VI: 293, l. 509; Exodus 3:14 "I am that I am") – testifies to Byron's lasting, keen, indeed "stern" and "stubborn" (*CPW* VI: 293, l. 503) interest in the Satanic as a purely intellectual ethos. Equally, "intellectual life ... is a perpetual *agon*, and Byron's Satan, at the end of Act II of *Cain*, gives the most complete expression to Byron's conception of a 'spiritual' or 'intellectual existence' – in praise of 'reason' as the 'one good gift.' "[14] For some readers of *Cain*, the "truly Satanic is the unresolved tension" "between God and Devil" – "[t]rue evil lies in the opposition of the two psychic principles, true good in their reconciliation."[15] Perhaps. What remains clear is that Byron's Lucifer sets up a false dichotomy: love or knowledge, happiness or freedom. The only possible paradise is "a Paradise of Ignorance!" (*CPW* VI: 262, l. 101), as Lucifer tells Cain. This paradigm pervades Byron's *oeuvre*, advocated by the Satanic: knowledge equals strife/war, only ignorance allows peace. The Satanic stands for "stern" and "stubborn," but also loyal and heroic – intellectual, agonistic. It excludes empathy while increasingly heralding sympathy, ultimately replacing both with a discourse epitomizing memory and power – Lucifer to Cain, the Satanic Spirits to Japhet in *Heaven and Earth*, various supernatural entities to Manfred. The agents of "the dark side" in *Manfred*, *Cain*, *Heaven and Earth* and *The Deformed Transformed* have one common denominator – keen sense and performance of agonism.

Byron's Satanism is replete with *agon*, combining the quest for meaning with an increasing threat of eternal boredom. We can discern a marked shift from the agonistic ontology of *Manfred* and *Cain*, where the Satanic both imbues and seeks to subdue the protagonist, to profound Satanic boredom, tackling eternity by meddling with God's creatures for a feeble pastime.

While critics have remarked that life in Milton's Paradise would be boring – most famously Tillyard, for whom Adam and Eve "are in the hopeless position of Old Age Pensioners enjoying perpetual youth"[16] – and Byron himself imaged, rather splendidly, a bored, bureaucratized Heaven in his *Vision of Judgment* – there is a line of purely Satanic boredom worth exploring. As C. S. Lewis remarks on Satan: "The Hell he carries with him is, in one sense, a Hell of infinite boredom."[17] "Boredom presupposes subjectivity, i.e. self-awareness ... To be able to be bored the subject must be able to perceive himself as an individual that can enter into various meaning contexts, and this subject demands meaning of the world and himself."[18] Byron's Lucifer holds an eternal existential grudge, and his essential agonism can also be interpreted as a desperate desire not to succumb to the boredom of immortality, a desperate desire to mean. This meaning can only be attained by extreme agonism, dissent by default. From Lucifer's intimations of "everlasting" existence (*CPW* VI: 236, l. 122), we may glean the cross-purposes of his discursive framing and the impulse to impress a mortal audience: "With us acts are exempt from time, and we / Can crowd eternity into an hour, / Or stretch an hour into eternity: / We breathe not by a mortal measurement – / But that's a mystery" (*CPW* VI: 250–1, ll. 535–9). Contrary to Blake's Zen agenda in *Auguries of Innocence* – to "Hold Infinity in the palm of your hand, / And Eternity in an hour" – Byron's theory of relativity tends toward auguries of *agon*- and angst-ridden experience. The "mystery" of the Satanic is intertwined with the exemption of "acts" from "time" here – and while there are consequences within God's narrative, Byron's Lucifer is loath to admit more than temporary defeat in what he sees as an eternal cosmic war between "the *two Principles!*" (*CPW* VI: 273, l. 404). The sole Satanic sympathy exists "in our conflict!" (*CPW* VI: 237, l. 146) and in "sorrow" (*CPW* VI: 235, l. 95).

This Satanic conflict is accompanied in Byron by the prevailing sense of meaninglessness: "Boredom masks uneasiness and intense boredom exhibits the signs of the most basic of modern anxieties, the anxiety of nothingness, or absence."[19] Playing on these "modern anxieties," and chan-neling history's perpetual proclivity to carnage, Byron's unfinished last drama, *The Deformed Transformed*, presents a distinctive departure from the intellectual gravity of Satanism. While agonism still reigns, it is now framed by the levity and *Schadenfreude* of *Don Juan* and Byron's letters:

> Well! I must play with these poor puppets: 'tis
> The spirit's pastime in his idler hours.
> When I grow weary of it, I have business
> Amongst the stars, which these poor creatures deem
> Were made for them to look at. 'Twere a jest now
> To bring one down amongst them, and set fire
> Unto their ant hill: how the pismires then
> Would scamper o'er the scalding soil, and, ceasing
> From tearing down each other's nests, pipe forth
> One universal orison! Ha! ha!
>   (*The Deformed Transformed*, Pt. 1, ll. 320–9 [*CPW* VI: 551])

As Schock notes, this "speech negates both of the Satanic roles already explored by Byron, the tempter and the Promethean mentor, substituting for them the leisurely play that staves off the boredom of an immortal."[20] The Stranger's / Caesar's *tour-de-force* view of civilization, by a devil-may-care, bored Satanic spectator, is Byron's ultimate addition to the "one page" of "History" (*CPW* II: 160, ll. 968–9). This shift, and the recurring ironies of Byron's biographical curse, are well reflected in Mary Shelley's letters to Byron: " 'The Eternal Scoffer' seems a favourite of yours. The Critics, as they used to make you Childe Harold, Giaour & Lara, all in one, will make a compound of Satan and Caesar to form your prototype"; she later adds that the drama "surpasses" "or at least fully equals" "[Byron's] former glorious style" (*LMWS* 289, 311). Byron's final Satanic note is, as ever, on the cusp of modernity.

Just over a hundred years later, the French theorist Roger Caillois summed up Romanticism's ramifications as follows:

> Romanticism ends in a theory of boredom, that characteristically modern sentiment; that is, it ends in a theory of power, or at least of energy … *Romanticism*, in effect, marks the recognition by the individual of a bundle of instincts which society has a strong interest in repressing; but, for the most part, it manifests the abdication of the struggle.[21]

Byron never belonged to any "school," but he was certainly part of a tradition, and a part of this tradition was the Romantic revaluation of the Satanic. Byron's Satanism ends in boredom, having begun as a great dramatic statement of imaginative power, transgression and creative comeback in *Manfred*. In between, there was an adventure to be had, and Byron had it. And in the end, Byron's idea of the Satanic, spanning from acute agonism to boredom, became yet another beacon of emergent modernity.

NOTES

1 Susan Wolfson, "*The Vision of Judgment* and the Visions of 'Author,'" in Drummond Bone (ed.), *The Cambridge Companion to Byron* (Cambridge, UK: Cambridge University Press, 2004), 171.

2 "*Sardanapalus, a Tragedy; The Two Foscari, a Tragedy; Cain, a Mystery.* By Lord Byron. 8vo. 439. London, 1821," in *European Magazine and London Review* 81 (January 1822), 64.

3 Clara Tuite, *Lord Byron and Scandalous Celebrity* (Cambridge, UK: Cambridge University Press, 2015), 233.

4 Jeffrey Burton Russell, "The Romantic Devil," in Harold Bloom (ed.), *Satan* (Philadelphia: Chelsea House, 2005), 164.

5 Joseph Hall, *Virgidemiarum* (London: Printed by John Harison, 1602), Prologue, 8.

6 "Lecture X: Donne, Dante, Milton, Paradise Lost," in T. Middleton Raysor (ed.), *Coleridge's Miscellaneous Criticism* (Cambridge, MA: Harvard University Press, 1936), 163.

7 T. Hutchinson (ed.), *The Complete Poetical Works of Percy Bysshe Shelley* (London: Oxford University Press, 1905), 205.

8 D. L. Clarke (ed.), *Shelley's Prose, or, the Trumpet of a Prophecy* (New York: New Amsterdam Books, 1988), 290.

9 Peter A. Schock, *Romantic Satanism: Myth and the Historical Moment in Blake, Shelley and Byron* (Basingstoke, UK: Palgrave, 2003), 87.

10 Tuite, *Scandalous Celebrity*, xx–xxi.

11 Jerome J. McGann, "Milton and Byron," in James Soderholm (ed.), *Byron and Romanticism* (Cambridge, UK: Cambridge University Press, 2002), 23, 22, 27.

12 Ralph Pite, "Byron Turning to Stone," in *The Circle of Our Vision: Dante's Presence in English Romantic Poetry* (Oxford: Clarendon Press, 1994), 227.

13 Schock, *Romantic Satanism*, 98.

14 Jerome J. McGann, "Hero with a Thousand Faces," in James Soderholm (ed.), *Byron and Romanticism* (Cambridge, UK: Cambridge University Press, 2002), 149–50.

15 Russell, "The Romantic Devil," 167.

16 E. M. W. Tillyard, *Milton* (London: Chatto & Windus, 1930), 239.

17 C. S. Lewis, *A Preface to Paradise Lost* (Oxford: Oxford University Press, 1961), 102.

18 Lars Svendsen, *A Philosophy of Boredom*, trans. John Irons (London: Reaktion Books, 2005), 32.

19 Thomas Weiskel, *The Romantic Sublime* (Baltimore: Johns Hopkins Press, 1976), 18.

20 Schock, *Romantic Satanism*, 169.

21 Roger Caillois, "Paris, Mythe Moderne," *Nouvelle Revue française* 25 (May 1, 1937), 284, cited in Walter Benjamin, *The Arcades Project*, trans. H. Eiland and K. McLaughlin (Cambridge, MA: Belknap Press, 1999), 110.

CHAPTER 23

The Lake Poets

Madeleine Callaghan

"If Southey had not been comparatively good," writes Herbert F. Tucker, "he would never have drawn out Byron's best in those satirical volleys that were undertaken, at bottom, in order to reprehend not the want of talent but its wastage."[1] And if Wordsworth and Coleridge had not been dangerously talented, Byron might have spared them some of his stinging sallies. In *Table Talk*, Coleridge proclaimed the conclusion of the "intellectual war" Byron threatened in *Don Juan* (XI. 62: 496), declaring Wordsworth the poet who "will wear the crown,"[2] triumphing over Byron and his ilk for the poetic laurels of the Romantic period. But Byron was not simply an opponent of his contemporaries. His responses to the Lake poets, particularly to Wordsworth, ran the gamut from "reverence" (*HVSV* 129) then "nausea" (Medwin 192) to *Don Juan*'s comical though cutting disdain, in under a decade. Focusing on Byron's relationship with Wordsworth and Coleridge, I will show how Byron's poetry and drama reveal the range and complexity of his dialogue with his older peers, where, even at their most apparently divergent, the conversation between the poets reveals the depth of the engagement across their works.

The simmering personal enmity between the Lake poets and Byron is well known. Byron had attacked, among many others, Wordsworth, Coleridge and Southey in his *English Bards and Scotch Reviewers* (1809), despite claiming a "reverence" for Wordsworth's poetry, donating £100 to a literary fund for Coleridge and presiding over the Drury Lane committee that accepted Coleridge's play, *Remorse*. The animus grew between the poets, especially after Southey labeled Byron and Shelley members of "the Satanic school" and accused them of writing poetry that "betrays the wretched feeling of hopelessness wherewith it is allied" (Southey X: 206). But Byron's relationship with Wordsworth was more remote than his relationship with Coleridge. Though Byron and Coleridge wrote some, if few, letters to one another, Byron and Wordsworth never corresponded. Wordsworth also never responded directly to Byron about his mockeries of or close resemblances to Wordsworth's work in epistolary or in poetic form. But Wordsworth had a hand in perpetuating what Jerome McGann terms a "campaign of vilification" against Byron.[3] Coleridge, too, after Byron's death, wrote that the dead poet would not be "remembered at all, except as a wicked lord who, from morbid and restless vanity, pretended to be ten times more wicked than he was" (*BCH* 266). Both provoking and provoked, if Byron was "born for opposition" (*CPW* v: 595, l. 176), he grew to relish clashing verbal swords with the "shabby fellows" who were "poets still" (*CPW* v: Dedication, 5, l. 47), despite his censure.

Byron's "conversational facility" (*CPW* v: 594, l. 155), showcased with witty verve and creative zest in *Don Juan*, has attracted the lion's share of modern plaudits of his work. Although he attacked Wordsworth and Coleridge along with Southey in the "Dedication" to *Don Juan*, they were more than the butt of his jokes. Seizing upon Wordsworth's maxim in his preface to *Lyrical Ballads* (1802) that the poet should write like a "man speaking to men," Byron in *Don Juan* insists on specifying the type of men speaking and listening, namely, himself and his chosen allies. Claiming that his method is: "never straining hard to versify, / I rattle on exactly as I'd talk / With any body in a ride or walk" (*CPW* v: 594, ll. 150–2), Byron carefully constructs the impression of a living, breathing and, above all, Byronic presence, speaking in his work. Yet Coleridge had managed a similar feat in his conversation poems, which move seamlessly from the personal, the domestic and themes warm with human touch to the philosophical, the divine and the poetic. Though Coleridge was gently self-mocking on the topic of his own possible contribution to the evolution of the epic, his conversation poems offered Byron possibilities for how the poet might weave together disparate strands of thought and emotion in wittily distinctive poetry. Influenced by the "divine Chit chat" of William Cowper (*BCH* 279), Coleridge might be said to have created the conversation poem, and Richard Holmes includes nine poems under this banner in his edition.

These poems, which Michael O'Neill aptly terms "performances,"[4] prefigure Byron's own exuberant exhibitionism in *Don Juan* and *Beppo*. Their conversational and philosophical beauties offer models for *Don Juan*'s musings on philosophy and religion. "The Eolian Harp" encapsulates Coleridge's ability to move effortlessly between levels in his conversation poems:

> And what if all of animated nature
> Be but organic Harps diversely fram'd,

> That tremble into thought, as o'er them sweeps
> Plastic and vast, one intellectual breeze,
>   At once the Soul of each, and God of all?
>
> But thy more serious eye a mild reproof
> Darts, O beloved Woman! nor such thoughts
> Dim and unhallow'd dost thou not reject,
>   And biddest me walk humbly with my God.[5]

Capturing the reader's attention by its dazzling philosophical and religious musings, the poem also anticipates our attempt to understand the relationship between its speaker and its interlocutor, "My pensive Sara" (l. 1). Coleridge's verbal gymnastics betray the restless intelligence of the poem even as the poetry never strains for but smoothly achieves its pantheistic heights. Philosophy's dizzying possibilities, where Coleridge dreams of "one intellectual breeze," is half-comically curbed by a "mild" glance from Sara, as the poem expands with his meditative excitement and deflates from her silent reproof. The poem's lightness of touch hints at (but does not utter) accusations of marital strife, as "The Eolian Harp" hovers above leaden pronouncement, maintaining mobility even as it remains affectingly tethered to the heights and depths of Coleridge's shifting thoughts.

Don Juan takes up such Coleridgean thinking in verse. After condemning his own self-proclaimed "tired metaphor" (*CPW* v: 534, l. 285), Byron gives the impression of fashioning his poetry before the reader, conjuring up "another figure in a trice" to offer us, in lieu of his hackneyed volcano image, "a bottle of champagne" (*CPW* v: 535, ll. 289–90). The poetry brims with effervescent brio as comic spontaneity meets poetic mastery, attesting to Byron's creative and dramatic powers. Seeming almost to wing it before his reader, Byron swiftly yokes metaphor to moral precept, claiming that such "moral lessons" are precisely those upon "which the Muse has always sought to enter" (*CPW* v: 536, ll. 301–2). Gathering all possible elements into his capacious epic, Byron follows and innovates upon Coleridge's model in his serio-comic masterpiece.

Wordsworth, though pilloried in *Don Juan*'s cutting mockeries, is also a vital presence in Byron's poetry. Philip Shaw notes that the competition between the poets extends into the present day, where "modern critics tend, on the whole, to prefer the unerring honesty of Byron to the uncertain equipoise of Wordsworth."[6] Yet the difference between Byron and Wordsworth is less profound than either poet would admit. By the time Shelley met Byron and dosed him with "Wordsworth physic even to nausea" (Medwin 192), Byron was already aware of and in dialogue with Wordsworth's poetry, as *English Bards and Scotch Reviewers* reveals; critics have noted and even complained of Byron's use of Wordsworth's poetry in poems such as the "Epistle to Augusta." But the similarities between the two poets led both to sharpen their differences before their reading public. Wordsworth espoused a teaching ethic, claiming that "Every Great poet is a Teacher: I wish either to be considered as a Teacher, or as nothing."7 By contrast, *English Bards and Scotch Reviewers*, Byron's energetic satire on the literary landscape, aims to dazzle dunces into silence in a manner that recalls Alexander Pope's *The Dunciad*. According to Byron, Wordsworth's example proves that "Poetic souls delight in prose insane" (*CPW* I: 236, l. 244). Wordsworth had introduced *Lyrical Ballads* as the site of "experiment[s]," which he says, might create both "feelings of strangeness and aukwardness [*sic*]," and Byron seemed to agree.8 But Wordsworth's presence in *Childe Harold's Pilgrimage* tells a different story. In poems such as "Lines Composed [originally "Written"] a Few Miles Above Tintern Abbey," Wordsworth creates a model of the self transfigured by nature against which Byron offers his own competing version. "Tintern Abbey," line by line, soars beyond pain to affirm, against all suffering, that "Nature never did betray / The heart that loved her" (ll. 123–4). *Childe Harold* III's dialogue with nature is rather different:

> I live not in myself, but I become
> Portion of that around me; and to me,
> High mountains are a feeling, but the hum
> Of human cities torture: I can see
> Nothing to loathe in nature, save to be
> A link reluctant in a fleshy chain,
> Class'd among creatures, when the soul can flee,
> And with the sky, the peak, the heaving plain
> Of ocean, or the stars, mingle, and not in vain.
> (*CHP* III, st. 72, ll. 680–8 [*CPW* II: 103–4])

Byron's method of avoiding linear trajectory, refusing the solving and simplifying temptation of systems and standing firm against untried axioms, shimmers in the above quoted lines. Byron opens the stanza with a blaze of self-transcendence. Though the urban world is firmly rejected as "torture," Byron is nevertheless forced to deal with it, even in lines that had seemed to promise nature as a means of escape, admitting the painful temporariness of transcendence. The stanza declines from its original height, where the blurring of self and world gives way to the speaker seeing "Nothing to loathe in nature," as the understatement underwhelms. Hating all that is creaturely here, Byron is selective in terms of the nature he would seek and find, and the alexandrine limps into the hushed hope that to mingle with "the sky, the peak, the heaving plain / Of ocean, or the stars" is "not in vain." The self-transcendence that had been affirmed at the start of the stanza leads only into doubt by its close. The poem seems locked into its presiding Byronic myth, that "to Sorrow I was cast, / To act and suffer" (*CPW* II: 104, ll. 692–3). Swithering between hope and doubt, aspiration and loss, *Childe Harold* shapes itself as moving away from the Romance genre's linear quest and away from the affirming structure of the Wordsworthian ode, where, as James Chandler writes of "Immortality Ode," by the final section of the poetry, "forms are all redeemed."[9] Byron denies his poetry the redemption that Wordsworth finds. Though Wordsworth is a vital presence in *Childe Harold*, particularly in Canto III, Wordsworth's solutions cannot be Byron's.

"Wordsworth's imagination," writes McGann, deals in "forms of worship," Byron's in "poetic tales."[10] Byron's imagination, with its determined individuation of the self, sees him depart from Wordsworth's generous universalizing gestures into meditations on the singularity of the poet. *The Prophecy of Dante* (published in 1821) and *The Lament of Tasso* (published in 1817) see Byron fashion a myth of the poet based on his poetics of personality. Even when writing from another perspective than his own, Byron's Dante and his Tasso are always primarily Byronic rather than distinctly separate from the self. Byron performs what he describes in *Childe Harold* as "gaining as we give / The life we image" (*CPW* II: 78, ll. 48–9). This emphasis on creation in the present tense, alight with excitement and potential that stem from the self, became a key part of the Byronic credo. If *The Excursion* was "singing old themes as though they were something new,"[11] Byron's imagination sought to quicken the epic to a new birth by insistently personalizing poetry's themes. Poetry, and its themes, would be made new by being colored by Byron's personality. Byron would rethink and individuate Wordsworth's and Coleridge's themes to achieve his ends, veering between challenging and adapting their works to make his work new.

Auden perceptively observes that "[w]hat Byron means by life – which explains why he could never appreciate Wordsworth or Keats – is the motion of life, the *passage* of events and thoughts."[12] But Byron also saw that life could be infused into poetry by transforming and adapting genres, from the satire and epic to the Gothic, into *Don Juan*'s forgivingly capacious structure. One of those elements was the supernatural. *Christabel* and *The Rime of the Ancient Mariner* claimed Byron's admiration for their evocation of Gothic mystery, and Byron would draw upon their ambiguity in poems such as "Darkness," *The Siege of Corinth* and *Manfred*. But in

Don Juan, Byron restyles the darkness of Coleridge's Gothic poems, with Juan ending up at a Norman Abbey, the seat of Lord Henry Amundeville. Byron makes use of Coleridge's Gothic machinery and Matthew Lewis' *The Monk* by making his stanzas sway between mockery of and immersion in the genre. Juan, having heard Lady Adeline's song about the ghostly Black Friar who stalks the halls, sits apprehensively, expecting and then receiving its visitation:

> Again – what is 't? The wind? No, no, – this time
>   It is the sable Friar as before,
> With awful footsteps regular as rhyme,
>   Or (as rhymes may be in these days) much more.
> Again, through shadows of the night sublime,
>   When deep sleep fell on men, and the world wore
> The starry darkness round her like a girdle
> Spangled with gems – the monk made his blood curdle.
>   (xvi, st. 113, ll. 945–52 [*CPW* v: 653–4])

Studded with Shakespearean allusions, these stanzas revel in the supernatural, drawing out its absurdity and terror, as the thrilling danger of the Black Friar's ghostly appearance assails Juan. Just as *Christabel*'s narrator asks: "Is it the wind that moaneth bleak? / There is not wind enough in the air" (i, ll. 44–5), *Don Juan* also holds out the immediately arrested possibility that the wind might be responsible for the sounds. Rather than dwelling upon or heightening the scene's uncanny atmosphere, the narrator insults contemporary poetry by claiming that poets do not use rhyme as well as they used to, before returning to its theme. The night's sublime, as Byron reminds us, to borrow Burke's definition, is "astonishing,"[13] and beyond the merely beautiful or simply terrifying. Likewise, Byron's ghost is not only ridiculous. Byron slips the yoke of completely undercutting the supernatural or satirizing the Coleridgean or any other form of the Gothic. Though the Black Friar turns out to be "her frolic Grace – Fitz-Fulke!" (*CPW* v: 656, l. 1032), Byron does not render Juan's intimations absurd. The Gothic shiver of the stanzas may culminate in farce, but not in a rejection of their emotional possibility. Byron brings "the motion of life" into *Don Juan* by packing verbal brio, ironic wit and wide-eyed fascination with the uncanny.

Though on the surface a thoroughgoing debunker of the Lake poets' "sect" and their "followers" (*CPW* v: 195, ll. 852, 851), Byron was far from ignorant or dismissive of their work. And he was highly attuned to their work's potential to be transformed into the Byronic mode. Though pulling in different poetic directions, Wordsworth, Coleridge and Byron attempted to mold poetry into their own image. Byron, like the Lake poets, aimed to dominate their shared poetic age, and each poet was profoundly invested in reaching and reshaping their respective audiences. Rather than viewing their relationship as Byron *versus* the Lake poets, instead, it seems that Byron *and* the Lake poets better encapsulates the nature of their complex dialogue.

NOTES

1　Herbert F. Tucker, "Southey the Epic-Headed," *Romanticism on the Net* 32–3 (2003–4), http://id.erudit.org/iderudit/009263ar.

2　Samuel Taylor Coleridge, *Specimens of the Table Talk of the Late Samuel Taylor Coleridge in Two Volumes*, ed. Harry Nelson Coleridge (London: John Murray, 1835), vol. II, 271.

3　Jerome McGann, *Byron and Wordsworth* (Nottingham: University of Nottingham, 1999), 9.

4　Michael O'Neill, "Samuel Taylor Coleridge, Conversation Poems," in Michael O'Neill and Madeleine Callaghan (eds.), *The Romantic Poetry Handbook* (Oxford: Wiley Blackwell, 2018), 179.

5　Samuel Taylor Coleridge, "The Eolian Harp," in H. J. Jackson (ed.), *Samuel Taylor Coleridge: The Major Works* (Oxford: Oxford University Press, 2000), 28–9. All quotations from Coleridge's poetry are from this edition unless specified otherwise.

6　Philip Shaw, "Wordsworth or Byron?" *Byron Journal* 31 (2003), 38–50 (38).

7　William Wordsworth, "Letter to Sir George Beaumont, February 1808," in Ernest de Selincourt (ed.), *The Letters of William and Dorothy Wordsworth: The Middle Years, Part 1*, 2nd ed. (Oxford: Clarendon Press, 1969), 195.

8　William Wordsworth and Samuel Taylor Coleridge, "Advertisement to *Lyrical Ballads*," in Stephen Gill (ed.), *William Wordsworth: The Major Works* (Oxford: Oxford University Press, 2011), 591. All quotations from Wordsworth's poetry are from this edition unless specified otherwise.

9　James Chandler, "Wordsworth's Great Ode: Romanticism and the Progress of Poetry," in James Chandler and Maureen N. McLane (eds.), *The Cambridge Companion to British Romantic Poetry* (Cambridge, UK: Cambridge University Press, 2008), 136–54 (150).

10　McGann, *Byron and Wordsworth*, 18.

11　Seamus Perry, "Coleridge's Disappointment in *The Excursion*," *Wordsworth Circle* 45.2 (2014), 147–51 (147).

12　W. H. Auden, *The Dyer's Hand and Other Essays* (London: Faber & Faber, 1975), 405.

13　Edmund Burke, *A Philosophical Enquiry into the Origin of our Ideas of the Sublime and Beautiful*, ed. Adam Phillips (Oxford: Oxford University Press, 2008), 53.

CHAPTER 24

Byron's Accidental Muse
Robert Southey

Susan J. Wolfson

My chapter takes our old friend Southey as a new "context" for Byron: not the well-known target of satiric abuse, but in surprises of sympathy, as an accidental muse for Byron's voice. This may seem ultra-counterintuitive for the famous butt of brutal, hilarious Byronic ridicule. The debut was *English Bards and Scotch Reviewers* (begun October 1807, published 1809): hailing the poet of ponderous Epics (*CPW* 1: 230, l. 25), the relentless Ballad-monger, the plodding long-winded Bard (*CPW* 1: 231–3, ll. 86–118). Southey wasn't the lone star in the abuse. It was a constellation, including Lakers Wordsworth and Coleridge. The irritation of Wordsworth's poetry was sharpened in the Regency for Byron by Wordsworth himself, his Tory-turn thanked with a patronage post. As for Coleridge, Byron apologized in 1815 for the "pert, petulant, and shallow" satire in *English Bards* (*BLJ* 4: 286), and stayed true to the best of the poet. Coleridge would stand by his Lordship in the Byrons' Separation scandal of 1816, with an essay in the April 18 *Courier* (unsigned, the author was legible to Byron).[1] Rapt by the "pathos and tenderness" of Byron's *Fare thee well!* to Lady Byron (privately circulated, quickly pirated), Coleridge defended its "touching and affecting" verses against charges of "affectation" and "hypocrisy." Byron had helped him financially, supported his playwriting, and persuaded John Murray (his own publisher) to issue a slim volume of Coleridge's poetry. This came out in May, leading with *Christabel*, the poem Wordsworth rejected, years ago, for *Lyrical Ballads*. Byron had read it in manuscript and praised it in an endnote in *The Siege of Corinth* (1816, 56). After it was roasted in the reviews, he defended it vigorously to Murray (*BLJ* 5: 108) and others – among these, Thomas Moore (*BLJ* 5: 150), whom Byron nudged for a favorable notice in the *Edinburgh Review*. Moore obliged, but hardly with favor (*ER* 27, September 1816, 58–67). When in 1819 Byron drafted a satirical "Dedication" of *Don Juan* to Southey, he let Coleridge off with a friendly jest just about his prose: "Explaining

metaphysics to the nation – / I wish he would explain his Explanation"
(*WLB* 15: 101).

Southey was a different case. This time, it was more than his poetry.
It was personal. With the force and authority of this office, Southey had
attacked not only Byron's poetry but also his character and his friends.
Byron's skewering of Southey – reprised in the trimmer poet of Canto III
(1821) and the sweaty, unprincipled hack of *The Vision of Judgment* (1822) –
sharply honed as it is and infamous as it would become, flexes some strange
angles that Jerome McGann has brilliantly elucidated, limning a dark self-
reckoning in Byron about his own political default and fatal facility of
talent. Yet even in this new view of Byron, it's still the same "Southey."
I hope to show a different "Southey," not the one in Byron's scathing sights
but a surprising brother in song. If, as Byron declares at the top of the last
canto of *Don Juan* that he saw into print (1824), his muse is "beyond all
contradiction / The most sincere that ever dealt in fiction" (*CPW* v: 619, ll.
15–16), the deepest contradiction, I'll argue, comes in two fictional duets
with Southey's voice in *Don Juan*, one ephemeral and one enduring.

Not that Dedication, of course. Turning the Laureate performance of
honors to a monarch onto the Laureate himself, Byron renders "good,
simple, savage verse" (he said to Moore, *BLJ* 6: 68):

> BOB SOUTHEY! You're a poet – Poet-Laureate,
>   And representative of all the race;
> Although 't is true you turn'd out a Tory at
>   Last, – yours has lately been a common case, –
> And now, my Epic Renegade! what are ye at?
> With all the Lakers, in and out of place?
>   (*WLB* 15: 101)

In this common case is Wordsworth, too, but it is the Laureate who takes
the chief fall, poetical, political, and sexual, "you soar too high, Bob, /
And fall, for lack of moisture, quite a-dry, Bob!" (*WLB* 15: 102). Instead of
rhyming the bobbed name, Byron just repeats it in a hilarity of scurrilous
slang. While *Don Juan* itself opens with the call, "I want a hero," it is met
here, anti-typed in Southey, the spur of Byronism at its sharpest and most
principled.

Byron decided to suppress the Dedication in 1819, but it appeared in
1833 (*WLB* 15: 101–8), in embarrassment to the still reigning Laureate (who
had heard about it in July 1819, when *Don Juan* I–II was published). When
Southey's Laureate call to elegize George III produced *A Vision of Judgement*
(April 1821), Byron had another shot. Southey's *Vision*, a mini-epic of the
late King's welcome at Heaven's gate, had a long, pompous Preface about

his own poetry, with a dedicated subsection (III) on the defilement of "English poetry" into a "brothel" of "monstrous combinations of horrors and mockery, lewdness and impiety" (XVII). Southey issued his first vision of judgment on the chief begetter. For such a sinner (unnamed but clearly coded) there can be "no after repentance": "Whatever remorse of conscience he may feel when his hour comes (and come it must!) will be of no avail" for this "pandar of posterity" (XVIII–XIX). Certain of eternal damnation, Southey still itched for temporal action: "Let the rulers of the state look into this, in time!" To help out, he tagged – with the seal of his office and the implied endorsement of the Church – "the Satanic school," a "moral virus" of "audacious impiety" (XX–XXII).

Southey's *Vision* would earn durable fame not for this judgment, but for inspiring *The Vision of Judgment* / SUGGESTED BY THE COMPOSITION SO ENTITLED BY THE AUTHOR OF "WAT TYLER." *Nom de plume* "Quevedo Redivivus" notwithstanding, Byron's authorship was transparent. The subtitle tweaks the chagrin of a monarch's Laureate at the recently pirated *Wat Tyler*, Southey's revolution drama from his hot youth in 1794. (The piracy was unpreventable, because a seditious work – which this was – forfeited copyright.) Byron worked on his counter-*Vision* across 1821, and, in an appendix to *The Two Foscari* (published in December) he inserted a few pages defending his patriotism and itemizing Southey's multiple hypocrisies, including "impious impudence." This deft doubled-dactyl signaled the arrows in Byron's quiver – so, too, the jab at Southey as a "renegado in his rancour" (p. 328). Expecting a Laureate rebuke, Byron was delighted by Southey's letter in the *Courier*, January 5, 1822, which unwisely challenged, "When he attacks me again let it be in rhyme." In a heartbeat Byron resumed his *Vision*.

But London publishers backed off. Murray was tied in with the monarchy, Longman had published Southey's *Vision*, and the radical press feared prosecutions that could result (if past were prologue on Southey's watch) in steep fines and imprisonment. Byron's *Vision* landed at last in the inaugural issue (October 1822) of the *Liberal*, published by courageous John Hunt. Byron discovered too late that Murray had remanded it to Hunt "without the *preface*, with which I had taken particular pains," and it debuted so curtailed (*BLJ* 10: 16–17). Hunt quickly remedied with a second edition (1 January 1823), now with this preface (i–v), a brisk parody of Southey's, lambasting the "attempt to canonize a Monarch" whose policies were distinguished by tyranny, then indicted his Laureate for "gross flattery," "dull impudence, and renegado intolerance and impious cant" (*Liberal* 1 [1822], i–v). Southey's "intolerance of Apostacy" was especially hateful. As Byron put it to Murray in 1817, when the piracy of *Wat Tyler* appeared: "it is no disgrace to Mr Southey to have written Wat Tyler – & afterwards to have written his birthday or Victory Odes (I speak only of their *politics*) but it is something [...] to have endeavoured to bring to the stake (for such would he do) men who think as he thought – & for no reason but because they think so still, when he has found it convenient to think otherwise" (*BLJ* 5: 220–1).

Byron's *Vision* needs little rehearsal these days. It's less about George III (pretty much a McGuffin) than about the politics of judgment, about droll Sathan as Byron's latest iteration of the Byronic hero and, most of all, about Southey's bad poetry, bad character, bad judgment. Southey called the "Demon" of his *Vision* "multifaced" (Southey X: 225); Byron assigns the versatility to "multo-scribbling Southey" (*Liberal* I, LXV, p. 25), panderer of "a pen of all work" (*Liberal* I, C, p. 36). Where Byron's trade in contradiction is an epistemological, philosophical principle, Southey's is the failure of principle itself. His résumé of service (for regicide and for kings; for and against republics; giving his pen to Wesley, then offering to present Sathan handsomely bound for the pious purchaser) is itemized in Byron's Preface (II–III) and submitted in his *Vision* to a relentlessly rhymed declension (*Liberal* I, XCVI–IX, pp. 35–6). Byron reiterated the charges in 1820 in an article intended for *Blackwood's*. This wasn't published until 1832 – in a double-whammy for the still regnant Laureate, in the same volume of Moore's *Byron* that unveiled the suppressed Dedication of *Don Juan* (*WLB* 15: 55–98 [see 73–6)]; 101–8). Meanwhile, Byron's *Vision* was quickly pirated, sometimes bound with Southey's. The capture of Southey was durable, and durably Byronic. In 1866 Swinburne could say that *The Vision of Judgment* had simultaneously demoted "the funeral and fate of George III" to "oblivion" and elevated Byron to fame: it "stands alone, not in Byron's work only, but in the work of the world."[2] The king is one thing; but the standing Swinburne accords rests on Southey's shoulders of inspiration. This is one kind of muse for sure.

And yet "Byron's Southey" is not entirely contained by this assignment. I want to mark two moments of tendered affiliation. As a preview, it's worth recalling Byron's admiration of Southey's "talents" in the privacy of a journal entry in the very month he became Poet Laureate (November 1813): "his prose is perfect," his "life of Nelson is beautiful," and "there are passages equal to any thing" in his poetry (*BLJ* 3: 214). At the end of *Don Juan* Canto 1 (1819), one thing (an equal thing, even) comes in an envoi that ironizes the poetic convention – but not completely:

> "Go, little book, from this my solitude!
>   I cast thee on the waters, go thy ways!
> And if, as I believe, thy vein be good,
>   The world will find thee after many days."
> When Southey's read, and Wordsworth understood,

I can't help putting in my claim to praise –
The four first rhymes are Southey's every line:
For God's sake, reader! take them not for mine.
(*DJ* 1: CCXXII, p. 114)

In the 1819 publication, this stanza has a page to itself, a status matched only by the first stanza.[3] For all the protest, the rhymes register as "mine" for the poet of *Don Juan*, woven into Byron's now signature *ottava rima*.

The lines in quotation reprise the closing stanza of the "Envoy" to Southey's *Carmen Nuptiale: The Lay of the Laureate.*[4] Byron implies a colossal false modesty in the cant of a Laureate casting his little book on uncertain waters. The public was agog for the nuptials of Princess Charlotte in May 1816 and the dynasty so promised. Reception was politically wired. The Tory *British Critic* loved *The Lay*, while the *Monthly Review* hooted at "the clumsy allegory." *The Champion* could only sigh that it sounded more like an "old gentleman's admonition to a school-girl, than a Poet's song on the Nuptials of his Sovereign." To Byronist Francis Jeffrey, it was consummately ridiculous, even for Laureate verse, rife with abominable egotism, conceit, and dogmatism.[5] Byron's champion Leigh Hunt parodied its proem in the *Examiner* (August 4, 1816); and James Hogg spoofed it in his *Poetic Mirror* with *The Curse of the Laureate: Carmen Judiciale* (1816). When death claimed the princess in stillborn childbirth on November 6, 1817, and took with this hopes of a monarchy restored to respectability and national affection, Byron and Southey were among the many poets to issue elegies. All this weighs on Byron's claiming and disclaiming of Southey's lines. By 1819, both poets are famous; both are infamous. And for Byron, anyway, the "if" of reception is patently ironized by the imminence of Canto II, in advance of the public's vision of judgment, two pages on in the 1819 edition.

But why is it Southey's rhymes – rather than verse from any of the raft of poets, from Chaucer on, who sing "go little book" – that Byron sets into his frame? It's not appropriation, an opportunistic venture into someone else's field; it's not allusion, a debt refinanced for new uses. Was he out to annoy Southey by Byronizing him? If so, the waver of *mine/not mine* can play another way. This is what happens in a strange arrest of Byronism, in the legible but totalized form of a Southey-Laureate in Canto III, published in 1821.[6] Southey had now been in his office for eight years, and *Don Juan* was so famous that Murray's warehouse was stormed by booksellers on the day that Cantos III–V were published.

The scene of arrest is pirate Lambro's estate in the Isles of Greece, at a banquet presided over by his princess daughter Haidée. Among the entertainers is a court poet, a "trimmer" (LXXXII, p. 44) ready to flatter any nation for his pudding: "He lied with such a fervor of intention –/ There was no doubt he earn'd his laureate pension" (LXXX, p. 43). No doubt, too, about the Southey-coding. This "poet" is "of great fame, and liked to show it" (LXXVIII, p. 42), a critical rhyme. McGann has incisively teased out a Byron-coding in this trimmer: a versatility in national idiom, problematic hosts – or worse, a figure of Byron's most hated self, the hired voice as a self-betrayer, by political principle and by poetic talent. Yet there is more at work than this dark aspect. This is a poet who, "seeming independent in his lays" (LXXIX, p. 42),

> Might for long lying make himself amends;
> And singing as he sung in his warm youth,
> Agree to a short armistice with truth.
> (*DJ* III: LXXXIII, p. 44)

In regimes that "Treat a dissenting author very martyrly" (*DJ* I: CCXI, p. 108), the epic narrator himself recalls that once

> I was most ready to return a blow,
> And would not brook at all this sort of thing
> In my hot youth – when George the Third was King.
> (*DJ* I: CCXII, p. 109)

George III still was King when Byron wrote Canto III. On the thermometer of warm youth to hot youth, Byron's repetition marks out a sympathetic track.

The *amende honorable* is a sixteen-stanza inset song that begins "The isles of Greece, the isles of Greece!" (*DJ* III, pp. 46–51). The theme and refrain voice fervent opposition to a decadent Greece complicit in its oppression and traitor to its glorious past. Is it a poet's truth, or a trimmer performance of "truth"? Or does its singing override such distinction? The epic poet gives the first review:

> Thus sung, or would, or could, or should have sung,
>   The modern Greek, in tolerable verse;
> If not like Orpheus quite, when Greece was young,
>   Yet in these times he might have done much worse:
> His strain display'd some feeling – right or wrong;
>   And feeling, in a poet, is the source
> Of others' feeling; but they are such liars,
> And take all colours – like the hands of dyers.
> (*DJ* III: LXXXVII, p. 52)

Much virtue in "or": on this swing, Byron expands the historical site of Juan's story, the late 1780s, to potential for any poet, including poets in "these times" for the reader (and Byron) of 1821. Opposition to Turkish domination plays as well in 1821, and in principle speaks to the politics of poetry in the post-Napoleonic restorations of Europe too. The couplet would shrug this off. Rhymed to *dyers*, *liars* also puns *lyres*, the instrument in the trimmer's hand ("Isles", fifth stanza, p. 48). But the riff on Shakespeare's self-satire in Sonnet III plays double, setting sentiment against reception. The poet of this sonnet concedes the bad trade: "Thence comes it that my name receives a brand, / And almost thence my nature is subdu'd / To what it works in, like the Dyers hand."[7] The simile became a famous trope for the soiling cost, right up there with "go little book."

While fame in posterity is no certainty, there are surprising turns and returns in the hazard, as the epic poet muses, against the containment by immediate situation:

> But words are things, and a small drop of ink,
>   Falling like dew, upon a thought, produces
> That which makes thousands, perhaps millions, think.
>   (*DJ* III: LXXXVIII, p. 52)

This is a productivity beyond parody, beyond even irony or indeterminacy. I dissent from the critic who calls "The isles of Greece" just so much "fantasy" nationalism, abstracted from and subtracted of social and historical context.[8] Writing this song, Byron must have sensed that out of a trimmer's lyre he had spun pretty amazing lyrical gold, born of and for opposition to a modern Greece forgetful of its glorious heritage, and in need of arousal. Everyone knows this stanza:

> The mountains look on Marathon –
>   And Marathon looks on the sea;
> And musing there an hour alone,
>   I dream'd that Greece might still be free;
> For standing on the Persian's grave,
> I could not deem myself a slave.
>   (*DJ* III, p. 47)

This singing is ignored by Juan, Haidée and everyone else; the singer is sole audience to his solitary swings of sarcasm and melancholy. His wide audience awaits on that unknown arc of "go little book." When the Greek War of Independence commenced in 1821, the song was ready to launch, trimmed of its trimmer. From 1824 on, it has been one of Byron's most famous, most anthologized lyrics. In 1824, Alfred Howard put it in *The Beauties of Byron*, and it was called into *The Oxford Entertaining Miscellany*. Thirty years later, Murray himself used some of the stanzas for a gloss in *Handbook for Travellers in Greece*. The trail of stand-alone prestige is paced out (inter alia) by its inclusion in Swinburne's *Selection from the Works of Lord Byron* and Arnold's *Selected Poems of Lord Byron*, published both in England and the United States – the last with a frontispiece, "The Isles of Greece"; F. W. Farrar's *With the Poets*; and at the turn of the century, Henry Van Dyke's *Little Masterpieces of English Poetry*.[9] "I want a hero" may have been preempted by the draft-Dedication's Bob Southey, but in the immediate arc of publication, it gets another answer in this briefly heroic poet, rendering "the single most important philhellenic text … the anthem of Greek renewal for Western readers."[10] Greek renewal shaped Byron, too: he went there to become his last Byronic hero, born for opposition and dying in the cause.

In "Discourse in the Novel," M. M. Bakhtin comments that language "lies on the borderline between oneself and the other. The word in language is half someone else's. It becomes 'one's own' only when the speaker populates it with his own intention, his own accent, when he appropriates the word, adapting it to his own semantic and expressive intention."[11] While Bakhtin is describing diminished authority, and sees lyric, by virtue of privacy and personal voice, as a more authoritarian mode, it is worth recalling Byron's dance with *mine/not mine* at the end of Canto I, and worth measuring the semantic and expressive force of "The isles of Greece" on this border – not least in the complex layerings of Canto III, itself a chapter in an epic that is arguably the first serialized "novel" in nineteenth-century English literature. Adapting comes in unpredictable public uses – by excerpt, by accent, by anthology, by political appropriation – for ends that Byron could not know, might marvel at. Roger Rosenblatt puts this case personally: "You write a book and send it into space. Go, little book. You have no idea where it lands – what effects it will have on a reader."[12] Trimming a trimmer for satire, Byron finds a voice he can call "genius" (*DJ* III: LXXXI, p. 43), with a generative force beyond its first stage. In this sway, the context of "Southey" wavers from the bitter inspiration of a despicable, pompous turncoat – the un-Byron – into a contradiction through which Byron gets to write a national poetry in the best philosophical-political sense: not of accommodation, but of passionate opposition, a surprise that turns ironic into iconic.

NOTES

1 Text and attribution of "Lord Byron" from David V. Erdman (ed.), *The Collected Works of Samuel Taylor Coleridge: Essays on His Time, in* The Morning Post *and* The Courier, 3 vols. (Princeton: Princeton University Press, 1978), vol. II, 427–9.

2 Algernon Chas. Swinburne, "Preface," in *A Selection from the Works of Lord Byron* (London: Edward Moxon, 1866), XXI.

3 Lord Byron, *Don Juan, Cantos I and II* (London: Davison, 1819), 3, 114.

4 Southey, *The Lay of the Laureate* (London: Longman, [June] 1816), 69.

5 *British Critic*, NS 6 (July 1816), 44; *Monthly Review* 82 (January 1817), 93–4; *Champion* (June 30, 1816), 206; Jeffrey, *Edinburgh Review* 26 (June 1816), 443.

6 Quotations follow *Don Juan, Cantos III, IV and V* (London, 1821), the edition Southey would have known.

7 William Shakespeare, *Sonnets* (London, 1609 quarto).

8 Charles Donelan, *Romanticism and Male Fantasy in Byron's "Don Juan"* (Basingstoke, UK: Macmillan, 2000), 72–3.

9 See Alfred Howard (ed.), *The Beauties of Byron* (London, 1824), 64–7; *The Oxford Entertaining Miscellany* (London, 1824), vol. 1, 21–2. *Handbook for Travellers in Greece* (London: John Murray, 1854), 211; Swinburne, *Selection*, 163–7; Matthew Arnold, *Selected Poems of Lord Byron* (London: Macmillan, 1881), 65–8; F. W. Farrar (ed.), *With the Poets: A Selection of English Poetry* (New York: Funk & Wagnalls, 1883), 214–16; Henry Van Dyke (ed.), *Little Masterpieces of English Poetry* (New York: Doubleday, 1905), 75–9.

10 David Roessel, *In Byron's Shadow: Modern Greece in the English and American Imagination* (New York: Oxford University Press, 2002), 51–2, 79–81.

11 Bakhtin, *The Dialogic Imagination* (Austin: University of Texas Press, 1981), 294.

12 Rosenblatt, "Seen and Unseen," *New York Times Book Review* (August 27, 2017), 8.

CHAPTER 25

"Benign Ceruleans of the Second Sex!"
Byron and the Bluestockings

Caroline Franklin

"Of all Bitches dead or alive a scribbling woman is the most canine," Byron commented to Hobhouse in 1811. His target was the author Anna Seward, whose books of sentimental poetry he derided as "6 tomes of the most disgusting trash" (*BLJ* 2: 132). Byron's antagonism to female rivals never let up. In 1813, when selecting his all-male gradus ad Parnassum, he declared: "I have no great esteem for poetical persons, particularly women; they have so much of the 'ideal' in *practics*, as well as *ethics*" (*BLJ* 3: 221). By 1820, when he was living in Italy, he instructed his publisher John Murray not to send him "feminine trash" especially verse by "Mrs. Hewoman" (Felicia Hemans, who had been heavily influenced by Byron and was now threatening to overtake him in popularity) – for if she "knit blue stockings instead of wearing them it would be better" (*BLJ* 7: 182–3). When embarking on drama, he pronounced: "Women (saving Joanna Baillie) cannot write tragedy; they have not seen enough nor felt enough of life for it" (*BLJ* 4: 290). Authorship derives from phallic power when he quotes Voltaire: " 'the composition of a tragedy requires testicles,' " speculating mischievously: "If this be true, Lord knows what Joanna Baillie does – I suppose she borrows them" (*BLJ* 5: 203). If this was hinting that Baillie was derivative, it may have been a smokescreen to divert attention from Baillie's influence on his own Venetian tragedies.

It would be a mistake to write off Byron's preoccupation with bluestockings as quaint belatedness, evidence of his supposed Augustanism. The bluestocking values of female intellectualism and philanthropy survived the antifeminist reaction following the French Revolution, and were morphing into a much broader movement for women's activism in nineteenth-century public life, fueled by the domestic ideology of bluestocking Hannah More rather than the Enlightenment feminism of Mary Astell or Mary Wollstonecraft. Indeed, Byron had entered a literary marketplace dominated by women. This was the context that shaped the poet's marked ambivalence toward female intellectuals. The first ten years of the nineteenth century saw the posthumous publication of the works, correspondence and memoirs of the original bluestockings Hester Chapone, Catherine Talbot, Elizabeth Carter and Elizabeth Montagu. The novelist Frances Burney, the playwright Joanna Baillie and the poets Anna Barbauld and Anna Seward were concluding long and successful careers, while educationalist and fiction writer Maria Edgeworth and salonnières Madame de Staël and Lady Morgan (Sydney Owenson) were still ascendant. "I had been the lion of 1812," the poet recalled in his journal; "Miss Edgeworth and Madame de Staël ... were the exhibitions of the succeeding year" (*BLJ* 8: 29).

In his early literary satire *English Bards and Scotch Reviewers* (1809), Byron attacked the most popular male poets of the day, Thomas Moore, Walter Scott, William Lisle Bowles and Matthew Lewis, for prostituting themselves "to please the females of our modest age" (*CPW* 1: 237, l. 272; see also ll. 182, 283–5, 299) – the very tactic he would adopt himself a few years later. He vehemently called upon William Gifford, famous for his misogynistic attacks on Della Cruscan poets Hester Thrale and Mary Robinson in the 1790s, to return to finish cleansing the literary Augean stables (*CPW* 1: 251, ll. 702–4). But Byron himself virtually ignored female writers. He singled out for ridicule only the "two volumes of very respectable absurdities in rhyme of Charlotte Dacre or Rosa Matilda" (*CPW* 1: 413, n. 758). This Gothic poet and novelist had been the principal inspiration behind his earliest publications: even the title of *Hours of Idleness* (1807) echoed Dacre's *Hours of Solitude* (1805). Byron's ambivalence about Della Cruscan sentimentalism and the Gothic – both literary modes dominated by women writers, but that also fired his imagination – would prompt his defensive turn toward the "masculine" genres of travelogue and the paean to past heroism in *Childe Harold's Pilgrimage* in 1812. Yet even here, his Whiggish anti-war rhetoric competed with Barbauld's visionary *Eighteen Hundred and Eleven* published the same year.

Byron's misogynistic comments in letters to male friends are in complete contrast to the very real reverence for the older generation of women writers he often expressed in his private journals, especially when he began his literary career. He believed Joanna Baillie to be "our only dramatist since Otway & Southerne – I don't except Home" (*BLJ* 3: 109). When *The Giaour* was published in 1813, Byron wrote in his journal of his particular pleasure that the Godwinian sentimental novelist Elizabeth Inchbald had praised the poem "because her 'Simple Story' and 'Nature and Art' are, to me, *true* to their *titles*" (*BLJ* 3: 236*)*. He confessed trepidation at the prospect of meeting Maria Edgeworth at a breakfast held by Sir Humphry and Lady Davy on May 17, 1813 (*BLJ* 3: 48). He later recalled the contrast between the unassuming novelist and the bombastic father who always accompanied her, with an ironic humour reminding one of the author of *Persuasion*: "Her conversation was as quiet as herself; no one would have guessed she could write *her name*. Whereas her father talked, *not* as if he could write nothing else; but as if nothing else were worth writing" (*BLJ* 8: 30). In 1811, Byron's then publisher James Cawthorn had hoped to obtain Frances Burney's *The Wanderer* for £1,000 and asked him to act as reader of the manuscript. Byron answered that he would do this "with pleasure, but I should be very cautious in venturing an opinion on her whose 'Cecilia' Dr Johnson superintended" (*BLJ* 2: 143). This did not materialize, but in 1813 Byron asked his publisher, John Murray, to send Burney's *The Wanderer* and Edgeworth's *Patronage* to Lord Holland, who was sick, adding that he himself would like the same works: "I would almost fall sick myself to get at Me. D'Arblay's writings" (*BLJ* 3: 204).

This, however, was a watershed moment when women authors began to lose their dominion even of the novel genre. In 1814, Walter Scott turned to prose and published the first of a series of historical adventurous tales, which were as wildly popular as Byron's and Moore's verse romances. There is no doubt that authors were conscious of the rivalry between male and female writers, and between masculine and feminine subject matter. Writing of Scott's *Waverley*, Byron now chauvinistically declared to Murray: "I like it as much as I hate Patronage & Wanderer – & O'Donnel [by Lady Morgan] and all the feminine trash of the last four months" (*BLJ* 4: 146). Meanwhile Jane Austen grumbled to Anna Austen: "Walter Scott has no business to write novels, especially good ones. It is not fair. He has fame and profit enough as a poet, & should not be taking the bread out of other people's mouths. I do not like him, & do not mean to like *Waverley* if I can help it – but fear I must."[1]

Byron's considered opinion of Edgeworth's moralistic fiction, which probably also applied to Jane Austen (two of whose novels he possessed), was confided to his journal in 1821: "they excite no feeling, and they leave no love – except for some Irish steward or postillion. However, the impression of intellect and prudence is profound – and may be useful" (*BLJ* 8: 30). He here registers his unease that a female should eschew sentimentalism, as women writers were traditionally associated with courtship novels. He recognized that Edgeworth's didactic fiction, aimed at young women readers, urged them to be rational and prudent rather than lovestruck, to help them survive in a patriarchal world where money and patrilineal power ruled. The word "useful" is ambiguous: these intelligent books have a moral use yet should fiction or morality be utilitarian? Byron probably preferred Germaine de Staël's romantic tragedy *Corinne* (1807), where a famous female poet is rejected by her lover and subsequently dies because she cannot conform to bourgeois norms. It is true that Byron voiced the view that fiction should have a moral purpose when he publicly lectured Staël in 1813, telling her that her novels were "very dangerous productions to put into the hands of young women."[2] But as his own poetry was criticized for immorality, we can hardly take this seriously. Six years later, he would inscribe his most impassioned declaration of unchanging love to his mistress Teresa Guiccioli in her copy of *Corinne*. The heroine of the book also symbolized her native land of Italy, and the poet was at one with its author in envisioning her freedom. Even in 1813 Byron had reluctantly admitted to his diary: "I do not love Mde. de Stael – but depend upon it – she beats all your Natives hollow as an Authoress – in my opinion – and I would not say this if I could help it" (*BLJ* 4: 25). Ironically, she later became a close friend when he resided in Switzerland in 1816 and frequently visited her salon at Coppet.

During the first fifteen years of the nineteenth century, Scott's, Moore's and then Byron's spectacular success with swashbuckling romantic verse tales was the result of a deliberate remasculinization of the literary scene combined with careful attention to pleasing the female readers who now dominated the reading public. Even though the male-dominated premises of publishers such as John Murray were taking over from the feminine spaces of salons as literary gathering places, the latter were still important, especially to an aristocrat. Byron had begun by satirizing Lady Holland's power over Whig writers in *English Bards and Scotch Reviewers* (*CPW* I: 246, ll. 557–9 and 410, n. 559), but her "set" was vital for his own political ambitions, so he needed to make peace with her (*BLJ* 3: 231). He might declare: "I don't much affect your blue-bottles" (*BLJ* 3: 228), but he often attended the salons of Lady Jane Davy, wife of the scientist, and Agnes Berry and her sister Mary, who edited the works and correspondence of their friend Horace Walpole.

Byron's dismissal of Lady Caroline Lamb after their tempestuous love affair inspired her to write a "silver fork" novel, *Glenarvon* (1816). She demonized the poet and caricatured his Whig hostess friends: Lady Holland as the Princess of Madagascar, Lady Oxford as Lady Mandeville and Lady Jersey as Lady Augusta. The latter remained loyal to Byron even when the scandal over his mistreatment of his wife Annabella Milbanke caused him to be ostracized among the *ton*, the fashionable elite. When he settled in Italy in 1817, Byron frequented the Venetian salon of Isabella Teotochi Albrizzi, who he noted "has written very well on the works of Canova"

(*BLJ* 5: 148). Her rival, Countess Marina Querini Benzoni, he described as "the oddest & pleasantest of elderly ladies – & her Conversazione better than the Governor's or the Albrizzi's" (*BLJ* 6: 37).

Byron's satire of the "loveliest Oligarchs of our Gynocrasy" (*CPW* v: 514, l. 524) in England is partly explained by their support of Annabella, but it also reflected the general disfavor now shown to nineteenth-century bluestockings. Salonnières such as Staël were criticized in the press for meddling in politics, while even a pious evangelical, such as More, who campaigned for Sunday schools, was rebuked for interfering in church affairs. Byron's method for cutting bluestockings down to size was to question their sexual attractiveness. Staël was as "frightful as a precipice" (*BLJ* 1: 9); "her books are very delightful – but in society I see nothing but a very plain woman forcing one to listen & look at her with her pen behind her ear and her mouth full of *ink*" (*BLJ* 4: 19).

He also brought in class. The privately circulated "A sketch from private life" (1816) portrayed a lower-class woman (his wife's former governess, Mrs. Clermont) as having dared to teach herself "penmanship":

> She taught the child to read, and taught so well,
> That she herself, by teaching, learn'd to spell.
> An adept next in penmanship she grows,
> As many a nameless slander deftly shows.
> (ll. 13–16 [*CPW* iii: 383])

Female intellectual ability is linked with unnatural cold-bloodedness:

> Mark, how the channels of her yellow blood
> Ooze to her skin, and stagnate there to mud,
> Cased like the centipede in saffron mail,
> Or darker greenness of the scorpion's scale –
> For drawn from reptiles only may we trace
> Congenial colours in that soul or face) –
> Look on her features! and behold her mind
> As in a mirror of itself defined.
> (ll. 65–72 [*CPW* iii: 384–5])

Even the veteran Juvenalian satirist William Gifford, Byron's "*literary father*" (*BLJ* 11: 117), wondered if any human being deserved this.

Mockery of bluestockings is a significant theme in Byron's poetry, as it was the impetus behind the poet's attempt to reposition himself as an alpha-male author after publishing the series of oriental verse romances he said he had written "to please the women" (Medwin 205). The poet told his friend Percy Shelley in Italy that "all I have yet written has been for

woman-kind."³ In Canto IV of *Childe Harold* he dedicated himself politically and poetically to his adopted home of Italy.

Byron next returned to the "masculine" genre of satire, but now on
an epic scale, selecting for its plot the adventures of the mythical libertine, Don Juan, specifically to exclude respectable female readers. His first
target was his bluestocking wife, the mathematician and educationalist
Annabella Milbanke, who was lampooned as Juan's mother, Donna Inez,
a supposed prodigy who turns out to be a hypocrite. Her prudishness is
responsible for turning first her husband and then her son into libertines:

> His mother was a learned lady, famed
>   For every branch of every science known –
> In every christian language ever named,
>   With virtues equall'd by her wit alone.
>   (*DJ* I, st. 10, ll. 73–6 [*CPW* v: 12])

Inez's favorite authors are the bluestocking moralists Maria Edgeworth,
Sarah Trimmer and Hannah More:

> In short, she was a walking calculation,
>   Miss Edgeworth's novels stepping from their covers,
> Or Mrs. Trimmer's books on education,
>   Or "Cœlebs' Wife" set out in search of lovers,
> Morality's prim personification,
>   In which not Envy's self a flaw discovers,
> To others' share let "female errors fall,"
> For she had not even one – the worst of all.
>   (*DJ* I, st. 16, ll. 121–8 [*CPW* v: 13])

These bluestockings attacked aristocratic libertinism, hoping that if the
upper classes reformed themselves, a revolution would be averted. Rather
than arguing for intellectual equality like Mary Wollstonecraft, they
positioned women on the moral high ground. *Don Juan* responds by
targeting the bourgeois hypocrisy and prudery that would dominate the
coming Victorian age.

When he reached England, the land of "white cliffs, white necks, blue
eyes, bluer stockings" (*CPW* v: 515, l. 535), Don Juan thought the females
not pretty. They insisted on cross-examining him about Spanish literature:

> The Blues, that tender tribe, who sigh o'er sonnets,
>   And with the pages of the last Review
> Line the interior of their heads or bonnets,
>   Advanced in all their azure's highest hue.
>   (*DJ* XI, st. 50, ll. 393–6 [*CPW* v: 481])

The narrator acknowledges that bluestocking circles make or break literary reputations:

> fame is but a lottery,
> Drawn by the blue-coat misses of a coterie.
>
> Oh! "darkly, deeply, beautifully blue,"
>   As some one somewhere sings about the sky,
> And I, ye learned ladies, say of you;
>   They say your stockings are so (Heaven knows why,
> I have examined few pair of that hue);
>   Blue as the garters which serenely lie
> Round the Patrician left-legs, which adorn
> The festal midnight, and the levee morn.
>   (*DJ* IV, st. 109–10, ll. 871–80 [*CPW* V: 238])

The narrator's lack of (erotic) experience with *blue* stockings is because they were everyday wear. Sporting them in the evening was a refusal of ceremony adopted by bohemian intellectuals, like wearing blue jeans today. The aristocratic poet would be more familiar with courtly grey silk – the men's stockings occasionally ornamented with blue enameled garters of the highest order of chivalry. The "blue-coat" of the coterie miss, in contrast, alludes to a charity-school education and sneers at upwardly mobile female intellectuals.

As late as 1823, Byron published *The Blues, A Literary Eclogue* in the *Liberal*, the journal he published with the Shelleys and Leigh Hunt, where the ridiculous Lady Bluebottle rhapsodizes on the Lake poets and "Wild Nature! – Grand Shakespeare!" (*CPW* VI: 306, l. 115). At this time Byron was a close friend of Mary Wollstonecraft's daughter, Mary Shelley, and an enthusiastic admirer of her novel, *Frankenstein* (1818), later recalling: "methinks it is a wonderful work for a Girl of nineteen – *not* nineteen indeed – at that time" (*BLJ* 6: 126). But Byron associated bluestockings with sexual convention, whereas Wollstonecraftian "feminists" such as Mary Shelley and his mistress Claire Clairmont followed their mentor's example by refusing to conform to conventional sexual mores.

Bluestockings were still a force to be reckoned with in the early nineteenth century, and Byron was not their only Regency satirist. The caricaturist Thomas Rowlandson portrayed a catfight of warring women in *The Breaking Up of the Blue Stocking Club* (1815). Byron's friend Thomas Moore wrote a successful comic opera *M. P. or The Blue-Stocking* (Lyceum Theatre, 1811), where a scientist Lady Bab Blue composes a poem personifying the chemical elements and allegorizes their reactions to one another as sexual

attraction. This idea shockingly implied that the behavior of human repro-
duction itself might be governed by the laws of biology. These were light-
hearted squibs. However, *Don Juan*'s prominent attack on bluestockings, in
what Jerome McGann has described as the most important English poem
published between 1667 and 1850 (*CPW* v: xvii), far from confirming the
diminishing of women's cultural capital, should be seen as evidence of a
well-founded masculine fear of intellectual rivals.

NOTES

1 Jane Austen to Anna Austen, September 28, 1814. *Jane Austen's Letters*, ed.
  Deirdre Le Fay, 4th ed. (Oxford: Oxford University Press, 2011), 289.
2 D. H. Reiman, *Shelley and his Circle 1773–1822*, 10 vols. (Cambridge, MA:
  Harvard University Press, 1986), vol. VII, 59.
3 Richard Henry Stoddard (ed.), *Anecdote Biography of Percy Bysshe Shelley*
  (New York: Scribner, Armstrong & Co., 1876), 219.

CHAPTER 26

The Pisan Circle and the Cockney School

Maria Schoina

In its August and September 1822 issues, the *Imperial Magazine* devoted a long, scathing memoir to Byron's life and works under the column titled "Memoirs of the Living Poets of Great Britain." The anonymous "W" concluded by drawing a telling comparison between the poet and Voltaire:

> [Byron's] moral failings are perceptible in all his writings; and it is but too plain that this licentiousness is connected with the darkest infidelity. There is a great similarity, in this respect, between the English peer, and his admired author, Voltaire; for though Lord Byron is not equal to the Frenchman in variety of talent, he is superior to him in poetry; and, like him, he has perverted a fine genius to the destruction of principles, and the depravation of manners. As Voltaire, in his exile at Ferney, appeared ambitious of standing at the head of the free thinking of his time, whose object was to overthrow religion; so, according to accounts, Lord Byron, in his retreat at Pisa, is engaged in forming a school of sceptics, who, it seems, are to club their wits in a journal, for the dissemination of what they are pleased to term liberal opinions.[1]

Having ascertained Byron's moral and religious dissent, the reviewer casts a suspicious eye on his latest association with like-minded expatriates at Pisa, "a school of sceptics" deemed keen to "overthrow religion" and propagate liberalism, a word Tory periodicals used to designate "otherness, dissent, and foreign, un-English sympathy."[2] The parallel with Voltaire's famously multicultural circle at Ferney suggests the threat such an association was thought to pose to the Anglo-centric religious and intellectual establishment. It also reveals the Tory anxiety over the formation of "free thinking" literary circles, which had the potential to gain considerable cultural influence and act powerfully upon the opinions of the British reading public. Thus, Byron's contentious association with the Pisan circle, and its affiliate, the Cockney School of poetry, illustrates the centrality of the group as a way of understanding not only certain phases of the poet's career but also Romantic literary and political culture in general.

Though not named, the "sceptics" alluded to in the passage above were Leigh Hunt and Percy Bysshe Shelley. While in Hampstead, the editor of the *Examiner* mobilized a large group of writers, artists and intellectuals who, despite their aesthetic divergences and changing allegiances, shared Hunt's enthusiasm for collective literary experience and joined his repeated appeals in the press for cultural and political reform. Hunt and the members of the group – John Keats, William Hazlitt, John Hamilton Reynolds, the Shelleys, Horace Smith, Charles Lamb and Benjamin Robert Haydon, among others – were mauled by reactionary periodicals led by *Blackwood's Edinburgh Magazine*, which contemptuously labeled them "The Cockney school of versification, morality, and politics" (*Blackwood's* 3, August 1818, 521). As a form of identity representation, the term "Cockney" has been subject to historical change, but in the 1818 edition of Dr. Johnson's dictionary, a cockney was defined as "a native of London, by way of contempt" and also as "any effeminate, ignorant, low, mean, despicable citizen."[3] Such a cluster of associations fed easily into the *Blackwood's* charges launched against Hunt and his collaborators: "1. The want and the pretence of scholarship; 2. A vulgar style in writing; 3. A want of respect for the Christian religion; 4. A contempt for kingly power, and an indecent mode of attacking the government of your country" (*Blackwood's* 2, October 1817, 415). The Cockneys' "faults," counted and detailed pedantically by the anonymous reviewer "Z" in *Blackwood's* October 1817 issue, suggest a broader spectrum of signification, uncovering arenas of severe ideological conflict. As Gareth Stedman Jones points out, cockney "was a term mediating between the aesthetic and the political."[4]

Despite their expatriate status and nomadic life in Italy (1818–22), Percy and Mary Shelley stayed closely connected with Hunt. When the couple decided to settle in Pisa in 1821, their circle began to form: it was an international group of friends from Britain (Thomas Medwin, Edward Trelawny, the Williamses, John Taaffe, Claire Clairmont), Italy (Francesco Pacchiani, Tommaso Sgricci, Emilia Viviani) and Greece (Alexandros Mavrokordatos). Interaction with the non-English members of this group shaped the Shelleys' thinking and enriched their aesthetic and cultural perspective, contributing to a stronger sense of their allegiance with the South. Being in favor of freely associating groups, which he saw as agents of cultural and political change, Percy Shelley envisioned Pisa as a hub of intellectual activity, peopled by personalities as different as Hunt, Byron, Keats, Horace Smith and Thomas Love Peacock, all of whom he tried to gather around him. Critics seem to agree that Byron's arrival at Pisa in October 1821 energized the Pisan group's social activities. More importantly, though, Shelley, Byron and Hunt founded a joint periodical work, *The Liberal: Verse and Prose from the South*, which epitomized the group's reformist tendencies.

Jeffrey N. Cox's important study, *Poetry and Politics in the Cockney School*, sees Shelley's Pisan group and the Hunt circle in London as interlinked, and as embodying an "ideal circle of liberal writers."[5] The *Liberal* in this respect carried on the work of the *Examiner*. This may explain why the reviewers' invectives and abusive comments targeted Pisa now instead of Hampstead: Pisa had become yet another "Cockney site."[6] This change in geographical location had several far-reaching implications; indeed, in a broader historical context, Pisa – hence Italian culture – was seen as an even greater threat than Hampstead because it undermined and "destabilize[d] an Anglo-centric vision ... posing ... the challenge of alien manners, politics and religion."[7] This elucidates what was at stake in the "war" waged against Hunt and his circle. Particularly indicative of the ferociousness directed against the circle's projected activities at Pisa is the vocabulary of intrigue and irreligion used by the Tory reviewers to caricature the three men. Hunt, Shelley and Byron were labeled the "Pisan Triumvirate" and the "grand Pisan conspiracy," while the *Liberal* was identified by "John Bull" as the "Italianized Cockney Magazine," the "Manifesto of the Pisan Conspirators," and the work of "translated cockneys."[8]

Byron's involvement in the Pisan circle was another reason why it received such a torrent of abuse. Byron was distantly connected with the Hunt circle at first, but his later involvement through the project of the *Liberal* was received with apprehension and suspicion by his London friends and his publisher John Murray. Alarmed by Byron's association with the radical Hunt brothers and Shelley, the "writer of infidel poetry," as he was labeled in the *Courier* (cited by Hunt in *Liberal* 1: xi), Murray wrote to Byron: "[R]eally Lord Byron it is dreadful to think upon your association with such outcasts from Society, it is impossible, I am sure, that you can conceive any thing like the horrid sensation created in the mind of the public by this connexion, unless you were here to feel it" (*LJM* 455). While Byron was often swayed by his London friends, and vacillated now over the fortunes of such a vulnerable association, he was hoping that the journal would grant him opportunities to regain control of the publication and editing of his poetry. This was a pressing concern in view of his break with Murray, who objected to publishing Byron's controversial Italianized poetry (*The Vision of Judgment* and the later cantos of *Don Juan*). Finally, nearly as important as the literary objectives were the economic motives, as the project was expected to bring in profits.

The plans to set up a new literary periodical had begun to look feasible after Byron's meeting with Shelley in Ravenna in August 1821. Leigh Hunt was invited from London to join the enterprise and finally agreed to move to Italy with his family, excited by the prospect of such a promising alliance. However, only Hunt and Byron lived to see the *Liberal* in print, as Shelley's death by drowning on July 8, 1822 marked the end of the Pisan circle and precipitated a series of complications. Nevertheless, Nikki Hessell describes Shelley's "lamented absence [as] a kind of shaping presence" in the periodical, which "became Hunt's elegy to Shelley's memory."[9] Caroline Franklin claims that Shelley's influence on Byron was profound: "Byron's confidence in himself as a Liberal poet had surged as a direct result of his friend's presence,"[10] a point extensively argued by Roderick Beaton in *Byron's War: Romantic Rebellion, Greek Revolution* (2013).

Following William Marshall's seminal 1960 study on the history of the journal and its collaborators, scholarly work on the *Liberal* has mostly focused on the reasons behind its premature failure after four issues, the negative reviews it attracted, its polemical character and the disputed quality of its contents. More recent criticism, however, has positioned the collaborative, transnational achievement of the *Liberal* at the heart of second-generation Romanticism, paying close attention to its symbolic significance. Thus, the Anglo-Italian nature of the journal and of the Pisan circle in general represents not only an aesthetic marker but an attempt by the expatriated poets to fashion a bicultural space, identity and literacy. Italy is evoked generously in the pages of the *Liberal*, but the periodical's contents reveal its dynamic openness to other cultures, ancient and modern, and manifest its writers' "mobile and culturally pluralistic viewpoints."[11] In spite of its designation as "cockney," the journal was anything but parochial; it was in fact contesting the idea of "a nationalized cultural capital."[12]

Having announced in the Preface that Italian, German and Spanish literature was a "favorite subject" of its contributors, the journal featured a considerable number of translations or short stories with an Italian theme (such as Shelley's "May-Day Night," Byron's translation of the first canto of Luigi Pulci's *Morgante Maggiore* and Hunt's translations of various minor pieces, mainly by Alfieri and Ariosto). Michael Scrivener stresses the importance of such literary treatments of cosmopolitanism as the one practiced by the Hunt and Shelley circles, within the climate of violent nationalisms that developed after the Revolutionary Wars in Europe: "When Britain found itself after 1815 the most powerful nation in the world, on the verge of an unprecedented economic take-off fuelled by the Industrial Revolution, with an empire that spanned the globe, it was not eager to embrace cosmopolitan political ideas that would weaken state sovereignty and promote international cooperation."[13] The *Liberal*'s open-minded and flexible attitude to language, style, genre and form reinforced the cosmopolitan ideal and undermined "essentialist constructions of national identity."[14]

As for the political orientation of the journal, in the disarming Preface to the first issue, Hunt famously denies the magazine's direct relation to politics; instead, he attempts to align it with a liberalism that champions intellectual freedom: "[W]e are advocates of every species of liberal knowledge, and ... we go to the full length in matters of opinion with large bodies of men who are called LIBERALS" (*Liberal* 1: ix). According to Daisy Hay, the conception of liberalism offered here "is an international one, which permeates linguistic and geographical divides to unite sympathetic minds to a cause which is international too."[15] It seems that the journal's political "program" was to advocate a model of political and cultural reform by appealing to the power of the group and of a supranational community.

Being disillusioned by the climate that surrounded his connection with the *Liberal* circle, and by Murray's delays in publishing his works, Byron must have found the journal emancipatory and inspiring, at least in the beginning. Hunt's strong advocacy of "liberal knowledge" energized Byron's opposition and defiance against "Thought's foes ... / Tyrants and Sycophants" (*CPW* v: 416, ll. 187–8), a point he reiterates in a letter to Douglas Kinnaird when publication plans for the *Liberal* were underway and Byron was composing Canto VII of *Don Juan*: "[Y]our present Public ... shall not interrupt the march of my mind – nor prevent me from telling the tyrants who are attempting to trample upon all thought – that their thrones will yet be rocked to their foundation" (*BLJ* 9: 152). The poet's opposition to political regimes, religious authorities and publishing networks that "trample upon" intellectual freedom is particularly resonant and finds powerful expression in the later cantos of *Don Juan*, for which the *Liberal* and its hostile reception provide a useful context. As Mary Shelley confessed in an 1832 letter, "the opposition he met concerning the Liberal made him defy the world in D. Juan" (*LMWS* II: 163–4).

Byron's contributions to the *Liberal* were designed to act as a focal point for each one of the four issues: *The Vision of Judgment*, "A Letter to the Editor of 'My Grandmother's Review'" and the epigram on Lord Castlereagh; *Heaven and Earth*; *The Blues, A Literary Eclogue*; and the translation of the first canto of Pulci's *Morgante Maggiore*. Despite their generic diversity and uneven distribution, these works, when viewed as a unified body, offer an alternative conception of literature and voice a powerful rejoinder to an age of failed revolutions, imperial reaction, aggressive nationalism and new market relations. Most of these works proclaim their political sentiments through an urbane, satirical tone, though there are cases where the attack is calculated and savage, as in the epigram on Lord Castlereagh. Robert Southey and George III feature unfavorably in *The Vision of Judgment*, while *The Blues* parody the Lake poets and the Bluestockings. In terms of stylistic experimentation, Byron's contributions encompass a wide range of literary forms originating in different traditions and ages: satire, verse drama, epigram and translation. In *Heaven and Earth* the poet mixes Greek choruses with Biblical diction. He also manipulates the *ottava rima* in *The Vision of Judgment* and in his translation of *Morgante*, adapting the Italian rhyme into English verse to admirable effect.

Stabler is right to point out that despite the *Liberal*'s support of revolution and reform, the journal's real "challenge [was] to the dogmatic authority of the established church."[16] Hunt answers the charge that the circle is planning "to cut up religion, morals, and everything that is legitimate" in a provocative passage in the Preface:

> When we know … that there is not a greater set of hypocrites in the world than these pretended teachers of the honest and inexperienced part of our countrymen; – when we know that their religion … means the most ridiculous and untenable notions of the DIVINE BEING, and in all other cases means nothing but the Bench of Bishops; … then indeed we are willing to accept the title enemies to religion, morals and legitimacy, and hope to do our duty with all becoming profaneness accordingly. (*Liberal* I: v, vi)

In similar vein, the translation of *Morgante* appeared with an "Advertisement" defending the Florentine poet Pulci from charges of immorality and irreligion:

> That [Pulci] intended to ridicule the monastic life, and suffered his imagination to play with the simple dulness of his converted giant, seems evident enough; but surely it were as unjust to accuse him of irreligion on this account, as to denounce Fielding for his Parson Adams, Barnabas, Thwackum, Supple, and the Ordinary in Jonathan Wild, or Scott, for the exquisite use of his Covenanters in the "Tales of my Landlord." (*Liberal* II: 194)

In defending Pulci, Byron was in fact defending himself and the values projected in his works and those of his collaborators: freedom of thought and expression, the creative merging of past and present poetic traditions and of native and foreign literatures, license in composition and style. By speaking in Pulci's favor and placing great faith in his translation of *Morgante*'s "half-serious rhyme," Byron rejects both traditions and contemporary systems that impose constraints and rigid doctrines on people's minds and imagination, preferring to align himself with a European Renaissance epic tradition that allows "a poet [to] be facetious about religious matters and still not incur the charge of blasphemy."[17]

The Pisan/Cockney project presented significant challenges and had a shaping influence on all those involved. Association with the Pisan circle and the *Liberal* led Byron to a new awareness of his role as a poet and catalyzed his sensibility and political thought. Specifically, the outcry against the periodical's literary freethinking and cultural pluralism strengthened the poet's opposition to oppression and injustice and aroused his interest in the current political affairs of Italy and Greece.

Notes

1 "W." "Memoirs of the Living Poets of Great Britain," *Imperial Magazine* 4 (September 1822), 825.

2 Daisy Hay, "Liberals, *Liberales* and *The Liberal*: a Reassessment," *European Romantic Review* 19.4 (October 2008), 310.

3 Samuel Johnson, *Dictionary of the English Language*, 4 vols. (Longman, 1818), vol. 1, www.hathitrust.org.

4 Gareth Stedman Jones, "The 'Cockney' and the Nation, 1780–1988," in David Feldman and Gareth Stedman Jones (eds.), *Metropolis, London: Histories and Representations since 1800* (London and New York: Routledge, 2017 [1989]), 284.

5 Jeffrey N. Cox, *Poetry and Politics in the Cockney School: Keats, Shelley, Hunt and their Circle* (Cambridge, UK: Cambridge University Press, 1999), 217.

6 Jeffrey N. Cox, "Cockney Cosmopolitanism," *Nineteenth-Century Contexts* 32.3 (September 2010), 254.

7 Jane Stabler, "Religious Liberty in the 'Liberal,' " in Dino Franco Felluga (ed.), *BRANCH: Britain, Representation and Nineteenth-Century History*, Extension of *Romanticism and Victorianism on the Net*, www.branchcollective.org/?ps_articles=jane-stabler-religious-liberty-in-the-liberal.

8 See Maria Schoina, *Romantic "Anglo-Italians": Configurations of Identity in Byron, the Shelleys, and the Pisan Circle* (Burlington, VT: Ashgate, 2009), 156.

9 Nikki Hessell, "Elegiac Wonder and Intertextuality in the *Liberal*," *Romanticism* 18.3 (2012), 239–40.

10 Caroline Franklin, *Byron: A Literary Life* (Basingstoke, UK: Macmillan, 2000), 159.

11 Stabler, "Religious Liberty in the 'Liberal,' " 5.

12 Cox, "Cockney Cosmopolitanism," 252.

13 Michael Scrivener, *The Cosmopolitan Ideal in the Age of Revolution and Reaction, 1776–1832* (Abingdon, UK: Routledge, 2015), 202, 201.
14 Scrivener, *Cosmopolitan Ideal*, 204.
15 Hay, "Liberals, *Liberales* and *The Liberal*," 313.
16 Stabler, "Religious Liberty in the 'Liberal,'" 7.
17 Peter Vassallo, *Byron: The Italian Literary Influence* (London and Basingstoke, UK: Macmillan, 1984), 153.

CHAPTER 27

Drama and Theater

Rolf P. Lessenich

All the major Romantic poets tried their hands at drama, expecting success in the theater to balance the frequent commercial failure of their poetic works. So Wordsworth invested his hopes in *Borderers*, Coleridge in *Remorse* and *Zapolya*, Shelley in *Cenci*, Keats in *Otho the Great* and Blake in his fragmentary *Edward the Third*. For the authors of transgressive dramas, however, the publicity surrounding theatrical exposure created a dilemma. On the one hand, provocative heresy had to be made public in order to question received opinions and create scandalous celebrity; on the other, publication and public performance risked intervention by the Examiner of Plays under Britain's 1737 Licensing Act, with the dangers of libel prosecutions and forced self-exile.

The problems Byron encountered with his eight subversive dramas were similar to those Horace Walpole met in 1768 when writing and publishing his only drama, the incest tragedy *The Mysterious Mother*. Walpole solved the problem by printing his tragedy on his own press and performing the work privately in his neo-Gothic mansion, Strawberry Hill, leaving it to posterity to decide whether the play should be staged in public. Like Walpole, who was the third Earl of Orford, Byron paraded his aristocratic licenses (including his same-sex leanings) as well as his skepticism, had a strong liking for the Gothic and had a keen interest in theater. Walpole's *Mysterious Mother* and Byron's first drama, *Manfred* (1817), share a Gothic setting and a provocative theme – incest – a tragic offence and aesthetic transgression for which they offered more apology than Sophocles in *Oedipus*. While Walpole never married and was cautious enough not to be socially ostracized, Byron's numerous affairs with both sexes and rumored incestuous relationship with his half-sister Augusta led to his separation from his wife and ultimate exile in April 1816.

In Byron's time, London had about thirty theaters: two "patent" theaters (Drury Lane and Covent Garden) as well as numerous "illegitimate" ones, and dramatists sought fame by writing and publishing plays with certain renowned actors in mind. From June 1815 to his exile, Byron was on the subcommittee of the (then gaslit) fourth Drury Lane Theatre, which had reopened in 1812 after a fire in 1809. It was amateur-run, and its most famous actor was Edmund Kean, who shared Byron's penchant for scandal and "illegitimacy."[1] Though often classified as a metaphysical closet drama, Byron very probably wrote *Manfred* with a view to Drury Lane, where Philippe de Loutherbourg had introduced the technique of stage illusions that he would have needed for his sublime Gothic and Alpine scenery. When the play was finally staged at Covent Garden ten years after Byron's death, Alfred Bunn converted it into a post-Gothic melodrama, dumping it in tame domesticity, followed by a popular burlesque, *Man-Fred*, at the illegitimate Strand Theatre.

Manfred was named after the Gothic villain of Walpole's *Castle of Otranto* (1764), a work surrealistically inspired by a dream and written in the solitude and gloom of Strawberry Hill. Byron's Manfred is a Faustian figure and typical Byronic hero – lonely and lost in his castle in the immensity of the towering Alps, a wild Gothic landscape that symbolizes unconquerable fate. Irresistible passions drive him into an incestuous love for his sister Astarte, mirroring Byron's love for his half-sister. "I loved her, and destroy'd her" (*CPW* IV: 74, l. 117). He is thus guilty without culpability. His pangs of conscience, his failed suicide attempt, his descent into the underworld, his invocation of spirits and his vision of his dead sister's ghost announcing his imminent death all evoke a sense of the created world's injustice, prefiguring Byron's *Cain*. Unlike Goethe's Faust, to whom Byron dedicated his tragedies *Sardanapalus* (1821) and *Werner* (1822), Manfred does not confess and repent. He proudly spurns an abbot's offer of repentance: "Old man, 'tis not so difficult to die!" Friedrich Nietzsche judged Byron's Manfred greater than Goethe's Faust for his rejection of the "slave religion of Christianity" – a character therefore progressing toward the status of a superman.

Byron's passion for drama prevailed during his exile in Italy, where he came under the influence of Vittorio Alfieri, an early Romantic tragedian in the German *Sturm-und-Drang* tradition, though his Italian tragedies, with their cult of melancholy and revolt, were cast into classical form. First in Venice and later in Ravenna, Byron became involved in the cause of the Italian Carbonari in their fight against Austrian rule and wrote the tragedy *Marino Faliero* (1820–1). Neoclassical in form – modeled on Alfieri – and Romantic in content, it featured a Venetian Doge who sided with the people against the *ancien régime* of the Forty. Murray published the play, together with *The Prophecy of Dante*, in 1821. In Ravenna, and later in Pisa, where Percy Shelley rented a house for Byron and Teresa Guiccioli's family, he wrote *The Two Foscari, Sardanapalus, Cain, Werner, Heaven and Earth* and the unfinished *The Deformed Transformed* – all in 1821–2, his *annus mirabilis* as a dramatist.

Murray published *Sardanapalus, The Two Foscari* and *Cain* in one volume in December 1821, eliciting a wave of vehement attacks on *Cain* for heresy. The scandal strained Byron's relationship with Murray, who was forced to weigh the risk of scathing reviews against the profit he expected from publishing the work of the "scandalous lord." Characteristically, Murray printed Byron's drama *Werner* but left the printing of *The Vision of Judgment* and *Heaven and Earth* – two politically dangerous and religiously heretical works – to Percy Shelley, Leigh Hunt, his brother John and their short-lived radical periodical the *Liberal* (1822–3).

Byron's dramas, rarely acted on stage if at all, were not very successful. *Werner*, later considered his weakest play, was the most popular on the nineteenth-century London stage, albeit in revised form. After a New York performance in 1828, Charles Macready played its title role in Drury Lane in 1830–1, then revived it a few times up until 1851. Other famous actors involved in nineteenth-century performances were Samuel Phelps, Edmund Kean's son Charles, Henry Irving and Ellen Terry. However, the play never ran for long before disappearing from the stage.

Robert William Elliston, lessee of Drury Lane Theatre from 1819, unsuccessfully staged an abbreviated version of *Marino Faliero* against the express wishes of Byron. After a French-language performance in Brussels in 1834, Macready acted the title role of *Sardanapalus* in Drury Lane, but only for a few nights. Again, this happened despite Byron's letter to Murray of May 31, 1821 stating that the play was "expressly written not for the theatre" (*BLJ* 8: 129). It is difficult to decide how serious Byron was in his preference for what he called "mental theatre" over a stage performance in London, such as he seems to have envisaged for *Werner*.[2] In fact, he feared failing on the stage and would rather not have his plays acted in London. The psychological explanation that his "neurotic fear of competition" and "hidden urge to reach the stage" was a typical Byronic paradox, due to his insecurity and hunger for applause, is quite convincing.[3]

Byron, an iconoclast and code-switcher mobile in all things, shifted his dramas between Romanticism and neoclassicism. Five of his dramas ignored the neoclassical rules observed by Alfieri (the five-act structure, probability, the unities of plot, time and place). Yet his three neoclassical dramas – *Marino Faliero, Sardanapalus* and *The Two Foscari* – combined the structure of Alfieri with a Shakespearean dramatic idiom and a Romantic disrespect for the rules. Byron blamed this formal experiment for the luke-warm reception of *Marino Faliero* in Drury Lane and changed back to free Romantic forms after that.

Romanticism was a counterculture, launching countercreeds in religion as well as poetics – even when later revoking them in a return to ortho-doxy (as occurred in the cases of Wordsworth, Coleridge and Southey). This included what I have called "Romantic disillusionism."[4] Placing himself in the skeptical tradition of Pyrrho and Montaigne versus Plato and Platonism, Byron produced dramas that challenged firm traditions, all the while drafting *Don Juan*. The only dogma the skeptical tradition knew was the doubt of fundamentalism, in religion as well as philosophy, distinguishable from an outright negation that comprises another kind of fundamentalism. This included doubting not only the truth of reve-lation and the divine foundation of the *ancien régime*, but also the dia-lectical justification that revolutions lead to a better world; doubt of the justness and justice of the world order; doubt of rational and emotional cognition; doubt of man's homogeneity; and doubt of humankind's ability to control its passions. Byron's so-called metaphysical dramas, which are in part parodies of medieval mystery plays, are meant as provocations of orthodoxy and not as manifestos propagating atheism. He was a would-be believer and a must-be skeptic in religious matters, just as he was a would-be positive-platonic Romantic and a must-be skeptic and realist in both the theory and writing of his poetry.

Manfred is a "dramatic poem" about the modern intellectual's loss of religious humility and orientation. If the strong passions of humankind are uncontrollable – as exemplified in the Oriental tales and the ship-wreck episode of *Don Juan*, as well as in Byron's own love affairs – then punishment is unjust: a creator would simply be punishing humanity for the unavoidable sins he had imposed on them. Divine predestination, as Byron learnt through his Calvinist upbringing, justified the "absolutism" of *ancien-régime* sovereigns, God and King being rulers "absolved" from obedience to laws (*legibus absoluti*). Manfred is a Byronic hero like his Prometheus of 1816: an offender against a law that his uncontrollable passions could not possibly allow him to obey, he is disorientated and out-cast, discontented with his lack of knowledge, enslaved by fate yet longing for liberty, proudly suffering unjust pangs of conscience and refusing con-fession even in the hour of his death. "Man," the abbreviated form of his name, suggests that he represents a modern human condition, a pre-Heideggerian "thrownness" (*Geworfenheit*), Martin Heidegger's term for man's existence in the world, thrown into a stretch of time between birth and death without any ascertainable purpose.[5] His suicide attempt fails. He cannot turn to religion to alleviate his world-weariness and yearning for death. Like Goethe's Faust, he traverses time and space, conjures up spirits and converses with the dead. His complaints about man's lack of knowledge are Faustian, yet he declines the devil's pact that would enslave him even more. This was Byron's answer to Goethe. Manfred bears the burden of the insight provided to him by the First Destiny in the terrible subterranean Hall of Arimanes:

> That knowledge is not happiness, and science
> But an exchange of ignorance for that
> Which is another kind of ignorance.
> (*Manfred* II, iv, ll. 61–3 [*CPW* IV: 83])

The Abbot's concluding words after Manfred's death express skepticism rather than doctrinaire negation: "He's gone ... Wither? I dread to think – but he is gone" (*CPW* IV: 102, ll. 152–3).

The Two Foscari foregrounds the problem of theodicy touched on in *Manfred* and elaborated in Mary Shelley's *Frankenstein*, which was written in Byron's presence (MS Villa Diodati June 1816), namely the fall and suffering of mortal creatures and the injustice of their creation. Doge Franceso Foscari, forced to punish his son Jacopo by sending him into permanent exile for faults that he had bequeathed him, reflects on the biblical creator of the world punishing his creatures for obeying the nature they inherited. They are slaves to absolutism and necessitarianism – a human nature that was never free.

A similar father–son constellation can be found in Byron's verse tale *Parisina* (1816). Like Blake in his comment on Michelangelo's *Creation* and Mary Shelley in her epigraph to Frankenstein, Byron reads the theodicy of Milton's *Paradise Lost* against the grain: "Did I request thee, Maker, from my clay To mould me Man?" (*Paradise Lost* x, ll. 745–6). The Gnostic Demiurge, Blake's Urizen, survived in the Pyrrhonian tradition.

Marino Faliero is a blank-verse tragedy about a fourteenth-century Venetian doge who fails in his revolutionary attempt to side with a popular insurrection against the injustice and corruption of the Forty. The history of Marino Faliero fascinated Byron during his stay in Venice because it recalled the failure of the French Revolution and cast doubt on the Platonic theory of a dialectical evolution of history toward its destined completion (as we find in Blake and Hegel). History, Byron suggested, moves instead in absurd circles of thesis and antithesis without the final synthesis of a millennium. The French Revolution had overcome the *ancien régime*, but ended first in the Terror and subsequently in the new feudalism of Napoleon. Significantly, Byron's Faliero is beheaded where he had been inaugurated.

Heinrich Heine quoted Byron's tragedy as supporting his own view of the simple circularity of history, a view later adopted by Byron's admirer Nietzsche. The elderly Marino Faliero is a tragic hero, "antithetically mixed" (*CPW* II: 89, l. 317), combining vices and virtues as in the skeptical anthropology of Montaigne and Hume. He is vigorous and passionate, necessitating a loss of control. Love and compassion alternate with hatred and rage. The tragic flaw that causes his downfall is due to human nature rather than personal culpability. His great revolutionary speech in the third act is a warning against the rash call for equality that later caused the failure of the French Revolution, a call the Whig aristocrat Byron vigorously opposed. Yet Faliero's warning goes unheard; his betrayal reestablishes Venice's *ancien régime*, which would later be abolished but not overcome by another tyrant, Napoleon:

> We will renew the times of truth and justice,
> Condensing in a fair free commonwealth
> Not rash equality but equal rights.
> (*Marino Faliero* III, ii, ll. 168–70 [*CPW* IV: 372])

Sardanapalus is another blank-verse tragedy concerning a hero of "antithetically mixed" character: Ashurbanipal, the last king of Assyria, who became known as the incarnation of sybaritism and decadence. Though married, he is in love with the Greek slave Myrrha, a woman of similarly changeable character – another pairing that evokes Byron's affair with Teresa Guiccioli at the time of writing in Ravenna. Sardanapalus starts out as effete and peaceful, but when a revolt against him breaks out, he unexpectedly turns manly and warlike, urged on by Myrrha, who also drops her initial slavish meekness. Defeated on the battlefield, Sardanapalus arranges for the safety of his queen Zarina before proudly committing suicide on a pyre together with Myrrha. Sardanapalus anticipates Nietzsche's injunction that man must accept his undeserved fate stoically rather than in tears. The Christian virtue of humility is called into question as well as the Christian doctrine of man's homogeneity.

Cain resumes a free Romantic drama form as well as revisiting the skeptical questions raised in *Manfred* and *The Two Foscari*. In this inverted mystery play with its parody of Milton's *Paradise Lost*, Cain is punished by God for slaying his brother Abel in a fit of passion without having known death before. Moreover, deviating from the biblical text, Cain makes his sister Adah the mother of an unhappy race without previous knowledge of the prohibition of incest. A spoiler rather than a noble rebel, yet also an intellectual doubter, Lucifer confirms that Cain feels aggrieved. Guilty without culpability, Cain comes to blame his father Adam, and ultimately God, much as Mary Shelley's Monster blames his creator Victor Frankenstein for the injustice of his miserable, bungling (and maybe even sadistic) creation:

> My father could not keep his place in Eden.
> What had *I* done in this? – I was unborn,
> I sought not to be born.
> (*Cain* I, i, ll. 66–8 [*CPW* VI: 234])

Heaven and Earth, another inverted mystery play, again questions the justice of God creating only to destroy. It presents a rereading and reinvention of the sixth chapter of *Genesis*. God repents that he had made man and perversely kills his creation by a Flood for the "wickedness" of making "love" – out of which he himself had created man. The drama ends in chaos, showing the mass murder of thousands, except for those arbitrarily saved in Noah's ark. The rebel angel Salmiasa poses the question of theodicy:

> Was not man made in high Jehovah's image?
> Did not God love what he had made? And what
> Do we but imitate and emulate
> His love unto created love?
> (*Heaven and Earth* I, iii, ll. 477–80 [*CPW* VI: 368])

Werner, or, The Inheritance, Byron's penultimate drama, revives the father-son configuration in a Gothic setting. Werner Siegendorf and his son Ulric are both caught in a web of injustice, bloodshed, robbery and chaos that dominates the end of the Thirty Years' War in Germany and does not end with the Westphalian Peace of 1648. Father and son are each other's doppelgangers in irresistible passion, insofar as they resemble their enemy, the villain Stralenheim:

> Ulric! – Ulric! – there are crimes
> Made venial by the occasion, and temptations
> Which nature cannot master or forbear.
> (*Werner* II, ii, ll. 147–9 [*CPW* VI: 432])

The Deformed Transformed, unfinished at Byron's death, reworks the Goethean Faust theme. The hunchback Arnold, rejected by his mother as Byron himself was for his club-foot, meets a stranger (the devil) who offers him the form of Achilles and follows him as the servant Caesar, just as Mephistopheles follows Faust. They take part in the Sack of Rome in 1527 where Arnold, like Byron's Don Juan in the battle of Ismail, follows "honour and his nose" (*CPW* v: 374, l. 255), irresistibly yielding to the passion of war after having just as irresistibly yielded to the passion of love. The praise of peace in the drama's last chorus is reminiscent of Byron's *The Island* – an imaginary paradisiacal millennium "devoutly to be wished" though ever dissolved in what Byron identified as "hope baffled" (*BLJ* 8: 37). With his knowledge of human nature, Mephistopheles-Caesar calls the Platonic doctrine of free will and dialectical historical meliorism into doubt:

> You must obey what all obey, the rule
> Of fix'd necessity: against her edict
> Rebellion prospers not.
> (*The Deformed Transformed*,
> Pt. I, ii, ll. 31–3 [*CPW* VI: 541])

NOTES

1 Jane Moody, *Illegitimate Theatre in London 1770–1840* (Cambridge, UK: Cambridge University Press, 2000), 236.
2 Richard Lansdown, *Byron's Historical Dramas* (Oxford: Oxford University Press, 1992), 51.
3 David V. Erdman, "Byron's Stage Fright: The History of his Ambition and Fear of Writing for the Stage," *ELH* 6 (1939), 219–43.
4 Rolf P. Lessenich, *Romantic Disillusionism and the Sceptical Tradition* (Göttingen: Bonn University Press, 2017), 129.
5 Martin Heidegger, *Being and Time*, trans. Joan Stambaugh (Albany: State University of New York Press, 2010), §81, 405.

CHAPTER 28

Autobiography

Alan Rawes

Though autobiography was first named as such in 1797, its history goes back to antiquity. The two principal models of "self-writing" handed down to the Romantics by the eighteenth century were Rousseau's *Confessions* (1782) and Sterne's *Tristram Shandy* (1759–67). Rousseau's model of autobiography sets "before my fellows the likeness of a man in all the truth of nature," that man being the author, who shows himself "as [he] was," "unveil[ing his] innermost self" and revealing "the secrets of [his] heart" – "mean and contemptible, good, high-minded and sublime" as these might be.[1] The Shandyean model of autobiography, offered through the novel's eponymous fictional autobiographer, explores and reflects on the complexities thrown up by any attempt to form, narrativize or communicate a coherent self and its history; with "fifty things to let you know," a "hundred difficulties" to "clear up," a "thousand distresses and domestic adventures crowding in," "thick and threefold, one upon the neck of the other," the "sport of small accidents, Tristram Shandy" repeatedly finds "I am lost myself."[2] Revealing the intimacies of the self and/or reflecting on selfhood per se (though not generally in Sterne's humorous mode) were to become key tropes of Romantic autobiography from Coleridge's *Biographia Literaria* (1817) to de Quincey's *Confessions of an English Opium Eater* (1821), William Hazlitt's *Liber Amoris* (1823) and Wordsworth's *Prelude* (1850).

Byron gave the first draft of his autobiography to Thomas Moore in 1819 and added to it over the following years (*BLJ* 7: 207, 219; *BLJ* 8: 196n). He did not, it seems, follow the model of Rousseau or Shandy, but rather "that of Gibbon – Hume – &c." (*BLJ* 6: 59). These "Memoirs" were then burnt on May 17, 1824, "three days after the news of Byron's death reached England" (*BLJ* 6: 235n), so we have no idea of what was in them beyond the hints Byron supplies in his letters. They were, says Byron, "full of many passions & prejudices of which it has been impossible for me to keep clear"

(*BLJ* 6: 64), though he claimed that his "first object" in writing was to give "the truth" (*BLJ* 7: 244) and that he wrote them "with the fullest intention to be 'faithful and true' in my narrative" (*BLJ* 7: 125). Writing to Lady Byron, he adds: "You will perhaps say *why* write my life? – Alas! I say so too – but they who have traduced it & blasted it – and branded me – should know – that it is they – and not I – are the cause" (*BLJ* 6: 261). Byron's autobiographical truth-telling, then, was to be less self-revelation than self-defense. Indeed, Byron wrote to Murray: "The life is *Memoranda* – and not *Confessions* – I have left out all my *loves* (except in a general way) and many other of the most important things ... – But you will find many opinions – and some fun – with a detailed account of my marriage and its consequences – as true as a party concerned can make such accounts" (*BLJ* 6: 236). While implicitly insisting that his autobiography is un-Rousseauean – "not *Confessions*" – Byron hints at a few traces of Shandyism in the "passions & prejudices" he says he could not keep out of the memoirs, as well as the "many opinions" and "fun" Murray will find there. But we shall never know.

We can more safely suggest that both Rousseau's confessional mode and Shandy's digressive, comic, "cock and bull" self-writing[3] influenced Byron's letters, which, together with his journals, have been described as "one of the ... most significant informal autobiographies in English."[4] The letters also tell us a lot about the influence of both Rousseau and Sterne on Byron's poetry (*BLJ* 5: 209; *BLJ* 10: 150), much of which has also long been read as thinly disguised autobiography. This began with Byron's contemporaries, driving Byron to write in the dedication to *Childe Harold's Pilgrimage* IV: "With regard to the conduct of the last canto, there will be found less of the pilgrim than in any of the preceding, and that little slightly, if at all, separated from the author speaking in his own person. The fact is, that I had become weary of drawing a line which every one seemed determined not to perceive" (*CPW* II: Dedication to *CHP* IV, 122). A similar determination stretches right up to our own time, to McGann's seminal readings of *Manfred* as "nakedly autobiographical" and *Sardanapalus* as autobiography "in masquerade,"[5] and Peter Graham's recent reading of *Parisina* as a tale in which "history gives Byron a discreet way of talking about himself."[6] And if Byron's poetry in these readings is thinly disguised autobiography, it can also be a form of fictionalized autobiographical confession – especially on the matter of Byron's incestuous relationship with his half-sister, Augusta Leigh.

Byron first "confessed" to this relationship in letters to Lady Melbourne in 1814. One of these letters offers us a good starting point for discussing

Byron's distinctive deployment of confessional autobiographical writing in his later poetry – a deployment that was very different from any previous autobiographical writing, and was to become one of his signature tropes:

> [I]t is *not* an "*Ape*" and if it is – that must be my fault – however, I will positively reform – you must however allow – that it is utterly impossible I can ever be half as well liked elsewhere – and I have been all my life trying to make some one love me – & never got the sort I preferred before. – But positively she & I will grow good – & all that – & so we are *now* and shall be these three weeks & more too. (*BLJ* 4: 104)

This appears to confess to a sexual relationship with Augusta, though we cannot be sure that Byron is being altogether honest here. Byron's own statements are the only evidence that he had a sexual affair with Augusta,[7] while

> Hobhouse records that Augusta herself used to say: "Byron is never as happy as when he can make you believe some atrocity against himself" … Moore [also] tells us that there was "hardly any crime so dark or desperate" of which he might not on occasion hint that he had been guilty … This is a trait everyone recognised, and evidence of it abounds.[8]

Nevertheless, Byron is clearly using a confessional, autobiographical mode of discourse to achieve un-autobiographical ends – to adopt a particular persona and solicit particular responses from his readers. The letter does not directly state what it appears to be confessing, but works through playful, teasing hints that pander to the reader's prurience and invite speculation. "*Ape*" may be a reference to Augusta's daughter, Medora, and the medieval use of the ape as a "symbol of the Fall of Man … of which incest was a prime example."[9] But perhaps it is not. What exactly does Byron mean by "love"? He does not say. The letter is suggestive but ambiguous.

It does solicit sympathy for the "sinner," though, and even some emotional complicity in the implied "sin": "I have been trying all my life to make some one love me." There is a sense of guilt – "my fault," "I will positively reform" – but a defiance of morality bubbles just under the surface in "you must allow" and in the off-hand, almost coarse, "the sort I preferred." Any resolution to reform seems fragile – Byron promises to be "good" for "these three weeks and more," but not longer, in a teasing suggestion of possible future sinning that seeks to involve the reader in a personal drama of high emotion, moral risk and possibly dire consequences for everyone concerned. Projecting Byron as excitingly "mad, bad and dangerous to know,"[10] the letter uses a seeming confession to offer its reader the prospect of a thrilling, intimate involvement in that madness, badness and danger.

This is a private "confession," but within two years Byron's private life had gone very public. In January 1816, Lady Byron left her husband in London to visit her parents in Leicestershire. On February 2, Byron received a letter from her father announcing her desire for a separation. Rumors immediately abounded of adulterous incest with Augusta (among other things) – rumors that, according to John Cam Hobhouse, "struck at the very existence of Lord Byron as a member of society" (quoted in MacCarthy 268). On April 8, 1816, Byron "appeared with Augusta, to general consternation, at a party given by Lady Jersey where they were cut by some of the guests" (MacCarthy 275). As Byron wrote, "I was advised not to go to the theatres lest I should be hissed, – nor to my duty in parliament lest I should be insulted by the way" (*CMP* 95). According to Byron, Hobhouse even "imagined I should be *assassinated*" (quoted in MacCarthy 276) and a "threatening crowd" was at his door when he departed for Europe on April 23 (MacCarthy 278). Once abroad, he "was pursued and breathed upon by the same blight" (*CMP* 95). Even where he was welcomed, as at Madame de Staël's salons, "he found the room full of strangers who had come to stare at him" (MacCarthy 301).

Byron first responded to this crisis in his relationship with his readers in two poems that John Murray printed for private circulation in March 1816: *Fare Thee Well!*, addressed to Lady Byron, and "A Sketch from Private Life," an attack on Lady Byron's governess. These poems toy with various voices and stances, from sentimentality and self-pity to aggressive, vengeful attack. They show Byron unsure of how to respond to public vilification, but testing out possibilities. Neither poem went down well with its test audience. In April he sent "Stanzas to Augusta" to Murray, but, again, was not hitting the right note: Murray showed the poem to Caroline Lamb, who told Byron that the stanzas were "beautiful" but "I do implore you for God sake not to publish them … I think they will prove your ruin" (quoted in MacCarthy 278). On his way to Ostend, Byron returned to *Childe Harold*, the poem that first made him famous, weaving in references to his wife, child and accusers, and again playing with various first-person, lyric responses to recent events, this time focusing not on his wife or Augusta so much as his daughter – his loss of her and her loss of him. But it was in *Manfred* – begun in September 1816 and published in June 1817 – that Byron finally found a way of facing down his critics, working with the accusations thrown at him, rather than against them, reseducing old readers and seducing new ones. And he did so by reworking, on a grand poetic scale, the confessional, autobiographical gestures of his letters to Lady Melbourne.

Manfred is manifestly not "nakedly" autobiographical, but its fictional eponymous hero is another of those distinctive Byronic heroes that readers had long read as thinly disguised versions of their author, and his hints of past crimes very deliberately evoke the rumors of incest surrounding Byron himself:

> Yet there was one –
> …
> She was like me in lineaments – her eyes,
> Her hair, her features, all, to the very tone
> Even of her voice, they said were like to mine
> …
> I loved her, and destroy'd her!
> …
> Not with my hand, but heart – which broke her heart –
> It gazed on mine, and withered.
>   (*Manfred* II, ii, ll. 104–19 [*CPW* IV: 73–4])

Here is another bad and dangerous "Byronic" figure, who breaks – indeed withers – a heart and has destroyed a life. Yet, like Byron's letter to Lady Melbourne, *Manfred* does not openly state its central crime, or the relation of its hero to his victim, but supplies just enough for contemporary British readers to fill in the gaps with what they think they know of the poet's life: "like me in lineaments" clearly suggests a sister, but does not say "sister"; "I loved her" suggests nothing sexual per se, but a love that breaks the heart of a sister might. Like the letter, Byron's play teasingly invites sexual speculation but confirms nothing.

It does, however, solicit sympathy for its eponymous "criminal" (*CPW* IV: 101, l. 124): "I have gnash'd / My teeth in darkness till returning morn, / Then cursed myself till sunset" (*CPW* IV: 74, ll. 131–3). If this man has committed a crime, he has suffered for it ever since. There is a sense of guilt, but also an ongoing defiance of conventional morality: "The mind which is immortal makes itself / Requital for its good or evil thoughts – Is its own origin of ill and end" (*CPW* IV: 101, ll. 129–31). And there is the display of "badness," as Manfred quests after "hidden knowledge" (II, ii, l. 110), summons the supernatural minions of "the Evil principle" (*BLJ* 5: 170), and demonstrates, ultimately, that he "can call the dead" (*CPW* IV: 76, l. 178).

Clearly this is not autobiographical, but just as clear is the fact that, on the issue of incest and its emotional consequences, the play deploys the idea of autobiography – the possibility that Byron is writing about himself – in ways that invite complicity and solicit sympathy, from within a fictional context that offers imaginative thrills beyond what is allowed by social norms. The manifest aim here is to face down the moral condemnation that led to Byron's self-exile by tapping into the fascination that was its flip-side – the fascination with the "mad, bad and dangerous to know" Byron that would lead crowds of tourists to watch him at Villa Diodati through "glasses" from "the opposite side of" Lake Geneva (Medwin 11). First of all, then, *Manfred*'s deployment of the idea of self-writing is part of its author's attempt to win back the complicity, sympathy and imaginative interest of his estranged readers.

However, Byron's evocation of autobiography in *Manfred* is also part of a larger battle for control over Byron's "bio" that began in his lifetime and continues today in biographies of the poet that base their narratives so centrally on Byron's own letters but seek to interpret them anew – a battle between the authority of biography versus that of autobiography in the public telling of private lives. According to Mary Godfrey, in February 1816 the "world [was] loud against" Byron and "vote[d] him a worthless profligate … I look on him as given up to every worthless excess" (quoted in MacCarthy 273). Byron himself said that in Switzerland there was "no story so absurd that they did not invent it at my cost … I was accused of corrupting all the *grisettes* in the Rue Basse." Back in Britain, Robert Southey, having returned from Switzerland in 1817, started spreading stories of Byron, the Shelleys and Claire Clairmont forming a "League of Incest" (MacCarthy 295, 296). This is not just condemnation, but the rewriting of Byron's life; like the poet's memoirs, *Manfred* is a response to those who have "traduced" that life and "branded" him.

Unlike the memoirs, though, *Manfred* does not aim to set the record straight. Rather, it brandishes the authority of autobiography against the claims of biography – the (re)writing of a life by someone else. The play does this, tantalizingly, by first suggesting an "autobiographical" confirmation of the "stories" told about the poet (in particular, about incest) but then withholding that confirmation. It stimulates the desire for a full, "autobiographical" confession that will prove beyond doubt that the "stories" are true, but, in the end, leaves the reader feeling the lack of that final, explicit proof.

In other words, Byron's evoking but then withholding autobiographical confession seeks to reveal biography's fundamental need of autobiography – a need of first-hand testimony, we might say – to supply it with its authority *as* biography, the writing of an *actual* life. Without autobiographical confirmation, *Manfred* implies, biography starts to feel like speculation. And, in this way, Byronic autobiography becomes, paradoxically and brilliantly, not a revelation of the private but a safeguard of privacy, precisely because it can be withheld. If the presence of autobiography has the authority to endorse, its absence has the power to undermine, to create doubt. In *Manfred*'s repeated, insistent withdrawal of autobiography behind the dashes that mark all the crucial "confessional" moments of the play, including those we have already looked at ("there was one –," "She was like me in lineaments –"), we thus see autobiography transformed into a defense against the "tales" told by biographies. These dashes, and the silence they point to, seek to make the reader begin to wonder whether, without the authority of a full autobiographical confession to support them, "stories" about Byron's personal life are anything more than "sound and fury / Signifying nothing" (*Macbeth* V, v, ll. 26–8).

Yet the overt withholding of autobiography naturally works the other way too, as it encourages the reader to wonder what other, true, perhaps even worse, "stories" Byron might tell us about himself, if he chose to – to wonder what really lies behind those dashes. Thus we might say, finally, that Byron's deployment of his own, highly distinctive "autobiographical" poetic, far from belonging to the confessional tradition of Rousseauean autobiography, is, rather, a high-wire act that self-consciously performs a Byron poised between self-revelation and self-concealment. It willfully, romantically, even aggressively, answers the Shandyean lament at a life being "put in jeopardy by words"[11] with a defiant cry of "Away with words!" – "I'll die as I have lived – alone" – while tantalizing us with the possibility that he might change his mind at any moment (*CHP* IV, st. 108, l. 972 [*CPW* II: 160]; *Manfred* III, iv, l. 90 [*CPW* IV: 100]).

NOTES

1 Jean Jacques Rousseau, *Confessions*, trans. John Grant (London: J. M. Dent, 1931), 1.
2 Laurence Sterne, *The Life and Opinions of Tristram Shandy, Gentleman*, Melvyn New and Joan New (eds.) (London: Penguin, 2003), 212, 149, 416.
3 Sterne, *Tristram Shandy*, 588.
4 Richard Lansdown, *The Cambridge Companion to Byron* (Cambridge, UK: Cambridge University Press, 2012), 47.
5 Jerome McGann, "Milton and Byron" and "Hero with a Thousand Faces: The Rhetoric of Byronism," in James Soderholm (ed.), *Byron and Romanticism* (Cambridge, UK: Cambridge University Press, 2002), 29, 142.
6 "*Parisina, Mazeppa* and Anglo-Italian Displacement," in Alan Rawes and Diego Saglia (eds.), *Byron and Italy* (Manchester: Manchester University Press, 2017), 151.
7 See my "'That Perverse Passion' and Benita Eisler's 'Byronic' Biography of Byron," in Arthur Bradley and Alan Rawes (eds.), *Romantic Biography* (Aldershot, UK: Ashgate, 2003), 74–92.

8 G. Wilson Knight, *Lord Byron's Marriage: The Evidence of the Asterisks* (London: Kegan Paul, 1957), 41, quoting John Cam Hobhouse and Thomas Moore.

9 Benita Eisler, *Byron: Child of Passion, Fool of Fame* (London: Hamish Hamilton, 1999), 424n.

10 Lady Caroline Lamb coined this famous phrase when she met Byron for the first time in 1812. See Elizabeth Jenkins, *Lady Caroline Lamb* (London: Victor Gollancz, 1932), 95.

11 Sterne, *Tristram Shandy*, 78.

CHAPTER 29

*"Litera*toor*" and Literary Theory*

Clara Tuite

This thing of rhyme I ne'er disdained to own.
English Bards and Scotch Reviewers (1809)

Contradiction was Byron's keynote. He initiated his career in rhyme with a gesture of disavowal: "Poetry, however, is not my primary vocation" (*CPW* 1: 33), the young Lord announced in the preface to *Hours of Idleness* (1807). Any consideration of Byron and literary theory needs to be alive to his testy relationship with what he famously dismissed as "the mart / For ... poetic diction" (*CPW* v: 391, ll. 685–6). But it is also clear that Byron lived and breathed literature, conceiving of it as a total system. It was the material system of publishing; a court-styled marketplace run by "the Allied Sovereigns of Grub-Street" (*BLJ* 8: 207); a social institution that transacted the business of authorial fame and afterlife; a conversation; an experiment in thought and sense; a tribute to and tributary of the flotsam and jetsam of everyday life; and a source of life itself. As Byron asked rhetorically of *Don Juan*, "is it not *life*, is it not *the thing*?" (*BLJ* 6: 232).

So committed was Byron to the idea of literature as a form of life that he rarely used the polite term *literature* without irony, often substituting trivializing terms like "scribblement" (*BLJ* 2: 20), "poeshie" (*BLJ* 7: 124) and "Literatoor" (*BLJ* 5: 198) – typographically mimicking a Scottish burr, paying tribute to the "colloquial powers" of the speaking voice (*BLJ* 2: 93), and putting into writing the effects of real speech. If literature was "high" writing, Byron went low.

In the Romantic period, the institution of literature and the field we know as literary theory had only just been invented. "Literature" was recognized as "a set of genres both segregated from, and elevated above, the general field of writing."[1] Philosophical or theoretical discussions of literature occurred under the rubric of "aesthetics," coined by the German philosopher Alexander Baumgarten in his *Reflections on Poetry* (1735). Byron produced important insights about all of these constitutive concerns of modern literary theory. Indeed, he anticipated many modern precepts by flouting them. Questioning the literary institution at the moment of its emergence, when traditional distinctions between classical and vernacular languages were giving way to a new hierarchy of imaginative (high) and non-imaginative (low) writing, Byron was immersed in debates about literary value, the creation of the English vernacular canon and its relation to the ancient classics. He celebrated the novelist Henry Fielding as "the *prose* Homer of human nature" (*BLJ* 8: 11–12), subverting the privileging of classical above vernacular language and poetry above the novel. In the essay *Letter to John Murray Esqre.* (1821), Byron offered a powerful defense of the low, in a discussion of social class and literary style: "there *is* a Nobility of thought and of Style – open to all Stations" and implicitly to all genders: "Gentlemanliness is … far more generally diffused among women than among men" (*CMP* 159–60).

The disavowal of interest that prefaced *Hours of Idleness* was spectacularly contradicted in *English Bards and Scotch Reviewers*, which surveyed the contemporary literary scene as a complex site of social, commercial and political transactions. Here, each fabled or excoriated authorial name is a hieroglyph indexing particular interrelations of social class, style, politics and religion. These tokens of literary currency testify to Byron's prodigious knowledge of literatures past and present. In *English Bards* and Byron's other satires, the Regency literary world is mapped with extraordinary power and intensity. Byron's all-encompassing response to any new book was also a response to its author. His sprawling multigeneric *oeuvre* is peopled by literary figures who appear like cameos in an epic picaresque: so Coleridge features as "Scamp" the lecturer in *The Blues* (the scamp was a highwayman in "flash" language) and Germaine de Staël is conflated with her most famous fictional protagonist as Corinna de Staël in "The Devil's Drive" (1811).

Fictional protagonist and author were strategically messed up in a way that urged readers to discriminate between them. In the Preface to *Childe Harold's Pilgrimage* IV (1818), Byron claims he was at pains to distinguish hero from author in previous cantos but isn't bothering any more because he has been ignored. Similarly, he often professed to be more interested in authors' lives than their works: "I have been turning over different *Lives* of the Poets. I rarely read their works" (*BLJ* 8: 21). In fact, Byron's reading was voracious and wide-ranging.

Byron follows his beloved Alexander Pope in presenting essays in poetic form; and the sustained self-reflexivity of his writing confutes the distinction between literary theory and practice. His writings across every genre are enactments of theoretical reflection and conversation about literature.

Byron's literary theory and criticism are by no means confined to his prose works, but these often-neglected works are important, both as essays in their own right and as part of the intertextual circuit of the Byronic *oeuvre*, as they elaborate the abiding theoretical topics of Byron's career. Their theoretical complexity is belied by their banally occasional titles: *To the Editor of the* British Review (written 1819, pub. 1822); *Letter to John Murray Esqre.* (1821); *Observations Upon Observations* (written 1821, pub. 1832); *Some Observations Upon an Article in* Blackwood's Edinburgh Magazine (written 1820, pub. 1833). Byron took his essays seriously enough to refer to them as "my prose tracts" (*BLJ* 8: 237) and to suggest that John Murray group them into a volume of "Miscellanies" (*BLJ* 9: 58). Two of the essays were occasioned by Byron's defense of Pope against W. L. Bowles' attack on the man (for bad morals) and his poetry (for allegedly following art over nature).

Byron's prose tracts, like his poems, insist upon the figurality of poetry and its powers – a form of *Don Juan's* "truth in masquerade" (*CPW* v: 476, l. 290). They foreground the relation between the author's life and work, employing a dialectical use of language to sustain critique and argument through parody and indirection. In *To the Editor of the* British Review (published as *Letter to the Editor of "My Grandmother's Review"*), Byron writes under the pseudonym "Wortley Clutterbuck" to defend *Don Juan* against an attack by *British Review* editor William Roberts. Teasing the reader to identify "the author whom I cannot find out – (can you?)" (*CMP* 84), Byron as Clutterbuck defends the theoretical principle of the author's right to be elusive, "unknown," a tissue of abyssal figurations. In the radical disingenuousness of his address as Clutterbuck to "My dear Mr Roberts," Byron gives a spectacular workout to what Michel Foucault calls the "author-function."[2]

Roberts was responding to a passage in which the narrator of *Don Juan* claimed to have bribed the editor to secure a positive review, and appears to out himself with a self-implicating confession: "I've bribed my Grandmother's review." But this powerful grenade of ambiguity proves too hard to pin down – not that this stopped Roberts from taking the bait, failing to see the claim "might have been in jest" (*CMP* 79). Parsing what may or may not be "a mere figurative allusion," Byron-Clutterbuck invents a "Conversazione" in which he was told that "my Grandmother" was the writer of the review – "thereby insinuating, my dear Roberts, that you were an old woman … so 'my Grandmother's review' and Roberts's – might be also synonimous" (*CMP* 82). But Byron-Clutterbuck insinuates only to disavow: "It is very unfair to judge of Sex from writings – particularly from those of the British review."

Byron was acutely preoccupied with the relationship between literature and the marketplace. When the *British Review* attacked *Don Juan* as "a poem so flagitious" that booksellers "disgrace themselves by selling it" (*CMP* 349), Byron pointed out that its sales were driven by his readers' desire: "there can be no very extensive selling … without buying" (*CMP* 80). Byron's engagement with the market was ambivalent and paradoxical: he was both a canny operator and hustler, and a satirical anatomist of nascent capitalist society. This ambivalent fascination with the workings of the market involves reworking the genre of the "puff," an excessive advertisement that inflates the value of its object. Here, Byron takes his cue from Richard Brinsley Sheridan's character Puff in *The Critic* (1779) and his parodic taxonomy of puffs ("the puff direct, the puff preliminary, the puff collateral, the puff collusive"). Invoking the "puff collusive," which "acts in the disguise of determined hostility" (*CMP* 352), Byron mischievously suggests that Roberts is secretly puffing Byron's work by drawing attention to it. This parodic invocation of appreciation in the guise of hostility demonstrates a fundamental principle of Byron's negative dialectics: that any attack betrays attraction. It exemplifies the parodic indirection and rhetorical contradiction that structures so much of Byron's philosophical thought and critical practice.

For Byron as a materialist, literary theory meant something different from the metaphysical abstractions that Coleridge produced in *Biographia Literaria* (1817), which celebrated the "dynamic philosophy" of Immanuel Kant, Johann Fichte and Friedrich Schelling.[3] Byron didn't like the *Literaria*'s metaphysics or its immersion in theoretical "obscurity." A similar obscurity marred Friedrich Schlegel's *History of Literature*: "[H]e always seems to be upon the verge of meaning; and, lo, he goes down like the sunset, or melts like a rainbow, leaving a rather rich confusion" (*BLJ* 8: 38). Philosophy for Byron was not about airy abstraction but the back and forth of argument: "I love a row" (*CMP* 79). His references to "the great Professor Kant" (*DJ* x, st. 60, l. 476) and "Philosopher Kant" ("The Devil's Drive," *CPW* iii: 102) are dismissively offhand. Satirically bandying about such honorifics, Byron resists the professionalization of philosophy, through which a domain that belongs to everyone was being turned into a specialized pursuit and appropriated through a rhetoric of expertise. In this sense, Byron is "antiphilosophical."[4]

A key Byronic contention is that theory belongs to everyone, as part of the sublimity and bathos of everyday life. The metaphysical is part of the physical, the soul part of the body. Aesthetics, too, refers not just to thought but also to perception and sensation; it was in this sense a form of sensuous knowledge and experience. These points are dramatized with great panache in *Don Juan* v's extended discussion of the interrelations between thinking and eating, which starts as a reflection about slavery and the appraisal of human flesh. When Juan is sold off at a Constantinople market and the merchant "began to think of dining" (*CPW* v: 250, l. 232), the narrator wonders "how far we should / Sell flesh and blood" (ll. 237–8) and whether such "odd thoughts might intrude" on the slaver's digestion (l. 235). Asking rhetorically, "who / Would pique himself on intellects, whose use / Depends so much upon the gastric juice?" (*CPW* v: 251, ll. 255–6), Byron prosecutes a powerful materialist case while playfully subordinating reason to the body. Emphasizing the genre of the argument as inherently sociable (unlike the philosopher's solipsistic abstraction), Juan's companion then "Said, 'In Heaven's name let's get some supper now, / And then I'm with you if you're for a row'" (*CPW* v: 256, ll. 375–6).

All for the convivial row, the narrator continues:

> Some talk of an appeal unto some passion,
>   Some to men's feelings, others to their reason;
> The last of these was never much the fashion,
>   For reason thinks all reasoning out of season …
>
> But I digress: of all appeals, – although
>   I grant the power of pathos, and of gold,
> Of beauty, flattery, threats, a shilling, – no
>   Method's more sure at moments to take hold
> Of the best feelings of mankind, which grow
>   More tender, as we every day behold,
> Than that all-softening, over-powering knell,
> The tocsin of the soul – the dinner bell.
>   (*DJ* v, st. 48–9, ll. 377–80, 385–92 [*CPW* v: 256])

Contrasting the philosophers' idealized Reason with ordinary common sense, Byron puns on "season" to mean out of fashion and out of taste (rhyming "reasoning" with the *seasoning* of food). He also implicitly refuses Kant's evaluative distinction between aesthetic and corporeal taste. Formulated in Kant's *Critique of Aesthetic Judgment* (1790), this distinction would go on to influence an entire tradition of bourgeois aesthetics; but as Pierre Bourdieu argues in his influential *Distinction: A Social Critique of the Judgment of Taste* (1979), such high-cultural judgments of taste are based on social exclusions.

The category of taste was set out in foundational works of literary criticism such as Lord Kames' *Elements of Criticism* (1762) and Hugh Blair's

Lectures on Rhetoric and Belles Lettres. Referring to Blair as one of "the highest reachers / Of eloquence in piety and prose" (*DJ* 11, st. 165, ll. 1318–20), Byron's mischievous pun on "poetry and prose" turns a compliment into a critique of Blair for replacing poetry with piety. At this time of profound social change, when religion was being displaced by literature, authors' religious views were fiercely scrutinized. Byron was routinely accused of blasphemy and retaliates here by calling out Blair's aesthetic blasphemy in twisting poetry into religion.

Byron's insistence on the autonomy of art anticipates the so-called art for art's sake movement of the mid-nineteenth century, which Bourdieu has described as enabling the "conquest" of aesthetic "autonomy" in its demand that art and literature be evaluated on their merits, without regard to morals or religion.[5] Musing over how Milton "shocks" "the Divines of his day" by "making the Devil his hero, and deifying the daemons," Byron reflected: "He certainly excites compassion for Satan ... I should be very curious to know what his real belief was" (Medwin 76). Underlying this offhand speculation is the serious question whether it is possible to read off authorial intention from the work.

Exploiting the generative capacity of the pun, Byron embeds a pun on "appeals" to refer to the *peals* of bells. In this chiming of "peals" with "appeals," the juxtaposition of the pealing dinner bell with the appeal to reason jolts "the reader out of complacency by insisting that objects or activities conventionally regarded as distinct may, in fact, be related in ways that do not necessarily end with their phonetic similarity."[6] Vitally, the play on words drives the conceptual investigation, dramatizing the profound intellectual agency of poetic form. A fascination with literature's capacity to compel and enchant informs this exuberant word play, which utilizes the serendipitous finding and forging of linguistic coincidence, connection and meaning. Such coincidence is dramatized by the openness of Byronic "Litera*toor*" to the winds of etymological change and the accrual of new meanings that could not possibly have been intended by the author. So, the 1889 coinage of "toxin" (by Ludwig Brieger) happily activates a pun on "tocsin" to mean both alarm bell and a poison produced by a living organism (especially one formed in the body). Here, the dinner bell as the toxin of the soul kills off pious Kantian and religious notions alike that the body is subordinate to the soul.

For all Byron's dismissive references to "poesy," it was his highest aspiration to produce a poem. As he writes in the quiet days before the publication of *Childe Harold*, "I know I have everything against me, angry poets and prejudices; but if the poem is a *poem*, it will surmount these obstacles, and if not, it deserves its fate" (*BLJ* 2: 92). What, then, made a poem a *poem*, even when it challenged conventional rules of genre? The distinguishing characteristic was "rhyme" itself. As Jane Stabler observes, Byron's texts are "energized conceptually and practically by strict adherence to verse structure."[7] Verse structure's paradoxical binding of rules and chance energized Byron's poetry in its evolution toward a form that best enabled their fortunate coincidence, thereby demonstrating the productive force and agency of poetry.

Like his contemporaries Wordsworth and Coleridge, Byron placed a premium on writing that captured the rhythms of speech. Paradoxically, writing *Beppo* and *Don Juan* in *ottava rima* – a challenging form that required an unusually high number of rhyming words – enabled him to express himself in poetry with the same freedom as in his letters, journals and conversation. His adoption of this demanding technique demonstrated his commitment to conversation and "colloquial powers" (*BLJ* 2: 93).

Byron was notoriously iconoclastic about the formal rules of genre, but he was also notoriously inconsistent. He would sometimes invoke the rules he broke, or use classical models to justify breaking the rules, as when he described *Childe Harold* I–II as "a poem on *Ariosto's plan* that *is* to *say* on *no plan* at all" (*BLJ* 2: 63). In the preface to his three tragedies (including *Sardanapalus*), Byron invoked Aristotelian classical "unities" (*CPW* VI: 16–17), implicitly against the Shakespearean traditions of the English stage, but wrote a Shakespearean play of mixed moods anyway. He worried over its reception in a letter to Murray:

> I trust that "Sardanapalus" will not be mistaken for a *political* play – which was so far from my intention that I thought of nothing but Asiatic history … My object has been to dramatize like the Greeks (a *modest* phrase!) striking passages of history, as they did of history & mythology. – You will find all this very *un*like Shakespeare – and so much better in one sense – for I look upon him to be the *worst* of models – though the most extraordinary of writers … The hardship is that in these times one can neither speak of kings or Queens without suspicion of politics or personalities. – I intended neither. (*BLJ* 8: 152)

Despite the seemingly open clarification of authorial intention against "mistaken" interpretation, we can read between the lines a *dis*avowal of allegorical intention, and the implicit suggestion that readers will read – regardless of authorial intention – in a variety of ways. In fact, when Byron sets out to explain his intentions, what follows is often anything *but*. Irony, the double negative and disavowal ("I intended neither") are all parts of Byron's habitual authorial practice, clarifying nothing except perhaps the intention to contradict.

Byron also had a habit of discounting – while enumerating – the very things he wanted readers to notice. The pious distinction between history and politics disavows what was in fact a well-established contemporary practice of reading historical plays allegorically. And "suspicion of politics and personalities" is precisely what he is soliciting. The consummate if often contradictory field of poetry, theory and critical practice that is Byronic "Litera*toor*" thrives in these spaces of open possibility that invite speculation and multiple interpretations. Its strenuous, exuberant self-reflexivity is no less enigmatic or urgent now than it was then.

NOTES

1 John Guillory, *Cultural Capital: The Problem of Literary Canon Formation* (Chicago: University of Chicago Press, 1993), 213.
2 Michel Foucault, "What Is an Author?," in *Textual Strategies: Perspectives in Post-Structuralist Criticism*, ed. Josué V. Harari (London: Methuen, 1979), 148.
3 Samuel Taylor Coleridge, *Biographia Literaria*, eds. James Engell and W. Jackson Bate (Princeton: Princeton University Press, 1983), vol. ii, 162, 89.
4 James Chandler, *England in 1819* (Chicago: University of Chicago Press, 1998), 263.
5 Pierre Bourdieu, *The Rules of Art: Genesis and Structure of the Literary Field*, trans. Susan Emanuel (Cambridge, UK: Polity Press, 1996), 47.
6 Anne Barton, *Byron*: Don Juan (Cambridge, UK: Cambridge University Press, 1992), 18.
7 Jane Stabler, *Byron, Poetics and History* (Cambridge, UK: Cambridge University Press, 2002), 17.

CHAPTER 30

Periodical Culture, the Literary Review and the Mass Media

Andrew Franta

Byron's career as a poet was bound up with the periodical reviews from the start. Beginning with the publication of *English Bards and Scotch Reviewers* in 1809 – and, even earlier, with the hostile review of *Hours of Idleness* in the *Edinburgh Review* that prompted it – Byron's identity as a poet was distinctly *public* – and public in a new way. In one sense, this goes without saying: Byron was famous, and famously so. In another sense, however, the public nature of Byron's career – and its close proximity to the developing culture of reviewing – has been difficult to see. Despite the long-standing critical interest in early nineteenth-century reviewing, we have only recently begun to appreciate the extent to which Romantic literature and periodical reviewing were reciprocal activities. Considering Byron's career in the context of the literary reviews and the emerging mass media discloses the sense in which the periodical culture of reviewing was transforming literary production in the Romantic period. Byron's poetry makes it dramatically clear that the literary world into which the new poet sought to introduce himself in the early nineteenth century was one that was in the process of being remade by the interconnection of poetry and the reviews.

English Bards has led something of a double life in Byron criticism. It has long been regarded as both a preview of the kind of wit and invective that would fuel much of Byron's subsequent poetry, especially *Don Juan*, and at the same time a disjointed, disorganized mess. As Mary Clearman observed in 1970, "the poem is confusing, and its failure to follow any logical plan or outline leaves even the careful reader grappling with a series of vivid but unrelated sketches."[1] Following Claude M. Fuess' account of the influence of Juvenal's first satire on *English Bards*, Clearman argued that the poem makes better sense if we recognize Juvenal as Byron's model; both poets, she claims, are "introducing" themselves as satirists, "and providing a preface for future satirical poems."[2] But, as Fuess argued, *English Bards* has a "double object." "[I]t is, in one sense," he wrote in 1912, "an attempt at retaliation upon the editors of the *Edinburgh Review*," and, "in another, an eager and deliberate defense of the Popean tradition in poetry."[3] This divided purpose reflects the poem's compositional history; provoked by the *Edinburgh*'s review of *Hours of Idleness*, Byron expanded the scope of *British Bards*, the satire on contemporary poets on which he was working, to include contemporary periodical reviewers as well (*BLJ* 1: 136). For many readers and critics, the poem's "double object" has been its principal defect and the chief souce of its incoherence. As Fuess put it, Byron was "posing as an overthrower of intolerant reviewers, and at the same time outdoing them in unjust and prejudiced criticism."[4] On the one hand, he rejects the *Edinburgh* reviewer's ungrounded assumption of authority. On the other hand, he assumes a similarly ungrounded authority in attacking his contemporaries. The combination of these two incompatible attitudes makes *English Bards* an incoherent poem.

The tension between poet and reviewer is central not only to *English Bards and Scotch Reviewers* but also to Byron's relationship with the reviews and to the place of the poet in the literary culture of the early nineteenth century. Put simply, Byron offers a picture of the poet not so much at odds with hostile reviewers as engaged with reviewers in a competition for literary authority. That poets and reviewers sought to occupy the same cultural space is what it means for poetry to be among the mass media. Thus, while *English Bards* might appear to be merely a circumstantial response to the *Edinburgh Review*'s provocation – the kind of "personal and occasional Satire" that Wordsworth claimed "rarely comprehend[s] sufficient of the general in the individual to be dignified with the name of poetry"[5] – in responding to the *Edinburgh*'s attack, and in combining his assessment of the contemporary world of letters with a critique of the contemporary practice of reviewing, Byron does more than merely take revenge on a reviewer. Instead, in *English Bards*, he yokes poets and reviewers together, and, in so doing, suggests that their relationship is symbiotic rather than antagonistic. From *English Bards* to *Don Juan*, Byron recasts the idea that reviewers are fundamentally parasitic, that they live on the literature they review (a view maintained by many early nineteenth-century commentators), into a critique of the groundlessness of judgment in a literary culture founded on the expression of opinion and a literary practice that capitalizes on the structural correlation between the position of the reviewer and that of the poet. "Moved by the great example" of the reviewers, Byron advances the ironic claim that he will "pursue / The self-same road, but make my own review: / Not seek great JEFFREY's yet like him will be / Self-constituted Judge of Poesy" (*CPW* 1: 231, ll. 59–62).

The tenor of the *Edinburgh*'s review of *Hours of Idleness* and its importance to Byron's career reflect key aspects of the reviews' central place in the literary landscape of early nineteenth-century Britain. The *Edinburgh Review* (established in 1802 by Francis Jeffrey, Sydney Smith, Henry Brougham and Francis Horner, and published by Archibald Constable) and its main rival, the *Quarterly Review* (founded in 1809 by Byron's publisher, John Murray, edited by William Gifford, and modeled on the *Edinburgh*), claimed a new kind of authority for the critic. It has long been accepted that the *Edinburgh* radically revised the traditional practice of literary reviewing it inherited from the eighteenth century. Derek Roper qualified this claim in *Reviewing Before the "Edinburgh," 1788–1802* (1978), but even his measured account confirms the difference in emphasis that distinguished the *Edinburgh* and the *Quarterly* from their precursors. The reviews of the eighteenth century sought to introduce readers to a wide range of works and provide them with a current, and cumulative, picture of "literature" in the broadest sense. Such established periodicals as the *Monthly Review* (founded by Ralph Griffiths in 1749) and the *Critical Review* (founded by Tobias Smollett, a contributor to the *Monthly*, in 1756) regularly reviewed forty or more works in a single monthly issue and often treated multiple works in a single article. By contrast, the *Edinburgh* and the *Quarterly* were ruthlessly selective in their coverage of new publications. The *Edinburgh* addressed a much smaller number of books from the outset and devoted most of its articles to a single work; the *Quarterly* followed suit, and by the 1810s each review normally published just twelve articles per issue.

The *Edinburgh* and the *Quarterly* also departed from the practice of earlier reviews in their emphasis on reviewers' opinions. Eighteenth-century reviews included some critical commentary, but they focused on summarizing the contents of the works under consideration and devoted considerable space to often lengthy extracts. Griffiths' description of the *Monthly*'s critical practice – "to enter no farther into the province of criticism, than just so far as may be indispensably necessary to give some idea of such books as come under our consideration" – stands in stark contrast to the authoritative critical posture assumed by the reviewers who wrote for the *Edinburgh* and the *Quarterly*.[6] The *Edinburgh*'s review of *Hours of Idleness* (which Byron assumed was Francis Jeffrey's work but was actually written by Henry Brougham) exemplifies this new practice of reviewing:

> The poesy of this young lord belongs to the class which neither gods nor men are said to permit. Indeed, we do not recollect to have seen a quantity

of verse with so few deviations in either direction from that exact standard. His effusions are spread over a dead flat, and can no more get above or below the level, than if they were so much stagnant water. (*BCH* 27)

As Marilyn Butler has written of the *Edinburgh*, "If a single characteristic accounts for the supremacy of this journal, it is arrogance."[7]

The *Edinburgh*'s and the *Quarterly*'s selectiveness about the titles they reviewed and their development of distinctive editorial voices both respond to the expansion of the reading public and of the literary marketplace at the end of the eighteenth century. While the success of the eighteenth-century reviews reflected the growth of the marketplace for books, the *Edinburgh* and the *Quarterly* were responding to a literary world that suddenly seemed overpopulated with readers and books, and they took advantage of the explosion in the supply of reading materials in a way that made the case for their own indispensability as arbiters of culture. William St Clair has powerfully described the "rapid expansion in reading" that began in the 1790s and continued throughout the Romantic period; and, as Leigh Hunt recognized in an 1817 review of Percy Shelley's *The Revolt of Islam*, "although the art of printing is not new, the Press in any great and true sense of the word is a modern engine in the comparison … *Books* did what was done before; they have now a million times the range and power."[8]

St Clair's account of the reading nation and Hunt's observation about the new "range and power" of the press both reflect the transformative effect of the French Revolution and the political discourse of the 1790s on literature and the reading public. From the beginning, the reviews organized themselves, and appealed to readers, along political lines: Ralph Griffiths was a nonconformist, and the political outlook of the *Monthly Review* was Whiggish; Smollett's *Critical Review* was Tory and High Church. Although less influential than the *Monthly* or the *Critical*, the *Analytical Review*, founded by the radical bookseller and publisher Joseph Johnson and Thomas Christie in London in 1788, established a place in the reviewing landscape for dissenting views. On the opposite side of the political spectrum were the *British Critic: A New Review*, established in 1793 by the conservative Society for the Reformation of Principles, and the *Anti-Jacobin, or, Weekly Examiner* (1797–8), a short-lived but influential political newspaper founded by William Canning and edited by William Gifford. Both the *British Critic* and the *Anti-Jacobin* participated in the British reaction against the French Revolution, and the *Anti-Jacobin* in particular embodied what William Hazlitt would later call "the invisible link, that connects literature with the police."[9] The *Anti-Jacobin* was important both for its politics and its emphasis on satire and poetry – a conjunction that would have a powerful influence on Byron's career. More broadly, its significance reflects the impetus provided by the French Revolution for an intensified politicization of the reviews – as well as the emergence of the mass public on which both the *Edinburgh* and the *Quarterly* would soon capitalize.

The intensity of the revolution controversy in Britain has been gauged by the sales figures for Tom Paine's *Rights of Man* and the number of radical pamphlets published in the 1790s. Paine estimated that *Rights of Man* had sold one-and-a-half million copies by 1809; Richard Altick gives a more conservative estimate, placing the number at a still-impressive 100,000.[10] This paper war served to fuel the growth of the reading public – and also to reveal its size and scope. Like their eighteenth-cenury precursors, the *Edinburgh* and the *Quarterly* were partisan publications. The *Edinburgh* promoted the Whig party and its contributors frequently argued for reform; the *Quarterly* was designed to give an equal voice to the Tory interest. But the most significant respect in which the *Edinburgh* and the *Quarterly* differed from eighteenth-century reviews and reflected the influence of the revolution debate of the 1790s was the extent of their circulation. The *Monthly*, the most successful of the eighteenth-century reviews, had a paid circulation of 5,000 subscribers in 1797; the *Edinburgh* grew from an initial print run of 750 (which quickly sold out) to 4,000 copies in 1805 and, at the height of its popularity, 13,000 copies in 1814.[11] The sales figures of the *Quarterly* rose even more rapidly and soon matched, or even surpassed, those of the *Edinburgh*. Although they never achieved the circulation of the *Edinburgh* and the *Quarterly*, the other major reviews of the Romantic period, *Blackwood's Edinburgh Magazine* (est. 1817), the *London Magazine* (1820–9) and the *Westminster Review* (est. 1824), each carved out its own literary and political niche in this greatly expanded marketplace.

In an unpublished response to a savage review of the first two cantos of *Don Juan* published in *Blackwood's*, titled *Some Observations Upon an Article in* Blackwood's Edinburgh Magazine (1820), Byron looks back on his departure from England and remarks, "The fashionable world was divided into parties" (*CMP* 95). He offers a picture of a literary world that is similarly divided, and returns, twelve years later, to the targets of his satirical attacks in *English Bards*. If the "double object" of satire in *English Bards* seems disjointed, *Some Observations* articulates the principle that connects Byron's response to the *Edinburgh Review* and his defense of Pope. "These three personages Southey – Wordsworth, and Coleridge," Byron writes, "had all of them a very natural antipathy to Pope, and I respect them for it … But they have been joined in it by those who have joined them in nothing else" (*CMP* 106). The distaste for Pope's poetry, in short, has itself become a fashion:

> [T]he Edinburgh Reviewers, and the Lakers – and Hunt and his school, and every body else with their School, and even Moore – without a School – and dilettanti lecturers at Institutions – and elderly Gentlemen who translate and imitate, – and young ladies who listen and repeat – Baronets who draw indifferent frontispieces for bad poets, and noblemen who let them dine with them – in the Country, the small body of the wits and the great body of the Blues – have latterly united in the depreciation of which their fathers would have been as much ashamed as their Children will be. (*CMP* 106–7)

The problem described in both the *Edinburgh*'s review of *Hours of Idleness* and *Blackwood*'s of *Don Juan* is that of a literary world divided into parties, factions and schools – interest groups whose individual members have nothing in common but their opinions and for whom communal identity has taken the place of individual judgment.

But it would be a mistake to suggest that nothing changes between *English Bards* and *Don Juan*. In fact, this is the period during which the reviews made their most significant contribution to British literary culture. The *Edinburgh* and the *Quarterly* made opinion, but they also made opinion-making central to the literary world, and Byron's satirical attacks on the reviews register their growing importance. In *English Bards*, he called out reviewers by name. In *Don Juan*, he calls out the reviews in general. In order to defend his poem in advance from charges of immorality, he hatches a plan designed to beat the reviews at their own game, claiming that he has "bribed my grandmother's review – the British":

> I sent it in a letter to the editor,
>   Who thank'd me duly by return of post –
> I'm for a handsome article his creditor;
>   Yet if my gentle Muse he please to roast,
> And break a promise after having made it her,
>   Denying the receipt of what it cost,
> And smear his page with gall instead of honey,
> All I can say is – that he had the money.
>
> I think that with this holy new alliance
>   I may ensure the public, and defy
> All other magazines of art or science,

> Daily, or monthly, or three monthly; I
> Have not essay'd to multiply their clients,
>   Because they tell me 'twere in vain to try,
> And the Edinburgh Review and Quarterly
> Treat a dissenting author very martyrly.
>   (*DJ* I, st. 210–11, ll. 1673–88 [*CPW* v: 76])

As the first canto of *Don Juan* draws to a close, Byron promises his "gentle reader! and / Still gentler purchaser" (ll. 1761–2) that he will only continue the poem if they approve – "and if not, I shall not try / Your patience further than by this short sample" (ll. 1766–7). But he claims that he has improved the odds of their approval by bribing a review editor; "this holy new alliance" (ll. 1681) between poet and reviewer will "ensure the public" (ll. 1682). His scheme casts doubt on the impartiality of the reviews – not because we believe that he has in fact bribed an editor but because the claim itself underscores the commercial basis of the reviews' pretense of disinterested judgment. That he accepts that it would be "in vain to try" to buy a positive review from the *Edinburgh* or the *Quarterly* is no testament to their impartiality (ll. 1686). Instead, it darkly insinuates that, like political parties and poetic schools, reviews like the *Edinburgh* and *Quarterly* make opinion by advancing their own.

NOTES

1 Mary Clearman, "A Blueprint for *English Bards and Scotch Reviewers*: The First Satire of Juvenal," *Keats–Shelley Journal* 19 (1970), 87.
2 Ibid., 89.
3 Claude M. Fuess, *Lord Byron as a Satirist in Verse* (New York: Columbia, 1912), 49.
4 Ibid., 50.
5 "Preface to the Edition of 1815," in W. J. B. Owen and Jane Worthington Smyser (eds.), *The Prose Works of William Wordsworth*, eds. 3 vols. (Oxford: Clarendon Press, 1974), vol. III, 28.
6 Quoted in Derek Roper, *Reviewing Before the "Edinburgh," 1788–1802* (Newark: University of Delaware Press, 1978), 20.
7 Marilyn Butler, "Culture's Medium: The Role of the Review," in Stuart Curran (ed.), *The Cambridge Companion to British Romanticism* (Cambridge, UK: Cambridge University Press, 1993), 131.
8 William St Clair, *The Reading Nation in the Romantic Period* (Cambridge, UK: Cambridge University Press, 2004), 11; and *Shelley: The Critical Heritage*, ed. James E. Barcus (London: Routledge & Kegan Paul, 1975), 114.
9 William Hazlitt, *Letter to William Gifford, Esq.*, in *The Complete Works of William Hazlitt*, ed. P. P. Howe, 21 vols. (London: J. M. Dent & Sons, 1930–4), vol. IX, 13.

10 For Paine's estimate, see Marilyn Butler, *Burke, Paine, Godwin, and the Revolution Controversy* (Cambridge, UK: Cambridge University Press, 1984), 109; for Altick's, see *The English Common Reader: A Social History of the Mass Reading Public* (Chicago: University of Chicago Press, 1957), 70.

11 For these figures, see Roper, *Reviewing*, 24, and John Clive, *Scotch Reviewers: The Edinburgh Review, 1802–1815* (London: Faber & Faber, 1957), 133–5.

PART IV

Reception and Afterlives

CHAPTER 31

Contemporary Critical Reception to 1824

William Christie

"As an author, I am cut to atoms by the E[dinburgh] Review," Byron wrote to John Cam Hobhouse a month after his twentieth birthday, "it is just out, and has completely demolished my little fabric of fame, this is rather scurvy treatment from a Whig Review, but politics and poetry are different things, & I am no adept in either, I therefore submit in Silence" (*BLJ* 1: 158–9). The savage attack on *Hours of Idleness* in the *Edinburgh Review* of January 1808, subjecting Byron to a rite of passage reserved by Romantic periodicals for select authors, was a defining moment in the young poet's career. If the author of *Childe Harold's Pilgrimage* would awake in 1812 to find himself famous, it was only after the author of *Hours of Idleness* had awoken one day early in 1808 to find himself humiliated. A harsh review of his first public poetic venture (*Fugitive Pieces* and *Poems on Various Occasions* had both been privately published), appearing in the leading periodical of the day and written (Byron assumed) by its editor, Francis Jeffrey, the man who for many of his contemporaries was or would become the leading critic of the day – all this clearly mattered to the young poet. As did the fact that the *Edinburgh* had recently "come out" as an unequivocally Whig review.

The review of *Hours* was not written by Jeffrey, as it happens, but by the *Edinburgh*'s most prolific contributor, Henry Brougham. What mattered at the time, however, was not so much who wrote it as the fact that a good review from the *Edinburgh* was sufficient, if not necessary, to establish a literary reputation. The cultural influence self-consciously exerted by the prominent periodicals of the day – primarily by the *Edinburgh* (1802) and *Quarterly Review* (1809), but also on occasion by the older *Monthly Review* (1749) and *Critical Review* (1756), the *British Critic* (1793), *Anti-Jacobin Review* (1798), *Eclectic Review* (1805) and *British Review* (1811), as well as by critical reviewing in postwar magazines such as *Blackwood's Edinburgh Magazine* (1817) and the *London Magazine* (1820) – confirmed the extent to which nineteenth-century Britain had become a periodical culture fighting "over economics and information," to quote Mark Schoenfield, "over political and aesthetic norms, over the control of public opinion and the boundary between public and private."[1] The influence of periodical reviewing was never limited to promoting books as commercial objects. From the beginning, reviews and magazines were also engaged in the culture of ideas and ideologies, reflecting and fueling political and cultural antagonisms that became more open and divisive after the French Revolution. Later, when he abandoned his conservative publisher and *Don Juan* became more openly radical and skeptical, Byron would feel the full force of this ongoing battle.

It was to realize the intellectual and political potential of book reviewing that the *Edinburgh* had been launched in October 1802.[2] Thanks to some clever, scathing, but well-informed and well-argued reviews, it had erupted into the intellectual life of early nineteenth-century Britain. The *Quarterly*, set up in emulation and political opposition, was the brainchild of a handful of Tory writers and intellectuals, including poet and novelist Walter Scott, John Murray, the second-generation Scot who would become both the *Quarterly*'s and Byron's publisher, and George Canning, the leader of the liberal conservative faction of the Tory party. Under the editorship of Canning's close literary associate William Gifford, with whom he had published the *Anti-Jacobin, or Weekly Examiner* in 1797–8, the *Quarterly* would begin a comparably wide-ranging, more politically conservative survey of contemporary literature. Byron's complicated relationships with the *Quarterly*'s publisher and editor make a simple political interpretation of the poet's critical reception impossible. Gifford, the author of the successful 1790s satire *The Baviad* (1791), would become Byron's literary mentor. The big reviews may have had barely concealed political priorities – their "Right leg is politics," as Jeffrey famously insisted[3] – but this did not always translate into predictable allegiances, as Byron discovered with the *Edinburgh*'s treatment of *Hours of Idleness*.

The *Edinburgh* and the *Quarterly* dominated the years of Byron's contemporary critical reputation (1807–24) – not just its book reviewing, but also its thinking. Book reviews gradually expanded in length, up to as many as sixty pages, with the reviewer and his ideas taking precedence over the book under review and assuming greater authority than the author and the reader: "he establishes his own claims in an elaborate inaugural dissertation," wrote Hazlitt, "before he deigns to bring forward the pretentions of the original candidate for praise, who is only the second figure in the piece."[4] The *third* figure, in fact: the editor took precedence over *both* reviewer *and* author, more or less subtly letting contributors know what approach and judgment he had in mind when commissioning a review, then often modifying them after submission. The *Edinburgh* and the *Quarterly* also paid astonishingly well, a fact that soon became part of the aura of periodical reviewing and integral to its authority and reputation. With comparative independence and a dramatic increase in financial remuneration came a dramatic rise in cultural and social status.

The final innovation attributable to the *Edinburgh* and characteristic of early nineteenth-century reviewing generally was the critical severity apparent in Brougham's review of *Hours of Idleness*, a severity foreshadowed in the *Edinburgh*'s motto *Judex damnatur cum nocens absolvitur* – "the judge stands condemned when the guilty are acquitted" – which literalizes the idea of the review as judicial enquiry and highlights the ethical and social accountability of the work under review. Preemptive appeals to reviewers for clemency and complaints about their malevolence were hardly new, but with the *Edinburgh* misrepresentation and severity become especially willful and especially skillful, politically calculated and sometimes vicious and inexcusable. It was a style best exemplified by Jeffrey himself in reviews of Walter Scott, Joanna Baillie, John Thelwall, Thomas Moore and (most notoriously) William Wordsworth. It was understandable that Byron assumed Jeffrey's authorship.

The conduct of the *Quarterly* confirmed critical severity as a cultural habit and it was not long before the Shelleys, Hunt and Hazlitt, Walter Savage Landor and Sydney Owenson were falling foul of its conservative attacks. The infamous attack on John Keats and the Cockney writers that began with John Gibson Lockhart in *Blackwood's Edinburgh Magazine* was taken up by John Wilson Croker and carried over into the *Quarterly*. Equally dismissive, not to say abusive on occasion, *Blackwood's* was only less predictable in its labile, upper-class critical hijinks, in which Wordsworth, Coleridge and Byron all suffered extremes of praise and abuse, sometimes in the same number. "Attacking persons as much as principles, the reviewers and critics of Romantic Britain positioned one another as often according to their social habitus as to their critical postures," writes Jon Klancher: "Class and gender associations became means of crediting or discrediting a bewilderingly various array of critical positions."[5]

Accordingly, Brougham mercilessly dissects the aristocratic pretensions and disingenuousness of *Hours of Idleness*, focusing on marginal aspects of the text – title, epigrams, preface, notes, dates – all of which are seen to signify in a psychological and ideological critique that rightly identifies the poet's self-projection as central to the volume. Where all but a couple of the other twenty reviewers who attended to *Hours of Idleness* took the unknown young poet largely at his own word, Brougham not only refused to indulge Byron but also critically probed the demand for indulgence itself. As for the poems: "His effusions are spread over a dead flat, and can no more get above or below the level, than if they were so much stagnant water" (*ER* 9, January 1808, 285). Byron was understandably and justifiably shocked. As a Whig, he had presumed upon the *Edinburgh*'s allegiance, but the figure of the insouciant patrician – of Byron straining to establish his credentials as an aristocrat and a poet (*Crede Byron*) – only provoked his reviewer. The Cambridge Whig Club that Hobhouse and Byron joined in 1807 might have been "typically Whig," but its "commitment to aristocratic manners and politeness"[6] meant that its members distinguished themselves from middle-class lawyers like the aspiring *Edinburgh* reviewers, who were already fast becoming the party's leading ideologues. It was not just that "politics and poetry are rather different things," as Byron surmised when attempting to come to terms with the *Edinburgh*'s dismissal, but that politics and politics were also different things.

The *Edinburgh*'s savaging of *Hours of Idleness* led first to despair, then to *English Bards and Scotch Reviewers*, in which Byron transformed his humiliation into an attack on Jeffrey and Scotland.[7] Byron and Jeffrey, however, did not remain enemies for long. Jeffrey assumed responsibility for reviewing Byron in the *Edinburgh* and went on to become his most consistent and astute contemporary critic, celebrating him as the most original and strongest poet of the day. Even in exile, Byron would make sporadic efforts to keep up with the reviews and, once Jeffrey had become "the monarch of existing criticism," happily circulated Jeffrey's opinion that he was himself the monarch of existing poets (*BLJ* 4: 87).

Jeffrey was not alone in celebrating Byron, of course. Byron may not always have been the most read poet of his generation – that was the privilege of Walter Scott[8] – but he was the most discussed and the most reviewed. Donald Reiman reprints over 500 separate contemporary articles in his multi-volume *Romantics Reviewed*. "Almost all his publications," writes Andrew Rutherford, "major or minor, failures and successes, were the subject of widespread critical discussion." And, as Rutherford also reminds us, that discussion took many different forms, including "tributes, attacks, and parodies in verse," "pamphlets" (especially later with highly controversial work like *Cain* and *Don Juan*), critical essays in cultural histories, and reflections in novels like Jane Austen's *Persuasion* – before we begin on letters and journals and dinner-table discussion (*BCH* 1). Reviews, then, constitute only a part of Byron's critical reception.

The overwhelming majority of reviews, moreover, were favorable. Even before the overnight sensation of *Childe Harold*, both *Hours of Idleness* and *English Bards* had met with praise, the latter almost universally. Not surprisingly, given the seductively autobiographical nature of the poetry and "the compulsion for public recognition,"[9] the fluctuations of Byron's critical reputation closely followed the fluctuations of his fame, leading to "the perfect bell curve of his reputation during the years 1812–1816."[10] If critical reception of his early volumes was flattering, with *Childe Harold* it becomes effusive, competitively so. Having bypassed *English Bards*, the *Edinburgh* and the *Quarterly* give the poem sustained attention. Speculation as to Byron's relationship with his hero gets under way, as does the reconstruction of his literary heritage in Milton's Satan, but what critics return to again and again in seeking to characterize the author's "genius" are the striking imagery, sublime descriptions, "impetuous feeling," and "tone of self-willed independence and originality" (*ER* 19, February 1812, 466–7). In wondering out loud whether the "gloominess" or melancholy that should detract from the poem are not central to its (and Byron's) attractiveness, Jeffrey captures the sado-masochistic fascination of his generation: "We do not know, indeed, whether there is not something *piquant* in the very novelty and singularity of that cast of misanthropy and universal scorn, which we have already noticed as amongst the more repulsive features of the composition. It ... gives such great effect to the flashes of emotion and oppressed sensibility that occasionally burst through the gloom" (*ER* 19, February 1812, 467).

Just as *Childe Harold* proves compelling beyond the critical shortcomings identified by the reviewers – its anti-heroic hero and absence of plot, Byron's handling of the Spenserian stanza – so a Turkish tale like *The Giaour* (1813) triumphs in spite of its fragmentariness and willful narrative obliquities, its arbitrary structure and morally dubious hero. After *The Giaour*, the comparative accessibility of *The Bride of Abydos* (1813) inspires a chorus of approval and *The Corsair* (1814) is celebrated as a consummation. Throughout this periodical chorus, Jeffrey welcomes "those deep and powerful emotions that alternately enchant and agonize the mind," while seeking a context for the Byron phenomenon in a history of the emotions and the temporal and cultural dislocations necessitated by a new structure of feeling (*ER* 23, April 1814, 198).

There is a clear falling off in Byron's poetic reputation with *Lara* (1814) and *The Siege of Corinth* (1816), a growing impatience among reviewers with the carelessness and repetition of the romances, along with occasional misgivings about Byron's politics, religious relativism and moral laxity that anticipate the outcry provoked in the first instance by *Manfred* (1817), with its existential hubris and hint of incest, then loudly and unremittingly by *Don Juan* (1819–) and *Cain* (1821). Before then, however, once the nation has recovered from the scandal of Byron's widely publicized separation and exile, the publication of *Childe Harold* Cantos III (1816) and IV (1818) represents the high point of Byron's contemporary critical reputation, as reviewers move beyond their infatuation with the novelty of the Byronic to take stock of his career, acknowledging *Childe Harold* "the finest, beyond all comparison, of Byron's poems" (*Blackwood's* 3, May 1818, 219). Not everyone, it should be said, but the majority of periodicals (and all the major ones) greet the final cantos with considered admiration. Reviewing Canto III in the *Quarterly*, Walter Scott is willing to forgo his own antipathy to its repugnant politics in order to salvage Byron's reputation: "we owe it to the pleasure he has bestowed upon us, and to the honor he has done to our literature" (*QR* 16, October 1816, 206). Jeffrey takes the opportunity to analyze in more detail "the temperament of Lord Byron's ideal hero," its literary genealogy and its social consequences, before declaring Canto III (against expectation) the most successful: "the same bright gaze on nature, and the same magic power of giving interest and effect to her delineations – but mixed up, we think, with deeper and more matured reflections, and a more intense sensibility to all that is grand or lovely in the external world" (*ER* 27, December 1816, 292). For John Wilson, who reviewed Canto IV in both the *Edinburgh* and *Blackwood's*, Byron is to be compared only with Rousseau "in the continual embodying of the individual character, – it might almost be said, of the very person of the writer." In arguably the most telling phrase in all the contemporary critical reception of Byron, Wilson's erotics of reading can stand for his generation: "we feel as if chosen out from a crowd of lovers" (*ER* 30, June 1818, 90).

With the advent of *Don Juan*, however, it really was downhill all the way, as periodical after periodical either regretted the sad demise of a once-great poet (especially reviewing the dramas) or execrated his moral corruption. When Byron deserted Murray in 1823 to embrace the radical John Hunt as his publisher, everything he wrote was damned by association. Having lived by publicity, he looked set to die by publicity, but the poet never wavered in his conviction of the originality and (ironically, in the light of the review reaction) moral probity of *Don Juan*. Perversely, *Blackwood's* characteristic ambivalence was able to come into its own and register, in its contempt no less than in its concessions, the courage and originality of Byron's final masterpiece: "Call things wicked, base, vile, obscene, blasphemous," wrote Lockhart, "but never say they are stupid when they are not." *Don Juan* is, "without exception, the first of Lord Byron's works" (*Blackwood's* 14, September 1823, 282–3).

With *Cain* and *Don Juan*, however, Jeffrey's "intellectual sympathy with Byron reached a crisis point."[11] Unfazed by its sexual explicitness, Jeffrey could not forgive "a tendency to destroy all belief in the reality of virtue" (*ER* 36, February 1822, 448). In the thirteenth canto of *Don Juan*, Byron returned to his original skirmish with the *Edinburgh* over *Hours of Idleness*, and though bruised by the alienation of Jeffrey's review of *Sardanapalus*, with its aside on *Don Juan*, nevertheless celebrated the curious kinship he felt with Jeffrey, whom he made the focus of a meditation on friendship, and of nostalgia for the land of Scotch Reviewers:

> And all our little feuds, at least all *mine*,
>   Dear Jeffrey, once my most redoubted foe,
> (As far as rhyme and criticism combine
>   To make such puppets of us things below)
> Are over. Here's a health to "Auld Lang Syne"!
>   I do not know you, and may never know
> Your face, – but you have acted on the whole
> Most nobly, and I own it from my soul.
>   (*DJ* x, st. 16, ll. 121–8 [*CPW* v: 441])

Notes

1 Mark Schoenfield, *British Periodicals and Romantic Identity: The "Literary Lower Empire"* (Basingstoke, UK: Palgrave Macmillan, 2009), 2.

2 Henry Cockburn, *Life of Lord Jeffrey, with a Selection of His Correspondence*, 2 vols. (Edinburgh: Adam & Charles Black, 1852), vol. I, 142.

3 Francis Jeffrey, *Contributions to the Edinburgh Review*, 3 vols. (London: Longman, Brown, Green, & Longmans, 1846), vol. I, xvii.

4 William Hazlitt, "On Criticism," in P. P. Howe (ed.), *The Complete Works of William Hazlitt*, 21 vols. (London: J. M. Dent, 1930–4), vol. VIII, 214.

5 Jon Klancher, "The Vocation of Criticism and the Crisis of the Republic of Letters," in Marshall Brown (ed.), *The Cambridge History of Literary Criticism: Vol. V: Romanticism* (Cambridge, UK: Cambridge University Press, 2000), 314.

6 T. A. J. Burnett, *The Rise and Fall of a Regency Dandy* (London: John Murray, 1981), 146.

7 William Christie, *The Edinburgh Review in the Literary Culture of Romantic Britain* (London: Pickering & Chatto, 2009), 123–46.

8 William St Clair, *The Reading Nation in the Romantic Period* (Cambridge, UK: Cambridge University Press, 2004), 632.

9 Schoenfield, *British Periodicals and Romantic Identity*, 130.

10 Clement Tyson Goode, Jr., "A Critical Review of Research," in Oscar José Santucho (ed.), *George Gordon, Lord Byron: A Comprehensive Bibliography of Secondary Materials in English, 1807–1974* (Metuchen, NJ: The Scarecrow Press, 1977), 6.

11 Jane Stabler, "Against Their Better Selves: Byron, Jeffrey and the *Edinburgh*," in Massimiliano Demata and Duncan Wu (eds.), *British Romanticism and the Edinburgh Review* (Basingstoke, UK: Palgrave Macmillan, 2002), 161.

CHAPTER 32

Byron, Radicals and Reformers

Jason Goldsmith

"He was a lover of liberty," observed Mary Howitt when Byron's funeral procession reached Nottingham, "which the Radical Corporation here thought made him their brother; therefore all the rabble rout from every lane and alley, and garret and cellar, came forth to curse and swear, and shout and push, in his honour."[1] Both during his life and after, Byron was venerated as the patron saint of radicalism. He was toasted at clandestine Tom Paine dinners in the 1820s. Incendiary works such as *Cain* (1821), *The Vision of Judgment* (1822) and *Don Juan* (1819) were pirated in cheap editions. His name decorated the walls of Chartist public houses alongside those of Paine, Jefferson and Washington, while selections of his verse emblazoned banners at demonstrations across the manufacturing districts of northern England.

From his maiden speech in the House of Lords to his death supporting the cause of Greek independence, it would be all too easy to map a trajectory of Byron's radical sympathies. Byron, the champion of the downtrodden and dispossessed, proved a potent public myth. Howitt's observation, though, suggests the tenuous nature of the poet's sympathy with those eager to make him over in their image. Byron's liberalism was genuine but highly qualified. He regarded plebian radicals such as William Cobbett and Henry Hunt with contempt, declaring, "I am and have been for *reform* always but not for the *reformers*" (*BLJ* 6: 166).

Just as it would be a mistake to distill Byron's politics to an unambiguous radical populism, it would be wrong to read a single imperative behind Byron's widespread appeal. The pressure for reform immediately after Waterloo was different from that later under the impulse of Chartism. The term "radical" variously characterized unskilled urban laborers, disaffected Whigs, Paineite populists, middle-class dissenters, skilled artisans, revolutionary Spenceans, moderate communitarian Owenites and physical-force Chartists – that is, anyone dissatisfied with the status quo. Not all radicals came from what we now call the working class, and not all working-class readers espoused radical politics, but these two populations were entwined in the public imagination.

If Byron comes to us today as a figure charged with political meaning, he does so because he reflected the hopes of his readers. That the man could never manifest these desires mattered not. A peer of the realm who left its shores amid scandal, Byron remained a ghostly presence on the English political stage, his very absence incorporating and nullifying the contradictions he seemed to embody: "And I will war, at least in words (and – should / My chance so happen – deeds)" (*CPW* v: 416, ll. 185–6). Such taunts amplified Byron's unprecedented celebrity, and reveal how far words might stand for flesh and blood.

England in 1819 was deeply divided. Widespread economic distress had fueled popular support for reform, and protests by disaffected workers had turned violent, stoking establishment fears that revolution was imminent. In this state of suspicion and alarm, the Manchester yeomanry forced their way into a crowd of 60,000 gathered at St. Peter's Square on August 16 to hear Henry Hunt address the need for parliamentary reform. As the soldiers drove their horses forward, the crowd seethed around them. Inexperienced and by most accounts inebriated, the cavalry lashed out with their sabers, leaving 15 dead and 600 injured.

The Peterloo massacre, as it became known, was the culmination of a series of events that set Britain on edge. Faced with public outrage, the Tory ministry doubled down on its policy of repressing dissent, drafting laws to limit public gatherings and curtail the radical press. For loyalists the specter of armed insurrection was real. One of many anti-radical satires that appeared at this time, *The Dorchester Guide* (1820) denounces the public as:

> a reprobate pack
> Who religion, Morality, Probity, lack; …
>
> Who Blasphemy, Treason, Rebellion, exhibit, –
> Are running a race which would end at the Gibbet.[2]

The Dorchester Guide is a parody of *The Political House That Jack Built* (1819) by William Hone, perhaps the most significant radical publisher of the day. In *The Political House*, he adapted the familiar nursery rhyme's insistent rhythm and cumulative structure to deliver a cutting indictment of government attempts to thwart reform through repressive legislation and blunt military force. Hone's pointed rhymes and George Cruikshank's stark woodcuts proved immensely popular, running through fifty-four editions and inspiring numerous imitations.

The Dorchester Guide repurposes this format to present a roll call of the day's foremost agitators – Richard Carlile, Henry Hunt, John Cartwright and William Hone – gleefully anticipating their arrival at Dorchester jail. Clad in the robes of "a Peer" and a baronial coronet, "The Devil" brings up the rear of this procession, his cloven hoof a conspicuous allusion to Byron's clubfoot.

That Byron would be associated with Hone is no surprise. Hone had published an unauthorized edition of Byron's *Fare Thee Well!* and "A Sketch from Private Life" (1816), a prose adaptation of *The Corsair* (1817) and *Don Juan, Canto the Third!* (1819). A meditation on the perilous position of radical publishing, *Canto the Third* places Byron in a network of associations with deep meaning in radical circles.

Appearing on July 15, 1819, the official version of *Don Juan* contained two stanzas parodying biblical language, and Hone saw John Murray's decision to publish the poem anonymously in an expensive quarto edition as an attempt to avoid prosecution for libel. Four days later, Hone issued a forty-page pamphlet protesting that *Don Juan* was going unprosecuted for its "immoral tendency" while a Birmingham printer was being detained for publishing a copy of "The Political Litany," for which Hone himself had been unsuccessfully tried the previous year.[3]

Hone's *Don Juan, Canto the Third* extends this critique. Having launched a radical newspaper called the *Devilled Biscuit*, Juan attends a meeting at Westminster Palace Yard on September 2, 1819, where Sir Francis Burdett and Byron's friend John Cam Hobhouse deliver speeches protesting against Peterloo and affirming the right of public assembly. Reporting on the event, Juan is detained on the word of an informer. The poem ends with the journalist, denied bail, asleep in a cell.

If *Canto the Third* considers how one might report on reform amid government efforts to suppress radical ideals, the solutions it proposes reveal its author thinking through the contingencies of voice. It begins with a typically Byronic performance dramatizing its legitimacy while simultaneously emphasizing its fabrication. The poem is little more than a series of speech acts that foreground the indeterminate nature of voice and, by extension, truth. *Canto the Third* is told by a figure who speaks as "Byron" and gives Juan's account of the Palace Yard meeting, including his *Devilled Biscuit*, which contains Burdett's speech, delivered in Spenserian stanzas to remind us of the poem's making.

This recursive structure extends beyond the text to incorporate Hone's trials and Murray's decision to publish *Don Juan* anonymously. What we hear, then, is a polyphonic voice that offers us nothing more than its insistent fact. The poem celebrates a voice as radical in its mode of delivery as in its political ideology. In Byron, Hone found a voice free to speak the truth that is its own being.

Seven indictments or informations were filed in 1819, forty-three in 1820 and thirty-two in 1821. Dorchester jail was becoming the "fashionable resort" described in *The Dorchester Guide*, which celebrates the imprisonment of Richard Carlile, found guilty of seditious and blasphemous libel in October 1819 for reprinting Paine's *Age of Reason* and Palmer's *Principles of Nature*.

Carlile single-handedly resurrected Paine's reputation. His 1818 edition of *Age of Reason* was the first openly published in England in over two decades, and Carlile ensured its dissemination by reading the entire work into the court record. "A Chief of Deistical Fame" (l. 16), Carlile was unsparing in his criticism of institutional Christianity, which he denounced as "a theatre of idolatry and superstition" bent on maintaining its material and political privileges by peddling mysteries that kept the people in thrall.[4]

The correlation of religious skepticism and political radicalism that Carlile represents helps us make sense of Byron's place in *The Dorchester Guide* and in the iconography of 1820s radicalism more generally. That the poem's sequence of radicals ends with Byron is telling. The cumulative design builds backwards, situating the poet as source of radical energies, each figure linked to a Byronic a priori. If *The Dorchester Guide* ends with Byron, it also, in a sense, begins with him, its final section progressing from Byron back to Carlile, an unholy alliance of devil and deist.

Carlile was quick to exploit these affinities, associating Byron with his own brand of Paineite deism that saw religion as a prop for political power. Byron appeared frequently in *The Republican*, and Carlile pirated two of his most controversial works, *Cain: A Mystery* (1822) and *The Vision of Judgment* (1824). Although Byron maintained that *Cain* was "a drama – not a piece of argument" (*BLJ* 9: 103), friends and critics alike perceived "a series of wanton libels upon the Supreme Being and His attributes."[5]

Cain revealed Byron to be of the devil's party, and Carlile presented its publication as a deliberate provocation. He praised it as "a ponderous blow at superstition," and stoked the controversy it aroused, reprinting in full Byron's letter to Murray assuming legal responsibility for *Cain* as "an open declaration of war against all delusion and superstition … a challenge to the Attorney General, or the Vice Society, to prosecute him."[6] Carlile's six-penny edition was designed to encourage this prosecution.

In contrast to Hone, who condemned church corruption but not the church, Carlile sought to raze the institution itself. A devil of Blakean temper, Carlile's Byron exposed priestcraft as a means of social control, but he sang his infernal song to little material effect. Its corroding fire burned brightly, yet briefly, tempered by more moderate calls for reform.

The passage of the Reform Act in 1832 and the rise of Chartism, Britain's first truly working-class political movement, altered Byron's appeal. "[I]t is the workers who are most familiar with the poetry of Shelley and Byron," observed Friedrich Engels.[7] The Reform Act extended the franchise to some 250,000 new voters and eliminated rotten boroughs, but it also made clear to plebeian reformers that their interests were incompatible with those of a middle class eager to promote its own political agenda. The radical working class would need to look after its own, and Byron was central to this development, helping to define a working-class community and articulate its demands.

Published in the *Northern Star* of April 29, 1842, John Watkins' untitled sonnet calls into being a Chartist community constituted through the struggle for political liberty:

> Chartists! what strive ye for? for liberty!
> Most glorious strife! more noble as more hard.
> 'Twas liberty inspir'd the British Bard
> Who surnam'd our Britannia – "The Free!"
> Byron! chiefest of poets! yes, 'twas he.[8]

Meant to rouse its working-class readers and unite them in a shared sense of purpose, the poem associates Chartist aspiration and poetic inspiration, situating Byron as the touchstone for an imagined Chartist community aligned with the national community of Britons. Byron's appeal here is his political orientation, divested of nobility, which has been transferred to the Chartist struggle: "more noble as more hard." No longer predicated on birth, nobility becomes a function of a very specific kind of labor.

So too is the Chartist Byron stripped of the profane religious hetero-doxy emphasized by Carlile. What Engels called Byron's "glowing sensu-ality"[9] needed to be tempered by a Chartist such as Watkins, who based his demand for universal male suffrage on a distinctly Christian ethic: "God waits to help you, for your cause is right, / And, to succeed, you have but to Unite!" (ll. 13–14). Watkins stresses the moral weight of the Chartist position, while recognizing that success will come only when the community imagined in the poem is realized in the world. Chartists like Watkins invoke Byron's celebrity to foster the emotional identifications through which political communities are constituted.

Launched with the express purpose of consolidating working-class factions into a cohesive bloc, the *Chartist Circular* refutes the attacks on Byron's character, displacing the emotional charge of Byron's celebrity to his poetry, which expresses sympathy with the oppressed and generates a corresponding response in its readers. "Nothing more is necessary for any unprejudiced mind to see the utter falsehood of these representations, than to read his works; and if the reader belong to the suffering class, he will find admiration and gratitude his prevailing sentiment towards Byron."[10]

Here, as elsewhere, it is Byron's voice that appeals. Emanating from his work, the Chartist Byron transcends time and geographical constraints to "raise his far-heard voice against the wretches who made their own gain and their country's ruin their study and practice." This voice speaks across the distance separating the poet from his homeland, and across the years since his death. Echoing Byron's correlation of Greece and England in *The Giaour*, the author prophesies that "[s]ome other Byron may yet weep over thy fallen cities, or warn some other people to avoid thy ambition, thy folly, and thy crime."[11] "Byron" no longer signifies a specific individual, but names a poetic praxis that voices a progressive political agenda.

Chartism's failure to achieve its political goals seems inscribed in its treatment of Byron. The Chartists were unable to harness Byron's "glowing sensuality" because they willed it out of existence. "[F]lowing with the celestial fire of liberty," the Chartist Byron transcends its material condition, denouncing tyranny and oppression with almost divine sanction. But political protest requires more than a voice. It demands physical presence.

Just as the Chartists were circulating their version of Byron, John Clare, a rural laborer turned poet who achieved fleeting celebrity as the "Northamptonshire Peasant," was locked in an asylum writing versions of *Childe Harold's Pilgrimage* and *Don Juan*. But where the Chartist Byron was a public creature, generating community and stimulating political action, Clare's Byron was a private figure, wrought from the tension between embodied individual and public spectacle.

Clare's Byron is bent on exposing hypocrisy. If imitations of *Don Juan* were a fashionable practice, perhaps none was so promiscuous as Clare's, a deliberately vulgar work meant to offend middle-class sensibilities. It also lamented the economic distress of the laboring poor: "I wish for poor men luck – an honest praxis / Cheap food & cloathing – no corn laws or taxes."[12] Despite such sentiments, Clare was no radical. Rather, he sought a return to older forms of community. His outlook was shaped by enclosure, which had transformed common fields to private farms, eroding the communal relationships based on the open field system and the social economy predicated on customary rights and privileges such as grazing, gleaning and fuel gathering, which had joined the nobility and the lower class in a mutually supportive relationship.

Clare was equally suspicious of Radicals, Whigs and Tories: "their discourse is of their country but when their parts are done we see they only meant themselves."[13] This skepticism extended to Byron, who, in supporting Greek independence, "achieved nothing more by the profession of arms than effect & applause for the intention when the intention appears to be the utmost extent of his ambition."[14] Byron played to an audience hungry for the sign of liberty, not necessarily its reality.

Clare recognized Byron's celebrity as emblematic of a shift in social relations, where appearances were increasingly expected to stand for things. Yet Byron offered Clare a way to counter this tension, if not quite to resolve it. Turning the effect of spectacle back on itself, Clare produces a visceral poetics that evokes a political economy of the open fields and the communities they sustained. His "Don Juan" articulates a confederacy of voice fitted to the ancient bond between manorial lord and tenant farmer: "Lord Byron poh – the man wot rites the werses / & is just what he is & nothing more" (ll. 263–4). Clare is Byron. Byron is Clare. Shifting registers as readily as Byron, Clare laments a rural England lost to industrialization.

Like Byron, Clare was an exile. "Don Juan" speaks of and from a distance. If it expresses Clare's disaffection, it did little to stem the changes that would produce the Victorian nation as civilized, decent and morally upstanding. This age had little use for Clare's Byron, one of many possibilities inscribed in "Byron" that remind us just how little we will ever know.

NOTES

1 Mary Howitt, *An Autobiography*, ed. Margaret Howitt (London: Wm. Ibister Limited, 1889), vol. 1, 185.
2 *The Dorchester Guide; or, A House that Jack Built*, 2nd ed. (London: Dean & Munday, 1820), ll. 6–10.
3 William Hone, *"Don John," or Don Juan Unmasked* (London: Author, 1819), 37.
4 Quoted in George Jacob Holyoake, *The Life and Character of Richard Carlile* (London: J. Watson, 1849), 7.

5 Review of *Cain, Gentleman's Magazine* (Supplement for December–July 1821), 91 (ii), 615.
6 *The Republican* (London: R. Carlile, 1822), vol. v, 192, 342.
7 Friedrich Engels, *The Condition of the Working Class in England*, trans. W. O. Henderson and W. H. Chaloner (Oxford: Blackwell, 1958), 273.
8 John Watkins, "Chartists! What Strive ye for? For Liberty!" in *An Anthology of Chartist Poetry: Poetry of the British Working Class, 1830s–1850s*, ed. Peter Scheckner (Rutherford, NJ: Farleigh Dickinson University Press, 1989), 315, ll. 1–5.
9 Engels, *The Condition of the Working Class*, 240.
10 "The Politics of Poets IV," *Chartist Circular* 49 (August 29, 1840), ed. William Thomson (Glasgow: W. & W. Miller, 1841), 198.
11 "The Politics of Poets IV," 198.
12 John Clare, "Don Juan," in Eric Robinson and David Powell (eds.), *The Later Poems of John Clare: 1837–1864* (Oxford: Clarendon Press, 1984), ll. 47–8.
13 John Clare, *A Champion for the Poor: Political Verse and Prose*, eds. P. M. S. Dawson, Eric Robinson and David Powell (Manchester: Carcanet Press, 2000), 293.
14 John Clare, *The Prose of John Clare*, eds. J. W. and Anne Tibble (London: Routledge & Kegan Paul, 1951), 224.

CHAPTER 33

European Reception

Peter Vassallo

In a chapter devoted to Byron in *A History of Western Philosophy*, Bertrand Russell remarked that Byron's posthumous reputation was more influential on the Continent than in England, and that it was there that his "spiritual progeny" was to be sought. His death at Missolonghi while supporting the Greek cause against the Ottoman oppressors contributed to the myth of Byron the Romantic poet and aristocratic rebel who gave his life to the cause of freedom against oppression; Russell concludes that as a myth Byron's importance on the Continent was "enormous."[1] To adapt Mircea Eliade's theory of archetypes, Byron could have been the exemplar of the poet as "historical personage" whose life history was metamorphosed by nineteenth-century criticism into an "archetype" of mythical status.[2]

For most contemporary readers interested in Byron's life and poetry, Amedée Pichot's prose translations in French (1819–21) were an essential introduction to the poet's "genius," despite the fact that the poems were translated into a hackneyed if readable language. Pichot's renderings, according to Therese Tessier, were on the whole reasonably accurate, even though Byron's subtle irony was missed when translated into "pedestrian" prose.[3]

In Italy in the late 1820s, during the struggle for liberation from Austrian rule, Byron was regarded as a champion of liberalism and nationalistic sentiment. Count Camillo Benso di Cavour, the Piedmontese diplomat who was eventually responsible for Italian unification under the Savoy king Vittorio Emanuele II, considered Byron an inspired promoter ("powerful genius") of patriotism. Giuseppe Mazzini, the founder of "Giovane Italia" and the ideologue of the *Risorgimento*, compared Byron with Goethe and thought of him as a champion of democratic movements in Europe. Mazzini's essay on "Byron and Goethe" (*Monthly Chronicle* 1839) was written when he was a refugee in London, as a political activist and man of letters campaigning for the liberation and unification of Italy. He saw Byron and Goethe as representing the *zeitgeist* of an entire epoch and the principle of individuality. He wrote: "This is at once the philosophical explanation of their works and the secret of their popularity. The spirit of an entire epoch of the European world became incarnate in them ere its decease."[4]

In Mazzini's view, Byron the man occasionally overtook the artist and was an example of "the eternal spirit of the chainless mind," whereas in the case of Goethe the man was completely lost in the artist. Goethe had diagnosed the malaise of his age (in *Werther* and *Faust)* but offered no solution. Byron, on the other hand, struggled energetically against "the falsehood and evil of the world around him." For Mazzini, as the theorist and ideologue of patriotic movements in Europe, Byron's death in Greece symbolized the supreme sacrifice of the artist. Mazzini, a democratic republican, acknowledged Byron's profound influence on himself and like-minded revolutionaries.

Concerning Byron's art in creating tyrannical characters, Mazzini makes these perceptive observations about Byron's poetic heroes: they are made to "drag through their useless and convulsed existence" and "Byron destroys them one after the other."[5] Most of his oriental tales in verse, Mazzini observed, proclaim in their own way the downfall of tyranny. By contrast, in Mazzini's view, Goethe was a cold spectator of the world's stage lost in inactive contemplation, surveying his world with an "Olympian calm." Byron, on the other hand, seeks action in "raking his harp to set forth in the struggle of the Greeks to regain their liberty." His tribute to Byron ends on a note of eloquent praise for the poet who combined thought and action, was sensitive to "the cause of the peoples" and, one must add, to Mazzini's own cause of agitating for the liberation of the Italians from foreign subjugation. Byron's death in Greece was to him "a beautiful symbol of the future destiny and mission of art."[6] The essay was written with an English audience in mind; Mazzini was attempting to counteract adverse criticism of Byron by his conservative contemporaries, "that mixture of cant and stupidity" which denied the poet his deserved place in Westminster Abbey, as well as the hostile reaction to his poetry by contemporary literary reviewers.[7] The essay ends on a note of high praise for the poet who heroically sacrificed his life espousing the Greek struggle for independence:

> I know no more beautiful symbol of the future destiny and mission of art than the death of Byron in Greece. The holy alliance of poetry with the cause of the peoples – the union – still so rare – of thought and action – which alone completes the human Word, and is destined to emancipate the world … all that is now the religion and the hope of the party of

progress throughout Europe, is gloriously typified in this image, which we, barbarians that we are, have already forgotten.[8]

Byron, in his view, was exemplary in combining thought with action in his heroic commitment to the Greek War of Independence.

In France, Alphonse de Lamartine, Byron's contemporary, was fascinated by the dominant figure of Byron, and in *Les Premieres Méditations Poétiques*, which was published in 1820 during Byron's lifetime, he characterizes Byron (in "L'Homme, a Lord Byron") as "chanter des enfers," much to Byron's chagrin. Later in 1825, the year after Byron's death, Lamartine composed a fifth canto of *Childe Harold* (*Le Dernier Chant du Pèlerinage d'Harold*) in which the hero travels to Greece to express his disillusion with the Italian revolutionaries and his disenchantment with politics and religion (see Figure 9.2 in Chapter 9).

The fall of Missolonghi in April 1826 was decisive in bringing the great powers Britain, Russia and France into concerted action against the Turks, culminating in the Ottoman naval defeat at Navarino (1827). The quasi-mythical figure of Byron, especially after the poet's death at Missolonghi, inspired Eugene Delacroix's painting of "Greece on the ruins of Missolonghi," which would give French Philhellenes a symbol of the necessity of rising against the oppressors of liberty. Delacroix produced many paintings of dramatic scenes suggested by Byron's Oriental tales (*The Giaour*, *The Corsair*, *The Bride of Abydos* and, later, the shipwreck scene in *Don Juan*) that focused on the prevailing notion that other European nations were shamefully permitting the savage hordes to crush the spirit of liberty that once illumined Greece.

The spirit of liberty had spread to Russia a few years after Byron's death in 1824. Alexander Pushkin was an admirer of Byron, and in his long narrative poem *Poltava* (1829) he retold the story of Mazeppa. In *Evgeny Onegin* (1832), an extended verse novel containing digressions on the contemporary Russian scene, he adopted Byron's aloof manner of telling a story in verse, "in the genre of *Don Juan*," but as he himself insisted, without Byron's cynical stance, only "half comic, half melancholic." The Byronic influence is especially noticeable in how the verse novel unfolds – the witty asides and personal observations, especially Pushkin's facetious comment, in a digression, that he knew the hero Evgeny personally and strolled with him on summer evenings along the banks of the Neva. But, unlike Byron, Pushkin lets events speak for themselves without digressing to comment critically (and self-consciously) on the political and social mores of his day. Like Byron in his later poetry, however, Pushkin frequently resorts to irony and innuendo, and presents Onegin, in Tatiana's eyes, as a Russian version of Childe Harold with half-angelic and half demonic attributes ("this angel, this proud devil"). Onegin, the reader is told, was fond of reading *Juan* and *The Giaour*, in which modern man is "put on parade," having adopted the Byronic mode of histrionic self-presentation. In the seventh section of the poem, Pushkin makes Tatiana, Onegin's rejected lover, exclaim that Onegin, "this freakish stranger" whom she still loves, is but "a Muscovite in Harold's dress."[9]

Mikhael Lermontov too was fascinated by Byron's vibrant personality and by his poems, some of which he read in the original. In his late teens he composed a "Byronic" narrative poem called *Ismael Bey* (1832), partly inspired by Byron's Oriental tale *The Giaour*, with its contrived Fall–Redemption pattern and its fragmented narrative. Apart from its melodramatic scenes, Byron's poem is also a romantic tale told from five different points of view about the clash of personalities from different cultures: the Muslim Hassan and the Giaour "the infidel," a renegade Christian, a friar and a Turkish fisherman. In *Ismael Bey* Lermontov imitates Byron's constant modulations of tone, as well as the digressive nature of the narrative, and transposes the setting to the Caucasus. The clash of cultures is represented in the characters who oppose each other – the Georgian and the Georgian renegade who has joined the detested Russians. Lermontov's *A Hero of Our Time* (1838–40) owes much to Byron's personality as filtered through his letters (published by Thomas Moore in 1830, and which Lermontov had read). The protagonist is cast into the mold of a Byronic hero at odds with his society, disillusioned and world-weary. Lermontov draws on the main characters in Byron's popular Oriental tales, especially Lara, the Corsair and the Giaour. There are elements derived from Byron's own complex character, his divided self, the inner contradictions and his contrariness. Lermontov based the Pechorin journal on Byron's journals, which he had read in Moore's life of Byron. Like Byron, Lermontov's hero Pechorin is in conflict with himself, torn between idealism and cynicism, full of dynamic energy but yielding to bouts of lassitude and ennui. Pechorin has most of the attributes one would associate with heroism, but, as Lermontov shows, the prevalent malady of the age dooms him to inactivity in a Tsarist Russia dominated by Western fashions, mediocrity and conformism.

In Germany the fascination with Byronism was less effusive than it was in France or Russia, with the exception of Goethe and Heine. Goethe openly expressed his admiration for Byron, especially the poetic drama *Manfred*, which he observed subsumed some of the themes of his own *Faust* in an original way. Byron for his part was pleased with Goethe's praise, and returned the compliment by dedicating his poetic drama *Werner* to the "illustrious Goethe." Goethe was fascinated by Byron's wit and praised *Don Juan*'s "strange wild, and merciless content" and its curious blending of "misanthropy and philanthropy."[10] Later, in *Faust*, part II, published in 1827, he went on to cast Byron as Euphorion, the child of Faust and Helen of Troy, who aspires to escape the confines of the visible world and fades into a blaze of light.

Heinrich Heine's response to Byron was mainly emotional, especially in relation to the dramatic circumstances of his colorful life. He thought that Byron was a misunderstood genius and compared him to Prometheus, the archetypal rebel who fought against the tyranny of the Gods – in Byron's case, social injustice, rampant officialdom and the oppressive Tory governments of his day. Heine felt an affinity with the English poet, considering himself a comrade-in-arms waging war against the religious conservatism of some contemporary German writers. His reflections on Byron and his poetry made him in turn reflect on the contradictory nature of his own feelings and attitudes. Some of Heine's critics have argued speciously that his admiration for Byron was his way of drawing attention to himself and his own works. Heine claimed that though he recognized an affinity with the English poet, he lacked the vibrant spleen with which Byron excoriated the old order of things. In his early twenties, piqued with his teacher, Professor August Wilhelm Schlegel, who claimed that Byron was unique and could not be translated into German, Heine embarked on a translation of some of Byron's better-known lyrics in 1819–20. His translation of Byron's *Fare Thee Well!* was deemed to be a remarkable feat for having successfully rendered Byron's conflicting emotions of wounded love, self-reproach and remembrance of past happiness as expressed in this poem.

The renowned Polish poet Adam Mickiewicz was born a Lithuanian Russian but considered himself a Polish patriot. In exile in Russia, he saw himself as the poet of Polish nationalism and like Mazzini grew to admire Byron. In 1832–3 he translated – or rather made a new version of – *The Giaour*. In his introduction to the poem, Mickiewicz defends Byron's brand of skepticism, observing that it was merely "the brief clouding of an early morning associated with an invigorating breeze which heralds the coming of the day." Byron's virtue, according to Mickiewicz, was that he wrestled with "all essential philosophical questions" against the grain of dogma or tradition. He also compares Byron with Napoleon as kindred spirits who were always in turmoil, always active – a comparison that Byron would have relished.[11] Significantly, he traces this energizing force of revolutionary movements to Napoleon who, he claims, not only influenced but "created Lord Byron." Byron's admiration for Napoleon, Mickiewicz maintains, made him write poetry, from *Childe Harold* onwards, dealing with real, lived experience. Byron's commitment to the Greek cause was, in his view, an extension of his literary pursuits.

In his version of *The Giaour*, Mickiewicz Christianizes the Giaour by allowing him to seek redemption – not in the original source. Mickiewicz adapts Byron's side comments on the plight of Greece by making them apply to the plight of Poland at the time. For Mickiewicz, Byron was the poet of action prepared to pay with his life for his ardent political beliefs. His heroes all had one particular emotion (one virtue), which though solitary and aloof, linked them with mankind: they were men of conscience.

Years later, when Mickiewicz was living in Paris, he discussed Byron in a lecture at the College de France, extolling the poet's willingness to "fuse the ideal (as imagined in his poetry) with the real" by serving the cause of the Greeks. Like Mazzini, Mickiewicz harnessed Byron, as the poet who seriously combined thought and action, to his own particular commitment to national liberty.[12]

In Greece, a decade after Byron's death, Byronism developed both as a literary movement and as an ideological one, especially after the 1827 battle of Navarino, as can be attested in Kyriakos Lambryllos' translations of *The Bride of Abydos* and *The Curse of Minerva*, which were published in Smyrna in 1836. These translations were intended to arouse patriotism and indignation in the Greeks of his day at the spoliation of ancient Greek works of art, especially the Parthenon marbles, by opportunistic foreigners such as Lord Elgin. As Lambryllos explains in his preface, these works would stimulate Greek intellectuals to agitate for the cultural awakening of contemporary Greece, and the texts were specifically chosen for their political import; *The Bride* for its defense of liberty against Oriental tyranny, and *The Curse* for Minerva's denunciation of Lord Elgin's despoliation of the Parthenon. Byron at the time was revered for his role as a martyr for the cause of Greek independence rather than appreciated for his poetical achievement.

The leading Spanish Romantic poet José de Espronceda read Byron's poems in exile in London in 1828. He had an affinity of temperament with Byron, as the adolescent Espronceda himself recognized, which caused him to imitate and appropriate Byron's verse. There are resonances of *The Corsair* in Espronceda's "Canción del Pirata" in the Pirate's anarchic song of Liberty "que es en mi barco, mi Tesoro, / que es mi Dios mi libertad … !" In most of his poems, particularly his long narrative poem *El Estudiante de Salamanca*, Espronceda rewrites the old legend of Don Juan

Tenorio in verse, consciously adopting Byronic attitudes such as irreverent mockery, exposure of political and religious hypocrisy, and contempt for the established order of things. Unlike Byron, who transforms Juan into a young man more seduced than seducing, Espronceda adapts the *leyenda* of Don Juan Tenorio, Tirso de Molina's drama about a handsome, callous philanderer from Seville (*El Burlador de Sevilla*) to his own times in Spain, shifting the original setting to the university city of Salamanca while preserving the characteristics of the immoral philanderer. Espronceda's Don Juan is a Spanish aristocrat, Don Felix de Montemar, who seduces and abandons the virtuous Elvira. She eventually goes mad and haunts Don Felix from the grave, leading him, as a demon, on a nightmare journey through the streets of Salamanca to hell. The Gothic elements of the narrative dominate the final section of the poem; and Don Felix's refusal to repent links the poem with the love affair of Manfred and Astarte, with its ultimate daredevil defiance of death.

This chapter has focused on the Byronic persona as perceived by foreign writers, and their reading, or misreading, of some of Byron's poems. Interestingly, each country created its own Byron or appropriated the Byronic hero as projected in Byron's earlier poems, especially *Childe Harold* and the Oriental verse narratives, mainly because the later poems, with their *chiaroscuro* blend of seriousness and flippancy, caused uneasiness among most readers who had been previously nourished on serious didactic poetry. To the Italians, Byron was a "carbonaro," under constant surveillance by the Austrians, a champion of freedom from foreign subjugation. To the French he became a symbol of the revolution, a pro-Bonapartist aristocrat. In Spain he was seen as a callous philanderer, a reincarnation of Don Juan Tenorio. In Germany he was a misunderstood genius, a Prometheus figure who defied autocratic rule. In Greece he was honored as a foreign patriot who was an inspiration in the struggle against the oppression of the Ottoman Turks; and in Russia he was a force of nature who inspired awe. For different reasons, he appealed to intellectuals on the Continent who had espoused the cause of political freedom and national identity, especially in countries where individual liberty was rigorously suppressed.

Notes

1 Bertrand Russell, *A History of Western Philosophy* (London: Allen & Unwin, 1979), 721.
2 Mircea Eliade, *Myths, Dreams and Mysteries*, trans. Philip Mairet (London: Collins, 1968), 32.

3 Therese Tessier, "Byron and the French Romantics," in Richard Cardwell (ed.), *Lord Byron the European* (Lewiston, NY: Edwin Mellen Press, 1997), 6, 7.

4 "Byron and Goethe," published anonymously in the *Monthly Magazine* (September 1839), reprinted in William Clarke (ed.), *Essays Selected from the Writings of Joseph Mazzini* (London: Walter Scott, 1887), 87.

5 Ibid., 92.

6 Ibid., 97.

7 Ibid., 107.

8 Ibid.

9 Alexander Pushkin, *Eugene Onegin*, trans. Charles Johnson (London: Penguin Books, 2003), vol. VII, st. 24.

10 E. M. Butler, *Byron and Goethe* (London: Bowes & Bowes, 1956), 18.

11 "On Lord Byron," in Stanislaw Helsztynsky (ed.), *Adam Mickiewicz: Selected Poetry and Prose* (Warsaw: Polonia, 1955), 185, 187.

12 Adam Mickiewicz, *Les Slaves. Cours professe' au College de France (1842–44)* (Paris: Musee' Adam Mickiewicz, 1914), 20. [My translation.]

CHAPTER 34

Recollections, Conversations and Biographies

Julian North

The many thousands of pages of biography devoted to Byron in the decades following his death formed the most substantial embodiment of his evolving cultural presence through the nineteenth century. Biographical narratives, often in the form of "recollections" or "conversations," picked up on the critical debates surrounding Byron's poetry in his lifetime and applied them to his behavior as a man. They included eyewitness accounts, letters and other documents that still inform biography and scholarship today. The story of Byron's biographies is one of passionate factionalism and conflicting vested interests, reflecting the extreme feelings he provoked, focused on contentious issues of class, gender, sexuality and religion. For all these reasons and more, the biographical literature is indispensable for understanding Byron and Byronism.

Two years before the publication of *Childe Harold's Pilgrimage*, Samuel Taylor Coleridge complained in an essay on "Modern Biography" that he was living in an "age of personality," dominated by a "mania" for gossip about the lives of the famous.[1] The thriving trade in literary *Lives* that lay at the heart of Coleridge's anxiety was produced by the same conditions that created Byron's celebrity. In a crowded and competitive literary market-place, it was an advantage for writers to construct strongly differentiated authorial identities and to foster illusions of personal relationship with their audiences – or to have such identities and relationships created for them. Biographical intrusions were risky, but they could also secure a reputation for posterity. Biographies of contemporary authors proliferated from the later eighteenth century, with production accelerating from the 1820s. They came in a variety of forms, including brief character sketches, memoirs, multi-volume *Lives and Letters* and biographical editions, with an emphasis on the testimony of family and friends.

The major Byron biographies were posthumous, but already in his life-time, Byron's poetry and its reviews taught his public to approach him biographically: to look for him in his fictional heroes and his lyric and narrative voices, and to find there what Andrew Elfenbein has called a "simulacrum of intimacy" with the poet.[2] The phrase acknowledges a relationship that was paradoxically genuine and illusory, in which Byron was both known and unknown to his readers: apparently flagrant in his self-exposure, but accused of theatrical insincerity after the publication of *Don Juan*. Byron wanted a *Life* to be written, and entrusted Thomas Moore with his journals, memoranda and manuscript "memoirs." Yet soon after his death the memoirs were burnt by a confederacy of friends, family and Byron's publisher, John Murray, who feared the consequences of the document's revelations. This attempt to frustrate the public appetite for knowledge of Byron only aroused it further.

Byron's early biographers were men and women who had known him personally, and each claimed to offer a uniquely intimate portrait. They detailed their impressions of his physical appearance and voice (with a "Northumbrian burr," as Leigh Hunt recalled), and his domestic habits, including what he had for breakfast ("a cup of strong green tea, without milk").[3] A recurring trope was the touch of hands between Byron and his future biographer, a gesture of trust as the poet's life was symbolically handed on. William Parry's title-page epigraph described how the dying Byron had "squeezed his hand, and tried to express his last wishes." The scene was illustrated in an engraving depicting the two with hands outstretched toward each other (see Figure 34.1), echoing Michaelangelo's "Creation of Adam."[4]

Intimacy was presented as a guarantor of truth. Byron biography was a lucrative business, and it paid to be reviewed as a more credible witness than one's competitors. Accordingly, biographers routinely questioned the veracity of rival memoirs, but, in doing so, tacitly admitted the provisional nature of their own truth claims. The limits of those claims were also signaled in other ways. The public did not see all the backstage dramas of censorship and suppression, but readers were made aware, for instance, that letters had been excluded from Robert Dallas' *Recollections* (1824), due to legal action; and Moore's *Letters and Journals of Lord Byron* (1830) marked cuts to the correspondence with scatterings of asterisks. Most significantly, biographers took Byron's own multiplicity and resistance to interpretation as a central theme. While they claimed to present the true Byron, their narratives formed an open-ended dialogue, reflecting on a man famed for his skeptical resistance to the single vision.

Shortly after Byron's death, Thomas Medwin, a cousin of P. B. Shelley, published his *Journal of the Conversations of Lord Byron* (1824), recording

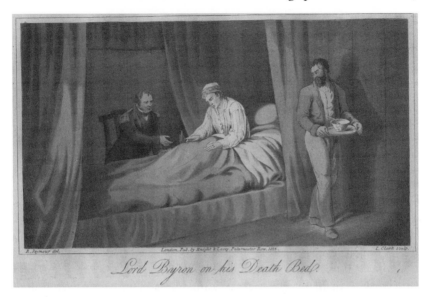

Figure 34.1 "Lord Byron on His Death Bed," engraving from William Parry,
The Last Days of Lord Byron (London: Knight & Lacey, 1825), University of Melbourne,
Baillieu Library Special Collections.

their friendship in Pisa in 1821–2. Medwin took on the role of Boswell to Byron's Johnson, transcribing the great man's words, seemingly as they issued from his mouth. Hobhouse attacked the book for inauthenticity, concerned that Medwin's casual attitude to truth-telling might be mistaken for Byron's own. Medwin's Byron, like the narrator of *Don Juan*, engaged in a theatrical performance of self, projecting a series of striking rhetorical attitudes. First encountered in the eccentric splendor of the Palazzo Lanfranchi, he was a lordly libertine who freely divulged his sexual secrets, including details of his marriage and his relationship with his mistress, Teresa Guiccioli. Medwin embraced this scandalous performance as proper to Byron's aristocratic masculinity.

By contrast, Robert Dallas' *Recollections*, published posthumously and edited by his clergyman son, portrayed Byron as a spoilt child of rank and fame, unable to follow Dallas' example of earnest Christian manliness. As Byron's literary adviser between 1808 and 1814, Dallas was one of relatively few nineteenth-century biographers to give detailed attention to the poetry; others included Moore and Isaac Nathan. Where Nathan found sincere religious feeling behind the *Hebrew Melodies*, Dallas, who had urged Byron to cut *Don Juan*'s skeptical stanzas, was less optimistic. The

Recollections ended with Dallas' deathbed regrets that he had ever helped Byron become famous by encouraging the publication of *Childe Harold*.

Most of the early memoirs reflected on Byron's involvement in the struggle for Greek independence. Some, by those who worked with him on the campaign, were devoted to this last phase of his life. Recollections by Colonel Leicester Stanhope and William Parry, fellow envoys of the London Greek Committee, were published in 1825, as well as a memoir by Pietro Gamba, Teresa Guiccioli's brother. Biographers portrayed Byron's final months in Greece as a redemptive turn from idleness to action, a rediscovery of his heroic soul. But those who had been there with him also detailed the tragicomic frustrations of a chaotic campaign and the medical incompetence that contributed to his death. James Kennedy, a Scottish doctor at Cephalonia, recorded conversations with Byron on religion, adding new evidence – but no resolution – to the controversy over whether he was a skeptic, an atheist or a believer. The partially ghosted memoir by William Parry, an engineer, was written in the voice of a practical working man, fiercely loyal to Byron, but with little time for genius or wit and equally unsympathetic to the values of fashionable society and the censoriousness of the middle classes. In a distinctive twist to the debates on Byron's mobility and masculinity, Parry countered "imputations of … conduct guided by caprice" with what he termed the "manly reality."[5] This was a Byron made in Parry's own image: a man of the people, hardworking and practical in the cause of liberty.

The most controversial memoir of the 1820s after Medwin's was by the radical poet and journalist Leigh Hunt, who described his time as Byron's guest in Pisa in 1822–3. *Lord Byron and Some of his Contemporaries* (1828) was fueled by resentment. Hunt believed that Byron and his friends looked down on him and his fellow "Cockney" poets, and had not adequately supported his journal, the *Liberal*. His vividly anecdotal but indiscreet recollections leveled class-based insults: Teresa was a "buxom parlour-border" with short legs; Byron had a despotic jaw.[6] Hunt associated the "mobility" of the poet's persona in *Don Juan* with Byron's inability to recognize the truth, and represented him as insincere and incapable of real love.[7]

Two years later Moore fought back with a biography that placed Byron's capacity for love at the center of his life. Moore's monumental two-volume *Letters and Journals of Lord Byron* (1830) remained the authoritative biography throughout the nineteenth century. For the first time readers had access to Byron's letters, journals and memoranda, interspersed with Moore's cradle-to-grave narrative, drawn from the testimony of the inner circle, including Teresa Guiccioli and Mary Shelley. Above all, audiences were given the thrilling revelations and myriad brilliance of the letters, in which a new medium of Byronic performance gave a fresh illusion of intimacy. Wanting his readers to love Byron, Moore presented his life as a quest for love, motivated in his early years by a cold mother and absent sister. Yet Byron's loves were tricky ground. Moore believed that he must preserve standards of decency to find favor with the British public, and he was under pressure from Hobhouse and others to leave out sensitive material. In his effort to present a favorable picture, Moore censored letters and tried to show that, despite his tendency to "self-libeling," Byron had "a heart sound at the core, however passion might have scorched it" (Moore 1: 302, 231–2). Volume one placed emphasis on the pure romantic attachments of Byron's youth and volume two stressed his genuine (albeit adulterous) relationship with Teresa. Byron's love for Moore himself was abundantly displayed in the letters to his future biographer.

Other affairs of the heart proved more awkward, including his relationship with Lady Byron and what Moore privately referred to as the "plagy Italian loves."[8] Moore strained to explain the separation without revealing the rumors of incest and sodomy. He argued that the marriage disintegrated because genius is by nature incompatible with domestic life, but this failed to address why Byron's relationship with Teresa had succeeded. Elfenbein has argued that Moore strove "to enclose Byron within the bounds of respectability," yet he did not always censor passages in the correspondence that went beyond those bounds.[9] He included one letter in which Byron compared his schoolboy relationship with Edleston to that of the lesbian Ladies of Llangollen, and the Greek loves of Playdes and Orestes, or Nisus and Euryalus (Moore 1: 113). There is evidence that some contemporary readers picked up on such hints. As volume two proceeded, Byron was increasingly allowed to speak for himself. The sheer size of the biography and its mass of detail resisted containment. In the end Moore surrendered his intermittent attempts to find a moral center to Byron's character and admitted "the extreme difficulty of analyzing, without dazzle or bewilderment, such an unexampled complication of qualities." He concluded that there was no one "pivot," unless it was, paradoxically, Byron's mobility (Moore 2: 782–3). Moore's effort to uncover "a heart sound at the core" gave way to the charm of Byron's performance.

The impact of Moore's biography was huge, partly because it was plundered by every subsequent biographer. John Galt's full-length *Life of Lord Byron* (1830), for example, was extensively based on Moore. Yet there were still new voices to be heard from the Byron circle. In 1832–4 the novelist and society hostess Lady Blessington published her *Conversations of Lord Byron*, an account of their daily exchanges in Genoa in 1823. Like Medwin, she emphasized Byron's indiscretion and theatricality, while her critique of his mobility and insincerity echoed Hunt's. This was also the first of several biographies that self-consciously tackled Byron's life from a woman's perspective. Lady Blessington compared herself not only to Boswell but to Mrs. Piozzi (Blessington iii). She wavered between adopting Byronic postures and exposing them. She participated in Byron's gossip and repeated his mockery of Madame de Stael. Yet her exasperation at his indiscretions and inconsistency suggested the point of view of a woman vulnerable to betrayal, in a way that none of the previous biographies had done: "there was no safety with him" (Blessington 59). Lady Blessington professed a sisterly empathy for Lady Byron and claimed to have instructed Byron on female feeling, since "[a] woman only can understand a woman's heart" (Blessington 26).

Women became the key players in Byron biography from the late 1860s, with Byron's conduct as a lover and husband the major themes; but in the 1850s Edward Trelawny published a memoir with a very different emphasis. *Recollections of the Last Days of Shelley and Byron* (1858) looked back to his time with the poets in Pisa in 1821–2 and his involvement in the aftermath of Byron's death in Greece. Trelawny had invented a swashbuckling, Byronic past for himself and was known as the "Cockney Corsair." His *Recollections* portrayed his hero as an adventurer and man of the world rather than a lover, and pictured the two of them competitively bantering and measuring up their masculine prowess in billiards, swimming and pistol firing. This model of masculinity did not go unchallenged. Throughout the memoir Trelawny compared the worldly Byron unfavorably to the ethereal Shelley, his ideal of what a poet should be. However, Trelawny's portrait of Byron was unusually free from concerns about his moral compass. This mood in Byron biography did not last.

The Countess Guiccioli's *My Recollections of Lord Byron* (1869) and her unpublished memoir "Vie de Lord Byron en Italie" (*c.*1869–70) were long polemics defending her former lover's character, drawing evidence of his saintly goodness from the work of previous biographers as well as her own memories. For Guiccioli, Byron was sincere and honorable; even in his weaker moments, he was the seduced rather than the seducer. Guiccioli tore down any biographer who dared question his virtue. She presented her *Recollections* as a "psychological study" and scorned "critics little versed in psychological science" (Guiccioli 399, 417). Where Lady Byron had been unable "to find the road to his heart or mind," Teresa would reveal the man behind the performance (Guiccioli 380). For Teresa, that performance could not be anything but superficial because his feelings for her had to be real. Her diagnosis was that Byron had "mobility of mind united to a constant heart" (Guiccioli 339). Contrary to Moore, she argued that he had a moral center in "his love of truth" (Guiccioli 471). Her memoirs were excessive in every sense: huge, repetitive, hagiographic, melodramatic: "when he wept his tears came from the heart, and were of blood" (Guiccioli 147). She tried to get around her own delicate position by referring to herself in the third person and suppressing the sexual nature of their relationship – a censorship that sat awkwardly with her insistence on the truth of her portrait. Yet her unpublished memoir included touching details of their courtship and life together that only she was in a position to give. As the only one of Byron's biographers to have been his long-term sexual partner, Guiccioli's perspective was unique, as was her belief in Byron's constancy.

Guiccioli's *Recollections* led to a new burst of biographical activity focused on Byron's conduct toward his wife. Harriet Beecher Stowe, the American novelist, campaigner and friend of Lady Byron, responded furiously in an article published simultaneously in *Macmillan's Magazine* and *Atlantic Monthly* (1869), followed by her book *Lady Byron Vindicated* (1870). Like Guiccioli, Stowe drew on the new science of psychology, specifically the work of Forbes Winslow, but this time to diagnose Byron as morally insane. Most sensationally, in this overtly feminist defense of the wronged wife, she reported that Lady Byron had left her husband because "[h]e was guilty of incest with his sister!"[10] The Earl of Lovelace, grandson of Lady Byron, produced more evidence for incest in *Astarte* (1905; revised 1921), a turgid character assassination of Byron and all his biographers. Compared with this, even the most censorious early memoirs looked enlightened. Yet the controversy initiated by Stowe reignited public and scholarly interest in Byron, leading to several more full-length biographies and the thirteen-volume *Works of Lord Byron* (1898).

It is ironic that this body of literature, which defined its objective as seeking truth through intimacy, persistently questioned Byron's own truthfulness and policed the boundaries of his intimate relationships. Nineteenth-century biographers of Byron searched for a moral center and did not find one. What we remember from these *Lives* are fleeting scenes: Byron, pursued by fans in Venice, jumping into a gondola and pulling down the blinds; Byron confiding in his dog Lyon in Greece; Teresa and Byron watching a thunderstorm. Many attempted grand theories of the true Byron, but these were less evocative than the shifting, fragmentary presence they created collectively, or the momentary illumination of first-hand observations and anecdotes.

Notes

1 Samuel Taylor Coleridge, "A Prefatory Observation on Modern Biography," *The Friend* 21 (January 25, 1810), 339.
2 Andrew Elfenbein, *Byron and the Victorians* (Cambridge, UK: Cambridge University Press, 1995), 53.
3 James Henry Leigh Hunt, *Lord Byron and Some of his Contemporaries; with Recollections of the Author's Life, and of His Visit to Italy*, 2nd ed., 2 vols. (London: Henry Colburn, 1828), vol. 1, 158.
4 William Parry, *The Last Days of Lord Byron: With His Lordship's Opinions on Various Subjects, Particularly on the State and Prospects of Greece* (London: Knight & Lacey, 1825), vol. III, 126.
5 Ibid., 100, 28.
6 Hunt, *Lord Byron*, vol. 1, 68–9, 150.
7 Ibid., 71, 11.
8 *The Letters of Thomas Moore*, ed. Wilfred S. Dowden, 2 vols. (Oxford: Oxford University Press, 1964), vol. II, 680.
9 Elfenbein, *Byron*, 79.
10 Harriet Beecher Stowe, *Lady Byron Vindicated: A History of the Byron Controversy from Its Beginning in 1816 to the Present Time* (London: Sampson, Low, Son & Marston, 1870), 155.

CHAPTER 35

Posthumous Reception and Reinvention to 1900

Eric Eisner

Just as the myth of Byron was not created by the poet alone during his lifetime, so after his death a whole industry kept the myth-making machinery running. Byronic aura was reproduced, challenged and reinvented throughout the nineteenth century, in new editions, portraits of the poet, accounts of his life and conversation, fictionalizations of his life story, continuations of his poems, adaptations, imitations, memorials and tributes. British and American tourists took Byron with them to the Continent, where his verse mediated their experience of natural landscapes and classical ruins. Byron and the heroes of his romances – so often blended together by the public – provided the template for both literary characters and real-life imitators who styled themselves after their idol. The many flavors, straight or parodic, of the "Byronic hero" suggest the range of nineteenth-century takes on the electric, contradictory, confounding Lord Byron himself: ruggedly handsome individualist, effeminate Regency fop, savage misanthrope, devilish charmer, demonic scoffer, hopeless romantic, seductive outlaw, perverse criminal, exilic wanderer, mad genius, noble revolutionary, egotistical poseur.

Within a strengthening critical hierarchy distinguishing commercial entertainment from "serious" literature, however, Byron's very popularity told against him. Even by the early 1830s, critics spoke of the embarrassing excesses of "Byromania" as a bygone fad, congratulating themselves on their more distanced, cool-headed view. Writing in the 1850s, the American author Samuel Goodrich recalled the days when the Byronic infection "could no more be kept at bay, than the cholera," but Goodrich contrasts the contagious appeal of Byronic transgression with the supposedly healthier reading habits that followed. At mid-century, he observes, "Byron is still read, but his immoralities, his atheism, have lost their relish, and are now deemed offenses and blemishes," while "the public taste is directing itself in favor of a purer and more exalted moral tone" exemplified in England by Tennyson, and in America by Longfellow and Willam Cullen Bryant.[1] The delirious heyday of Byronism had given way, it seemed, to a more soberly reflective outlook. Projecting a path beyond Romantic "self-tormenting" to an objective vision of useful work and action, Thomas Carlyle's *Sartor Resartus* (1833–4) encapsulated this shift in the famous formula, "Close thy *Byron*; open thy *Goethe.*"[2]

In truth, however, nineteenth-century responses to Byron were more complex than such a neat divide might suggest. Across the century, Byron's writing, and his myth, were active in a variety of contexts and guises, from abolitionist political discourse to aestheticism. Many later nineteenth-century authors – Tennyson, Longfellow, Bryant, the Brontës, Felicia Hemans, Carlyle himself – were seriously hooked on Byron when they were young. While Victorians often cast Byron worship as an adolescent phase, many never got over their feeling for the poet, even as their view of his work and character grew conflicted. Other writers, more resistant, still read Byron closely and contended with his charismatic example. The incessant returns to Byron's writing and his life story across the century have to do not only with commercial possibility or readerly curiosity, but also with the fact that "Byron" names an ensemble of cultural and psychological materials that many Victorian readers and writers continued to find relevant and sometimes needed to work through.

The most significant immediate successors to Byron's popularity were, in fiction, the silver-fork novel of fashionable high society, and in poetry, the writing of women such as Hemans and Letitia Landon (L. E. L.), who, reformulating the motifs of Byronic sensibility, dominated the market for verse in the 1820s. L. E. L.'s smash hit *The Improvisatrice: And Other Poems* (1824) was touted as picking up where Byron left off. A mash-up of tropes from Byron and Mme. de Staël's *Corinne*, L. E. L.'s work also forecasts the prominence of female poets in the post-Byronic cultural landscape. In *The Improvisatrice*, for example, the Byronic hero Lorenzo is left mute and forlorn while the eponymous heroine gets all the operatic fun, and L. E. L.'s narrative voice gets the last word. Like Landon, Hemans is an attentive, admiring and critical reader of Byron; her textual dialogue with the aristocratic poet begins during the Regency, and she continues to respond to his poetry throughout her career, submitting Byronic themes of alienation, autonomy, violence and female self-sacrifice to gender-conscious critique and revision.

The young Benjamin Disraeli (the future Prime Minister) helped launch the silver-fork genre with his scandalizing *roman-à-clef Vivian Grey* (1826) promoted by its publisher Henry Colburn as a novelistic successor to *Don Juan*. Yet while *Vivian Grey* is written under Byron's sway – and borrows

Don Juan's self-ironizing voice – the Byronic also appears in the novel as strangely attenuated, spectral or parodic. Despite many Byronesque characters, we encounter the "actual" Byron only in report, as older, corpulent and graying, no longer recognizably Byronic. Near the close of the novel's 1827 continuation, the hero Vivian, self-exiled on the Continent, watches a ballet version of *The Corsair*, eerie in its muteness. In moments like these, the novel draws attention to the active remediation of Byronic charisma in which it participates, in which versions of "Byron" – the poet and his texts – are translated into ever-multiplying images of images, at many removes from the original figure they conjure.

Silver-fork fiction returns obsessively to Byron's legend, as in Disraeli's later *Venetia* (1837), which cribs ostentatiously from Moore's *Life* of Byron. In Edward Bulwer-Lytton's bestseller *Pelham* (1828), the gloomy, aloof Byronic aristocrat of high passions and dark secrets literally exhausts itself in the character of Sir Reginald Glanville, whose body wastes into infirmity, while the novel presents an alternative model for the modern gentleman in the dandified title character, who underneath his outward posture of nonchalance and self-regard has a friendly desire to do practical good. The ambitious Disraeli and Bulwer were both notorious dandies and dedicated Byronists, who found in Byronic performance a model for their own play with norms of class and sexuality. Byronic performance of cosmopolitan masculinity was perhaps an even more significant model for American writers, including the journalist and dandy Nathaniel Parker Willis (who published a short-lived newspaper called the *Corsair*) or the popular poet Fitz-Greene Halleck, the "American Byron," whose intense identification with the sexually ambiguous Byron was partly a means of negotiating his love for other men.

For nineteenth-century audiences, Byron's glamour was caught up with charges that his writing, and perhaps his character, were blasphemous, criminal or otherwise morally tainted. Either Byron's writing uncontrollably spoke the truth of his deranged mind and haunted soul, or was all "humbug," or somehow both diseased and insincere. However, a strict dichotomy between sincere self-expression and calculated imposture leaves no room for the important, complex play with masks and masking, doubles and "double-disguise" Jerome McGann recognizes as the staging of Byronic "masquerade."[3] Byron's experimentation with performative personae helps shape cultural forms from the Victorian dramatic monologue to the theatrical celebrity of writers like Oscar Wilde.

The idea that there was a danger in merely reading Byron seems mostly to have made surreptitious reading more exciting. Byronic affect was channeled by feminized, mass-cultural forms such as the sensational romance novels of Ouida (Maria Louise Ramé). Byron's presence is also felt in boundary-challenging work that explores the Gothic terrains of violence and passion: Heathcliff in Emily Brontë's *Wuthering Heights* (1847) and Rochester in her sister Charlotte's *Jane Eyre* (1847) are two of the century's most famously Byronic creations. Edgar Allan Poe, whom Baudelaire called a "Byron astray in a wicked world," fashioned his own fascinating authorial image through a Byronic assemblage of Gothic conventions: dark, haunted, mesmerizing.[4] Absorbed into the touristic experience of Europe, Byron is an element of the heady romance atmosphere suffusing the Italy of Nathaniel Hawthorne's *The Marble Faun* (1860) and Henry James' *The Aspern Papers* (1888), the setting for dramas of sexual desire, guilt and transgression, and interchanges between life and art.

Yet the Satanic bad boy could also be a Promethean voice of freedom: a lover *and* a fighter. In 1838 the American George Bancroft attributed "the secret of Byron's power" to "the harmony which existed between his muse and the democratic tendency of the age."[5] Byron's association with the struggle for Greek liberation focused Philhellenic sentiment in Britain and America. Nationalist and liberationist movements around the world rallied to his lines from *Childe Harold's Pilgrimage* that called on oppressed peoples to take action in their own liberation – "Hereditary bondsmen! know ye not / Who would be free themselves must strike the blow?" (*CPW* II: 69, ll. 720–1). Taken up by rhetorical traditions in African American political discourse, the verse is given prominent citation by writers including Frederick Douglass and W. E. B. Du Bois, who uses it as the epigraph to his chapter on Booker T. Washington in *Souls of Black Folk* (1903).

For Elizabeth Barrett Browning, Byron was a powerful symbol of both political ideals and artistic aspiration. To the young Barrett, the noble poet represents a romantic possibility for action and freedom in the wider world: as a child, she even fantasized about disguising herself as a boy to run off as Lord Byron's page (in an interesting echo of Byron's lover Caroline Lamb, who dressed as a page to visit him surreptitiously). In her "Stanzas on the Death of Lord Byron" (1824), the teenage Barrett mourns "that generous heart where genius thrill'd divine," calling Byron "Britannia's Poet! Graecia's hero" (l. 16, 19).[6] Three decades later, she turns to Byron's epic example in setting out to write "a poem of a new class, in a measure – a Don Juan, without the mockery & impurity" that will "touch this real everyday life of our age."[7] Like *Don Juan*, the resulting verse-novel *Aurora*

Leigh (1856) aggressively mixes genres and registers. The eponymous poet-heroine steels herself to

> Never flinch,
>   But still, unscrupulously epic, catch
>   Upon the burning lava of a song
>   The full-veined, heaving, double-breasted Age.[8]

Recalling Byron's volcanic images for his own poetry, she also audaciously feminizes the figure.

Like Barrett Browning, many women writers, including Hemans, the Brontës and Margaret Fuller, found in Byron "a model ... for the rebellion implicit in the fact of female ambition."[9] Yet it is a model that provokes conflicting feelings: women writers repeatedly test Byronic ambition, recklessness and independence against familial and social structures of mutual obligation and care – a pattern in Mary Shelley's fiction from *Frankenstein* (1818), for example. In her novels *The Last Man* (1826), *Lodore* (1835) and *Falkner* (1837), Shelley uses fiction both to mourn and to revisit an experience of Romanticism to which Byron was integral, trying out in fantasy alternative plots for figures of Byronic capability and charisma.

The last decades of the century saw the publication of a series of important critical statements on Byron, prompted in part by the appearance of new editions and biographies in the 1870s and 1880s. Liberal and radical critics especially found Byron a sympathetic figure and demonstrated their independence from orthodox opinion by rescuing his work from charges of indecency. Harriet Beecher Stowe's controversial *Lady Byron Vindicated* (1870) also spurred impassioned responses from Byron's defenders. Critics arrived at widely varying opinions on how to understand his place in literary history and the relation of his life, work and reception to larger historical movements.

In the influential preface to his 1881 edition of Byron's verse, Matthew Arnold classed Byron as second only to Wordsworth among the century's British poets. Arnold contends that Wordsworth "has an insight into permanent sources of joy and consolation for mankind which Byron has not."[10] As Arnold's poem "Memorial Verses (April 1850)" had earlier declared, Byron's power lies instead in his ability to give voice to his own feeling, in which alienated, skeptical and searching Victorian readers like Arnold might find their own emotion echoed. Arnold admires Byron's valiant, if doomed, struggle against cant, hypocrisy and complacency, but argues that he lacks artistic sensibility or self-discipline. He describes Byron's poetry as uneven and wearying in the mass, best appreciated as his own edition presents it: in disconnected excerpts, freeze-frame moments of feeling.

The historian Thomas Babington Macaulay's 1831 description of Byron as a mediating figure among the competing positions within British culture presents a contrast to Arnold's vision of Byron's Promethean, oppositional role. Macaulay points out that Byron proves common ground for an establishment figure such as William Gifford and a radical such as Percy Shelley, because his spirit of resistance consorts with his curiosity and openness: his impulse to independence and stubborn opposition is expressed in his classical taste (posed against Romantic fashion) as much as in his posture of Romantic rebellion. For Macaulay, Byron's work synthesizes and expresses the whole run of British literature from Pope's "Essay on Man" to Wordsworth's *Excursion*.

Italian reformer Giuseppe Mazzini offered an even more dialectical understanding of Byron's relation to his era, which he argues condenses and makes visible the exhaustion of the previous era's ideologies. Taking individualism to its extreme, Byron throws back to us the insufficiency of the isolated individual, thus forecasting the demand for a more communal social order. Noting Byron's lasting influence on Continental reformers, the journalist (and later Liberal politician) John Morley identified Byron in 1870 with the spirit of protest launched by the French Revolution. For Morley, Byron is a fundamentally social poet who never loses sight of the "round earth and the civil animal who dwells upon it. Even his misanthropy is only an inverted form of social solicitude."[11]

Similarly, John Ruskin celebrated the revolutionary agency of Byron's poetry. In a wonderful phrase, he describes Byron, Robert Burns and Walter Scott as part of Britain's "carnal orchestra," their writings the British equivalent of France's stirring revolutionary songs like "La Marseillaise."[12] Byron's great gift in Ruskin's view is his elastic sympathy, which allows the aristocratic writer to think from the point of view of others, whether the lower classes in his own time or actors far removed in history. He is "the first great Englishman who felt the cruelty of war, and, in its cruelty, the shame."[13] While Arnold privileges the "Titanic" Byron of *Childe Harold*, Ruskin's emphasis on Byron's comic and satiric writing, especially *Don Juan*, matches a late-century critical consensus also reflected in Algernon Swinburne's 1866 appreciation. *Contra* Arnold, both Swinburne and Ruskin emphasize Byron's artistry, seeing his poems as organic wholes damaged by excerption. In Swinburne's insouciant account, playing off *Don Juan*'s own maritime metaphorics, the work is compared to the ocean's "wide wholesome air, full of vivid light," with a "tidal variety of experience and emotion," its stanzas "like waves that sound or that subside" offering, in his strikingly physicalized description, "a delicious resistance, an elastic motion."[14]

Ruskin and Swinburne here fit within a liberal and radical trad-ition that associates Byron with a particularly "healthful" masculinity, countering the discourse that linked Byron with diseased sensibility. Charles Kingsley in 1853 derided the "effeminacy" of an age that could prefer the "extravagance" of Shelley to the "sound shrewd sense" of "the sturdy peer, proud of his bull neck and his boxing" (quoted in *BCH* 355). For the novelist William Hale White ("Mark Rutherford"), Byron "was a mass of living energy," and his "power" and "force" make him an antidote to a "sickly age."[15]

Yet two decades after Swinburne praised Byron's "sincerity and strength," he launched a virulent attack on the poet for dishonesty and egotism. The university professor George Saintsbury's 1896 literary his-tory similarly criticizes Byron's theatricality: "the roses are rouged, the cries of passion even sometimes (not always) ring false." Byron appears "a poet distinctly of the second class, and not even of the best kind of second."[16] Saintsbury articulates a view that would hold for much of twentieth-century criticism as well.

NOTES

1 S. G. Goodrich, *Recollections of a Lifetime*, 2 vols. (New York: C. M. Saxton, 1859), vol. II, 106–7.

2 Thomas Carlyle, *Sartor Resartus*, eds. Mark Engel and Rodger L. Tarr (Berkeley and Los Angeles: University of California Press, 2000), 142–3.

3 Jerome J. McGann, "The Hero with a Thousand Faces: The Rhetoric of Byronism," in *Byron and Romanticism* (Cambridge, UK: Cambridge University Press, 2002), 154.

4 Eliza Richards, *Gender and the Poetics of Reception in Poe's Circle* (Cambridge, UK: Cambridge University Press, 2004), 31–2; Baudelaire qtd. on 31.

5 "On the Progress of Civilization," *Boston Quarterly Review* (October 1838), 400.

6 Elizabeth Barrett Browning, *Selected Poems*, eds. Marjorie Stone and Beverly Taylor (Peterborough, Ontario, Canada: Broadview, 2009), 54.

7 Barrett Browning to Mary Russell Mitford, December 30, 1844, in Philip Kelley and Scott Lewis (eds.), *The Brownings' Correspondence* (Winfield, KS: Wedgestone Press, 1991), vol. IX, 304.

8 Barrett Browning, *Aurora Leigh*, ed. Margaret Reynolds (New York: W. W. Norton, 1996), 150.

9 Dorothy Mermin, *Godiva's Ride: Women of Letters in England, 1830–1880* (Bloomington: Indiana University Press, 1993), 8.

10 Matthew Arnold, *Complete Prose Works*, ed. R. H. Super (Ann Arbor: University of Michigan, 1973), vol. IX, 236.
11 John Morley, *Critical Miscellanies* (London: Macmillan, 1886), vol. I, 215.
12 John Ruskin, "Fiction – Fair and Foul" (1880), in *Ethics of the Dust, Fiction: Fair and Foul, The Elements of Drawing* (New York: Bryan, Taylor, 1894), 195.
13 Ibid., 202.
14 Algernon Swinburne, "Byron," in Clyde K. Hyder (ed.), *Swinburne as Critic* (London: Routledge & Kegan Paul, 1972), 40.
15 William Hale White, "Byron, Goethe, and Mr. Matthew Arnold," *Contemporary Review* 40 (1881), 184–5.
16 George Saintsbury, *A History of Nineteenth-Century Literature (1780–1895)* (New York: Macmillan, 1896), 80–1.

CHAPTER 36

Popular Culture

Lindsey Eckert

Lord Byron's contemporaries frequently noted (and often lamented) his popular appeal, which had made him, according to one reviewer of *Childe Harold's Pilgrimage* III, a "remarkable phenomenon of the time" (*RR* 1966). By the time *Manfred* appeared in June 1817, the "remarkable phenomenon" had grown into a disturbing frenzy, affecting not only readers but also members of the public without direct knowledge of Byron's literary works. "There is a moral disease abroad," another critic wrote, "contagious and pretty prevalent, that may be termed the *Byromania*" (*RR* 1223). People infected by the "Byromania" simply could not get enough of the poet, with those severely afflicted sending him fan letters in droves. But Byromania – a condition often associated with indiscriminating and frantic female fans who, some complained, read Byron's poems for all the wrong reasons – is not limited to his original audience. Much like Jane Austen's famous "Janeites," Byron's admirers and readers from the Romantic period onward have created and consumed a wide variety of printed materials and other Byron-related artifacts, or Byroniana, evidencing Byromania's multimedia impact. From books to beard oil, films to figurines, statues to soup bowls, Byron and the forms of the Byronic hero that he popularized have consistently pervaded popular culture since he catapulted to fame following the publication of *Childe Harold* I–II in 1812. Byron's popular reception history reveals itself most strikingly through a methodology that looks beyond the literary and printed to the variety of quirky and kitsch, serious and sensational, digital and decorative adaptations indebted to his life and works. Though the specific forms that Byroniana takes have changed over time, clear trends emerge that demonstrate how and why Byron has fascinated popular audiences so intensely and for so long.

Byron's popularity can be measured in part by the number of volumes in which his literary works circulate. Published in impressively large first editions, revised editions and reprints (not to mention pirated publications), his poems immediately found a large readership during his life. William St.

Clair estimates that by 1815 the "fourteen apparent editions" of *The Giaour* and "eleven apparent editions" of *The Bride of Abydos* resulted in circulation of 12,500 copies of each text; 25,000 copies of *The Corsair* were also published by 1815.[1] Such figures are particularly remarkable in an era in which "most books were published in runs between 500 and 1,500 copies."[2] Byron's posthumous publication history is similarly impressive. When his works began to come out of copyright in the mid-nineteenth century, competing publishers produced volumes in different physical formats (quartos, octavos, duodecimos) and at different price points to fit diverse reading habits and budgets. For instance, Routledge's *Poems of Lord Byron*, originally released in 1859 as part of their "Poets for the People" series, sold 116,000 copies.[3] A decade later, Frederick Warne's edition of *Byron's Poetical Works* offered the complete poems for as little as three and a half shillings, and publishers in the United States produced similarly inexpensive volumes. By the 1870s, just half a shilling could buy a heavily illustrated edition of *Don Juan* from John Dicks' *English Classics* series.

The low cost of these texts reflects Byron's appeal to a broad readership, and his works were collected and excerpted to meet the demands of changing nineteenth- and twentieth-century audiences. Even religious communities adapted his works to suit their needs, exposing the poet's mediated words to huge nonacademic and perhaps even illiterate popular audiences. The famous Victorian preacher Charles Haddon Spurgeon frequently drew on Byron in his writings and sermons, which attracted thousands of listeners. More recently, more than a billion annual commuters on the London Tube have encountered Byron's poetry as part of Transport for London's "Poems on the Underground" series.

As Byron's literary texts have circulated among mass audiences, so too has information about Byron. Though not necessarily accurate, this information, particularly salacious details about his life, solidified Byron's place in the public imagination. Texts such as Thomas Moore's *Letters and Journals of Lord Byron* (1830), Lady Blessington's *Conversations with Lord Byron* (1834) and Harriet Beecher Stowe's *Lady Byron Vindicated* (1870) all offer hungry readers private information about the poet and his scandalous life. Likewise, successful works of fiction such as Lady Caroline Lamb's novel *Glenarvon* (1816) and John Polidori's novella *The Vampyre: A Tale* (1819) tease readers into recognizing loosely biographical Byronic characters, thus feeding and exploiting the period's growing Byromania.

More modern factual and fictional works about Byron are indebted to his literary fame and personal infamy, both firmly established in the Romantic period. Many twentieth-century representations of Byron continue to portray his literary achievements as secondary to his vibrant life. Cult classic films such as Robert Bolt's *Lady Caroline Lamb* (1972), Kenneth Russell's *Gothic* (1986) and Ivan Passer's *Haunted Summer* (1988) depict flagrantly fictionalized versions of Byron that largely sideline his authorial achievements. The trend is much the same in our own century when Byron's popularity seems only tangentially related to the poetry he wrote, showing how his representation in popular culture has shifted as new information about his romantic intrigues has been made publicly available. Indeed, rumors of his radical life that circulated during his own time are now supported in our own by more concrete textual evidence (letters, journals, commonplace books). For instance, Edna O'Brien's *Byron in Love: A Short Daring Life* (2009) makes rather quick work of his poems in favor of his amours, while in the National Portrait Gallery's exhibition *Mad Bad and Dangerous to Know: The Cult of Lord Byron* (2002–3), references to his poetry in the exhibition catalog are sparse when compared to details about Byron's biography and romantic relationships.

The poet's love life has found a keen audience online as well. The webcomic *Hark! A Vagrant* features a cartoon Byron asking people to "try and find a place here that I haven't put my penis in," while the website *The Toast* has published several comedic pieces about the poet, including "Texts From Lord Byron."[4] In one text exchange, Byron complains that choosing his favorite canto of *Childe Harold* is "like asking someone to pick who's hotter / his half-sister or his cousins / it's literally impossible."[5] Similarly, a 2016 episode of Comedy Central UK's popular series *Drunk History* highlights Byron's supposed affair with his half-sister, Augusta Leigh. In the episode, Byron, described as "suffering from infamy," defiantly tells two of his disapproving contemporaries, "Yeah I fucked my sister, but in years to come you'll be studying me."[6] Taken together, such representations of Byron do more than offer audiences intriguing biographical information; they point to complex links between Byron's scandalous life, his popularity and his continued literary canonicity.

Key to his canonicity are the mysterious, charismatic Byronic heroes from works like *Childe Harold*, *The Corsair*, *Lara* and *Manfred*, all of whom seem to offer veiled allusions to the poet himself. Like Byron's life, the characters he created have appeared in adapted forms for more than 200 years. Indeed, the Byronic hero has become so ubiquitous in popular culture that it can be easy to overlook. We see him – solitary, intelligent, rebellious and seductive – in nineteenth-century figures like Emily Brontë's Heathcliff in *Wuthering Heights* (1847) and Bram Stoker's title character in *Dracula* (1897). In the twentieth and twenty-first centuries, he emerges in characters such as the Byron scholar Bernard Nightingale in Tom Stoppard's play *Arcadia* (1993); the flawed superhero Tony Starke/ Ironman from the Marvel Comic universe; Edward Cullen, the heartthrob vampire in Stephanie Meyer's *Twilight* series of teen novels (2005–8) and its film adaptations; and the tavern-owning, gun-slinging Al Swearengen in the HBO show *Deadwood* (2004–6; 2019). What makes these Byronic heroes so compelling is their varying degrees of separation from Byron and the characters he created. Bernard Nightingale is self-consciously Byronic, whereas Edward Cullen's Byronism is mediated through references to *Wuthering Heights'* Heathcliff. In other instances, the poet's influence is obscured, leading to a new type of Byronic hero with the potential to (partially) reform. Thus, those like Tony Starke and Al Swearengen are as dark as Manfred or Childe Harold, yet their character trajectories ultimately reveal a social conscience that motivates them to help and lead others. The variety of characters indebted to Byron signals his wide-ranging influence beyond the texts that he wrote and their continued circulation in print.

Indeed, to assess Byron's cultural influence accurately, one must look beyond print, digital literature and film to an interconnected media landscape that also includes clothes, statues and other material objects. Matthew Arnold complained that Byron's visual popularity created imitators who "caught the fashion of deranging their hair or of knotting their neck handkerchief or of leaving their shirt collar unbuttoned."[7] The sartorial disease plaguing Victorian England was only possible because so many people knew what Byron looked like and how he dressed. Throughout the nineteenth century, Byron was often featured in a black robe with a white shirt left open at the collar in imitation of Thomas Phillips' famous "cloak" portrait of 1813 (see Figure I.1 in the Introduction). Changing technologies in the nineteenth century made printed portraits, caricatures and other illustrations more widely available than ever before, and by the 1830s his image had been "engineered" until it "was sufficiently simple and memorable to recognise in silhouette" alone.[8] Even those unfamiliar with the characteristics of his poetry could recognize his physical characteristics, with his dark curly hair, receding hairline and cleft chin. In addition to Byron's hair, his hand and his home were widely represented. The *Illustrated London News* printed facsimiles of Byron's signature, feeding directly into the popular practice of autograph collecting. Illustrations and later photographs of his ancestral seat, Newstead Abbey, appeared in periodicals, newspapers and luxury books, capitalizing on the growing vogue for domestic tourism.

It was not just printed likenesses, signatures and landscape photography that kept and continue to keep Byron in the public eye; since the mid-nineteenth century, monuments and memorials have circulated his image in public spaces and discourses both at home and abroad. Since 1845, visitors to the Wren Library at Trinity College, Cambridge, have been able to view the marble statue of Byron by Bertel Thorvaldsen. Commissioned by Byron's friends and admirers shortly after his death, it was moved to Cambridge only after its previous rejection from more prominent public spaces: St. Paul's Cathedral, the British Museum, the National Gallery and Westminster Abbey. After more than a century of public controversy, Byron was admitted into Poets' Corner at Westminster Abbey in 1968; his floor memorial was installed the following year. New monuments and accompanying publicity in popular news outlets have appeared as recently as 2016 with the unveiling of David Gross' wooden statue of Byron and his wife, Annabella Milbanke, in Seaham, England. The erection of such monuments and their coverage in newspapers and periodicals throughout Britain, the United States and Europe demonstrate the interplay between media forms that circulated Byron's image and information about him to popular audiences worldwide. Some of the most lively published descriptions of these monuments criticize their placement, decorousness and artistry. One writer in 1880 bemoaned the bronze statue of Byron in Hyde Park Corner (then Hamilton Gardens), claiming that the seated poet looked "like a hapless shipwrecked sailor" and that the "red and white streaks" on the statue's pedestal were "painfully suggestive of sausage."[9]

These sailor and sausage qualities seemed not to bother the wider nineteenth-century public, who continued to celebrate Byron's likeness in parks and in their private homes. Statues and portraits inspired small replicas that were sold on a large scale. Reproductions of Thorvaldsen's statue of Byron were produced in white bisque, an unglazed porcelain material evocative of marble. Made by the prestigious Royal Copenhagen Factory in 1835, they were reproduced hundreds of times for more than a decade to meet consistent consumer demand. Other bisque Byrons that imitate the later statue in Hyde Park appeared throughout the nineteenth century, including several by firms in North America and Europe, indicating his international popularity.

So prominent were these figures that the nineteenth-century comic Thomas Hudson opened his satirical song about inexpensive portrait busts, *Buy My Images*, with an extended reference to Byron:

> Will you buy Images? I Images cry,
> Very fine very pretty, very cheap will you buy? …
>
> Firs one *Prima* LORD BYRON head,
> BYRON live longtimes after him dead

Love tales *Poeta* – all very true one,
Every body's knows him call DON JUAN,
Will you buy Images?[10]

The title page of *Buy My Images* pictures a street hawker carrying busts, including one based on Phillip's "cloak" portrait of Byron, further demonstrating how his popularity traveled across different media forms. His image even appeared on fashionable finger rings, cravat pins and cameo pendants, keeping Byron close to the hands and hearts of his fans.

Byron also joined the ranks of military men, actors and authors depicted in the popular nineteenth- and early-twentieth-century Staffordshire style of pottery commonly displayed in middle- and lower-class homes. Produced in the Staffordshire region in England, these seven- to ten-inch detailed and brightly glazed earthenware statuettes appealed to consumers unable to afford expensive porcelain busts. Now collectors' items that are sold by prestigious auction houses and sellers on eBay and Etsy unsure of what they have, these busts still have a place in private homes and museums (see Figure 36.1). At least seven different Staffordshire-style Byrons were made in the nineteenth and early twentieth centuries. These ceramic figures of Byron were clearly inspired by portraits as well as the engravings of public monuments that circulated widely in the pages of the *Illustrated London News*. So fluid and multilayered are these transitions that today it is sometimes unclear which image of Byron inspired another. The fact that these objects are heavily mediated – with ceramic figures imitating statues that imitate illustrations of a painting – further confuses matters. For instance, one mid-nineteenth-century bust by an unknown firm seems to be a cheap, garish imitation of bisque busts of Byron made by European firms, which were themselves replicas of public monuments and paintings, including Phillips' "cloak" portrait and Thorvaldsen's statue.

Contemporaneous with ceramic likenesses of the poet were those of notable characters from his works. Several different group statuettes produced by different potters depict Selim and Zuleika as well as Giaffir and Zuleika from *The Bride of Abydos*. It is likely that more Staffordshire figures of Byron's characters were sold, since those that have been identified replicate almost exactly images from popular dinnerware sets sold in the same period.

Scenes from *The Bride of Abydos*, *Beppo*, *Mazeppa*, *Hebrew Melodies* and *Don Juan* appeared on soup plates, sauceboats and other dishes in two separate nineteenth-century transferware series of china both entitled "Byron Gallery," one produced by the firm Goodwins & Harris and the other by an unidentified manufacturer. Many of the pieces in these series take their lead from the illustrated edition of Byron's works *The Byron Gallery*, first

Figure 36.1 Lord Byron, Staffordshire ceramic statue (n.d., probably nineteenth century).
25.1 × 9 × 9.3 cm. Eckert Collection, Florida.

published in 1838. Such goods kept pace with new methods for producing
reasonably affordable commodities for popular audiences and an upwardly
mobile public.

As with the nineteenth-century adaptations of Byron's works and likeness,
the Byroniana circulating more recently often does so in a highly mediated
way. Adding to printed editions of Byron's works are modern digital editions,

facsimiles and interactive adaptations. Ichiro Lambe and Ziba Scott's award-winning videogame *Elegy for a Dead World* (2013) allows players to navigate and write about defunct civilizations on imagined planets inspired by Romantic poems. Byron's "Darkness" (1816) provides the inspiration for one of the game's three worlds. Related to Arnold's dreaded Byron-styled dandies, today's bearded Byromaniacs can purchase a variety of grooming products, including items from Lord Byron's Brand Beard Oil, which advertises scents inspired by Byron's poetry: "Don Juan 133" (tobacco and cedarwood), "Giaour 51" (patchouli and lavender) and "Darkness" (clove and cinnamon bark). While few today may wear their shirts open and hair deranged in an intentionally Byronic fashion, many can purchase sweatshirts featuring his face, scarves with quotations from his poetry, and even a shirt screen-printed with a facsimile of his marriage license. Byron's continued role in popular culture for more than two centuries exemplifies how literary texts and authorial reception are embedded in a diverse media landscape of texts and objects that have kept his poetry, life and likeness in the public eye.

Notes

1 William St Clair, *The Reading Nation in the Romantic Period* (Cambridge: Cambridge University Press, 2004), 586–7.
2 Lee Erickson, *The Economy of Literary Form: English Literature and the Industrialization of Publishing, 1800–1850* (Baltimore: Johns Hopkins University Press, 1996), 5.
3 St Clair, *The Reading Nation*, 716.
4 Kate Beaton, "Mary Shelley Quite Contrary, no. 56," *Hark! A Vagrant*, copyright 2006–16, harkavagrant.com/index.php?id=56.
5 Mallory Ortberg, "Texts from Lord Byron," *The Toast* (November 7, 2013), the-toast.net/2013/11/07/texts-lord-byron.
6 *Drunk History: UK*, series 2, episode 6, directed by Tom McKay, aired March 2, 2016, *Comedy Central UK*.
7 Matthew Arnold quoted in Frances Wilson, "Introduction: Byron, Byronism, and Byromaniacs," in Frances Wilson (ed.), *Byromania: Portraits of the Artist in Nineteenth-and Twentieth-Century Culture* (New York: St. Martin's Press, 1999), 5.
8 Tom Mole, *Byron's Romantic Celebrity: Industrial Culture and the Hermeneutic of Intimacy* (New York: Palgrave Macmillan, 2007), 79.
9 "The Statue of Lord Byron," *New York Times* (June 8, 1881), 2, ProQuest Historical Newspapers: The *New York Times*.
10 Thomas Hudson, *Buy My Images* (London: Brewer, [c.1842]), repr. in P. D. Gordon Pugh, *Staffordshire Portrait Figures and Allied Subjects of the Victorian Era, Including the Definitive Catalogue* (Woodbridge, UK: Antique Collectors Club, 1995), 11.

CHAPTER 37

Byron Now

Ghislaine McDayter

When asked to write an overview of contemporary Byron scholarship for this collection, I first turned to my predecessor Maureen M. McLane's Wordsworth essay for this same series for inspiration. Her essay on "Wordsworth Now" opens with the following compelling statement on the Lake poet: "It is striking that, however much he has been historicized, psychoanalyzed, deconstructed, queered, eco-criticized, eulogized, interred and revived, Wordsworth in many ways remains 'Wordsworth,' the elaborately consolidated figure who emerges in the reviews and poetries (his own and others') of the early nineteenth century."[1] As eloquent and insightful a piece as McLane's essay is, it was clearly not going to provide any kind of template for my review of Byron since, whatever else might be said about the mad, bad lord, he was rarely if ever thought to be consistent. As he remarks in *Don Juan*, it is *in*consistency that should be celebrated as nothing less than the "adoration of the real" and "the fine extension of the faculties" (*CPW* v: 155, ll. 1687, 1690). In short, "mobility" enables us to see and embrace the richness of a life worth living, and it was, arguably, only with a great deal of cajoling that Byron could be relied upon to consistently "remain" anywhere or be anything for a protracted period. Thus if, as McLane suggests, Wordsworth has come to represent a "consolidated" poet of the Romantic movement for us, then Byron stands before us as its most capricious and *un*consolidated participant.

It is no surprise that Byron and Wordsworth, two of the most influential and mutually hostile poets of the Romantic period, appear to us today as writers and thinkers utterly at odds, even in the world of criticism. Wordsworth's poetry has been celebrated for its centrality to the definition of the Romantic project since his own lifetime. Wordsworth scholars have authoritatively situated his *oeuvre* within the context of every major critical school to emerge over the last century, as McLane suggests above. By way of contrast, Jane Stabler observes that Byron remains the "wild card of English Romantic studies";[2] and in a recent study of Byron and genre, Dino Franco Felluga confesses that he has set himself the unenviable task of discerning "why Lord Byron was for so long a mystery to, or simply ignored by the dominant critical schools of the twentieth century, from New Criticism to phenomenology to psychoanalysis and post-structuralism."[3] It is not, I hasten to add, that there have not been equally important critical studies on the subject of Byron's work, nor that scholarship on his poetry has somehow been wanting. On the contrary, Byron studies have enjoyed a rich and theoretically sophisticated period of growth over the last few decades, as the preceding chapters in this collection amply attest. Byronists have made foundational contributions to digital scholarship, disability and celebrity studies and have also continued to contribute valuable scholarship to a growing body of queer, psychoanalytic, cultural, new-historical and formalist scholarship.

The recent acquisition of the Murray Archives by the National Library of Scotland has made the poet's work and documents far more easily accessible to the public and to scholars alike. Not that Byron has ever been hard to find in popular culture: he continues to appear with phenomenal regularity in graphic novels, anime, feature films and steampunk art as everything from a vampiric, rakish anti-hero to a gritty political revolutionary. Byronic literary lore is thus kept alive in fictional worlds. Even in Susanna Clarke's resurrection of the poet in her magical world of *Jonathan Strange and Mr. Norrell* (2004), the novel's British tourists travelling in Venice echo the rumours about the "dangerous" poet that were voiced by their historical counterparts during Byron's life. One matronly figure asks of her ingenue niece, for example, "should not you be afraid to look at him, my love? Lord Byron, I mean?"[4] And in such fictional repetitions of the gossip circulated about the poet by his contemporaries, Byron's mythic sexual presence is established as "real" to a whole new generation of readers. The recent "discovery" of Ada Lovelace, as one of the promoters and "programmers" of Babbage's Difference Engine, has also provoked a resurgence of interest in her father, and here too Byron's importance is established through his notoriety. The chapter heading introducing Ada's father in a study about the birth of the digital age is, notably, "Lord Byron: A Scandalous Ancestry."[5] Even readers with little interest in Byron's poetry for its own sake have a hard time avoiding his legendary presence.

And yet, despite a large scholarly and artistic output, what strikes one most about Byron studies is *not* a shared sense of the poet's "gigantic" Wordsworth-like presence, but rather the cacophony of voices, proliferation of views and seemingly endless quest to get to the "truth" of Byron. As so many critics have observed, it must be one of the greatest ironies of literary studies that the poet most renowned for his "self-conscious" biographical impulses and "egotism," whom critics from Northrop Frye to William Hazlitt have accused of "mak[ing] man after his own image," has nonetheless inspired a deep sense of mystery about the "truth" of his character, his poetic process and his art.[6] We as readers and scholars endlessly circle around Byron without ever having a sense that we have finally reached him or his truth. Biographies and commentaries on the poet's life and loves continue to be written and published despite the very real sense that whatever could be said about the poet has surely already been said. And yet this is evidently not the case. No matter how much ink is spilled in aid of our attempt to "get at" the real Byron, we don't seem to be able to "get" there from here. Whenever we try, we are confronted by an absence, a void, the unspoken, the unspeakable. At the heart of Byron studies, I would argue, is a vacuum that might easily be emblematized by the famous "Memoir" of Byron burned by Hobhouse and Murray shortly after the poet's death. We feel that there is a truth to be had, but that we are never to be given full access to it. As Corin Throsby puts it, "It is a wonderful dramatic irony, then, that Byron's memoirs – which might have finally provided the 'truth' about his life – were destroyed soon after his death."[7] Notably, the word "truth," even here, remains in scare quotes.

Arguably, it is precisely this mythic "void" at the heart of Byron studies that best stands in for the poet's greatest power. It is the reason critics keep returning, transfixed, to Byron's poetry and life, but it is also responsible for the suggestiveness that his writing still has for a twenty-first-century readership. Byron continues to fascinate because he is the poet par excellence of wanting. When Byron famously embarked on his great epic, *Don Juan*, with the line: "I want a hero. An uncommon want," scholars were quick to identify the double meaning of "desiring" and "lacking" in this poem, but they were less alert to the centrality of this idea throughout the entire body of the poet's work. For it is, I would argue, in this voided space appearing throughout Byron's poetry that we find the structural operations that describe the emergence of modern subjectivity itself. For many prior scholars, what makes Byron "wanting" as a poet might have been the fact that he could not be situated within their own paradigms of Romanticism; for a new generation of scholars, however, the poet's resistance to such universalizing theories is his greatest appeal. What makes Byron so moving to modern readers is his ability to explore and articulate the growth not of any particular poet's mind, *pace* Wordsworth, but rather the very process by which we become subjects at all. Byron's poetry is always on some level about how we become who we are, whether the subject be heroic, disabled, queer, revolutionary, insane, a genius, narcissistic, famous, or a combination of all of the above. In short, what Byron "wants" is what we all "want" and struggle to achieve: a liberating "mobility" of subjectivity that does not surrender the very necessary psychological fantasy of an identifiable and coherent self. Thus, to paraphrase Marx via Slavoj Žižek, there is a spectre haunting Byron's poetry – the spectre of the Cartesian subject. What lurks at the heart of Byron's texts is the fear that we might become fixed in a stable subjectivity that privileges the rational mind over our desires.

Mine is not a particularly new claim; many critics have brilliantly illuminated the many ways in which Byron's poetry and prose open up a space for the exploration of Romantic identity and subjectivity, from Jerome McGann and Louis Crompton to Andrew Elfenbein and Andrea K. Henderson. But what I would like to point out are the particular ways in which this exploration of subjectivity is inextricably bound to the experience of radical loss. *Manfred*, published in 1817 after Byron's self-imposed exile from England and the scandal of his separation from Annabella Milbanke, is an ideal place to begin, marking as it does a new self-consciousness in the poet's representation of identity. As Andrew Elfenbein has remarked, it is in the writing of this dramatic poem that Byron shifts from the third to the first person when describing his hero. Conrad is always "he," Manfred notoriously and insistently is an "I."[8]

Countless examinations of *Manfred* have appeared in recent years focusing specifically on Manfred's tortured emotional state due to the tragic demise of his sister, Astarte, dead by Manfred's fault, though "Not with my hand" (*CPW* IV: 74, l. 118). His immortal suffering, Manfred insists, isolates him from the rest of mankind. To the bemused priest who visits him, he explains his self-exile as being inevitable, since he is now of an altogether different species or order: "I disdained to mingle with / A herd, though to be leader – and of the wolves. / The lion is alone, and so am I" (*CPW* IV: 92, ll. 121–3). And, at first, it does indeed seem as if Manfred is in this tortured state of isolated despair because of the loss of his beloved sister, with whom he presumably wishes to reunite. Many critics have spoken compellingly on this subject from (among others) psychoanalytic, queer and feminist perspectives. But what becomes interesting upon a close reading of this poem's investment in loss as a category is that (despite Manfred's often histrionic speeches) his much-vaunted despair does not so much serve to eulogize or mourn his absent sister as to revel in the experience of loss – to invite it and reenact it. It is very similar to what Stephen Bruhm has observed about the mourning narrative voice in the early Thyrza poems, a series of elegiac poems written after the death of Byron's schoolboy friend, John Edleston, the choirboy for whom he expressed "a violent, though *pure* love and passion" (*BLJ* 8: 24). Manfred's emotional intensity and trauma should be traced not to the mourning of the lost object itself – in this case the once beloved Astarte – but rather to the all-encompassing *experience* of this loss. For Bruhm, "[r]ather than bemoan the loss [of the loved one], the poem seems instead to celebrate the intensity with which the loss is felt and the intensely individual subject that such loss constructs."[9]

While this experience of loss might help to construct the individual subject, this process goes well beyond the prosaic sentiment that personal loss builds character. Rather, Manfred, no less than the poetic voice in the Edleston poems, engages in a highly dramatic renunciation of life itself, retreating into himself and thereby severing all links to his fellow man, his world and his god. "Good, or evil, life, / Powers, passions, all I see in other beings, / Have been to me as rain unto the sands" he says (*CPW* IV: 53, ll. 21–3). In sleep even his "eyes but close / To look within" (*CPW* IV: 53, ll. 6–7) But while it is tempting to argue that he can see nothing as he gazes with his mind's eye into the interior of his soul, it becomes evident that there is, on the contrary, something "within" that dominates that space, making it impossible for him to see himself at all. He might wish to retreat into an inner void, but while the figure and memory of Astarte is invisible to readers, this is what preoccupies and haunts Manfred. When asked by the Spirit what he wants, he replies, "Forgetfulness," but when asked to specify "Of what – of whom – and why?" his only response is: "Of that which is within me; read it there – / Ye know it, and I cannot utter it" (*CPW* IV: 57–8, ll. 136–8).

What Manfred "wants" then is not Astarte, the physical manifestation of this haunting "residue," but her obliteration. She has filled the space of Manfred's being to the point that his own subjectivity is jeopardized and thus it is not the actual loss of Astarte that haunts him. Rather it is the unspeakable desire *for her loss*, for true forgetfulness, that will make possible the emergence of his own subjectivity. As Elfenbein observes, "Astarte, even as a memory, challenges the supremacy of his narcissism,"[10] and so Manfred's erasure of Astarte is essential. Until such a moment, it is impossible for him to speak her name or his own desires since, as Tony Myers explains, "words can only exist if we first murder the thing, if we create a gap between them and the things they represent. This gap, the gap between nature and the beings immersed in it, is the subject."[11] Only by voiding his interiority of this powerful spectral "thing" can Manfred begin the process of moving from a state of wanting (desire for the lost object) to a secondary state of wanting, (desire for the *loss* of that object), because as it stands, the ghostly, immovable trace of Astarte has left him no space, no interiority within which to emerge as his own subject.

Thus, when Manfred confesses to having "destroyed" Astarte "not with my hand but heart," this Byronic hero, and, more specifically, Byron himself, reveals the violence in the very creation of all subjectivity. We must murder, not to dissect, but to create – and more specifically to create the word that enables us to take our place as an independent subject in the world. Astarte, the sister whose every feature was, in Manfred's words, "like to mine," blurs the lines between the subject and any possible signifier of the self. Her presence takes its place, if you will, standing in *for* him. Thus, although Astarte resides in the heart of Manfred as the unspeakable, she nonetheless *speaks him*. She has become a threat to Manfred's own ability to articulate self and he must rid himself of her enthralling presence in order to make space, and to embrace the radical loss that enables subjectivity and desire to emerge. Notably, in its final appearance, the apparition of Astarte does not give Manfred the forgiveness that he requests; what she does give him is the word – his own name – and with her disappearance, his self.

Just as scholars continue to grapple with and tease out the essence of this Byronic self, the poet himself makes it clear in *Don Juan* that the word not only makes our identity possible, but also stands in *for* our identity when we are gone:

> But words are things, and a small drop of ink,
>   Falling like dew, upon a thought, produces
> That which makes thousands, perhaps millions, think;
>   'Tis strange, the shortest letter which man uses
> Instead of speech, may form a lasting link
>   Of ages; to what straits old Time reduces
> Frail man, when paper – even a rag like this,
> Survives himself, his tomb, and all that's his.
>   (*DJ* III, st. 88, ll. 793–800 [*CPW* v: 192–3])

Our desires and considerations, when fixed by the written word "like dew, upon a thought," become that "thing" which we, as material beings, can never become – a "lasting link" with the minds of the future. In short, there is no need to despair that scholars and critics will never find the "truth" of Byron – whether buried in the words of the lost memoirs or elsewhere. For while words may become incarnated as things, what makes them worthy of eternity and fame is not their ability to produce reassurance and satisfaction in the reader, but rather their ability to inspire thousands, maybe millions, to "think."

NOTES

1 Maureen M. McLane, "Wordsworth Now," in Andrew Bennet (ed.), *William Wordsworth in Context* (Cambridge, UK: Cambridge University Press, 2015), 78–88.
2 Jane Stabler, "Introduction," in Jane Stabler (ed.). *Byron* (London: Longman, 1998), 1.
3 See Dino Franco Felluga, "Truth Is Stranger Than Fiction: *Don Juan* and the Truth Claims of Genre," *Modern Language Quarterly* 77 (2016), 105–20.
4 Susanna Clarke, *Jonathan Strange and Mr. Norrell* (London: Bloomsbury Publishing, 2004), 761. We see similar echoes in the highly successful computer-animated BBC web movie series and role-playing game *The Ghosts of Albion* (2007) created by Amber Benson and Christopher Golden, www.bbc.co.uk/cult/tamaraswift.
5 Most recently, the life and work of Ada Lovelace have been documented by James Essinger in *Ada's Algorithm: How Lord Byron's Daughter Ada Lovelace Launched the Digital Age* (London: Melville House, 2015) and by Sydney Padua in a graphic novel, *The Thrilling Adventures of Lovelace and Babbage: The (Mostly) True Story of the First Computer* (New York: Pantheon, 2015).
6 See Northrop Frye, *Fables of Identity: Studies in Poetic Mythology* (New York: Harcourt Brace & Co., 1963), 172–4; William Hazlitt, *The Spirit of the Age: Or, Contemporary Portraits* (London: Printed for Henry Colburn, 1825), 160.
7 Corin Throsby, "Byron Burning," *Times Literary Supplement* (June 8, 2016), 2.
8 Andrew Elfenbein, *Byron and the Victorians* (Cambridge, UK: Cambridge University Press, 1995), 34.
9 Steven Bruhm, *Reflecting Narcissus: A Queer Aesthetic* (Minneapolis: University of Minnesota Press, 2001), 41.
10 Andrew Elfenbein, *Byron and the Victorians*, 37.
11 Tony Myers, *Slavoj Žižek*, Routledge Critical Thinkers (London: Routledge, 2003), 37.

Further Reading

CHAPTER 1 EARLY YEARS

Boyes, Megan, *My Amiable Mamma: The Biography of Mrs. Catherine Gordon Byron* (London: privately published, 1991).

Calder, Angus, *Byron and Scotland: Radical or Dandy?* (Lanham, MD: Roman & Littlefield, 1990).

Crompton, Louis, *Byron and Greek Love: Homophobia in Nineteenth-Century England* (Berkeley, CA: University of California Press, 1985).

Douglass, Paul, "Byron's Life and his Biographers," in Drummond Bone (ed.), *The Cambridge Companion to Byron* (Cambridge, UK: Cambridge University Press, 2004), 1–26.

Elledge, Paul, *Lord Byron at Harrow School: Speaking Out, Talking Back, Acting Up, Bowing Out* (Baltimore: Johns Hopkins University Press, 2000).

Marchand, Leslie, *Byron: A Biography* (New York: Random House, 1957).

McGann, J., "Byron, George Gordon Noel, Sixth Baron Byron (1788–1824), poet," in *The Oxford Dictionary of National Biography* (Oxford: Oxford University Press, 2004), https://doi.org/10.1093/ref:odnb/4279.

Pratt, Willis W., *Byron at Southwell: The Making of a Poet, with New Poems and Letters from the Rare Books Collections of The University of Texas* (New York: Haskell House, 1973).

Walker, Viola, *The House of Byron* (London: Quiller Press, 1988).

CHAPTER 2 THE YEARS OF FAME

Cochran, Peter (ed.), *Byron in London* (Newcastle upon Tyne, UK: Cambridge Scholars Publishing, 2008).

Dart, Gregory, *Metropolitan Art and Literature, 1810–1840: Cockney Adventures* (Cambridge, UK: Cambridge University Press, 2012).

Gross, Jonathan D., "Epistolary Engagements: Byron, Annabella, and the Politics of 1813," in William D. Brewer and Marjean D. Purinton (eds.), *Contemporary Studies on Lord Byron* (Lewiston, NY: Edwin Mellen, 2001), 17–36.

Heinzelman, Kurtz, "Byron and the Invention of Celebrity," *Southwest Review* 93 (2008), 489–501.

Kelly, Lynda, *Holland House: A History of London's Most Celebrated Salon* (London: I. B. Tauris, 2015).

McDayter, Ghislaine, *Byromania and the Birth of Celebrity Culture* (Albany: State University of New York Press, 2009).

Murray, Venetia, *High Society: A Social History of the Regency Period, 1788–1830* (London: Viking, 1998).

Quennell, Peter, *Byron: The Years of Fame* (London: Faber & Faber, 1935).

Rendell, Jane, *The Pursuit of Pleasure: Gender, Space and Architecture in Regency London* (London: Athlone Press, 2002).

Saglia, Diego, "Touching Byron: Masculinity and the Celebrity Body in the Romantic Period," in Rainer Emig and Antony Rowland (eds.), *Performing Masculinity* (Basingstoke, UK: Palgrave Macmillan, 2010), 13–27.

Simpson, Michael, "Byron in Theory and Theatre Land: Finding the Right Address," in Jane Stabler (ed.), *Palgrave Advances in Byron Studies* (Basingstoke, UK: Palgrave Macmillan, 2007), 191–212.

Soderholm, James, "Lady Caroline Lamb: Byron's Miniature Writ Large," *Keats–Shelley Journal* 40 (1991), 24–46.

Chapter 3 Exile

Beaton, Roderick, *Byron's War: Romantic Rebellion, Greek Revolution* (Cambridge, UK: Cambridge University Press, 2013).

Guiccioli, Teresa, *Lord Byron's Life in Italy*, ed. Peter Cochran, trans. Michael Rees (Newark: University of Delaware Press, 2005).

Luzzi, Joseph, *Romantic Europe and the Ghost of Italy* (New Haven: Yale University Press, 2008).

Miranda, Omar F., "The Celebrity of Exilic Romance: Francisco de Miranda and Lord Byron," *European Romantic Review* 27.2 (2016), 207–31.

Rawes, Alan and Diego Saglia (eds.), *Byron and Italy* (Manchester: Manchester University Press, 2017).

Schoina, Maria, *Romantic "Anglo-Italians": Configurations of Identity in Byron, the Shelleys, and the Pisan Circle* (Farnham, UK: Ashgate, 2009).

Stabler, Jane, *The Artistry of Exile: Romantic and Victorian Writers in Italy* (Oxford: Oxford University Press, 2013).

Chapter 4 Texts and Editions

Fraistat, Neil and Julia Flanders, *The Cambridge Companion to Textual Scholarship* (Cambridge, UK: Cambridge University Press, 2013).

Higashinaka, Itsuyo, "Byron and William Gifford," *Byron Journal* 30 (2002), 21–8.

Levy, Michelle and Tom Mole, *The Broadview Introduction to Book History* (Peterborough, ON: Broadview, 2017).

McGann, Jerome J. (ed.), *Lord Byron: The Complete Poetical Works*, 7 vols. (Oxford: Clarendon Press, 1980–93).

Byron and Romanticism, ed. James Soderholm (Cambridge, UK: Cambridge University Press, 2002).

Poole, Gabriele, "'Hidden Secrets': The First Manuscript Version of *The Giaour*," in M. B. Raizis (ed.), *Byron: A Poet for all Seasons* (Messolonghi, Greece: Messolonghi Byron Society, 2000), 76–89.

Poole, Roger, "What Constitutes, and What is External to, the 'Real' *Childe Harold's Pilgrimage, A Romaunt: and Other Poems* (1812)?" in Richard A. Cardwell (ed.), *Lord Byron the European: Essays from the International Byron Society* (Lampeter, UK: Edwin Mellen, 1997), 149–207.

Pratt, Willis W. and Guy Steffan Truman (eds.), *Don Juan: A Variorum Edition*, 3 vols. (Austin: University of Texas Press, 1957).

Reiman, Donald (ed.), *Manuscripts of the Younger Romantics: Lord Byron*, 13 vols. (New York: Garland, 1980–98).

CHAPTER 5 BYRON AND HIS PUBLISHERS

Benedict, Barbara, "Publishing and Reading Poetry," in John Sitter (ed.), *The Cambridge Companion to Eighteenth-Century Poetry* (Cambridge, UK: Cambridge University Press, 2001), 63–82.

"Readers, Writers, Reviewers, and the Professionalization of Literature," in Thomas Keymer and Jon Mee (eds.), *The Cambridge Companion to English Literature, 1740–1830* (Cambridge, UK: Cambridge University Press, 2004), 3–23.

Carpenter, Humphrey, *The Seven Lives of John Murray: The Story of a Publishing Dynasty, 1768–2002* (London: John Murray, 2008).

Graham, Peter W., "Byron and the Business of Publishing," in Drummond Bone (ed.), *The Cambridge Companion to Byron* (Cambridge, UK: Cambridge University Press, 2004), 27–43.

Isaac, Peter, "Byron's Publisher and His Printers," in Peter Cochran (ed.), *The Newstead Byron Society Review* (July 2000), 86–96.

Jack, Ian, *A Poet and His Audience* (Cambridge, UK: Cambridge University Press, 1984).

Mason, Nicholas, "Building Brand Byron: Early Nineteenth-Century Advertising and the Marketing of *Childe Harold's Pilgrimage*," *Modern Language Quarterly* 63.4 (2002), 411–40.

Mole, Tom, *Byron's Romantic Celebrity: Industrial Culture and the Hermeneutics of Intimacy* (Basingstoke, UK: Palgrave Macmillan, 2007).

Newlyn, Lucy, *Reading, Writing and Romanticism: The Anxiety of Reception* (Oxford: Oxford University Press, 2000).

St Clair, William, "The Impact of Byron's Writings: An Evaluative Approach," in Andrew Rutherford (ed.), *Byron: Augustan and Romantic* (Basingstoke, UK: Macmillan, 1990), 1–25.

The Reading Nation in the Romantic Period (Cambridge, UK: Cambridge University Press, 2004).

CHAPTER 6 PIRACIES, FAKES AND FORGERIES

Baines, Paul, *The House of Forgery in Eighteenth-Century Britain* (Aldershot, UK: Ashgate, 1999).

Dyer, Gary, "The Circulation of Satirical Poetry in the Regency," *Keats–Shelley Journal* 61 (2012), 66–74.

"Publishers and Lawyers," *Wordsworth Circle* 44 (2013), 121–6.

"What is a First Edition? The Case of Don Juan, Cantos VI. – VII. – and VIII," *Keats–Shelley Journal* 60 (2011), 31–56.

Ehrsam, Theodore G., *Major Byron: The Incredible Career of a Literary Forger* (New York: C. S. Boesen, 1951).

Garside, Peter, James Raven and Rainer Schöwerling (eds.), *The English Novel 1770–1829: A Bibliographical Survey of Prose Fiction Published in the British Isles*, 2 vols. (Oxford: Oxford University Press, 2000).

Groom, Nick, *The Forger's Shadow: How Forgery Changed the Course of Literature* (London: Picador, 2002).

Lynch, Jack, *Deception and Detection in Eighteenth-Century Britain* (London: Ashgate, 2008).

McGann, Jerome J., *Introduction to Lord Byron: A Collection of 429 Items* (Dorking: C. C. Kohler, 1980).

Randolph, Francis Lewis, *Studies for a Byron Bibliography* (Lititz, PA: Sutter House, 1979).

Russett, Margaret, *Fictions and Fakes: Forging Romantic Authenticity, 1760–1845* (Cambridge, UK: Cambridge University Press, 2006).

Soderholm, James, *Fantasy, Forgery, and the Byron Legend* (Lexington, KY: University Press of Kentucky, 1996).

Chapter 7 Politics

Beckett, John, *Byron and Newstead: The Aristocrat and the Abbey* (Newark: University of Delaware Press, 2001).

"Byron and Rochdale," *Byron Journal* 33 (2005), 13–24.

"Politician or Poet? The 6th Lord Byron in the House of Lords, 1809–13," *Parliamentary History* 34.2 (2015), 201–17.

Davis, Richard W., "The House of Lords, 1801–1911," in Clyve Jones (ed.), *A Short History of Parliament* (Woodbridge, UK: Boydell Press, 2009), 193–210.

"The House of Lords, the Whigs and Catholic Emancipation, 1806–1829," *Parliamentary History* 18 (1999), 23–43.

Kelsall, Malcolm Miles, *Byron's Politics* (Brighton: Harvester Press, 1987).

MacCarthy, Fiona, *Byron: Life and Legend* (London: John Murray, 2002).

Chapter 8 War

Bainbridge, Simon, *Napoleon and English Romanticism* (Cambridge, UK: Cambridge University Press, 1995).

"'Of War and Taking Towns': Byron's Siege Poems," in Philip Shaw (ed.), *Romantic Wars: Studies in Culture and Conflict, 1793–1822* (Aldershot, UK: Ashgate, 2000), 161–84.

Beaton, Roderick, *Byron's War: Romantic Rebellion, Greek Revolution* (Cambridge, UK: Cambridge University Press, 2013).

Bell, David A., *The First Total War: Napoleon's Europe and the Birth of Modern Warfare* (London: Bloomsbury, 2007).

Clubbe, John, "Napoleon's Last Campaign and the Origins of *Don Juan*," *Byron Journal* 25 (1997), 12–22.

Coletes-Blanco, Agustín, "Byron and the 'Spanish Patriots': The Poetry and Politics of the Peninsular War (1808–1814)," in Roderick Beaton and Christine Kenyon (eds.), *Byron: The Poetry of Politics and the Politics of Poetry* (Abingdon, UK: Routledge, 2017), 187–99.

Shaw, Philip, "Byron and War: Sketches of Spain: Love and War in *Childe Harold's Pilgrimage*," in Jane Stabler (ed.), *Palgrave Advances in Byron Studies* (Basingstoke, UK: Palgrave Macmillan, 2007), 213–33.

Watson, J. R., *Romanticism and War: A Study of British Romantic Period Writers and the Napoleonic Wars* (Basingstoke, UK: Palgrave Macmillan, 2003).

Webb, Timothy, "Byron and the Heroic Syllables," *Keats–Shelley Review* 5.1 (1990), 41–74.

CHAPTER 9 GREECE'S BYRON

Beaton, Roderick, *Byron's War: Romantic Rebellion, Greek Revolution* (Cambridge, UK: Cambridge University Press, 2013).

Dakin, Douglas, *The Greek Struggle for Independence, 1821–1833* (London: Batsford, 1973).

Finlay, George, *History of the Greek Revolution and of the Reign of King Otho*, 2 vols. (London: Zeno, 1971).

Gordon, Thomas, *History of the Greek Revolution* (Edinburgh: Blackwell; London: Cadell, 1832).

Kelsall, Malcolm, *Byron's Politics* (Brighton: Harvester Press, 1987).

Kenyon Jones, Christine (ed.), *Byron: The Image of the Poet* (Newark: University of Delaware Press, 2008).

MacCarthy, Fiona, *Byron: Life and Legend* (London: John Murray, 2002).

Minta, Stephen, *On a Voiceless Shore: Byron in Greece* (New York: Henry Holt & Company, 1998).

Rosen, F., *Bentham, Byron, and Greece: Constitutionalism, Nationalism, and Early Liberal Political Thought* (Oxford: Clarendon Press, 1992).

St Clair, William, *That Greece Might Still Be Free: The Philhellenes in the War of Independence* (Oxford: Oxford University Press, 1972).

Trueblood, Paul G. (ed.), *Byron's Political and Cultural Influence in Nineteenth-Century Europe* (London: Macmillan, 1981).

CHAPTER 10 BYRON'S ITALY

Angeletti, Gioia, *Lord Byron and Discourses of Otherness: Scotland, Italy, and Femininity* (Edinburgh: Humming Earth, 2012).

Buzard, James, *The Beaten Track: European Tourism, Literature, and the Ways to Culture, 1880–1918* (Oxford: Clarendon Press, 1993).

Rawes, Alan and Diego Saglia (eds.), *Byron and Italy* (Manchester: Manchester University Press, 2017).

Redford, Bruce, *Venice and the Grand Tour* (New Haven: Yale University Press, 1996).

Vassallo, Peter, *Byron: The Italian Literary Influence* (New York: St. Martin's Press, 1984).

Webb, Timothy, "Haunted City: The Shelleys, Byron, and Ancient Rome," in Timothy Saunders, Charles Martindale, Ralph Pite and Mathilde Skoie (eds.), *Romans and Romantics* (Oxford: Oxford University Press, 2012), 203–24.

"'Soft Bastard Latin': Byron and the Attractions of Italian," *Journal of Anglo-Italian Studies* 10 (2009), 73–100.

CHAPTER 11 ORIENTALISM

Beaton, Roderick, *Byron's War: Romantic Rebellion, Greek Revolution* (Cambridge, UK: Cambridge University Press, 2013).

Cohen-Vrignaud, Gerard, *Radical Orientalism: Rights, Reform, and Romanticism* (Cambridge, UK: Cambridge University Press, 2015).

Leask, Nigel, *British Romantic Writers and the East: Anxieties of Empire* (Cambridge, UK: Cambridge University Press, 1992).

Makdisi, Saree, *Romantic Imperialism: Universal Empire and the Culture of Modernity* (Cambridge, UK: Cambridge University Press, 1998).

Said, Edward, *Orientalism* (New York: Vintage, 1979).

Schwab, Raymond, *The Oriental Renaissance: Europe's Rediscovery of India and the East, 1680–1880*, trans. Gene Patterson-King and Victor Reinking (New York: Columbia University Press, 1984).

CHAPTER 12 RELIGION

Ashton, Thomas L., *Byron's Hebrew Melodies* (Austin: University of Texas Press, 1972).

Beatty, Bernard, "Calvin in Islam: A Reading of *Lara* and *The Giaour*," in Martin Procházka (ed.), *Byron: East and West. Proceedings of the 24th International Byron Conference* (Prague: Charles University, 2000), 79–94.

Butler, Marilyn, "The Orientalism of Byron's *Giaour*," in Bernard Beatty and Vincent Newey (eds.), *Byron and the Limits of Fiction* (Liverpool: Liverpool University Press, 1988), 78–96.

Donnelly, William J., "Byron and Catholicism," in Angus Calder (ed.), *Byron and Scotland: Radical or Dandy?* (Edinburgh: Edinburgh University Press, 1989), 44–50.

Franklin, Caroline, "'Some Samples of the Finest Orientalism': Byronic Phillhelenism and Proto-Zionism at the Time of the Congress of Vienna," in Tim Fulford and Peter J. Kitson (eds.), *Romanticism and Colonialism: Writing and Empire, 1780–1830* (Cambridge, UK: Cambridge University Press, 1998), 221–42.

Hopps, Gavin and Jane Stabler, *Romanticism and Religion from William Cowper to Wallace Stevens* (Aldershot, UK: Ashgate, 2006).

Kenyon Jones, Christine, "'I was Bred a Moderate Presbyterian': Byron, Thomas Chalmers and the Scottish Religious Heritage," in Gavin Hopps and Jane Stabler (eds.), *Romanticism and Religion from William Cowper to Wallace Stevens* (Aldershot, UK: Ashgate, 2006), 107–19.

Looper, Travis, *Byron and the Bible: A Compendium of Biblical Usage in the Poetry of Lord Byron* (London: Scarecrow Press, 1978).

Said, Edward, *Orientalism* (New York: Pantheon, 1978).

Thorslev, Peter L., Jr., "Byron and Bayle: Biblical Skepticism and Romantic Irony," in Wolf Z. Hirst (ed.), *Byron, The Bible and Religion* (Newark: University of Delaware Press, 1991), 58–76.

CHAPTER 13 NATURAL PHILOSOPHY

Chandler, James, "'Man Fell with Apples': The Moral Mechanics of *Don Juan*," in Alice Levine and Robert N. Keane (eds.), *Rereading Byron: Essays Selected from Hofstra University's Byron Bicentennial Conference* (New York: Garland, 1993), 67–85.

de Almeida, Hermione, "Between Two Worlds: Evolution, Speciation, and Extinction in Byron," in Bernard Beatty and Jonathon Shears (eds.), *Byron's Temperament: Essays in Body and Mind* (Newcastle upon Tyne, UK: Cambridge Scholars Publishing, 2016), 138–57.

Horová, Mirka, "Byron and Catastrophism," in Peter Cochran (ed.), *Byron's Religions* (Newcastle upon Tyne, UK: Cambridge Scholars Publishing, 2011), 253–61.

Hubbell, J. Andrew, *Byron's Nature: A Romantic Vision of Cultural Ecology* (Cham, Switzerland: Palgrave Macmillan, 2018).

Kenyon Jones, Christine, "Byron, Darwin, and Paley: Interrogating Natural Theology," in Cheryl A. Wilson (ed.), *Byron: Heritage and Legacy* (New York: Palgrave Macmillan, 2008), 187–96.

"'When This World Shall Be Former': Catastrophism as Imaginative Theory for the Younger Romantics," *Romanticism on the Net* 24 (2001), https://doi.org/10.7202/006000ar.

O'Connor, Ralph, *The Earth on Show: Fossils and the Poetics of Popular Science, 1802–1856* (Chicago: University of Chicago Press, 2008).

"Mammoths and Maggots: Byron and the Geology of Cuvier," *Romanticism* 5.1 (1999), 26–42.

Stauffer, Andrew, "Redressing 'The Edinburgh Ladies' Petition,'" *Byron Journal* 31 (2003), 61–65.

CHAPTER 14 SEXUALITY

Crompton, Louis, *Byron and Greek Love: Homophobia in Nineteenth-Century England* (Berkeley, CA: University of California Press, 1985).

Elfenbein, Andrew, *Romantic Genius: A Prehistory of a Homosexual Role* (New York: Columbia University Press, 1999).

Gross, Jonathan D., *Byron: The Erotic Liberal* (Lanham, MD: Rowman & Littlefield, 2001).

Sha, Richard C., "Othering Sexual Perversity: England, Empire, Race, and Sexual Science," in Michael Sappol and Stephen Rice (eds.), *The New Cultural History of the Human Body in an Age of Empire* (Oxford: Berg, 2010), 87–106.

  Perverse Romanticism: Aesthetics and Sexuality in Britain, 1750–1850 (Baltimore: Johns Hopkins University Press, 2009).

Sigler, David, *Sexual Enjoyment in British Romanticism: Gender and Psychoanalysis, 1753–1835* (Montréal: McGill-Queen's University Press, 2015).

CHAPTER 15 LIBERTINISM

Augustine, Matthew and Steven Zwicker (eds.), *Lord Rochester in the Restoration World* (Cambridge, UK: Cambridge University Press, 2015).

Chernaik, Warren, *Sexual Freedom in Restoration Literature* (Cambridge, UK: Cambridge University Press, 1995).

Cryle, Peter and Lisa O'Connell (eds.), *Libertine Enlightenment: Sex, Liberty and Licence in the Eighteenth Century* (New York: Palgrave, 2004).

Cusset, Catherine (ed.), "Libertinage and Modernity," Special issue, *Yale French Studies* 94 (1998).

DeJean, Joan, *Libertine Strategies: Freedom and the Novel in Seventeenth-Century France* (Columbus: Ohio State University Press, 1981).

Gonsalves, Joshua, "Byron – In-between Sade, Lautréamont, and Foucault: Situating the Canon of 'Evil' in the Nineteenth Century," *Romanticism on the Net* 43 (2006), https://doi.org/10.7202/013591ar.

Hunt, Lynn (ed.), *The Invention of Pornography: Obscenity and the Origins of Modernity, 1500–1800* (New York: Zone, 1993).

Mudge, Bradford, *The Whore's Story: Women, Pornography and the British Novel, 1684–1830* (Oxford: Oxford University Press, 2000).

Pal-Lapinski, Piya, "Byron avec Sade: Material and Spectral Violence in *Childe Harold's Pilgrimage* Canto IV," in Gavin Hopps (ed.), *Byron's Ghosts: The Spectral, the Spiritual and the Supernatural* (Liverpool: Liverpool University Press, 2013), 131–43.

Turner, James Grantham, *Libertines and Radicals in Early Modern London: Sexuality, Politics and Literary Culture, 1660–1685* (Cambridge, UK: Cambridge University Press, 2002).

Vanhaesebrouck, Karel and Pol Dehert (eds.), "Libertine Bodies or the Politics of Baroque Corporeality," Special issue, *Journal for Early Modern Cultural Studies* 12.2 (2012).

Webster, Jeremy, *Performing Libertinism in Charles II's Court: Politics, Drama, Sexuality* (New York: Palgrave, 2005).

CHAPTER 16 FASHION, SELF-FASHIONING AND THE BODY

Barker, Clare and Stuart Murray (eds.), *The Cambridge Companion to Literature and Disability* (Cambridge, UK: Cambridge University Press, 2017).

Bradshaw, Michael (ed.), *Disabling Romanticism*, Literary Disability Studies, (London: Palgrave Macmillan, 2016).

Elfenbein, Andrew (ed.), "Byron and Disability," Special issue, *European Romantic Review* 12.3 (2001).

Hollander, Anne, *Sex and Suits: The Evolution of Modern Dress* (New York: Alfred A. Knopf, 1994).

Kenyon Jones, Christine, *Byron: The Image of the Poet* (Newark: University of Delaware Press, 2008).

Kuchta, David, *The Three-Piece Suit and Modern Masculinity: England, 1550–1850* (Berkeley, CA: University of California Press, 2002).

Lynch, Tony, "The Heretical Romantic Heroism of Beau Brummell," *European Romantic Review* 27.5 (2016), 679–95.

McNeill, Peter and Vicki Karaminas (eds.), *The Men's Fashion Reader* (London: Bloomsbury, 2009).

Moers, Ellen, *The Dandy: Brummell to Beerbohm* (New York: Viking, 1960).

Purdy, Daniel Leonhard (ed.), *The Rise of Fashion: A Reader* (Minneapolis: University of Minnesota Press, 2004).

CHAPTER 17 CLASSICISM AND NEOCLASSICISM

Beatty, Bernard, "Authenticity Projected: Byron, Pope, and Cardinal Newman," in Michael Davies, Ashley Chantler and Philip Shaw (eds.), *Literature and Authenticity 1780–1900* (London: Routledge, 2011), 67–80.

"Byron and the Eighteenth Century," in Drummond Bone (ed.), *The Cambridge Companion to Byron* (Cambridge, UK: Cambridge University Press, 2004), 236–48.

Beaty, Frederick L., *Byron the Satirist* (Oakland: University of California Press, 1985).

Erskine-Hill, Howard, "Pope and the Poetry of Opposition," in Pat Rogers (ed.), *The Cambridge Companion to Pope* (Cambridge, UK: Cambridge University Press, 2007), 134–49.

Gayle, Nicholas, *Byron and the Best of Poets* (Newcastle upon Tyne, UK: Cambridge Scholars Publishing, 2016).

Isbell, John, "Romantic Disavowals of Romanticism 1800–1830," in Steven P. Sondrup and Virgil Nemoianu (eds.), *Nonfictional Romantic Prose: Expanding Borders* (Bloomington: Indiana University Press, 2004), 37–55.

Kahn, A. D., "'Seneca and Sardanapalus': Byron, the Don Quixote of Neo-Classicism," *Studies in Philology* 66.4 (July 1969), 654–7.

Knight, G. Wilson, "The Book of Life: Byron's Adulation of Pope," in *The Poetry of Alexander Pope: Laureate of Peace, Chapter IV* (1955) (repr. London: Routledge Revivals, 2017).

McGann, Jerome, "The Anachronism of George Crabbe," *ELH* 48.3 (1981), 555–72.
Lessenich, Rolf, *Neoclassical Satire and the Romantic School 1780–1830* (Bonn: Bonn University Press, 2012).
Magnuson, Paul, *Reading Public Romanticism* (1998) (repr. Princeton: Princeton University Press, 2014).
Tomalin, M., "French Poets and British Reviewers, 1814–30," *Romanticism* 98.3 (2001), 506–9.

CHAPTER 18 EPIC (AND HISTORIOGRAPHY)

Cantor, Paul A., "The Politics of the Epic: Wordsworth, Byron, and the Romantic redefinition of heroism," *Review of Politics* 69 (2007), 375–401.
Curran, Stuart, *Poetic Form and British Romanticism* (Oxford: Oxford University Press, 1986).
DuBois, Page, *History, Rhetorical Description and the Epic from Homer to Spenser* (Cambridge, UK: D. S. Brewer, 1982).
Halmi, Nicholas, "Byron Between Ariosto and Tasso," in Frederick Burwick and Paul Douglass (eds.), *Dante and Italy in British Romanticism* (New York: Palgrave Macmillan, 2011), 39–53.
Lauber, John, "*Don Juan* as Anti-Epic," *Studies in English Literature, 1500–1900* 8 (1968), 607–19.
O'Neill, Michael, "Romantic Re-Appropriations of the Epic," in Catherine Bates (ed.), *The Cambridge Companion to the Epic* (Cambridge, UK: Cambridge University Press, 2010), 193–210.
Pomarè, Carla, *Byron and the Discourses of History* (Farnham, UK: Ashgate, 2013).
Quint, David, *Epic and Empire: Politics and Generic Form from Virgil to Milton* (Princeton: Princeton University Press, 1993).
Rawson, Claude, "Mock-Heroic and English Poetry," in Catherine Bates (ed.), *The Cambridge Companion to the Epic* (Cambridge, UK: Cambridge University Press, 2010), 167–92.
Reiman, Donald H., "*Don Juan* in Epic Context," *Studies in Romanticism* 16 (1977), 587–94.
Stabler, Jane, *Byron, Poetics and History* (Cambridge, UK: Cambridge University Press, 2002).
Tucker, Herbert F., *Epic: Britain's Heroic Muse 1790–1910* (Oxford: Oxford University Press, 2008).

CHAPTER 19 ROMANCE

Bloom, Harold, "The Internalization of Quest-Romance," in *The Ringers in the Tower: Studies in Romantic Tradition* (Chicago: University of Chicago Press, 1971), 13–35.
Curran, Stuart, *Poetic Form and British Romanticism* (Oxford: Oxford University Press, 1986).

Duncan, Ian, *Modern Romance and Transformations of the Novel* (Cambridge, UK: Cambridge University Press, 1992).

Duff, David, *Romance and Revolution: Shelley and the Politics of a Genre* (Cambridge, UK: Cambridge University Press, 1994).

Frye, Northrop, *Anatomy of Criticism* (Princeton: Princeton University Press, 1957).

Kucich, Greg, *Keats, Shelley, and Romantic Spenserianism* (University Park: Pennsylvania State University Press, 1991).

Miranda, Omar F., "The Celebrity of Exilic Romance: Francisco de Miranda and Lord Byron," *European Romantic Review* 27 (2016), 207–31.

Sánchez, Juan L., "Byron, Spain, and the Romance of *Childe Harold's Pilgrimage*," *European Romantic Review* 20 (2009), 443–64.

CHAPTER 20 BYRON'S LYRIC PRACTICE

Abrams, M. H., "Structure and Style in the Greater Romantic Lyric," in *The Correspondent Breeze: Essays on English Romanticism* (New York: W. W. Norton, 1984), 76–108.

Ashton, Thomas L., "Byronic Lyrics for David's Harp: The Hebrew Melodies," *Studies in English Literature, 1500–1900* 12.4 (1972), 665–81.

Culler, Jonathan, *Theory of the Lyric* (Cambridge, MA: Harvard University Press, 2015).

Duff, David, "The Combination Method," in *Romanticism and the Uses of Genre*, (Oxford: Oxford University Press, 2009), 160–200.

Findlay, L. M., "Culler and Byron on Apostrophe and Lyric Time," *Studies in Romanticism* 24.3 (1985), 335–53.

Gleckner, Robert F., "*Hebrew Melodies* and Other Lyrics of 1814–1816," in *Byron and the Ruins of Paradise* (Baltimore: Johns Hopkins University Press, 1967).

McGann, Jerome, "Byron and the Anonymous Lyric," in *Byron and Romanticism*, ed. James Soderholm (Cambridge, UK: Cambridge University Press, 2002), 93–112.

  "Byron and the Lyric of Sensibility," *European Romantic Review* 4.1 (1993), 71–83.

  "Byron's Lyric Poetry," in Drummond Bone (ed.), *The Cambridge Companion to Lord Byron* (Cambridge, UK: Cambridge University Press, 2004), 209–23.

Soderholm, James, "Byron's Ludic Lyrics," *Studies in English Literature, 1500–1900* 34.4 (1994), 739–51.

St Clair, William, "The Impact of Byron's Writings: An Evaluative Approach," in Andrew Rutherford (ed.), *Byron: Augustan and Romantic* (London: Macmillan, 1990), 1–25.

White, Adam, "Identity in Place: Lord Byron, John Clare and Lyric Poetry," *Byron Journal* 40.2 (2012), 115–27.

CHAPTER 21 SATIRE

Abrams, M. H., *Natural Supernaturalism: Tradition and Revolution in Romantic Literature* (New York: W. W. Norton, 1971).

Abrams, M. H. and Geoffrey Galt Harpham, "Satire," in *A Glossary of Literary Terms*, 9th ed. (Boston: Wadsworth Cengage Learning, 2009).

Canuel, Mark, "Race, Writing, and Don Juan," *Studies in Romanticism* 54.3 (2015), 303–28.

Chandler, James, "The Pope Controversy: Romantic Poets and the English Canon," *Critical Inquiry* 10.3 (1984), 481–509.

Christensen, Jerome, *Lord Byron's Strength: Romantic Writing and Commercial Society* (Baltimore: Johns Hopkins University Press, 1995).

Dyer, Gary, *British Satire and the Politics of Style, 1789–1832* (Cambridge, UK: Cambridge University Press, 1997).

Jones, Steve, "Intertextual Influences in Byron's Juvenalian Satire," *Studies in English Literature, 1500–1900* 33.4 (1993), 771–83.

McGann, Jerome J., *The Romantic Ideology* (Chicago: University of Chicago Press, 1983).

Wolfson, Susan, Borderlines: *The Shiftings of Gender in British Romanticism* (Palo Alto: Stanford University Press, 2006).

CHAPTER 22 THE SATANIC SCHOOL

Camilleri, Anna, "Byron, Milton, and the Satanic Heroine," in Peter Cochran (ed.), *Byron's Poetry* (Newcastle upon Tyne, UK: Cambridge Scholars Publishing, 2012), 70–81.

Hirst, Wolf Z. (ed.), *Byron, the Bible, and Religion* (Newark: University of Delaware Press, 1991).

McGann, Jerome J., *Byron and Romanticism*, ed. James Soderholm (Cambridge, UK: Cambridge University Press, 2002).

Parker, Fred, "Between Satan and Mephistopheles: Byron and the Devil," *Cambridge Quarterly* 35.1 (2006), 1–29.

Russell, Jeffrey Burton, "The Romantic Devil," in Harold Bloom (ed.), *Satan* (Philadelphia: Chelsea House, 2005), 155–92.

Shears, Jonathon, *The Romantic Legacy of* Paradise Lost: *Reading Against the Grain* (Farnham, UK: Ashgate, 2009).

Schock, Paul, *Romantic Satanism: Myth and the Historical Moment in Blake, Shelley and Byron* (Basingstoke, UK: Palgrave, 2003).

Svendsen, Lars, *A Philosophy of Boredom*, trans. John Irons (London: Reaktion Books, 2005).

Tuite, Clara, *Lord Byron and Scandalous Celebrity* (Cambridge, UK: Cambridge University Press, 2015).

Wolfson, Susan, "*The Vision of Judgment* and the Visions of 'Author,'" in Drummond Bone (ed.), *The Cambridge Companion to Byron* (Cambridge, UK: Cambridge University Press, 2004), 171–85.

CHAPTER 23 THE LAKE POETS

Callaghan, Madeleine, "Forms of Conflict: Byron's Influence on Yeats's Poetry," *English* 64.245 (2015), 81–98.

Chandler, James, "The Pope Controversy: Romantic Poetics and the English Canon," *Critical Inquiry* 10.3 (1984), 481–509.

Griggs, Earl Leslie, "Coleridge and Byron," *PMLA* 45.4 (1930), 1085–97.

Harson, Robert R., "Byron's 'Tintern Abbey,'" *Keats–Shelley Journal* 20 (1971), 113–21.

McGann, Jerome J., *Byron and Romanticism*, ed. James Soderholm (Cambridge, UK: Cambridge University Press, 2002).

  Byron and Wordsworth: The Annual Byron Lecture, Given in the University of Nottingham on 27 May 1998 (Nottingham: School of English Studies, University of Nottingham, 1999).

O'Neill, Michael, *The Human Mind's Imaginings: Conflict and Achievement in Shelley's Poetry* (Oxford: Clarendon Press, 1989).

Shaw, Philip, 'Wordsworth or Byron?' *Byron Journal* 31 (2003), 38–50.

Stabler, Jane, "Transition in Byron and Wordsworth," *Essays in Criticism* 50.4 (2000), 306–28.

Stevenson, Warren, "Byron and Coleridge: The Eagle and the Dove," *Byron Journal* 19 (1991), 114–27

CHAPTER 24 BYRON'S ACCIDENTAL MUSE: ROBERT SOUTHEY

Graham, Peter W., "Two Dons, a Lord, and a Laureate," in *Don Juan and Regency England* (Charlottesville: University Press of Virginia, 1990).

McGann, Jerome J., *Byron and Romanticism*, ed. James Soderholm (Cambridge, UK: Cambridge University Press, 2002).

  "Mobility and the Poetics of Historical Ventriloquism," *Romanticism, Past and Present* 9.1 (1985), 67–82.

Wolfson, Susan J., "*The Vision of Judgment* and the visions of 'author,'" in Drummond Bone (ed.), *The Cambridge Companion to Lord Byron* (Cambridge, UK: Cambridge University Press, 2004), 171–85.

CHAPTER 25 "BENIGN CERULEANS OF THE SECOND SEX!": BYRON AND THE BLUESTOCKINGS

Brewer, William D., "Joanna Baillie and Lord Byron," *Keats–Shelley Journal* 44 (1995), 165–81.

Camilleri, Anna, "Byron and the Politics of Writing Women," in Roderick Beaton and Christine Kenyon Jones (eds.), *Byron: The Poetry of Politics and the Politics of Poetry* (New York: Routledge, 2016), 44–56.

Clery, Emma, *Eighteen Hundred and Eleven* (Cambridge, UK: Cambridge University Press, 2017).

Elfenbein, Andrew, *Byron and the Victorians* (Cambridge, UK: Cambridge University Press, 1995).

Franklin, Caroline, *The Female Romantics: Nineteenth-Century Women Novelists and Byronism* (New York: Routledge, 2013).

Lau, Beth (ed.), *Fellow Romantics: Male and Female British Writers 1790–1835* (Farnham, UK: Ashgate, 2009).

Wilkes, Joanne, *Lord Byron and Madame de Staël: Born for Opposition* (Aldershot, UK: Ashgate, 1999).

Wolfson, Susan, "Hemans and the Romance of Byron," in Nanora Sweet and Julie Melnyk (eds.), *Felicia Hemans: Reimagining Poetry in the Nineteenth Century*, (Basingstoke, UK: Palgrave, 2001), 155–80.

Wootton, Sarah, *Byronic Heroes in Nineteenth-Century Women's Writing and Screen Adaptation* (Basingstoke, UK: Palgrave, 2016).

Chapter 26 The Pisan Circle and the Cockney School

Cline, C. L., *Byron, Shelley and their Pisan Circle* (London: John Murray, 1952).

Cox, Jeffrey N., "Communal Romanticism," *European Romantic Review* 15.2 (2004), 329–34.

 "Leigh Hunt's Foliage: A Cockney Manifesto," in Nicholas Roe (ed.), *Leigh Hunt: Life, Poetics, Politics* (London: Routledge, 2003), 58–77.

Craig, D. M., "The Origins of 'Liberalism' in Britain: The Case of *The Liberal*," *Historical Research* 85.229 (2012), 469–87.

Curreli, Mario and Anthony L. Johnson (eds.), *Paradise of Exiles: Shelley and Byron in Pisa*, papers from the International Conference Held in Pisa, May 24–6, 1985 (Salzburg: Institut für Anglistik und Amerikanistik, 1988).

Gross, Jonathan, "Byron and *The Liberal*: Periodical as Political Posture," *Philological Quarterly* 72.4 (1993), 471–85.

Kucich, Greg, "Keats, Shelley, Byron, and the Hunt Circle," in Thomas Keymer and Jon Mee (eds.), *The Cambridge Companion to English Literature 1740–1830* (Cambridge, UK: Cambridge University Press, 2004), 263–79.

Rawes, Alan and Diego Saglia (eds.), *Byron and Italy* (Manchester: Manchester University Press, 2017).

Reiman, Donald, *The Romantics Reviewed: Contemporary Reviews of British Romantic Writers*, Part A, 2 vols, Part B, 5 vols, Part C, 2 vols. (New York: Garland, 1972; repr., Abingdon, UK: Routledge, 2016).

Schoenfield, Mark, *British Periodicals and Romantic Identity: The "Literary Lower Empire"* (New York: Palgrave Macmillan, 2009).

Schoina, Maria, "Byron and *The Liberal*: A Reassessment," *Litteraria Pragensia* 23.46 (2013), 23–37.

Waters, Lindsay, "Pulci and the Poetry of Byron: 'Domestiche Muse,'" *Annali d'Italianistica* 1 (1983), 34–48.

Chapter 27 Drama and Theater

Booth, Michael R., *The Revels History of Drama in English: Volume VI, 1750–1880* (London: Methuen, 1996).

Burwick, Frederick, *Playing to the Crowd: London Popular Theatre 1780–1830* (Basingstoke, UK: Palgrave Macmillan, 2011).

Romantic Drama: Acting and Reacting (Cambridge, UK: Cambridge University Press, 2009).

Chew, Samuel C., *The Dramas of Lord Byron: A Critical Study* (1915) (repr., New York: Russell & Russell, 1964).

Cochran, Peter, *Byron and the Theatre* (Newcastle upon Tyne, UK: Cambridge Scholars Publishing, 2008).

Esterhammer, Angela, *The Romantic Performative: Language and Action in British and German Romanticism* (Palo Alto: Stanford University Press, 2000).

Gleckner, Robert F., *Byron and the Ruins of Paradise* (Baltimore: Johns Hopkins University Press, 1967).

Lansdown, Richard, *The Cambridge Introduction to Byron* (Cambridge, UK: Cambridge University Press, 2012).

Worrall, David, *The Politics of Romantic Theatricality, 1787–1832* (Basingstoke, UK: Palgrave Macmillan, 2007).

CHAPTER 28 AUTOBIOGRAPHY

Graham, Peter, "*Parisina, Mazeppa* and Anglo-Italian Displacement," in Alan Rawes and Diego Saglia (eds.), *Byron and Italy* (Manchester: Manchester University Press, 2017), 149–65.

Lovell, Ernest J. (ed.), *His Very Self and Voice: Collected Conversations of Lord Byron* (New York: Palgrave Macmillan, 1954).

McGann, Jerome J., "Milton and Byron" and "Hero with a Thousand Faces: The Rhetoric of Byronism," in James Soderholm (ed.), *Byron and Romanticism* (Cambridge, UK: Cambridge University Press, 2002), 19–35, 141–59.

Mole, Tom, *Byron's Romantic Celebrity: Industrial Culture and the Hermeneutic of Intimacy* (Basingstoke, UK: Palgrave Macmillan, 2007).

Moore, Dorothy Langley, *The Late Lord Byron* (London: John Murray, 1961).

Rawes, Alan, "Byron's Love Letters," *Byron Journal* 43.1 (2015), 1–14.

"'That Perverse Passion' and Benita Eisler's 'Byronic' Biography of Byron," in Arthur Bradley and Alan Rawes (eds.), *Romantic Biography* (Aldershot, UK: Ashgate, 2003), 74–92.

Throsby, Corin, "Being Neither Here Nor There: Byron and the Art of Flirting," in Gavin Hopps (ed.), *Byron's Ghosts: The Spectral, the Spiritual and the Supernatural* (Liverpool: Liverpool University Press, 2013), 202–14.

"Flirting with Fame: Byron's Anonymous Female Fans," *Byron Journal* 32.2 (2004), 115–23.

Tuite, Clara, *Lord Byron and Scandalous Celebrity* (Cambridge, UK: Cambridge University Press, 2015).

Knight, G. Wilson, *Lord Byron's Marriage: The Evidence of the Asterisks* (London: Kegan Paul, 1957).

Wu, Duncan, "Myth 16: Byron Had an Affair with His Sister," in *30 Great Myths About the Romantics* (Chichester, UK: Wiley Blackwell, 2015), 132–9.

Chapter 29 "Litera*toor*" and Literary Theory

Bourdieu, Pierre, *Distinction: A Social Critique of the Judgment of Taste*, trans. Richard Nice (1979) (repr. London: Routledge, 1984).

Cochran, Peter (ed.), "Byron's Library: The Three Book Sale Catalogues," https://petercochran.files.wordpress.com/2009/03/byrons_library.pdf.

Derrida, Jacques, "'This Strange Institution Called Literature': An Interview with Jacques Derrida," in Derek Attridge (ed.), *Acts of Literature* (New York: Routledge, 1992), 33–75.

Foucault, Michel, "What Is An Author?" in Josué V. Harari (ed.), *Textual Strategies: Perspectives in Post-Structuralist Criticism* (London: Methuen & Co., 1979), 141–60.

Guillory, John, *Cultural Capital: The Problem of Literary Canon Formation* (Chicago: University of Chicago Press, 1993).

McGann, Jerome, *Byron and Romanticism*, ed. James Soderholm (Cambridge, UK: Cambridge University Press, 2002).

Patterson, Annabel, "Intention," in Frank Lentricchia and Thomas McLaughlin (eds.), *Critical Terms for Literary Study* (Chicago: University of Chicago Press, 1995), 135–46.

Ross, Trevor, "The Emergence of 'Literature': Making and Reading the English Canon in the Eighteenth Century," *ELH* 63 (1996), 397–422.

Chapter 30 Periodical Culture, the Literary Review and the Mass Media

Altick, Richard, *The English Common Reader: A Social History of the Mass Reading Public, 1800–1900* (Chicago: University of Chicago Press, 1957).

Butler, Marilyn, "Culture's Medium: The Role of the Review," in Stuart Curran (ed.), *The Cambridge Companion to British Romanticism* (Cambridge, UK: Cambridge University Press, 1993), 120–47.

  (ed.), "Introduction," in *Burke, Paine, Godwin, and the Revolution Controversy* (Cambridge, UK: Cambridge University Press, 1984), 1–17.

Christensen, Jerome, *Lord Byron's Strength: Romantic Writing and Commercial Society* (Baltimore: Johns Hopkins University Press, 1993).

Clive, John, *Scotch Reviewers: The Edinburgh Review, 1802–1815* (London: Faber & Faber, 1957).

Dyer, Gary, *British Satire and the Politics of Style, 1789–1832* (Cambridge, UK: Cambridge University Press, 1997).

Franta, Andrew, *Romanticism and the Rise of the Mass Public* (Cambridge, UK: Cambridge University Press, 2007).

Klancher, Jon P., *The Making of English Reading Audiences, 1790–1832* (Madison: University of Wisconsin Press, 1987).

Roper, Derek, *Reviewing Before the "Edinburgh," 1788–1802* (Newark: University of Delaware Press, 1978).

St Clair, William, *The Reading Nation in the Romantic Period* (Cambridge, UK: Cambridge University Press, 2004).

CHAPTER 31 CONTEMPORARY CRITICAL RECEPTION TO 1824

Butler, Marilyn, "Culture's Medium: The Role of the Review," in Stuart Curran (ed.), *The Cambridge Companion to British Romanticism*, 2nd ed. (Cambridge, UK: Cambridge University Press, 2010), 127–52.

Christie, William, *The* Edinburgh Review *in the Literary Culture of Romantic Britain* (London: Pickering & Chatto, 2009).

Goode, Clement Tyson, Jr., "A Critical Review of Research," in Oscar José Santucho (ed.), *George Gordon, Lord Byron: A Comprehensive Bibliography of Secondary Materials in English, 1807–1974* (Metuchen, NJ: Scarecrow Press, 1977), 1–166.

Klancher, Jon P., *The Making of English Reading Audiences, 1790–1832* (Madison: University of Wisconsin Press, 1987).

Martin, Philip W., *Byron: A Poet Before His Public* (Cambridge, UK: Cambridge University Press, 1982).

Mortenson, Robert, *Byron's Waterloo: The Reception of* Cain, A Mystery (Seattle: Iron Press, 2015).

Reiman, Donald H. (ed.), *The Romantics Reviewed: Contemporary Reviews of British Romantic Writers*, Part B, 5 vols. (New York: Garland, 1972).

Rutherford, Andrew (ed.), *Byron: The Critical Heritage* (London: Routledge & Kegan Paul, 1970).

Schoenfield, Mark, *British Periodicals and Romantic Identity: The "Literary Lower Empire"* (Basingstoke, UK: Palgrave Macmillan, 2009).

Stabler, Jane, "Against Their Better Selves: Byron, Jeffrey and the *Edinburgh*," in Massimiliano Demata and Duncan Wu (eds.), *British Romanticism and the* Edinburgh Review (Basingstoke, UK: Palgrave Macmillan, 2002), 146–67.

CHAPTER 32 BYRON, RADICALS AND REFORMERS

Collins, Philip, *Thomas Cooper, the Chartist: Byron and the "Poets of the Poor,"* Nottingham Byron Lecture (Nottingham: University of Nottingham, 1969).

Erdman, David V., "Byron and 'The New Force of the People,'" *Keats–Shelley Journal* 11 (Winter 1962), 47–64.

Felluga, Dino, "'With a Most Voiceless Thought': Byron and the Radicalism of Textual Culture," *European Romantic Review* 11.2 (2000), 150–67.

Gilmartin, Kevin, *Print Politics: The Press and Radical Opposition in Early Nineteenth-Century England* (Cambridge, UK: Cambridge University Press, 1996).

Goldsmith, Jason N., "Celebrity and the Spectacle of Nation," in Tom Mole (ed.), *Romanticism and Celebrity Culture, 1750–1850* (Cambridge, UK: Cambridge University Press, 2009), 21–40.

Grimes, Kyle, "Verbal Jujitsu: William Hone and the Tactics of Satirical Conflict," in Steven E. Jones (ed.), *The Satiric Eye: Forms of Satire in the Romantic Period* (Basingstoke, UK: Palgrave Macmillan, 2003), 173–84.

Harling, Philip, "The Law of Libel and the Limits of Repression, 1790–1832," *Historical Journal* 44.1 (2001), 107–34.

Kovalev, Y. Y., "The Literature of Chartism," *Victorian Studies* 2.2 (1958), 117–38.

Manning, Peter J., "The Hone-ing of Byron's *Corsair*," in *Reading Romantics: Texts and Contexts* (Oxford: Oxford University Press, 1990), 216–37.

Murphy, Paul Thomas, *Toward a Working-Class Canon: Literary Criticism in British Working-Class Periodicals, 1816–1858* (Columbus: Ohio State University Press, 1994).

Ruddick, William, "Byron and England: The Persistence of Byron's Political Ideas," in Paul Graham Trueblood (ed.), *Byron's Political and Cultural Influence in Nineteenth-Century Europe: A Symposium* (Atlantic Highlands, NJ: Humanities Press, 1981), 25–47.

Shaaban, Bouthaina, "The Romantics in the Chartist Press," *Keats–Shelley Journal* 38 (1989), 25–46.

CHAPTER 33 EUROPEAN RECEPTION

Bayley, John, "Pushkin and Byron: A Complex Relationship," *Byron Journal* 16 (1988), 47–55.

Cardwell, Richard, "Lord Byron's Gothic Footprint in Spain: José de Espronceda and the Re-Making of Horror," in Peter Cochran (ed.), *The Gothic Byron* (Newcastle upon Tyne, UK: Cambridge Scholars Publishing, 2009), 129–44.

Diakonova, Nina, "Byron and Lermontov: Notes in Pechorin's Journal," in Charles Robinson (ed.), *Lord Byron and His Contemporaries* (Newark: University of Delaware Press, 1982), 148–56.

"Heine as an Interpreter of Byron," *Byron Journal* 22 (1994), 63–9.

Kephallineou, Eugenia, "Neohellenic Translations of Byron's Works in the Nineteenth Century," in Marius Byron Raizis (ed.), *Lord Byron: Byronism – Liberalism – Philhellenism, Proceedings of the 14th International Byron Symposium* (Athens: Ministry of Culture and Science, 1988), 94–103.

Miroslava, Modrzewska, "Polish Romantic Translations of 'The Giaour,'" in Martin Prochazka (ed.), *Byron: East and West, Proceedings of the 24th International Byron Conference* (Prague: Charles University, 2000), 141–56.

Nicholson, Andrew, "European Reactions to Byron: Mazzini and Mickiewicz," in Peter Vassallo (ed.), *Byron and the Mediterranean* (Msida: Malta University Press, 1986), 89–99.

CHAPTER 34 RECOLLECTIONS, CONVERSATIONS AND BIOGRAPHIES

Cochran, Peter, "Introduction to Teresa Guiccioli," in *Lord Byron's Life in Italy (Vie de Lord Byron en Italie)*, trans. Michael Rees, ed. Peter Cochran (Newark: University of Delaware Press, 2005), 1–60.

Douglass, Paul, "Byron's Life and his Biographers," in Drummond Bone (ed.), *The Cambridge Companion to Lord Byron* (Cambridge, UK: Cambridge University Press, 2004), 7–26.

Elfenbein, Andrew, *Byron and the Victorians* (Cambridge, UK: Cambridge University Press, 1995).

Moore, Doris Langley, *The Late Lord Byron: Posthumous Dramas*, rev. ed. (London: John Murray, 1976).

North, Julian, *The Domestication of Genius: Biography and the Romantic Poet* (Oxford: Oxford University Press, 2009).

St Clair, William, "Postscript to *The Last Days of Lord Byron*," *Keats–Shelley Journal* 19 (1970), 4–7.

Vail, Jeffery W., *The Literary Relationship of Lord Byron and Thomas Moore* (Baltimore: Johns Hopkins University Press, 2001).

CHAPTER 35 POSTHUMOUS RECEPTION AND REINVENTION TO 1900

Chew, Samuel C., *Byron in England: His Fame and After-Fame* (London: John Murray, 1924).

Cronin, Richard, *Romantic Victorians: English Literature, 1824–1840* (Basingstoke, UK: Palgrave, 2002).

Elfenbein, Andrew, *Byron and the Victorians* (Cambridge, UK: Cambridge University Press, 1995).

Felluga, Dino, *The Perversity of Poetry: Romantic Ideology and the Popular Male Poet of Genius* (Albany: State University of New York Press, 2005).

Leonard, William Ellery, *Byron and Byronism in America* (Lynn, MA: Nichols Press, 1905).

Rutherford, Andrew (ed.), *Byron: The Critical Heritage* (New York: Barnes & Noble, 1970).

Wolfson, Susan, *Romantic Interactions: Social Being and the Turns of Literary Action* (Baltimore: Johns Hopkins University Press, 2010).

CHAPTER 36 POPULAR CULTURE

Ascari, Maurizio, "'Not in a Christian Church': Westminster Abbey and the Memorialisation of Byron," *Byron Journal* 37.2 (2009), 141–50.

Bond, Geoffrey. "Byron Memorabilia," in Christine Kenyon Jones (ed.), *Byron: The Image of the Poet* (Newark: University of Delaware Press, 2008), 79–87.

Kenyon Jones, Christine (ed.), *Byron: The Image of the Poet* (Newark: University of Delaware Press, 2008).

Oliver, Anthony, *The Victorian Staffordshire Figure: A Guide for Collectors* (New York: St. Martin's Press, 1971).

McDayter, Ghislaine, *Byromania and the Birth of Celebrity Culture* (Albany: State University of New York Press, 2009).

Modrzewska, Mirosława, "The Transformations of the Byron Legend: Methodological Reassessment," in Cheryl A. Wilson (ed.), *Byron: Heritage and Legacy* (New York: Palgrave Macmillan, 2008), 61–9.

Mole, Tom, "Spurgeon, Byron, and the Contingencies of Mediation," in Andrew Piper and Jonathan Sachs (eds.), "Romantic Cultures of Print," Special issue, *Romanticism and Victorianism on the Net* 57–8 (2010), 1–27, https://doi.org/10.7202/1006518ar.

Stein, Atara, *The Byronic Hero in Film, Fiction, and Television* (Carbondale: Southern Illinois University Press, 2004).

Wilson, Frances (ed.), *Byromania: Portraits of the Artist in Nineteenth- and Twentieth-Century Culture* (New York: St. Martin's Press, 1999).

CHAPTER 37 BYRON NOW

Bruhm, Stephen, *Reflecting Narcissus: A Queer Aesthetic* (Minneapolis: University of Minnesota Press, 2001).

Cochran, Peter, *The Burning of Byron's Memoirs: New and Unpublished Essays* (Newcastle upon Tyne, UK: Cambridge Scholars Publishing, 2014).

Felluga, Dino, "'With a Most Voiceless Thought': Byron and the Radicalism of Textual Culture," *European Romantic Review* 11 (2000), 150–67.

Kenyon Jones, Christine, "'An Uneasy Mind in an Uneasy Body': Byron, Disability, Authorship, and Biography," in M. Bradshaw (ed.), *Disabling Romanticism* (London: Palgrave Macmillan, 2016), 147–67.

Mole, Tom, *Byron's Romantic Celebrity: Industrial Culture and the Hermeneutic of Intimacy* (Basingstoke, UK: Palgrave Macmillan, 2007).

Richardson, Alan, "Romanticism and the Colonization of the Feminine," in Anne Mellor (ed.), *Romanticism and Feminism* (New York: Routledge, 1993), 13–25.

Sha, Richard, *Perverse Romanticism: Aesthetics and Sexuality in Britain, 1750–1832* (Baltimore: Johns Hopkins University Press, 2009).

Stabler, Jane (ed.), *Byron*, Longman Critical Readers (London: Longman, 1998).

Stein, Atara, *The Byronic Hero in Film, Fiction and Television* (Carbondale: Southern Illinois University Press, 2009).

Index